Natural Law and Political Realism in the History of Political Thought

Major Concepts in Politics and Political Theory

Garrett Ward Sheldon
General Editor

Vol. 25

PETER LANG
New York • Washington, D.C./Baltimore • Bern
Frankfurt am Main • Berlin • Brussels • Vienna • Oxford

R. W. Dyson

Natural Law and Political Realism in the History of Political Thought

Volume I
From the Sophists to Machiavelli

PETER LANG
New York • Washington, D.C./Baltimore • Bern
Frankfurt am Main • Berlin • Brussels • Vienna • Oxford

Library of Congress Cataloging-in-Publication Data
Dyson, R. W.
Natural law and political realism in the history of political thought / R.W. Dyson.
p. cm. — (Major concepts in politics and political theory; v. 25)
Includes bibliographical references and index.
Contents: v. 1. From the sophists to Machiavelli
1. Political science—Philosophy—History. 2. Natural law.
3. Realism—Political aspects. I. Title. II. Series.
JA71.D97   320'.01'1—dc22   2004027473
ISBN 978-0-8204-7824-1
ISSN 1059-3535

Bibliographic information published by **Die Deutsche Bibliothek**.
Die Deutsche Bibliothek lists this publication in the "Deutsche
Nationalbibliografie"; detailed bibliographic data is available
on the Internet at http://dnb.ddb.de/.

The paper in this book meets the guidelines for permanence and durability
of the Committee on Production Guidelines for Book Longevity
of the Council of Library Resources.

© 2005, 2009 Peter Lang Publishing, Inc., New York
29 Broadway, 18th floor, New York, NY 10006
www.peterlang.com

All rights reserved.
Reprint or reproduction, even partially, in all forms such as microfilm,
xerography, microfiche, microcard, and offset strictly prohibited.

Printed in Germany

For
Val Dyson

Contents

Preface		ix
Chapter 1:	Political Realism in Fifth-Century Athens: Origins and Rationale	1
Chapter 2:	Plato's 'Republic': The Sovereignty of Philosophy	33
Chapter 3:	Aristotle: The Ethical Necessity of Politics	67
Chapter 4:	Stoicism: Equality, Cosmopolitanism and the Law of Right Reason	101
Chapter 5:	The Transvaluation of Classical Anthropology	137
Chapter 6:	The Augustinian Conception of Politics	167
Chapter 7:	St Thomas Aquinas: The Recovery of Aristotle and the Rehabilitation of Politics	209
Chapter 8:	Machiavelli: Virtù, Fortune and the Autonomy of Politics	245
Notes		271
Select Bibliography		327
Index		339

Preface

SOCRATES THOUGHT it impossible to dissociate the study of politics from questions of justice and the human good. Whether we agree with him or not, his maxim remains true after more than two millennia: that in exploring the implications of whatever definition of politics is proposed, 'no small matter is at stake: nothing less than the governance of human life.'[1] Those who set themselves to define politics undertake a great responsibility.

Defining politics is one of the oldest of all intellectual endeavours. It is hardly surprising that the task should have proved so contentious. Central to it is the question of whether political behaviour is rooted in enmity or amity. Does politics manifest itself in peace or war? Should the etymology of the word 'politics' be traced back to πόλεμος (*polemos*), 'battle,' or πόλις (*polis*), 'city'? Few have favoured a simple answer in terms of either of these alternatives. On the one hand, exponents of even the most bellicist views acknowledge that the political actor needs allies and that war cannot be perpetual war. On the other, peace tends to be regarded as a regulative idea to which we can hope to approximate but which we can never fully attain. To many, a preferable solution, neither too horrifying nor too utopian, is to conceive of politics as something like 'the constrained use of social power.'[2]

These issues raise a number of complicated and contested questions. Should the use of power be constrained by moral considerations and ordered towards moral ends? If so, how might one go about identifying such considerations and ends and translating them into practice? Are there timeless moral truths to which access is possible and in the light of which we can and should conduct our affairs? Or is political activity, whether at the level of individuals or States, to be understood only in terms of the constraints of power, security, self-interest, 'checks and balances'? Or is it driven not by cold calculation but by passion, pride, status and the pursuit of glory? In turn, these questions invite us to think about the nature and scope of political science. Is it a means of instruction in the art of wielding power—a science in the 'modern' sense of the term, affording predictability and certainty? Or is it a form of reflection upon how the political community ought to be organised and what kind of persons are fit to inhabit that community? These are among the most important and revisited themes of political writing. For the most part they were thought significant in classical antiquity, and they are no less significant in the twenty-first century: arguably, they are more so. No doubt there can be no definitive answers; but a historical treatment of the ways in which such issues have been addressed is of more than antiquarian interest.

Our concern in these pages is with the approach to these questions exhibited by two persistent streams of thought: the natural law tradition, and the tradition now most often called political realism. The two are not always distinct in reality, but it is convenient for the purposes of exposition to treat them as if they were. The expression 'natural law' is not entirely satisfactory; notoriously, it invites confusion and equivocation. Nonetheless, we prefer it to the several possible alternatives—utopianism, rationalism, universal moral order[3]—because it is on the whole the most comprehensive and best understood way of expressing the idea that we wish to investigate: that there are universal and non-conventional moral standards that lie, or should lie, behind conventional political arrangements and constrain the behaviour of political actors. 'Natural law' has also the advantage that it or closely similar terms have been used by most of the authors whom we wish to associate with the natural law tradition. The same cannot be said of 'political realism.' The currency of that term is more recent. It too invites confusion and equivocation, but there is no obvious alternative to it. We use it to designate the tradition that denies that there are universal standards of political morality and accounts for the constraints that exist on the behaviour of political actors in terms of power, interest and authority.

This is the first of two volumes in which we propose to examine the history of these traditions from classical antiquity to the present day. In doing so, we shall try to bring out the main implications for government, social organisation and international relations that have been attributed to them. We shall consider the political and social contexts that have enabled their various expressions to seem persuasive.

We shall look closely also at their intellectual contexts, treating them in relation to the theories of knowledge, ethics and human nature with which they have at different times been associated. We subscribe to the belief that no political doctrine can be understood adequately except by attention to such contexts, and this belief will be reflected in our treatment throughout. For the purposes of this work, we have adopted a 'commanding heights' approach to intellectual historiography. We have, that is, tried to avoid grand generalisations, and we have for the most part dealt systematically and in detail with specific authors. In adopting this selective method, we have inevitably omitted much; but the alternative, given the time-span involved and the complexity of the evidential literature, would have been to produce a history too diffuse and imprecise to be informative.

Perhaps the word 'tradition' needs some explanation. In using it, we do not make essentialist assumptions about the identity of what is described. On the contrary, we shall show that each 'tradition' has exhibited a range of historically conditioned forms, displaying different emphases, arising from a range of philosophical standpoints, and directed to different ends. Yet clearly there is continuity of a kind. The currents of thought that we shall delineate have been present in western political philosophy from the beginning. They are capable, as we shall suggest in a moment, of being expressed as Weberian 'ideal types' or, in Professor Oakeshott's phrase, 'ideal representations.' In view of their continuity in this sense, the term 'tradition' seems appropriate. We consider the expression 'political philosophy' justified also. Each of the two traditions has implications of a practical kind, and neither has ever been wholly abstracted from the 'real world' of politics. Each, however, has been elaborated by writers more immediately concerned with abstract justification than with concrete application. Most of the authors whose thought we shall examine have been philosophers *ex professo*, or have been engaged in an activity cognate to philosophy. We are to that extent concerned with an aspect of the history of political philosophy. We shall not attempt to deal with the large subjects of myth and literature; Homer and Sophocles will receive only passing mention. We do not, incidentally, take the view that political philosophy has nothing to say to the 'real' world. We remain open to the possibility that the kind of study here undertaken may enable that world to be understood more clearly and organised more rationally.

Stating it as an 'ideal type', then, we take the natural law tradition to include the following propositions:

1. That there are universal and objective moral principles that underlie—that are 'prior' to—all conventional arrangements. These principles are 'universal' in that they apply always and everywhere; 'objective' in that they exist (in some metaphysical sense that no one is ever quite clear about) regardless of what anybody thinks or wills; and 'moral' in that they prescribe how political life ought to be conducted, how people ought to treat one another, and how they ought to be treated.
2. That these principles are 'natural' in the sense of being (a) not created by human enactment or agreement: they are, according to the venerable distinction, 'natural' as distinct from 'conventional'; (b) indispensable to the meeting of needs characteristic of human nature; and (c) accessible to the capacity for reason which is part of that nature. Those who appeal to natural law arguments usually mean by 'natural' all three of these things.
3. That they have a critical function. Natural law is not a substitute for positive law, but it can and should be used as a standard against which to assess the moral adequacy of conventional arrangements.
4. That human beings are by nature co-operative, and that a vital part of the activity of politics is to enable co-operation to be undertaken successfully in pursuit of common goals.
5. That the natural norms which reason discloses apply to all human beings equally, and that all are therefore entitled to be treated as moral equals. If discrimination between individuals and groups is to be justified at all, it must be justified on morally relevant grounds lying behind or above positive law. In post-Renaissance political thought, this idea comes increasingly to be expressed in terms of natural *rights*.

We emphasise, however, that this description is intended only to map out a 'pure form' of natural law theory. It does not in any uncomplicated sense portray a reality, nor does it purport to express a standard to which some thinkers measure up and from which others

Preface

fall short. It depicts a generality not found in its completeness in any one text but which may be observed, in variants linked as it were by family resemblance, as a recurrent theme of political and moral discourse. We shall from time to time provide summaries that can be referred back to our 'ideal type' as a reference point; but it is, we stress, an artificial frame of reference imposed for the sake of convenience upon a long and diverse history.

Treating the tradition of political realism in the same fashion, and with the same qualification, we suggest that its perspective may be expressed generally as follows:

1. That it is not possible to identify objective moral standards of the kind that the natural law tradition supposes to exist.
2. That such principles of law and conduct as are acknowledged are conventional, and are the products of emotion, reason or a combination of both, 'reason' being understood as a calculative faculty wholly or mainly directed to the realisation of the interests of the rational agent.
3. That what passes in the world for political morality is no more than a polite device by which motives of individual and national self-interest are dignified.
4. That law is the command of some authority and that there is no appeal beyond that authority. All law is positive law; what gives it obligatory force is command, not truth.
5. That we should regard conflict, not co-operation, as the natural condition of humanity. This is so because either (a) we have reason to believe (or find it prudent to assume) that individuals are mostly competitive, selfish, and actuated by self-interest, or at least by shared interests tied to loyalties of a narrow national or economic kind; or (b) even if individuals are not so actuated, the social and political conditions under which they live require them to act as if they were.
6. That political order and law are geographically and chronologically determinate. They do not embrace all mankind but, rather, involve discrimination between individuals or groups. Even such moral and legal constraints as are acknowledged within groups may be set aside in their dealings with outsiders.

Our subject then, is what may be called the dialectical interplay of these two traditions in the history of political thought. To put it at its broadest, we, like Plato in the *Republic*, are concerned with an investigation of the nature of justice. Both traditions are still very much with us. On the one hand, the twentieth- and twenty-first century language of 'human rights,' 'crimes against humanity' and 'humanitarian intervention' is the language of the natural law tradition. This is true even where this tradition is not in so many words recognised and where its philosophical assumptions are not articulated and defended explicitly. On the other hand, twentieth- and twenty-first century political realism assumes that such language simultaneously reflects and disguises the hegemonic interests or ambitions of individuals or groups. It prefers instead the language of interests, security, necessity. If it uses the language of 'laws of nature,' it understands 'law' as referring to a set of invariant traits in human nature, or a set of invariant constraints, that drive individuals and groups to competitive and conflictual behaviour. Knowledge of such laws at best enables individuals and groups to manipulate each other to their own advantage. This language of political realism has also undergone significant changes but, again, is clearly recognisable. It is a central aim of this work to show how these two traditions have been intertwined from the earliest point in European thought at which they can be identified. Natural law, despite its own claims to timelessness, arose in specific conditions and in direct relation to what are recognisable as doctrines of political realism. Understanding natural law and the language that today often silently assumes natural law principles requires us to recall the history of natural law in detail.

In this volume, all the authors whose work we shall discuss use gender-specific language either consistently or mainly, and perforce we follow them. Revising the language of the past in order to make it conform to current preferences is an increasingly common error, but an error nonetheless. For instance, the habit of translating Aristotle's ὁ ἄνθρωπος φύσει πολιτικὸν ζῷον as 'human beings are by nature political animals' is a serious misrepresentation of what Aristotle says and means. A simple principle has been adopted throughout: that intellectual history must convey what past authors actually said rather than what present historians think they should have said.

Chapter 1

Political Realism in Fifth-Century Athens: Origins and Rationale

THE FIRST extant western attempt to develop what is, in effect, a philosophical theory of natural law is found in the *Republic* of Plato. The *Republic* is a 'middle-period' dialogue, written in about 375 BCE, when Plato was more than fifty years old. But it is the product of extended reflection on the Athenian political culture of his youth. It is a response to the political realism prevalent in Athens during the second half of the fifth century BCE: a realism that Plato associates with the group of teachers called the Sophists, though it is not attributable to them alone. Strictly speaking, it may not be attributable to them at all; but Plato represents the more radical of the Sophists as being convinced exponents of it, and he regards the Sophists in general as having a malign influence on public life. In this chapter, we shall describe the development and theoretical foundations of this Athenian version of political realism. We shall deal especially with the epistemology of the Sophists and its emergence in the context of presocratic Greek culture, and we shall examine the apparent consequences of that epistemology for moral judgment and political practice. We shall do these things partly with a view to clarifying the position that Plato is resolved to undermine; but the insights arising from such a prolegomenon will have broader implications also.

From 'Mythos' to 'Logos': the Rise and Failure of Presocratic Science

The three centuries after 800 BCE witnessed two developments that were in important respects to create 'classical' Greece as an intellectual milieu. On the one hand, the period was one of extensive colonial expansion out into the Mediterranean basin and beyond. This expansion, driven by population increase and territorial ambition, was begun by a few intrepid seafarers but gained momentum rapidly. By 500 BCE, Magna Graecia had come into being. Greek colonies were founded along the coasts of Macedonia and Thrace, of the Black Sea and its approaches, of Cyrenaica, Sicily and Southern Italy. On the other hand, during the same period the social arrangements of the Greek tribes underwent a far-reaching change. The tribal villages of earliest times began to coalesce into larger and more organised concentrations of population. These migrations from the countryside—these συνοικισμοι (*synoikismoi*): literally, mergers of households—were driven mainly by the need of the tribes to achieve security against one another, and they produced cities built in easily-defended locations. So began the most characteristic and intellectually fruitful form of Greek political organisation, the πόλις (*polis*) or city-State. The *poleis* were at first governed by βασιλεῖς (*basileis*), 'kings': personages not much different from the military chieftains of Homeric times. In some cases, the office of kingship became hereditary, but by 600 BCE most of the *poleis* were in practice ruled by aristocratic assemblies such as the Areopagitic Council at Athens. In response to internal and external pressures, there subsequently emerged the various constitutional forms and permutations which in the fourth century were to be analysed in such detail by Aristotle.[1]

It is impossible to exaggerate the importance of this period of expansion and change for the course of Greek history. Contact with other cultures and their accomplishments conferred upon the Greeks practical and technological benefits that they were not slow to exploit. They acquired mathematics from the Babylonians and Egyptians, and shipbuilding, navigation and alphabetic writing from the Phoenicians. Colonial expansion, commerce and the multiplying amenities of civic life brought the wealth and leisure that made study and reflection possible, and an omnivorous curiosity emerged. Contact with peoples beyond the sea proved to be corrosive of established beliefs and a stimulus to intellectual independence. The earliest Greek philosophers were polymaths with a pronounced inclination to seek the truth outside the received orthodoxies. Their speculations were unsystematic and indiscriminate; they did not make the distinctions that come so readily to us between the various modes of intellectual enquiry. It seems clear that their interests included a degree of reflection on politics, and a number of them are said to have been active in the political lives of their own communities; but of this incipient political philosophy only a few tantalising hints remain. We are most fully acquainted with what they have to say about mathematics and the origin and composition of the material world. Their studies were in part directed towards practical ends: warfare, navigation, architecture, land measurement; but they were undoubtedly motivated also by a pure desire for knowledge.

The first product of this burgeoning curiosity has come to be called 'presocratic philosophy' or 'presocratic cosmology.'[2] These expressions are in a sense regrettable. They create the impression that the earliest Greek philosophers are of interest only as precursors of Socrates. It is unfortunate also that, without exception, their writings, if they wrote anything much at all, have survived only as fragments transmitted by witnesses often lacking in sympathy and understanding or whose interest in them is auxiliary to other concerns.[3] The presocratic philosophers are interesting in their own right, and they have a definite scientific project. They were the first western thinkers to try to find a rational order in nature. In this sense, they are the forerunners of everything that we shall be exploring in these pages. As far as we can tell, their main preoccupation was with the phenomena of change. In particular, they were intrigued by the relation between change and stability. Everything in the world comes into being, undergoes transformations of various kinds, and passes away; yet the world itself seems to be a continuous and enduring whole. The reality that presents itself to our experience is simultaneously evanescent and constant, changing yet stable. How can this be?

Broadly speaking, the instinct of the presocratic philosophers was to look for a first cause or ruling principle, an ἀρχή (*arché*), lying behind the changing nature of the perceptible world. They hoped that such an *arché* might serve also as a principle of explanation: a λόγος (*logos*). *Logos* is a word of many meanings, and we shall encounter it frequently.[4] On the whole, the presocratics addressed their task by seeking to identify the primal matter, the *Urstoff*, of which the world is made. We can illustrate this by a glance at the group of individuals usually called the Milesian monists or materialists: Milesian because they were citizens of the city-State of Miletus on the western coast of

Asia Minor; monists because they tried to explain the world in terms of a single substance; materialists because they believed this substance to be a material substance. The eldest member of this group was Thales (ca 624–547 BCE), one of the 'seven sages' of antiquity: an individual of wide interests and abilities, which he is said to have put to a range of military and practical uses.[5] His method seems to have been a commonsense and unsystematic empiricism. According to Aristotle and others, he believed that 'water is the first principle.' Apparently he thinks that everything is made of water in various states or configurations, and that change occurs when these states or configurations alter.[6] 'Perhaps,' says Aristotle, 'he came to this conclusion when he saw that the food of everything is moist...and that the seeds of everything have a moist nature, and that water is the origin of the nature of moist things.'[7] Thales's younger contemporary Anaximander (ca 610–546 BCE) postulated as an *Urstoff* not any of the visible elements—water, earth, air or fire—but a mysterious invisible substrate which he called τὸ ἄπειρον (*to apeiron*), 'the unlimited.'

> He says that [the *arché*] is neither water nor any of the other things called elements, but something different from them: something unlimited by nature that is the origin of all the heavens and the worlds in them. He says moreover that the first origin of existing things is what existing things eventually fall back into 'according to necessity'; for he says in somewhat poetical terms that 'they give justice and make reparation to one another for their injustice according to the ordinance of time.'[8]

Here is one of those tantalising pieces of information to which we referred a few moments ago. Simplicius, from whom this testimonium comes, seems to make a point of the word ποητικωτέροις (*poetikoterois*); Anaximander speaks, we are told, 'in somewhat poetical terms.' Possibly a note of disparagement is intended, as if to say that this is no sort of language for a scientist to use. One has to wonder, though, if Anaximander's language is intended to be figurative only. It is tempting to see in it a suggestion that the balance of nature is maintained according to a sort of cosmic justice. There is, however, no point in placing more weight on this fragment than it will bear. Perhaps we are entitled to read his remark about justice and reparation as an early and oblique reference to a natural law; but, if Anaximander had any sort of moral or political theory, we cannot claim to know anything about it.⁹ In the literary remains of his pupil Anaximenes (d. ca 528 BCE), we find no trace of an interest in ethics or politics. Anaximenes thought that the *Urstoff* is air, manifesting itself in different states of condensation and rarefaction. If Anaximander believed in a cosmic justice regulating the way in which natural transformations occur, there is no evidence to suggest that this line of thought was continued by his pupil.

As well as the Milesian monists, we mention the famous Heraclitus of Ephesus (ca 535–475 BCE).¹⁰ Diogenes Laertius tells us that Heraclitus was the hereditary *basileus* of Ephesus, but resigned in favour of his brother. Apparently he was too proud to bother with public affairs.¹¹ Heraclitus is reputed to have written a treatise called Περὶ φύσεως (*Peri physeos*), *On Nature*: a work that has survived only as a collection of formidably obscure fragments and testimonia. If the fragments are representative of the whole, he well deserves the sobriquet σκοτεινός (*skoteinos*), 'dark' or 'obscure.'¹² Once again, we can only try to retrieve from these scraps as convincing an account as possible of what he may have meant. According to Plato (and a similar remark is recorded in several other sources), he thinks that 'all things are in flux and that nothing remains still. In likening existing things to the flowing of a river, he says that you could not step into the same river twice.'¹³ He too is a monist. 'The wise, who listen not to me but to the *logos*, agree that the first principle of everything is One.'¹⁴ Again, there is an *Urstoff*. The world is made of eternal cosmic fire, 'kindled in measure and quenched in measure.'¹⁵ The state of things at any moment is as it is because the forces of coming to be and passing away, of kindling and quenching, are so exactly balanced that the one cannot overcome the other. The *logos*—the 'Divine law,' the principle of 'the One'—underlying and governing the perceptible world is, it seems, the creative opposition of one cosmic force to another:

> It is not generally recognised that what makes a thing coherent is internal tension. Harmony consists in tension between opposites, as in the case of the bow or the harp.¹⁶

What makes a piece of wood and a piece of string into a bow is a relation of opposition or tension between its components; and the same is true, Heraclitus thinks, of everything in the universe. Once that constitutive tension has gone—once one force has overcome the other, as will inevitably happen eventually—stability is at an end; things pass away once more into the primal fire. 'When fire comes, it will judge and condemn all things.'[17] The world and everything in it is finely balanced and impermanent.

To the historian of political thought, the most interesting feature of Heraclitus's cosmology is that, in it, 'ethics is for the first time formally interwoven with physics.'[18] Much more clearly than anything previously encountered, Heraclitus's philosophy of nature appears to include certain ethical and political principles; though, again, only tantalisingly. The following fragments in particular are suggestive:

> It is necessary to know that war is common and justice is strife and that all things come about by strife and necessity.[19]
>
> War is the father of all and the king of all. Some he reveals as gods, others as men; some he makes free, others slaves.[20]
>
> Those who speak with intelligence must look to what is common to all, as a city must look to its law: indeed, more so, for all the laws of men are nourished by one law, the Divine law, which has as much power as it wills, is an unfailing defence for all laws, and prevails over all laws.[21]
>
> It is also law to follow the plan of the One.[22]

Given the difficult and disconnected nature of the fragments, we cannot be certain as to whether Heraclitus had a definite political 'philosophy' or not, or, if so, what it was. But it is not unreasonable to guess that he has in mind something along the following lines. Reality as we experience it is constituted by a harmony of opposing forces. When the equilibrium of forces changes, reality changes. But the *logos*, the 'Divine law,' is 'One'; it is 'common to all': it applies in the world of human affairs as well as to the material cosmos. The natural condition of mankind is one of strife or opposition. Such strife is inevitable and invigorating, and it is foolish to deplore it. Opposition is as much constitutive of political order as it is of the bow or harp. There is stability—stability seems to be what Heraclitus means by 'justice'—for as long as the forces of strife balance or check one another. For as long as they do so, everything remains in its proper order. When they cease to do so, the result is instability or injustice. We may conjecture, therefore, that to follow 'the plan of the One' is to manage the city's affairs in such a way that things remain as they are. It is a matter of seeing to it that no social force becomes strong enough to be disruptive. Perhaps also it is a matter of ensuring that change is creative rather than destructive. The art of maintaining stability is, Heraclitus seems to think, one that can be practised only by the wisest and best, and it should be practised as subtly as possible: 'Non-apparent harmony is better than apparent.'[23] Perhaps the mass of people should have no inkling of what is going on behind the scenes: of matters that they are not equipped to understand. Ordinary people, Heraclitus says several times and with scorn, have no insight into the nature of things.

> One ought to follow what is common to all; but though the *logos* is common to all, the mass of people live as though they had an understanding peculiar to themselves.[24]
>
> What intelligence or understanding do [the masses] have?...They take the mob for their teacher, not realising that most men are bad and few good.[25]
>
> To me, one man is worth ten thousand, if he is outstanding.[26]

Politically, Heraclitus—Heraclitus the hereditary *basileus*—is apparently a conservative and an aristocrat. This is a highly speculative account of what he means; but it is not an unpersuasive one. At all events, it seems clear that his *logos* or 'Divine law' or 'One' functions at least partly as a natural law in the sense in which we are interested: as a universal standard to which we may in some way look for guidance in the conduct of practical life. As we shall see in Chapter 4, Heraclitean ideas were to surface again in the philosophy of Stoicism, though they were there to contribute to a conception of human relations very different from the apparently morose conservatism of their originator. We shall also come across something rather similar in Chapter 8, in the thought of Machiavelli.

Why, for our purposes, are these *disiecta membra* of ancient philosophies interesting? Taken together, the intellectual developments that we have outlined represent a significantly broadened conception of what is to count as an explanation. In the earliest Greek literature—the *Iliad* and *Odyssey* of Homer are usually held to date from ca 850 BCE—the favoured mode of explanation is the *mythos*: the imaginative poetic story intended to enable its audience to understand the world and their place in it.[27] This literature is dramatic; it is not philosophical or political. The *Iliad*, inasmuch as it is the story of tribal warfare, contains themes—power, security, alliance, identity, loyalty—in which we are now interested as students of politics and international relations;[28] but these themes are not theorised or treated abstractly. Greek myths dramatise and convey a naturalistic religion. They offer a universal morality, but it is a morality grounded not in reason but in fate or the will of supernatural beings. They hold up to us the traditional standards of behaviour to which we should conform; they teach us the laws that have been given to mankind by the gods. They also relieve us of the feeling that the world is incoherent or chaotic. The forces of nature are persons, sometimes benevolent, sometimes vindictive, but open to persuasion and manipulation. The sky is Zeus; the sea is Poseidon; Achilles summons the North and West Winds to the pyre of Patroclus with promises and libations.[29] But during the sixth and fifth centuries BCE, thanks to widening horizons and emerging curiosities, we encounter a new and quite different attempt to explain the world: including, though in sources now seriously faulty, 'the laws of men.' Here is a form of explanation that proceeds not by narratives about gods and heroes, but by invoking an impersonal *logos* capable of being known and investigated. It is not stretching the imagination too far to suggest that this *logos* is the origin of the natural law tradition as we understand it. *Logos* did not, of course, supplant or replace *mythos*. But a central feature of the renaissance of 800–500 BCE is the rise, alongside *mythos*, of a genuine, if halting and rudimentary, scientific rationality.[30]

It seems plain, however, that, in an immediate sense, the enterprise of the presocratics failed. If some of them hinted at certain natural political or moral principles as part of their view of reality, these principles were for the time being to remain unelaborated. It may be that their enquiries were more sophisticated than the paucity of their remains allows them to seem. But it is clear that they provoked, in the Eleatic school of philosophy, a reaction amounting to a wholesale repudiation of the claims of empirical science and a retreat into what looks very like the absurd. Why is this? Why did presocratic science fail? The clue, surely, lies in Aristotle's *Metaphysics*.

> Most of those who first sought after knowledge recognised only first principles of a material kind as being the first principles of all things. For that

out of which all existing things are formed, from which their existence originates and into which they are at last destroyed, whose substance persists while changing its qualities: this, they say, is the element and first principle of everything...But they disagree about how many first principles there are, and about what they are like.[31]

The final sentence of this paragraph is the key. Thales had supposed the *Urstoff* to be water; Anaximander *to apeiron*; Anaximenes air; Heraclitus fire. How are we to decide which, if any, of these explanations is correct? Made increasingly aware of the 'otherness' of societies different from their own — of the range of possible versions of the truth — the presocratic philosophers found themselves lacking any principle or method that might enable different versions of the truth to be distinguished. The attempt to create accounts of the order of nature that did not depend on traditional myths could not appeal to the authority of tradition. But without the authority of tradition there was no way of choosing between these alternative accounts: no means of establishing any one of them as more satisfactory than any other. The modern philosopher of science would perhaps express this difficulty in terms of Professor Popper's principle of falsification.[32] Presocratic science has no procedure by which its hypotheses may be tested; the criteria that would enable its conclusions to count as knowledge are absent.

But if the study of the material world leaves us with nothing that can be held as incontestable, where can knowledge lie? This is the question that lies behind the doctrines of Parmenides of Elea (ca 510–450 BCE), the founder of the Eleatic school.[33] Parmenides's ideas are exceptionally difficult and quite unlike anything that had gone before. They are not made more accessible by being set forth in passages of hexameter verse so obscure that 'the meaning of some of his sentences will never be unanimously agreed.'[34] The Eleatic philosophy may plausibly be understood as a counsel of despair in the face of the inability of contemporary science to provide definitive explanations. Parmenides's fragments certainly contain unfavourable, though only glancing, references to Anaximenes and Heraclitus.[35] As we remarked a moment ago, his thought amounts to a root-and-branch rejection of empirical enquiry. It is an attempt to set off in a completely new direction: a direction relying not upon observation, which Parmenides insists is fruitless, but upon logical inference and linguistic analysis. Much of the difficulty of his language is due to the fact that the Greek of his day lacked a vocabulary adequate to express the novel meanings that he wishes to convey. The questions that concern him are the same as those that concerned the presocratic cosmologers. What can we know about the nature of the world and how it works? What *logos* is there? His answer, however, is that, when all is said and done, we can know very little, and nothing that is of any use to anyone. Anyone who thinks otherwise is following 'the way of seeming': a way that is, Parmenides tells us, impossible and unthinkable. His own philosophy is 'the way of truth.' Possibly as a literary conceit, but perhaps also as a way of lending authority to his utterances or indicating their momentous character, he presents it as having been revealed to him by a goddess.[36]

Reduced to as simple a paraphrase of it as can be made, the 'way of truth' is as follows. Anything that is an object of thought or speech must exist, precisely because it *is* an object of thought or speech. The 'something' about which we think or speak must *be* a 'something.' 'Nothing' therefore, is literally unthinkable: οὐκ ἔστι (*ouk esti*), 'it is not,' is, Parmenides says, πανταπευθέα (*pantapeuthea*), 'wholly inconceivable.' Clearly so: it is impossible to have an object of thought that is non-existent. We are therefore bound to affirm that the world, inasmuch as it is an object of thought, exists; or, as Parmenides chooses to express it, we are bound to affirm that it is 'Being.' This, however, is all we can say. To say more about Being—to try to add anything to the statement that Being exists—at once involves us in difficulties. Suppose we hold, as common sense seems to require, that Being is manifold: that it has parts. To say that the parts of Being are separated by Being is the same as saying that they are not separated. But we cannot think that they are separated by nothing, because 'nothing' is not capable of being an object of thought. Being, therefore, must be One. By a similar process of reasoning, it must be eternal. It cannot have come into being, since we should then have to think that, before it did so, it was not: that there was nothing. By the same token, it cannot cease to exist, for then it would leave behind nothing. We are inclined to suppose that there is such a thing as motion; but we find that this supposition too evaporates in the presence of Eleatic logic. If Being were to move from one place to another, what would it leave behind? Evidently, not-Being or nothing, which won't do. Parmenides's pupil Zeno of Elea (b. ca 490 BCE) produced, in his famous paradoxes, a series of arguments intended to illustrate and reinforce Parmenides's doctrines. If you try to walk across a racecourse, how long will it take you to reach the other side? The answer, of course, is that you never will reach the other side, because motion is impossible. In order to get across, you must first get half way across. But before you can get half way across, you must get a quarter of the way, and an eighth of the way, and so on *ad infinitum*. There is no distance, however small, that cannot be halved, and before you can go any distance, you must first go half of that distance. Because the number of halvings is infinitely great, it follows that it is impossible to cover any distance at all. QED.[37]

The Being of Parmenides, then, is a motionless plenum devoid of all sensible qualities and functions. It is one with itself, completely homogenous, without any distinctions or differences. Being is the totality of all things that exist. It is everything, and because it is everything it cannot be any one of the things that exist to the exclusion of the rest; it cannot be water, earth, air or fire. Being can have no determinate characteristics precisely because those characteristics would be determinate, and so would force us to think about 'what is not.' It cannot be red, blue or any other colour; it cannot be dry or wet, hot or cold; it can have no shape, size or, in fact, any observable attributes whatsoever. Sensory experience can tell us nothing about it. Any true information we have about what exists is obtained not by observation but by reason alone: by a logical analysis of what is involved in using the word ἐστι (*esti*), 'it is' or 'it exists.'

Where does Parmenides's remarkable ontology leave us? The presocratic cosmologers had offered order and *logos*: rational understanding, perhaps including a modicum of moral and political understanding. Parmenides too offers *logos*, but his *logos* can only bewilder. We find ourselves occupying a reality that our senses tell us is manifold, yet which intellect purports to demonstrate is One. We find ourselves occupying a reality in which we move about, yet in which motion is impossible; in which we are born and die, yet in which there can be no coming to be nor passing away. What has all this to do with ethics and politics? If Parmenides's 'way of truth' is indeed the truth, it seems that the only truth available to us is at odds with the promptings of common sense and the needs and circumstances of practical life. If we accept Parmenides, we inevitably accept that the world of everyday experience—the world that the Milesian monists had sought to understand—is a kind of illusion. There is no reason to suppose that the Eleatic philosophers really behaved as though this were true; but it is the only conclusion that their remarks ultimately support. Given, then, that this is the world in which we have to make our way, what can we do? On the face of it, it looks as though our reaction to the Eleatic philosophy has to resemble that philosophy's own apparent reaction to presocratic science. We can only throw up our hands in despair. We must conclude that there is no worthwhile connection—indeed, no connection at all—between philosophical enquiry and practical life. This, of course, is exactly the conclusion that Plato was to challenge, in adopting as his philosophical project the goal of building a bridge between the mental world of Parmenides and what Plato habitually calls 'the world of sight.' But why did Plato think this specific project worthwhile? The answer lies largely, if not quite entirely, in the response that the Eleatic philosophy seems to have provoked in certain figures prominent in the intellectual life of Athens during the second half of the fifth century BCE.

Gorgias and Protagoras: Scepticism and Ethical Relativism

Despite the common assertion to the contrary, it is not Socrates but the Sophists of fifth-century Athens who inaugurated the systematic study of morals and politics. For our purposes, two preliminary points may be made about the Athens in which the Sophists for the most part worked. First, she had emerged from the Persian wars of 499–479 BCE as a major maritime and military power. The great victories at Marathon (490 BCE), Salamis (480 BCE) and Plataea (479 BCE) had established her as the most influential of the Greek *poleis*, to the resentment of her militaristic neighbour Sparta. When the Delian League of Ionian cities was formed in 478 BCE for the purposes of defence against the continuing Persian threat, Athens was chosen as its ἡγεμών (*hegemon*): its organisational and military leader. The Delian League was originally a confederation, a συμμαχία (*symmachia*), of free allies with a federal constitution of its own: an early example of concerted action by a group of autonomous States exhibiting a high level of conscious political development. But its military commanders were all Athenian, its fleet was largely Athenian, and Athens controlled its treasury. By the middle of the fifth century, the Delian League had for all practical purposes become an Athenian empire, paying her enormous sums in tribute.

Second, between 800 BCE and 500 BCE the constitutional history of Athens is the history of more or less continuous, and sometimes revolutionary, change.[38] The names and vestiges of older governmental forms endured, but they underwent a series of transitions from monarchy through aristocracy and tyranny to democracy. The phases of this evolution are known to us in detail, not least from the treatise on the Athenian constitution usually attributed to Aristotle. Broadly speaking, we can describe Athenian constitutional history as the progressive displacement of the gentleman by the citizen. Reforms of a democratic character were first enacted in 594 BCE by Solon. After the tyranny of Peisistratus (560–528 BCE), a more broadly democratic constitution was established in 507 BCE by Cleisthenes, though with the higher magistracies remaining in the hands of wealthy families. The growth of democracy was much strengthened by the Persian wars. The wars had been won not by old-style Homeric noblemen and their feudal retainers, but by well-armed and well-trained citizen armies. Athens was above all indebted to the successes of her navy, and the crews of the navy had been recruited from the poorer citizens. After the war, these citizens began to look for a larger share of political rights and duties as the reward of service, and they found a champion in Cleisthenes's great-nephew Pericles—a pupil, incidentally, of Zeno of Elea—who by common consent carried Athenian democracy to the extreme point of its development. The reforms of Pericles after 461 BCE created a constitution under which every free-born native male was entitled to hold office and to serve on the Βουλή (*Boulé*), the Council, consisting of five hundred elected representatives. The recommendations of the *Boulé* were enacted into law by the Εκκλησία (*Ecclesia*), the Popular Assembly, which met forty times a year and which any citizen might attend. In addition to its legislative function, the *Ecclesia* was the highest court of appeal. Every citizen over the age of thirty might be selected by lot to sit as a judge on one of the panels (δικαστήρια: *dikasteria*) that comprised the people's court, the court of first instance. In short, every citizen might participate in the city's corporate life, and might hope to do so to good effect. Lest the poor be excluded from these arrangements, participation was recompensed by a small fee. The traditional stronghold of aristocracy, the Areopagitic Council, whose powers had been diminishing over many years, now served as a court to try offences of homicide only.

By about 450 BCE, then, Athens was a prestigious, powerful and thriving *polis* made wealthy by the income from her empire and by the growth of trade after the Persian wars, with the most advanced democratic constitution yet devised. In these circumstances, her prosperous young men began to look for a particular kind of education: an education that might equip them for a career in such a setting. To meet this demand there arose the class of teachers known to posterity as the Sophists. We must approach the Sophists with some circumspection. For one thing, our knowledge of them is limited, as it was in the case of the presocratic philosophers, by the fact that their writings survive only as fragments.[39] Anything we say about them has necessarily a certain provisionality. Another and more important consideration is that much of what we know about them is mediated to us through hostile sources. Such hostility is particularly associated with Socrates and Plato.[40] Xenophon reports Socrates as saying that 'the people called 'Sophists' offer wisdom for sale to anyone who will pay for it' and that all right-thinking persons regard the name with dislike.[41] Diogenes Laertius says of the Sophist Protagoras of Abdera (ca 485–415 BCE) that 'he neglected meaning in favour of merely verbal distinctions.'[42] There is something to be said for the view that the picture that Plato gives of the Sophists is a caricature; but it is at all events clear that they were a prominent and influential class into whose hands the education of the politically ambitious youth of Athens had passed. They were professional educators whose services were available for a fee, sometimes a considerable one.[43] Civic virtue, Protagoras tells us, is not the exclusive preserve of the rich and well born, as has for so long been thought. By the disposition of the gods it can be taught, and it can be learnt regardless of birth. The myth of Prometheus and Epimethius by which Protagoras justified his profession may be read in the Platonic dialogue named after him.[44]

The Sophists who are from our point of view most interesting are Protagoras, Gorgias of Leontini (ca 480–375 BCE),[45] Gorgias's pupil Callicles,[46] and Thrasymachus of Chalcedon (fl. ca 420). It is generally agreed that Protagoras and Gorgias were the most influential of the Sophists in terms of their effect on their younger colleagues; and it is clear that the intellectual standpoint of Protagoras and Gorgias is in important respects related to the ontology of the Eleatics. Gorgias wrote a treatise called Περὶ τοῦ μὴ ὄντος (*Peri tou mé ontos*) or Περὶ φύσεως (*Peri physeos*): *On Not-Being* or *On Nature*, a work evidently intended as a response to Parmenides. The treatise itself has not survived, but we have two lengthy epitomes of it.[47] Its ostensible purpose is to show that, by using the techniques of reasoning favoured by the Eleatics, we can appear to demonstrate that even manifest absurdities are true. Whereas Parmenides had held that only Being exists, Gorgias proposes that it is just as easy to demonstrate, by deploying the same sort of language, that only *not*-Being exists. Some have regarded *On Not-Being* as an elaborate send-up, and this judgment is up to a point convincing. Like Parmenides's poem, the treatise is mannered, intricate and obscure. Some of its arguments are so patently fallacious that it is hard to imagine that Gorgias intended them to be anything other than satirical.[48] Gorgias does, however, have a philosophical point, and in making it he contrives to complicate still further the problems posed by Eleatic logic.[49] When we try to get beneath his analysis of Being and not-Being, we notice that, in developing it, he has put his finger on an obvious flaw in Parmenides's reasoning. One is inclined to suspect that, satire apart, identifying this flaw is the true purpose of his treatise. Parmenides, we remember, holds that every object of thought has a necessary existence because it *is* an object of thought. But, on Gorgias's showing, not-Being itself is an object of thought. The mere fact that we can think about it establishes it as such. According to Parmenides's own argument, therefore, not-Being or 'nothing' exists; or, to put the same point more comfortably, non-existence is a possible object of thought. Existence, it seems, is a predicate like any other. We are no more compelled to say of anything that it exists than we are to say that it is blue or old.[50]

What is the consequence of this conclusion? It terms of epistemology, matters are now even more perplexing than Parmenides had left them. Clearly, any given thing must either be or not be; but if nothing has a necessary existence (because it is not absurd to conceive of its non-existence), we cannot *know* that anything at all exists, and ultimately we have no way of telling whether any particular thing is or is not. We can question the existence of anything whatsoever without self-contradiction. Implicitly at least, Gorgias's view as it is inferable from the treatise *On Not-Being* is a version of the philosophical position known as solipsism. As Descartes was later to observe, it is possible in principle to doubt the existence of everything except the doubting self. For all anyone can know to the contrary, the doubting self is alone in the void. Gorgias observes moreover that even if something exists and can be known to exist, we cannot communicate our knowledge of it to anyone. Speech, our only means of communication, cannot directly transmit our sensory experience to another. An exclamation of pain or pleasure is a sound; it is not pain or pleasure. Our experiences, it seems, are private to ourselves. In the nature of the case, no one else can know them, or at any rate no one else can have direct or immediate knowledge of them, because language conveys only our account of our experiences: it does not convey the experiences themselves. The treatise *On Not-Being* may well have been meant as a joke or an exercise, typical enough of Gorgias, in rhetorical virtuosity. It seems incontestable, however, that its philosophic core is a comment on the nature of reality that has a clear bearing on Gorgias's view of practical activity and how it is to be conducted.

In practice, of course, Gorgias is no more inclined than anyone else is to suppose that life is unreal or illusory; nor is it his view that our ordinary contact with things and people teaches us absolutely nothing. But he thinks that no part of what it teaches can be regarded as fixed or indubitable. We have to take the world as we find it. Each individual has to deal with whatever is presented in immediate experience, and each has to make pragmatic assumptions about the reality and uniformity of nature. But no experience that we can have is such as to exclude the possibility of our experiencing its opposite. It follows that, ultimately, no assertion that we can make about the world can be shown to be more or less true than its opposite.

Protagoras of Abdera appears to have thought along similar lines. The famous aphorism attributed to him by both Plato and Sextus Empiricus again seems to be a comment on the ontology of Parmenides: 'Man is the measure of all things: of that which is, that it is; of that which is not, that it is not.'[51] According to Sextus Empiricus, this was the opening sentence of a book of Protagoras's called Καταβάλλοντες (*Kataballontes*).[52] What, exactly, is the meaning of this *homo mensura* doctrine? The view ascribed to Protagoras by Socrates in Plato's *Theatetus* is that 'things are to you as they appear to you to be, and to me as they appear to me to be.'[53] Suppose—it is not clear from the text of the *Theaetetus* whether Socrates is devising the illustration himself or paraphrasing Protagoras—that two people step out into the street at the same time, but one of them is cold and the other not. The breeze blowing in the street will strike one of them as warm and the other as cool. There is no point in asking whether the breeze is 'really' warm or cool. Obviously, it is in a sense both. It is cool from the standpoint of one man, warm from that of the other, and there is nothing to be gained by asking whether one or other of them is right. The example chosen, whether it is to be attributed to Protagoras or Socrates, is not a happy one. This kind of thing is, after all, not something that we would normally think problematical; everyone is at home with the idea that some things are in this sense 'relative.' But as far as we can judge, Protagoras believed that *all* the information that our senses give us about the external world is subjective or relative in this way; and this, of course, is a conclusion with momentous consequences. Protagoras, like Gorgias, seems to have thought that all perceptions of the world are private to the individual whose perceptions they are, and incommunicable to others.[54] Honey is sweet to me and fire is hot to me, but I have no way of knowing what they are like to you, or what they are like independently of my own perceptions of them. I cannot know that my future perceptions will resemble my past ones; nor can I know whether anyone else has the same experiences as I, similar experiences to mine, or any experiences at all.[55] Stated at its most general, Protagoras's position is that, strictly speaking, no one can really *know* anything at all. What this implies is that no one can say anything that is objectively true or false. It is impossible to make any statement that is not a statement of belief merely, having no warrant beyond the speaker's own immediate perceptions and wholly subjective interpretations. Some beliefs may be more convenient or expedient than others in terms of their immediate consequences; but no belief can be shown to be more true or more false than any other.[56] 'He used to say,' Diogenes Laertius reports, 'that everything is true';[57] and we may take it that some version of what Protagoras taught was held as a doctrine by the Sophists at large.[58]

Protagoras and Gorgias, then, embrace a thoroughgoing epistemological scepticism or subjectivism. Their philosophical position is, we have suggested, a response to the ontology of Parmenides. For Protagoras and Gorgias, not even the strange, remote and abstract knowledge that the Eleatics propose is available to us. According to Gorgias, if the Eleatic position is carried to the farthest extent of its implications, we have no reason for supposing that anything at all exists. Both he and Protagoras believe that sense-perceptions have no necessary meaning beyond their meaning to the percipient. We may, and for practical purposes do, believe that there is a 'real' world, and we deal with it as it presents itself to our senses; but we cannot strictly speaking know anything about it or say anything true about it. There is no knowledge, no ἐπιστήμη (*epistemé*): only δοξα (*doxa*), opinion or belief, beyond which it is impossible to pass. Protagoras is said to have compiled a volume of ἀντιλογίαι (*antilogiai*) intended to demonstrate by example that nothing can be asserted as an unassailable truth. As far as we can tell, the book consisted of a series of demonstrations that any possible argument can be met by an equally credible counter-argument by anyone with sufficient skill or ingenuity to devise it.[59] As Diogenes Laertius puts it:

> He was the first to say that there are two mutually-opposed *logoi* about everything. It was by means of these *logoi* that he went on to develop his arguments in sequential stages; and he was the first to do this.[60]

Where does all this take us? Protagoras and Gorgias hold that we cannot discover, and therefore that speech cannot convey, any absolute certainty. The study of φύσις (*physis*), nature, has nothing to tell us that is not irredeemably contestable. Any statement about what is the case, any one *logos*, can always be matched by another and antithetical one that might equally well be true, and which may indeed *be* true from the standpoint of whoever utters it. However unsatisfactory this scepticism may be as a general theory of knowledge,[61] its importance to us lies in what it implies for the activity of *moral* judgment. It is this aspect of the matter that, in practice, interested the Sophists most; and it is in this sphere, after all, that it seems most plausible to suggest that certainty is not available. Plato attributes to Protagoras the following remark: 'Whatever seems right and praiseworthy to a particular city *is* right and praiseworthy to it, for as long as it holds it to be so.'[62] There is no objective morality to which appeal can be made in the event of disagreement. If two people—or, at least, two people who do not share a broadly similar perspective—differ over a matter of moral judgment or evaluation, there is no way of demonstrating that either of them is right or wrong. Strictly speaking, neither of them *is* right or wrong. Is it pious to eat your dead or bury them? The only possible answer is that it all depends. It is pious to bury them if you live in Greece and pious to eat them if you live in India. The example is from Herodotus;[63] but it illustrates what Protagoras has in mind. No indicative statement can convey anything more than the opinion of the individual whose statement it is. There may be difficulties in the way of saying that *all* 'knowledge' is really only a matter of opinion or belief, but something of the kind *is* arguably true in the sphere of morality. If it is true, then law, custom and our most ancient and hallowed practices rest on no sure foundation. It is for this reason that Plato perceives the Sophists as the enemies of an entire culture.

On the face of it, Plato's hostility seems a little overdone if we consider it only with respect to Protagoras and Gorgias. As far as we can tell, both Protagoras and Gorgias were responsible teachers, and neither of them encouraged extreme or disruptive political tendencies. On the contrary: Protagoras's view, as represented especially in Plato's *Protagoras*, reminds us somewhat (though the parallels must not be overdrawn) of Burke's *Reflections on the Revolution in France* or the case more recently made out by Professor Popper for 'piecemeal social engineering.'[64] There are no true principles in the light of which we can know that a course of action is right. But our concern as practical beings is not to know what is true but to contrive things in whatever ways happen to suit our requirements. It will be prudent, therefore, for as long as our existing arrangements are working satisfactorily, to leave well enough alone. Protagoras's emphasis is upon traditional institutions and practices. He stresses the value of education; of learning and practising the norms of the community of which you are a member; of worshipping the gods even though we cannot know anything about them, or even that they exist. In Protagoras's case—and the remark probably applies to Gorgias too, though we know less about Gorgias's specifically political views—moral relativism seems to have led to the conclusion of conservatives everywhere: that, in the absence of general certainties, the aim of politics and political education should be to foster cautious, responsible and tradition-honouring behaviour.⁶⁵ But the relativism of which Gorgias and Protagoras are exponents is also capable of subverting the shared beliefs that make social relations possible; and Plato regards this relativism as a decisive component of the cynicism and opportunism that he found in the Athenian politics of his youth.

Having sketched something of the intellectual standpoint of the two most influential and respected of the Sophists, we may now return to their educational programme. As educators, the Sophists, as Plato represents them, were for the most part concerned with teaching what they called ἀρετή: *areté*. Custom has made 'virtue' the usual English translation of this word, but, in modern English, 'virtue' has shed most of the meanings that *areté* has. In Greek literature *areté* means different things in different contexts: merit, goodness, excellence, effectiveness, valour, prowess, manliness, nobility. In the post-Aristotelian moral schools, as we shall see in Chapter 4, it means something like resignation or acceptance. In the context of Sophist education, *areté* is a strictly practical accomplishment.⁶⁶ It is the kind of forensic and political skill that equips its possessor for success in the public life of a democracy, where anyone with the right talents and accomplishments can rise regardless of birth. *Areté* is, one might say, the quality 'by virtue of which' success is attained. And what this 'virtue' chiefly consists in, as far as the Sophists are concerned, is rhetoric: oratory, the art of public speaking.⁶⁷ The Sophist is 'a master of the art of producing clever speakers.'⁶⁸ Indeed, Gorgias, whom we are probably right to regard as the most intellectually gifted of the Sophists, tells us that he, at any rate, is *not* a teacher of *areté*: that all he teaches, and all anyone needs to learn, is rhetoric. With rhetoric, and nothing else, you can achieve whatever you want to achieve, no matter what it is.

> I have many times done the rounds with my brother...or other physicians and found a patient reluctant to take medicine or undergo surgery or cauterisation. And where the physician has failed to persuade him, I have succeeded, simply and solely by the art of rhetoric. I give you my word that if a physician and a rhetorician were to go together into any city you care to name, and there speak against one another before the Assembly...in competition for the job of physician, you would find the physician beaten hands down, and the rhetorician having the job for the asking.⁶⁹

A lengthy example of Gorgias's rhetorical art exists in the form of an elaborate oration called *Encomium of Helen*. In it, Gorgias undertakes the task, plainly chosen as unpromising, of defending Helen of Troy against the charge of having brought about the ten-year Trojan war.[70] She is not to be blamed; she had no choice. Not only was she physically abducted. Also, and more important, her free will was taken from her. It was taken from her, Gorgias maintains, by the persuasive power of speech. Λόγος δυνάστης μέγας ἐστίν (*logos dynastes megas estin*): 'The word is a mighty ruler.'[71] We may take it that his choice of the word δυνάστης — lord, master, ruler — is deliberate and significant. The effect of rhetoric is to dominate the mind. Its action is like that of drugs on the body. It is a kind of master-profession. The skilled exponent of it is able to subdue all purposes to his own.[72]

The importance that the Sophists attach to rhetoric is perfectly comprehensible in the light of their moral relativism. Whether they embraced the relativism to justify the profession of rhetoric or the profession of rhetoric in the light of the relativism is something that we cannot know; nor, of course, does it much matter. The connection between moral relativism and rhetoric is clear. For the ordinary purposes of life we find it convenient to act on some beliefs and discard others; but your beliefs have no more claim to be thought true than mine have. All that the individual can know and respond to is what is given immediately in experience; there is no absolute knowledge of any kind. Whatever else successful practical activity may be, therefore, it cannot be a matter of identifying general truths and acting on them. The conclusion suggests itself that it must be a matter of persuading people to do what you want them to do. To the extent that I can convince you that one opinion is better than another, I can take control of what you do. I can shape the beliefs that you act on, and your behaviour becomes to that extent subject to my will, as Helen's had become subject to the will of Paris. It is impossible to show that anything is true; but it is possible to present one side of a question more effectively than its alternatives and so to determine which side is discarded and which upheld. This, to be sure, is a kind of deception. It entails concealment, the deliberate suppression of one argument in favour of another. But it is an unavoidable and not necessarily ill-intentioned deception. The man of practical experience will see that some courses of action are more advantageous in the circumstances than others, and these are the courses that he will champion. In a sense, rhetoric is a poetic or dramatic art. It is an art that enables its exponents to take command of the imagination and feeling of an audience; and it is an art that can be acquired through teaching. If Gorgias's thesis in the *Encomium of Helen* is to be taken seriously, persuasion can, literally, determine how those who are exposed to its influence will behave.

This, then, is why the Sophists attach so much importance to the art of public speaking as part of their educational curriculum. The ability to address law courts and assemblies persuasively is not only the best asset that the ambitious citizen of a democracy can acquire. There is also a sense in which it is the only asset worth acquiring. To Plato, who finds this whole view of things contemptible, the Sophist is an imitator of wisdom: a seller of false virtue, a charlatan who reduces important and complex matters to triviality in order to make money.[73] The Sophist, he says, is like a man in charge of a great and powerful beast. His profession requires him to say and do whatever will keep the beast pacified.[74]

The 'Radical' Sophists

But it is not really with Protagoras and Gorgias that Plato has a quarrel. They, as we have noted, were by all accounts moderate and conservative individuals who did not see, or at least did not explore, the more extreme practical consequences of their relativism. Some of the younger generation of Sophists, however—commonly referred to as the 'radical' Sophists—held a number of drastic beliefs, or made some drastic assumptions, about human nature and motivation; and these beliefs seem clearly connected with what their elders taught. Evidently they regarded these beliefs as having major implications for social and political relations; and the 'radical' Sophists are the ones to whom Plato is most hostile. It is their standpoint, as represented in the *Gorgias* by Gorgias's pupil Callicles and in the *Republic* by the orator Thrasymachus, that he is most determined to undermine.

The most fundamental of the radical Sophists' beliefs about human relations arises directly from the sceptical epistemology that we have outlined. Moral relativism led them to the straightforward conclusion that right and wrong are simply what those strong enough to enforce

Political Realism in Fifth-Century Athens

their will say they are. In the absence of incontrovertible moral standards, what else can they be? Might is right. The study of nature, of *physis*, is not quite pointless, but it has nothing to add to morality. It discloses only a particularist ethic of hedonism and self-interest. If nature teaches us anything, it is that the strong invariably dominate the weak in order to gratify their own desires.[75] This is a lesson of experience, and there is no point in wringing one's hands about it. We have to accept that right and wrong have no meaning unless accompanied by the power to get one's way. The radical Sophists are nominalists in much the way that Thomas Hobbes is. 'Right' and 'wrong' are not essences, but names. 'Right' means 'what the strong command' and 'wrong' means 'what the strong forbid.'[76]

A further and related assumption is that human beings are by nature greedy, selfish, competitive and ruthless. In strict consistency, this belief has no more claim to be thought true than any other; but every experience that we have encourages us to accept it as a working principle. Wherever you look, you see the same patterns of behaviour. Only those who are failing in life's struggle deplore such behaviour, and the sour-grapes morality to which they resort is a self-serving delusion. In the *Gorgias*, the following speech—no doubt it is intentionally outrageous—is put into the mouth of Callicles.

> How can anyone be happy if he is the servant of anything?...I tell you plainly that he who wishes to live well must allow his appetites to grow strong and not restrain them. When they have grown as large as they can be, he should have the courage to serve them and gratify all his desires: this is what I call natural justice and nobility. But the masses cannot achieve it, and they blame the strong man because they are ashamed of their own weakness, which they desire to conceal. For this reason they say that lack of self-restraint is base...They enslave nobler natures and, because they are not able to secure the full enjoyment of their own pleasures, they praise [conventional] justice and temperance out of their own cowardice...But in truth, Socrates...luxury and lack of self-restraint, and freedom, together with the means to enjoy them, *are* virtue and happiness.[77]

We note the distinction that Callicles here draws between natural justice and conventional justice. The good life, the life of *natural* 'justice and nobility,' consists not in any relationship of mutuality or service with one's fellow citizens, but in being free: in being free to do whatever one wants to do. Freedom is 'negative' freedom. It is a matter of not having to accept any limit or constraint. Callicles is moreover a hedonist, in both the psychological and ethical senses. Not only is it true in fact that human beings seek always to gratify their desires as completely as they can; it is according to nature, and therefore right and good, that they should. Again, we see in his use of language a nominalism that enables a straightforward connection to be made between fact and value. 'Natural justice,' 'nobility,' 'virtue,' 'happiness': these are names that human beings use in relation to the gratification of their appetites. By the same token, such things as conventional justice and temperance are verbal devices invented by the unsuccessful to solace their frustrations. Human potential is realised most fully in those 'nobler natures' who are most resourceful in defying whatever stands between them and the gratification of their every wish. Despite all our protestations to the contrary, Callicles suggests—and his viewpoint is repeated in its essential respects by Thrasymachus in Book 1 of the *Republic*—we all know this and, in our heart of hearts, we all desire this condition of unlimited personal supremacy for ourselves. Everyone wants a life of complete and unobstructed self-indulgence at the expense, where necessary, of his fellows. Everyone holds those weaker than himself in contempt. It is better to do injury than suffer it. Whoever denies this is a fool, a liar or a weakling. Anyone who denies it moreover lays himself open to exploitation or worse. Experience teaches that everyone grabs for himself. If we do not follow suit, we can only harm ourselves: self-restraint and consideration for others are folly.[78]

It is usual to attribute to the Sophists in general the doctrine that the *polis* is an artificial creation of expediency, and not a natural phenomenon. Political arrangements come about as a matter of νόμος (*nomos*), not *physis*: by convention, not nature. In the case of the radical Sophists, this attribution requires a degree of modification. They believe on the whole that the *polis* is artificial, but their views about human nature and motivation imply a limiting case: namely, that of the unfettered and exploitative tyranny. If, according to nature, every man wishes to have as much as he can for himself and be subject to no one, then the natural state of affairs among human beings is for the more powerful to exploit the less powerful and for the most powerful to exploit everybody. Freedom to exploit is what Callicles calls natural as distinct from conventional justice. To his mind, it is not that justice and government are unnatural as such, but that their natural forms are realised only under the government of the tyrant. The radical Sophists take it for granted that a natural ruler is a natural predator. As for non-tyrannical forms of political organisation, they come into being, Callicles suggests, as a result of σύνθηματα (*synthemata*), 'agreements.' These agreements occur when the weak band together for the purposes of mutual defence against the strong.

> It is the majority who [as individuals] are weak who lay down the laws; and they make laws and distribute praise and blame with reference to themselves and their own interests. They are hostile to stronger men who have the prowess to get more, and they say that self-interested ambition is disgraceful and unjust, meaning, by injustice, a man's desire to have more than his fellows. Equality pleases them because they are aware of their own inferiority. The endeavour to have more than the many is conventionally (νόμῳ, i.e. by *nomos*) said to be shameful and unjust, and is called injustice, whereas nature (*physis*) herself shows us that it is just for the better to have more than the worse, the more powerful than the weaker, and...that justice consists in the superior ruling over and having more than the inferior...But if there were a man born with enough ability, he would shake off all [artificial restraint] and break free and escape it.[79]

On this view, the *polis*, insofar as the *polis* is a commonwealth or association as distinct from a case of natural despotism, is the result of a compact between vulnerable people who have agreed to combine forces to limit the freedom of the strong by laws. The word 'compact' perhaps begs the question, but Callicles's understanding of the origin of political association reminds us in certain respects of Hobbes's account of why and how human beings co-operate. The non-tyrannical *polis*—we may take it that Callicles has the democratic constitution of Athens in mind—comes about when those who are naturally weak unite to make themselves artificially strong: when conventional or legal justice is created at the expense of natural justice.[80] A different formulation of what is fundamentally the same idea is put into the mouth of Plato's brother Glaucon, who represents it as being a Sophist doctrine, at *Republic* 358E–359A. Political arrangements come into being, Glaucon suggests, as a result of agreements not to harm each other made between people who, alone, are not strong enough either to do harm with impunity or avenge themselves when they suffer it. On either view, the non-tyrannical *polis* comes about not as a natural growth, but by human contrivance: not by nature, but by convention. Its justice, Glaucon says, 'is a mean or compromise between being able to do injury without punishment, which is the best thing of all, and having to suffer it without being able to retaliate, which is the worst thing of all.'

Not only is the non-tyrannical *polis* not natural, then: it is positively *un*natural. It comes into being when people try to tamper with the natural play of forces according to which the strong rule and the weak submit. It arises when the constraint of legal justice is created to restrict the freedom of the vigorous and ambitious. *Physis* and *nomos* are not only separate; they are fundamentally at odds. The radical Sophists believe that the natural (and, by implication, good and healthy) impulse of human beings is to strive to outdo one another and that political co-operation is the process by which this natural impulse is thwarted and controlled. What the Greeks call στάσις (*stasis*), conflict, is therefore not an avoidable misfortune, but an inevitable part of a vigorous political life, as the weak try to control the strong and the strong try to break free and assert their natural superiority. This theme may be an intentional reference to the opinion of Heraclitus: 'War is the father of all and the king of all. Some he reveals as gods, others as men; some he makes free, others slaves.' We might say that, according to the natural order of things, every *polis* that is not already a tyranny is striving to turn into one. If we extrapolate this doctrine into the field of international politics, the conclusion is plain: the natural condition of human life is one of war. Each State, as an international actor, will, and indeed should, seek to dominate its neighbours. Any State that does not heed this advice will not remain an independent State for long.

The Peloponnesian War

Considered as a political theory, then, the *Realpolitik* associated with the radical Sophists is grounded in a sceptical epistemology and the moral relativism implicit in it. We have suggested that this sceptical epistemology has its origins in the actions and reactions of Greek intellectual life during the sixth and fifth centuries BCE. But however much they may draw upon the resources of philosophy, political theories are characteristically *responses* to something. It would be naive to suppose that Athenian political realism emerged simply *in abstracto* from the speculation of intellectuals. Its topicality in the late fifth century must be understood in terms of the circumstances of strife and external threat in which its exponents found themselves. For the sake of completeness, we must pay some attention to these circumstances.

Militarism born of rivalry between tribes and tribal alliances had been a persistent feature of the culture of Homeric Greece; and we should not underestimate the continuing influence of the Homeric epics in fostering an admiration for martial prowess. 'Most of the central figures of classical Greece "had all been brought up on Homer...they had learned to look to the *Iliad* and the *Odyssey*, not merely for historical facts but for ethical principles".'[81] That the growth of the *polis* intensified the potential for conflict is a generalisation easy to infer from the astute commentary of the Athenian historian Thucydides.[82] The *poleis* were sovereign communities organised to acquire, exploit and defend the resources necessary to them. They were communities committed to territorial security and the interests of their citizens. Those citizens easily acquired a sense of their own identity and of the 'otherness' of rival communities. They were aware of the importance of power, aggressive diplomacy and, where opportunity served, active imperialism. Thucydides knows, as clearly as Heraclitus had known, that ἔρις (*eris*), strife, is an inescapable part of life: that peace is only the anteroom of war and that there will always be causes (αἴτιαι: *aitiai*) and pretexts (πρόφασεις: *prophaseis*) for war.[83] You see human nature at its clearest and most real, Thucydides remarks, in time of war.[84] The sentiment is like Carl Schmitt's: the true nature of power is revealed only in crisis, in 'a state of exception,' a 'state of emergency,' a 'state of siege'; the essential distinction in politics is the distinction between friend and enemy.[85]

The half-century of uneasy peace that followed the Persian wars ended in 431 BCE. For more than a quarter of the fifth century BCE, Athens was involved in a long, exhausting and ultimately unsuccessful contest with Sparta and her allies: the Peloponnesian War. The war began as a result of diplomatic and military complications described in detail by Thucydides. It dragged on through a series of treaties and vicissitudes, including the disastrous Athenian plague of 430 BCE, until the final siege and humiliating defeat of Athens in 404

BCE. This is a crucial part of the background against which the Sophists thought and taught. Their views as we have described them are of a kind that one might associate with a sense of moral disintegration. It is a safe conjecture that the disruptions of war called into question traditional assumptions about justice and right conduct, just as the broadening of geographical and cultural horizons had called into question traditional assumptions about the nature of the world and the gods. Even aside from questions of culture or background, it is hardly surprising that, at such a time, there should have been a marked current of opinion that saw the world as a cruel and merciless place: an arena in which the strong survive and the weak do not. Thucydides's own appraisal of the relation between war, amoralism and the use of language is revealing:

> War, in destroying the comfort of ordinary life, is a harsh teacher, and it adapts the temperament of most men to the conditions in which they find themselves...The usual meaning of words was changed as men claimed the right to use them as they pleased in justifying their actions. Rash daring was now called courage and party loyalty; prudent delay became an excuse for cowardice; moderation and self control came to be regarded as a mere disguise for timidity...In short, praise went to those who were foremost in performing some evil deed, and to him who incited another to commit some crime that he had not been contemplating.[86]

Also, of course, 'When a democracy is at war, oratory becomes of greater importance, because more vital issues are debated and more stirring leadership is demanded.'[87]

Athenian diplomacy during the war—a diplomacy practised by exactly the kind of careerists at whom the Sophists' educational curriculum was aimed—exhibited realism of the most uncompromising sort. The 'Athenian thesis' was that, at any rate in foreign affairs, the governing principle of conduct is not ethics but necessity. A famous incident, the so-called Melian debate, is recorded by Thucydides.[88] This episode is of interest to us because it has always been believed that the line taken in the debate by the Athenian emissaries reflects attitudes typical of, or inculcated by, radical Sophist teaching.[89] As Professor Guthrie remarks, Thucydides's reports of the Melian debate 'supply the necessary background to an outburst like that of Thrasymachus in the *Republic.*'[90] The inhabitants of the small island State of

Melos had resisted all efforts to persuade them to join the Athenian confederacy. After an initial attempt at neutrality, they began to drift towards an alliance with Sparta. Envoys were sent from Athens to reason with some of the leading citizens of Melos (the envoys were not allowed access to the *Ecclesia*, in case they should prove too persuasive). Thucydides describes the conversation in detail. Near the beginning of the debate, the Athenians observe that there is no point in appealing to fine moral sentiments or talking about justice. Everybody knows 'that men arrive at "just" settlements only when the parties involved are of equal strength. Otherwise, the strong take what they can and the weak give what they must.'[91] Justice, it seems, is what happens when no one is strong enough to impose his will on the other parties. But, the Melians reply, the strong may not be strong for ever. By being cruel and unmerciful now, the Athenians could be setting an example to others by which they will one day suffer themselves. Even at the level of utility it is a good idea for the strong to extend to the weak τὰ εἰκότα καὶ δίκαια (*ta eikota kai dikaia*), 'fairness and justice.'[92] After a good deal of argument, during which the Melians, with something of an air of desperation, claim to be on the side favoured by the gods,[93] the Athenian envoys retort:

> We know it to be true of the gods, and we believe it to be true of men, that as a matter of natural necessity they always rule wherever they have power to do so. We did not make this law, nor are we the first to take advantage of it. We found it already in existence, and we expect that it will remain in existence for ever. We therefore follow it, and so would you [if you could] and [so would] anyone else who had as much power as we…And the Spartans will not help you either…for they more than any others think that 'pleasant' is the same as 'good' and 'interest' as 'justice.'[94]

The only law of nature is that might is right. Whether Thucydides himself subscribes to this position or is merely reporting it is a matter of some debate;[95] but this oft-quoted passage may be taken as the *locus classicus* of Athenian political realism in practice.[96]

In the Melian debate, we notice that three different conceptions of justice make an appearance; we notice also that they do so to no real purpose. The Athenians suggest, as Glaucon does in the *Republic*, that justice is what emerges from a condition of stalemate, 'when the parties involved are of equal strength' and both sides have to compromise. They mention also the view that 'justice' and 'interest' are the same, by which they mean that each party will believe, as the Spartans apparently do, that 'justice' is what serves his own interest. This is something like the position that Thrasymachus defends in Book 1 of Plato's *Republic*. To the Melians, justice is neither of these things. It is fairness: fair treatment extended to the weak by the strong; not, to be sure, without an eye to the long-term advantage of the strong, but nonetheless willingly extended to those who are in no position to demand it. There is, it seems, no one conception of justice capable of commanding everyone's assent. Ultimately, the Athenians dismiss discussion of justice entirely, in favour of a maxim that might have come from Callicles himself: 'men...always rule wherever they have power to do so.' In 416 BCE, diplomatic resources having failed, Melos was besieged by Athens and surrendered to the Athenian general Philocrates. The Athenians 'slew all the men of military age and enslaved the women and children. Later, they settled the place themselves, sending five hundred colonists to it.'[97]

To some extent, this chapter was intended as a prolegomenon to Plato's *Republic*. Let us now try to sum it up with that purpose in mind. The Sophists entertain a range of beliefs, and at least some of them endorse standards of conduct, which Plato regards as morally and politically disastrous. They were not, moreover, a lunatic fringe. They were not a handful of cranks who could be laughed out of court. The fact that both Protagoras and Gorgias have Platonic dialogues named after them is enough to show how seriously Plato took them. The Sophists were intellectually respectable; some of them were intellectually formidable: and they were the professional educators of their day. Was their educational activity actually responsible for creating standards of behaviour, or did it only articulate attitudes long present in Greek culture and given immediacy by the necessities of war? There is no way of answering this question clearly. But it is to their influence, and especially to the influence of the 'radical' Sophists, that Plato attributes the violent and capricious style of politics that afflicted Athens towards the end of the fifth century BCE. According to the Sophists, there are no moral absolutes. Public life cannot be conducted according to objective standards of right and wrong because there are no objective standards of right and wrong. Government and submission to government rest on nothing more than human agreement, belief and, ultimately, force. Men are assumed to be selfish and tyrannical by nature, and politics is about exploitation and control. The Sophists can offer no clear account of what justice is. Is it following the established customs of one's city? Is 'natural' justice the freedom to exploit others with impunity? Is legal or conventional justice a compromise forced upon us by expediency? Or a means of thwarting the healthy desires of the strong? Or the perceived interest of whoever is using the word 'justice'? To cap it all, the Sophists insist that success in the public sphere depends not upon probity or reputation, but upon one's ability to manage public opinion through persuasion. They are professionally committed to the view that even the most disreputable and base-born can acquire this ability for a fee. Not surprisingly, Plato regards the Sophists as being, literally, in the business of training demagogues and political adventurers.

Plato's dislike of the Sophists is related closely to his conviction that democracies are especially vulnerable to subversion by those who have acquired the art of manipulating the beliefs of ordinary citizens. The problem with 'democratic man,' as Plato calls him, is not that he is committed to values that are wrong or unsound. Rather, it is that he is not committed to any particular values at all. The democratic personality is a disordered and undisciplined one. Democratic man is demoralised man, weak-willed and irresolute. He is dominated by unnecessary and frivolous desires. His life is characterised by the aimless pursuit of every passing fancy.[98] The very open-mindedness and versatility upon which Pericles had congratulated the Athenians in his *Funeral Oration* are, to Plato, disadvantages.[99] The possessor of a democratic 'personality' is a blank page waiting to be written on by whoever has the greatest plausibility or eloquence. Democracy, Plato suggests, has the self-destructive effect of undermining the characters of its citizens. It is for this reason, he thinks, that democratic constitutions are so notoriously liable to subversion by the unscrupulous.

This, in outline, is the intellectual context of Plato's *Republic*; though we shall have a little more to say by way of contexualisation in the next chapter. In the light of this context, the *Republic's* objectives as a philosophical essay become intelligible. Plato's purpose is to establish:

1. That there are non-relative standards of justice that political communities and individual human beings must acknowledge if they are to achieve their purposes successfully.
2. That these standards are capable of being understood and applied by those whose reason has been developed by a specialised kind of education and training.
3. That the *polis*, properly understood, is a community dedicated to the common good: a community that exists by nature and not by convention merely.
4. That the possibility of discovering absolute moral standards has a definite bearing upon the question, What is the best form of government?

An important part of the Sophists' project, according to Plato's understanding of it, is to show that morality has no footing independent of the opinions of those who create and sustain it. But their contention, expressed as the maxim of Protagoras that 'man is the measure of all things,' cannot be answered by a simple counter-assertion. Any such counter-assertion would plainly succumb at once to the objection that man is the measure of all things. If there is no real difference between one opinion and another, to argue about differences of opinion is to argue about nothing. To this extent, therefore, Plato realises that 'contradiction is impossible.'[100] With an optimism not entirely vindicated by his attempt actually to do it, he sets out to vanquish the Sophists by logical demonstration rather than by the futile opposition of one rhetoric to another. The Sophists' moral relativism, and the consequence of that relativism in making mere contradiction fruitless, was therefore an important stimulus to the first extended attempt to think philosophically about politics.

Chapter 2

Plato's 'Republic': The Sovereignty of Philosophy

PLATO WAS born in Athens in 427 BCE, four years after the outbreak of the Peloponnesian War. At the end of the war, he was twenty-three. As far as we can tell, the war itself had little effect on the development of his political ideas. Much more important is the fact that his early adulthood coincided with the period of extreme political dislocation following the defeat of Athens in 404 BCE. An immediate consequence of defeat was the overthrow of the democratic constitution of Pericles and the establishment of a ruling council of thirty oligarchs. This council was established, at the instance of the Spartan general Lysander, ostensibly to restore order, but with the clear intention of intimidating and demoralising the Athenian people. Especially in the behaviour of the 'radical' Sophist Critias, its most prominent member, it was distinguished by an extreme disregard for ordinary standards of morality.[1] In Critias—who was, we note, for some time a pupil of Gorgias—'we find a union of all the impulses of the sophistic movement.'[2] Critias was an exponent of the principle that we encountered in Callicles and the Athenian diplomats at Melos: might is right; the world belongs to the strong and masterful; it behoves the weak only to submit. He is said to have written a scandalous play called *Sisyphus* in which he suggested that the gods are an invention of legislators to frighten the masses into obeying the laws.[3] The 'Thirty Tyrants,' as they are called, adopted policies of government so ferocious that they alienated many of those prosperous Athenians who had initially regarded their rule with optimism. The new constitution drawn up by Critias and his colleague Charicles prescribed that only the 3000 full citizens of Athens might have a legal trial, and that anyone else could be put to death by summary order of the government.[4] It forbade 'instruction in the art of disputation': a prohibition possibly directed against Socrates, as Xenophon suggests,[5] but probably indicative of a more general resolve to stifle argument by eradicating the techniques and attitudes that make it possible. The short and discreditable life of the oligarchy was punctuated by show trials, confiscations, executions and onerous laws. [6]

Plato tells us that he himself almost played a part in this oligarchic government.[7] Members of his family were prominent in it—Critias was his great-uncle[8]—and offered to arrange a suitable career for him. The prospect was not without its attractions. Plato's family was wealthy and aristocratic; he was no lover of democracy, and he had youthful high hopes that the new regime might preside over a successful post-war reconstruction. The ruling council's deterioration in less than a year into rapacious tyranny taught him a vivid and remembered lesson in 'how difficult it is to take part in public affairs and remain an honourable man.' This feeling 'grew stronger the more I observed and the older I became.'[9] He was, he tells us, relieved when, in 403 BCE, a counter-revolution under the soldier and politician Thrasybulus swept the Thirty Tyrants away and reinstated the democratic constitution.

But it was under this restored democracy that Plato's revered teacher Socrates perished. At the instance of three citizens of Athens called Meletus, Anytus and Lycon, Socrates was tried on a charge of 'not recognising the gods that the city recognises...introducing new gods [and] corrupting young men.'[10] As capital charges go, this sounds unconvincing. Perhaps Socrates had come to be perceived as a bad influence on the young, but it seems likelier that he was a political casualty. Though not personally associated with the excesses of the Thirty, he was known to be a friend and teacher of Critias; the oligarch Charmides was a member of his circle;[11] he was also an intimate companion of Alcibiades, a person of pronounced anti-democratic tendencies.[12] Socrates was condemned to death and executed by self-administered poison in 399 BCE. The story of his final days and of the dignity with which he comported himself is told in Plato's *Euthyphro*, *Apology*, *Crito* and *Phaedo*. The orator Aeschines, speaking in 345 BCE, remarks, as though it were a matter of common knowledge, that Socrates was condemned because of his association with Critias.[13]

Plato: The Sovereignty of Philosophy

The death of Socrates was a defining moment in Plato's career. The celebration of his teacher's life and the propagation of his doctrines became his mission (although he also created a Socrates of his own: a kind of imaginary friend who came to embody everything that he wanted to believe in).[14] In 399 BCE, Plato and other companions of Socrates left Athens. He remained in voluntary exile until 386 BCE. It is not difficult to imagine his feelings. Having spent his formative years in a city at war, he had then seen the oligarchy of the Thirty, which he had hoped might 'lead men out of a bad way of life into a good one,'[15] turn into a sanguinary fiasco; he had moreover seen his friend and teacher tried and condemned under the ensuing democracy. Not surprisingly, the conclusion formed in his mind that all existing governments are bad. 'I never ceased to think about how an improvement might be made to this particular state of affairs and to politics in general, and I remained vigilant for the right moment to act.'[16] While still a young man, he came to believe that 'mankind's troubles will never have an end until either true and genuine philosophers achieve political power or, by some dispensation of providence, rulers of States become genuine philosophers.'[17] This conviction was to remain with him for the rest of his life. But what, exactly, does he mean by 'true and genuine philosophers'? Why does he regard philosophy as indispensable to good government, and how are we to understand this conviction in the light of its background? These are the questions that we must now examine.

The Argument with Thrasymachus

The actual date of the *Republic* is different from its 'dramatic' date. The dialogue was written in about 375 BCE, but it is set in the Athens of the late fifth century.[18] The political milieu that it addresses is one shaped by the Peloponnesian War and by the currents of epistemological and moral opinion that we examined in the previous chapter. It is no accident that the literary device by which it is got properly under way is an aggressive challenge to Socrates by the radical Sophist Thrasymachus of Chalcedon.[19] Plato's purpose is to refute the dangerous relativism of the Sophists and to correct the disintegration of morality that he takes them to represent. But the dialogue does not focus upon Athenian affairs as such. Plato is concerned with 'politics in general'; the *Republic* is a general contribution to the debate between *physis* and *nomos*, and it is this fact that gives it its lasting philosophical interest. Viewed in the context of Greek intellectual history, the Sophists occupy a transitional position. The forces of science, philosophy, war and domestic strife have shaken old assumptions about men and the gods. The way is open for something new. Plato is not a mere conservative. He wishes to effect a revolution in moral theory, 'a shift of perspective on the whole question of the right way to live.'[20] His objective is to discover an enduring formula for political order, stability and rationality, and to investigate the conditions under which these qualities might flourish. This desire for stability and order is Plato's central motivation as a political philosopher.

Although it turns into a great deal more, the *Republic* begins as an enquiry into the meaning of δικαιοσύνη (*dikaiosyné*), justice or right conduct: the concept about which there was so much diversity of opinion in contemporary circles. The dialogue is narrated by its chief protagonist, Socrates, the day after it is supposed to have taken place. This literary form is undeniably clumsy. As we shall notice, its clumsiness has no little bearing on the philosophical clarity of the *Republic*. The other main characters are an elderly acquaintance of Socrates called Cephalus, Cephalus's son Polemarchus, Plato's older brothers Glaucon and Adeimantus, and the Sophist Thrasymachus. The figure of Cephalus represents the old ways and beliefs that were being so much challenged by contemporary circumstances. The fact that his family was to suffer persecution, and Polemarchus to lose his life, under the Thirty Tyrants, is not without dramatic significance. Despite its length and often unhelpful complexity, the political point of the *Republic* is simple enough: Socrates is the White Knight of truth ranged against Sophist villainy in the shape of Thrasymachus. In the following pages, we shall take it for granted that Plato's opinions are the ones expressed in the *Republic* by Socrates.

On their way home from a religious ceremony at the Piraeus, Socrates and Glaucon are persuaded to go back to Cephalus's house, where they find the other protagonists assembled. After a certain amount of amiable conversation, the floor is seized by Thrasymachus. Plato's hostility to him is obvious from the outset, as is the extent to which Book 1 of the *Republic* is an *ad hominem* argument. This is a fact to be borne in mind by anyone who wishes properly to understand the nature of Book 1 as a controversial document. At least partly, Plato wants to undermine Thrasymachus's version of radical Sophist *Realpolitik* by diverting attention away from his argument and presenting him to us as boorish, intolerant and sarcastic. Talking to Thrasymachus, Socrates observes, is like having a bucket of water thrown over you.[21] Thrasymachus has been listening with growing irritation to the desultory attempts made so far to discover what justice is, bursting to interrupt but not allowed by the others to do so. Cephalus the traditional thinker holds that justice is a matter of giving to men and the gods what is due to them; his mind is grounded in the standards of the Homeric epics. Polemarchus, inclined to be a realist, thinks that it is helping friends and harming enemies. Finally losing patience, 'like a wild beast about to tear us to pieces...shouting at everybody,'[22] Thrasymachus offers his own uncompromising definition:

> *Thras*: You can see how wise Socrates is! He refuses to be the teacher and always learns from others, with never a word of thanks!
> *Soc*: It is true enough that I learn from others. But I certainly don't agree that I'm ungrateful. I have no money, so I pay with what I have, which is praise. When you answer me you will see how I ready I am to praise anybody who seems to me to speak well; for I'm sure your answer will be a good one.
> *Thras*: Well listen to this: I say that justice is nothing else than the interest of the stronger party. Why do you not praise me, then? You won't, though, will you?[23]

Socrates, though affecting to be frightened of Thrasymachus, then conducts a long and intricate analysis of his definition of justice. During his cross-examination by Socrates, Thrasymachus is made to shift his ground several times: not, in fact, in ways that alter his central realist contention, though the exact nature of his position has been much discussed. What he has in mind, it turns out, is not quite that justice is 'nothing else than the interest of the stronger party.' Rather, he thinks that it is in the interest of the stronger party for *others* to be just and he himself unjust. Justice and the just, he says,

> are in reality another's good, that is to say, the interest of the ruler and stronger, and the loss of the subject and servant; and injustice is the opposite. For the unjust man is lord over the truly artless and just. He is the

stronger, and his subjects do what serves his interest, and minister to his happiness, which is very far from being their own.

He is therefore led into the superficially curious position of having to say that injustice is better than justice.

> Injustice on a large enough scale is stronger, freer and more masterful than justice. As I have said already, justice is that which is subservient to the interest of the strong. But what really profits a man from his own point of view and secures his own interest is injustice.[24]

On the face of it, we are by the end of Book 1 supposed to believe that Socrates has defeated his flustered and ungracious opponent. But one is left with the impression that Socrates has been allowed to win rather easily; and this is something of which Plato is not unaware. The debate is on one level plainly intended to make Thrasymachus look foolish; but this is only a preliminary, and not a particularly successful, form of attack. For all his attempts to undermine it by portraying Thrasymachus unfavourably, Plato understands that Thrasymachus does have an intelligible and persuasive view that cannot be made to look ridiculous merely. What, then, is Thrasymachus's case, when all is said and done? Of what version of the radical Sophist standpoint is he an exponent? If we try to extract its essence from the complexities of the dialogue in which it is embedded, his position may be reduced to the following related points.[25]

1. He offers a conventionalist or positivist account of justice. When we say of someone that he is just, what we mean is that he is dutiful in obeying the city's law. 'Justice' is the state of affairs created by an artificial system of constraints, and the 'just' individual is one who allows his conduct to be circumscribed by its rules. Thrasymachus glosses this definition (though the gloss is not part of the definition) with the observation that anyone who willingly allows his conduct to be so circumscribed is either a weakling who has no choice or a kind of amiable fool: a simpleton who does not realise where his interests lie.
2. He observes that it is according to nature that the weak are ruled by the strong. He assumes moreover (though the assumption is not implicit in the statement — the truism — that the strong invaria-

bly rule the weak) that the strong will always rule in their own interest, or at any rate in what they believe to be their own interest.[26] Thrasymachus's assumptions are the radical Sophist ones that we considered in the previous chapter: that the strong dominate wherever they can, that they do so by nature, and that they always do so with a view to their own advantage. Everywhere you look, this is nature's way and hence, according to the kind of nominalism that we mentioned in connection with Callicles, the right way. What else could 'right' mean? The point of ruling, Thrasymachus thinks, is to secure profit for yourself by exploiting those over whom you have power.

3. Where does law come from? We notice that Thrasymachus's view differs somewhat from that of Callicles. Callicles had suggested that the laws by which conventional justice is expressed are devices produced by the concerted efforts of the weak to shackle the strong. Thrasymachus suggests that they are the means by which the strong control and take advantage of the weak. Law is a system of conventional rules imposed by those strong enough to enforce it upon those too weak or too foolish to resist. Law, as we might now say, institutionalises the dominant ideology. We can most easily explain the difference between Callicles and Thrasymachus in terms of a difference of perspective. Callicles's account of how law arises seems intended as a comment on Athenian democracy: as a complaint about the way in which democracy stifles vigour and ambition. By contrast, Thrasymachus is evidently thinking of law as the tyrant would make it. The difference is unimportant for our purposes. The assumption in both cases is the same: that conventional law exists to thwart and control those subject to it.

4. Thrasymachus holds, as Callicles does, that the most natural, and therefore the best, kind of life is one from which all restraint, all limitation, is absent. It is for this reason that injustice is better than justice. To Thrasymachus's mind, injustice is a 'virtue' in the instrumental, Sophist, sense. It is a virtue because it enables us to achieve our goals. According to the same reasoning, justice is a vice. The terminology is odd and paradoxical, no doubt intentionally so: Thrasymachus, like Callicles, wants to shock. But his meaning is not hard to see. What Thrasymachus means by 'injus-

tice' is exactly what Callicles had meant by 'natural' as distinct from conventional justice. The individual who is unfettered by any restriction is better off and happier than someone whose freedom of action is limited by his having to obey the law.[27] By nature, we all want to be free in the sense of exempt from the 'justice' of the law. Wherever law comes from, we are made subject to it only by convention or human enactment. Law itself, because it curtails our natural freedom, is an unnatural superimposition upon our true desires.

It comes as no surprise to find that Thrasymachus is a frank admirer of tyranny. The happiest and most successful man, he asserts, is the ruler who has succeeded in turning those subject to him into slaves.[28]

Justice as a Natural Principle

In Thrasymachus, we are presented, in a setting of deliberately staged confrontation, with another statement of the realism that we encountered in Callicles and in Thucydides's report of the Melian debate. There are differences, but only superficial ones. The good life is a matter of maximising power: of being able to liberate oneself from the limitations to which only the weak and pusillanimous defer, and of using one's power to the full and to one's own advantage. It is through the successful disregard of limitation that human beings express their true nature as exploitative and self-seeking. We note once again that, if we extend this argument into the international sphere, its implication is that war is the natural, and indeed the right and healthy, condition of mankind, and that its casualties are those too weak to enjoy the triumph that is the meed of the strong. The 'good' ruler or statesman is the individual strong enough or astute enough successfully to impose his will on others for his own purposes. Subjects, on the other hand, will inevitably — will by definition — be people who live stultified and frustrated lives. This is the kind of view that Plato, speaking through Socrates, wishes to confute.

After some preliminary skirmishing, Socrates embarks on his first major line of counter-attack: a challenge to Thrasymachus's assertion that the *point* of ruling is to achieve profit at the expense of one's subjects. If this is so, then, as we have noted, prowess in the art of ruling is displayed to perfection in the successful tyrant, and political philosophy as a normative enterprise is revealed as futile: might is right, and the student of politics can do no more than explore the realities and expediencies of power and security. But surely, Socrates urges, there is a distinction to be drawn here. One must distinguish between the practice of an art and the making of profit from it. Those who practise any art may indeed derive gain from their practice; but would one really want to say that the deriving of gain is the point or definition of the art? Strictly speaking, Socrates suggests, deriving gain is a separate kind of activity in itself. Consider the physician. When we say that someone is a good physician, what do we mean? Do we mean that he makes a fortune in fees, or that he is a successful healer of his patients? The point can be generalised to apply to any art. Do we say that a man is a good shepherd because he makes a lot of money out of wool and mutton, or because he cares for his sheep well? We might develop the point by remarking (though Socrates does not do this) that we can perfectly well conceive of an amateur shepherd or physician: of someone who practises the art of medicine or shepherding without pay. Marie Antoinette kept sheep at Le Petit Trianon *for fun*. Such an amateur might be considered an outstanding practitioner of the art even though deriving no material gain from it. If ruling is a technique like medicine, therefore (and Socrates tends to think that it is), then surely we shall have to say that a good ruler is defined not as one who derives gain from his subjects, but as one who looks after their interests. Any gain he derives is separate from or contingent to the art of ruling; in which case it is not as obvious as Thrasymachus thinks it is that 'justice is...the interest of the stronger party' and that the good ruler is only an effective exploiter of those under his power.[29] On the contrary: justice is the interest not of the strong, but of the weak.

This, it must be said, is not a promising beginning. Even when we help it out by additions to what he actually says, Socrates's argument is remarkably poor. Thrasymachus thinks it childish: Socrates has a negligent nursemaid, he says unpleasantly, who lets him wander around drivelling.[30] The weakness of Socrates's position surely lies in the fact that there is no reason why an art should not also be a commodity. He is, of course, right to point out that deriving gain from an art is not the *same thing* as practising the art. But it does not follow that an art should not be practised, nor is it true on the whole that arts are not practised, *for the sake of* gain. Yet this is the conclusion that Socrates needs, and which he apparently believes himself to have secured. In reality, it is hardly controversial to say (as Thrasymachus does) that a good shepherd might care for his sheep well while—indeed, by—fattening them up for market, or that a good shoemaker might make excellent shoes for no other purpose than that of selling them. And there is no reason why something similar should not be true of the ruler in relation to his subjects. A further point here, of which neither Socrates nor Thrasymachus seems aware, is that they are in any case at cross-purposes. Socrates's reply to Thrasymachus is an *ignoratio elenchi*. Thrasymachus is talking about what rulers actually do; Socrates is talking about what rulers *ought* to do. Even if Socrates's argument were better than it is, it would not be an answer to Thrasymachus.

So far, then, despite Plato's attempt to make Socrates's side of the debate look convincing, the reader is left with the impression that no great headway has been made against Thrasymachus's sturdy realism. But Socrates goes on to develop, at 349A–354B, a line of reasoning that looks altogether more worthwhile; and it is at this point that the real thrust of the *Republic* begins. In this part of the debate, Socrates is replying to Thrasymachus's version of the radical Sophist belief that an individual's true interest lies in transcending limits and outdoing others. Modern commentators have tended to think ill of Socrates' argument; but the weaknesses to which they call attention are not intrinsic to it. For the most part, they arise out of the limitations of the dialogue form as a mode of exposition. An interpretation that tries to look beyond those limitations discloses a rejoinder more effective than Socrates is commonly credited with.[31] Disentangled from its unhelpful setting, the pith of what he has to say is as follows.

A central feature of Thrasymachus's argument is that the unjust man is clever and wise and the just man a fool. The unjust man is clever because he succeeds in achieving his desires by outdoing everybody else: by disregarding the restrictions by which others are bound. The just man willingly remains within the limits of legal or conventional behaviour even though to do so is at odds with his true interests and the promptings of nature. He is a casualty of his own ingenuousness; he allows himself to be controlled and exploited by someone else, and thinks himself virtuous for doing so. Injustice is better and 'stronger' than justice because it is by behaving unjustly that we get what we want, whereas justice is submission to another's will. But, Socrates asks, what sort of behaviour do we normally expect the expert at something—the clever or wise man—to exhibit? Do we not regard the expert as being precisely someone who *knows how far to go*? Part of his cleverness lies in understanding that the mere pursuit of excess is futile: that simply trying to outdo everyone is self-defeating. Expertise, Socrates suggests, consists typically in *measure*. When he tunes his harp, there is certainly a sense in which the musician is trying to outdo the non-musician. He wishes to do it better than the non-musician would. But he does not screw the strings up ever tighter in the belief that he is now outdoing other musicians too. He tightens them to the appropriate pitch, and neither higher nor lower. The consequence of not doing this is that the instrument cannot be played properly. When the physician treats his patient, he tries to outdo the non-physician by curing the patient more effectively than the non-physician could. But he does not pour ever larger doses of medicine into his patient in the belief that he is now stealing a march on other physicians also. He administers as much as is necessary, and neither more nor less. Again, if he fails to do this, all he will accomplish is his own downfall: his own failure to do what he set out to do. So it is also, Socrates suggests, with the just man considered as an 'expert' in the art of living. He will try to 'outdo' unjust men in the sense of being just whereas they are unjust. But he will not try to outdo other just men in the sense of grabbing for himself more than his fair share. He will recognise that not remaining within the limits of justice—not giving due consideration to the claims of others—makes purposive interaction with others impossible, and so is subversive of his own interests. Even a band of robbers has to exhibit justice of a kind, if by 'justice' we mean limitations on one's freedom to do as one likes. It has to exhibit justice in this sense because it cannot operate successfully unless its members work together for a common purpose. Even those whose purpose is bad must acknowledge the rules that govern the band, determine the distribution of the loot, and so on. 'Injustice creates divisions and hatreds and fighting, and justice imparts harmony and friendship.'[32] Far from being ignorance and folly, therefore, justice turns out to be wisdom and virtue. The art of living well lies not in surpassing or ignoring limits, but in recognising what the proper limits are, and remaining within them. It lies in recognising the rules or parameters that make it possible to achieve the goals that human beings characteristically have.

The argument of *Republic* 349A–354B is corroborated by similar references to measure or limit elsewhere in Plato. In the *Gorgias*, when Callicles is defending a position essentially the same as that of Thrasymachus, it is urged against him that a life lived without a kind of geometric proportion—ἰσότης γεωμετρικη (*isotes geometriké*)—can only be self-defeating.[33] Temperance or self-restraint is the foundation of everything that makes us happy. You cannot satisfy all your desires at once; you cannot, indeed, satisfy *all* your desires at all. Anyone who tries to do so— anyone who insists on acting disproportionately—will end up displaying none of the qualities that even he would wish to applaud. In the *Philebus*, limit—πέρας (*peras*)—is represented as the principle upon which all arts, and nature herself, depend.[34] A similar point is made at length in Plato's late dialogue called the *Statesman*.[35] This line of reasoning is reminiscent of the doctrine of the presocratic philosophers that the natural order both displays and depends on measure. For our purposes, the conclusion to which it points is that justice, understood as a life-skill consisting in knowing how far to go, is both natural and desirable. And this, of course, is a direct rebuttal of Sophist relativism and amoralism. Socrates does not quarrel with Thrasymachus's understanding of justice as limit. But he holds that the restrictions that it imposes are not artificial and irksome constraints inflicted by the strong on the weak. Justice is a natural principle, but not in the way that Callicles had meant in speaking of natural justice; it is not simply the freedom to do whatever one wants. Regardless of what anybody thinks or wills, no activity can be performed successfully unless the limits that constitute the possibility of that activity are observed. Justice is moreover desirable in the sense that, if we do not recognise the truth that limits must be adhered to, we will not be able to do and get what we want, and to that extent will not live happy and successful lives. The just man certainly tries to outdo the unjust man by being more just than he. But the unjust man who strives to outdo everybody is only showing his own ignorance and folly.

It is therefore not true that injustice is stronger and more profitable than justice and that justice is at odds with the true nature of mankind; nor is it true that justice lies merely in complying with conventional laws or rules. Justice is the quality that enables us to achieve our purposes, and to be just is to conduct oneself in the light of the principle that measure or self-restraint is a necessary condition of successful living. It is the unjust man who will live in a way that is frustrating and self-defeating. Far from being free and happy, as Thrasymachus and Callicles think, the supremely unjust man—the tyrant—will be a kind of slave. He will be the slave of his own insatiable desires, like a man who fills up leaky barrels only to watch them empty again.[36] Why should the individual be just? Partly, at least, because it is in his own interest, not in the interest of the strong, that he should be so. Also, Socrates argues—in a way with which modern readers perhaps find it difficult to sympathise—the very fact of being just will make a man happy. Justice is to be valued not only for its consequences, but for itself also.[37]

But if Socrates's understanding of justice is to have any force, his definition needs to be given content as well as form. What specific qualities will have to be present in the individual if he is to display the requisite skill in knowing how far to go? Socrates's preferred way of investigating this question is to ask what kind of *soul* an individual must have if he is to live well. 'Soul' as a translation of ψῦχή (*psyche*) tends to create several wrong impressions in the minds of modern English readers, susceptible as they are to the word's religious connotations. It is necessary to bear in mind that *psyche* has much the same plurality of meaning as the Latin word *anima* does. By *psyche*, Socrates means something like 'mind' or 'temperament' or 'personality.' Justice, he suggests, is a virtue of the soul in this sense. As we saw in the case of the Sophists, *areté*, 'virtue,' is a word capable of having a number of meanings; and here, as in the former case, Socrates is using it to mean not moral virtue, but a quality or excellence that enables something or someone to perform a task well. Justice is that attribute 'by virtue of which' the soul performs its function, the soul being an instrument for living in much the way that a pruning-knife is an instrument for pruning and the eye an instrument for seeing.[38] An unjust soul is therefore like a blunt knife or a shortsighted eye. It lacks its necessary 'virtue,' and so will not be able to perform the function of enabling its possessor to live properly. You can live life after a fashion with an unjust soul, just as you can prune a tree after a fashion with a chisel; but a life so lived will not be a good and happy life.[39]

Where in the soul, in what features of the soul, are we to find its characteristic virtue of justice? This, Socrates says, is not a question that we should try to answer directly. His advice is that we should look at the justice of the city, the *polis*, before trying to describe justice in the individual human being. Those who have poor eyesight find it easier to read large letters than small; if we study justice on a large scale, we shall be better placed to understand it on a small, individual scale.[40] This methodological observation is imported into the conversation almost imperceptibly, but it carries with it an important presupposition: namely, that the just community is only the just individual writ large. The radical Sophists believe that political conflict is inevitable, or even creative, because civic life is intrinsically or naturally a contest between individuals who wish to dominate one another. By approaching individual justice along the broader road of political justice, Socrates invites us to take it as read that justice is a unitary concept. There are not different *kinds* of justice. Self and *polis* need the same virtue if they are to flourish, and, considerations of scale apart, injustice within the *polis* is the same as injustice within the self. If, therefore, as we have now established, injustice—the absence of measure—within the self is destructive and self-defeating, the same must be true of conflict within the *polis*.

Political Justice

What are the purposes of political life? It is by answering this question that we shall be able to identify the virtue that enables those purposes to be met. Socrates's answer takes its departure from a truism that has been appealed to often in the history of political thought. Human beings are not isolated individuals. We have to live in association with others because, apart from any higher consideration, we have material needs that can be supplied only through co-operation. The 'first' city, the most rudimentary community capable of being imagined,[41] would come into being because 'it is, as it happens, true that no one is self-sufficient and that each of us lacks many things.' We need food, shelter, clothing: necessities that cannot be produced other than by a division of labour.[42] The division and specialisation of

Plato: The Sovereignty of Philosophy

labour, and hence the *polis* considered as an organised citizen body, is therefore necessary to fulfil needs that are natural to us. As collective life becomes more established and complex, it generates further needs: needs, now, not for things necessary for survival, but for the accoutrements of luxury and sophistication. Socrates the ascetic regrets the growth of luxury: of what he calls 'unnecessary' needs. To him, the best, the 'healthiest,' city would be one in which there were no superfluous needs. This is the kind of frugal community in which philosophers would live if they had a choice. But Socrates accepts that such needs are for most people an inseparable part of life, and he is concerned with life as a whole rather than with the interests of a special minority.[43]

Socrates insists moreover that the needs that the *polis* must meet are not exclusively material ones. There is a need also for processes of moral formation that enable individuals to find happiness and a sense of self through making a contribution to the life of the whole. Where such processes are absent or defective, there is alienation, resentment and strife; people feel exploited and consider themselves justified in exploiting others. The successful *polis* will be more than the set of economic arrangements by which we are fed, clothed and protected. It will be an ethical community, extending to us the means of living a worthwhile and contented life with others of our kind. It will provide the good life for every individual insofar as he or she is capable of attaining it; and we must here stress the phrase *every* individual. The material and psychological needs to which Socrates points are needs that all human beings have in common. The *polis* should therefore not exist to gratify its rulers or please minorities. Beneath external differences of strength and ability there subsists a natural moral equality. 'In founding a city, we are not looking for the exceptional happiness of any one group among us, but, as far as possible, for that of the city as a whole...We are here devising the happy city not...for the sake of creating a few happy citizens, but as a whole.'[44]

What constitutional features must the *polis* embody if it is to be happy and successful? What is political justice, understood in the now familiar sense as the kind of measure by which the *polis* is enabled to function effectively? On the face of it, the most straightforward way of answering this question would be to examine existing constitutions with a view to isolating their strengths and weaknesses and making suitable recommendations. But Socrates does not do this. The fact that he does not is most readily explicable in terms of the opposition against which he conceives himself to be arguing. The most influential of the Sophists, we recall, are epistemological subjectivists. 'Man is the measure of all things.' There would be no point in trying to ground an argument against them on an analysis of the facts of life in Athens or any actual *polis*. Such an argument would at once fall foul of the objection that no one analysis can be shown to be any more correct than another. An empirical procedure is therefore ruled out. Socrates has to proceed by the method of *logical* inference from the general first premiss (granted that this premiss has to be accepted as self-evident) that human beings have natural needs that they cannot satisfy alone. He offers a description not of an actual *polis*, but of what, given this premiss, the logically self-consistent *polis* would be. He devises, as the theatre of his political prescriptions, an ideal or imaginary *polis* called Kallipolis—'Beautiful City':[45] a city that, he readily admits, may not be realisable in any earthly form. For explanatory purposes, though, this does not matter.

> Perhaps it exists only as a heavenly model. Whoever wishes to do so may see it and make himself a citizen of it; but it does not matter whether there really is such a city, or whether or not it could ever come into being.[46]

Socrates's ideal city is intended as a model of everything that might possibly be: a model more complete and incontestable than any actual city could provide.

When fully evolved—when it had passed beyond the provision of basic needs and become the kind of city in which most people would want to live—such a city would contain four virtues and three occupational groups. (The expression 'classes,' though often used, is best avoided here; the groups whose rôles Socrates wishes to elucidate are not differentiated according to economic relations.) The four virtues are wisdom (σοφία: *sophia*), courage (ἀνδρεία: *andreia*), self-restraint (σωφροσύνη: *sophrosyné*) and justice. The three groups are Guardians (φύλακες: *phylakes*), Auxiliaries (ἐπίκουροι: *epikouroi*) and Producers (πολλοι: *polloi*).[47] Socrates does not tell us why he thinks the *polis* would contain only four virtues or only three groups; but his analysis is allowed to pass unchallenged, and there is nothing in it to which

Plato: The Sovereignty of Philosophy

we need raise an objection.[48] His method is a process of elimination. He suggests that, if we can find out where wisdom, courage and self-restraint lie in terms of their distribution between the three groups, justice will be what is left over. The wisdom of the *polis* would be embodied in the Guardians or rulers.[49] The Auxiliaries, the military group, whose task it is to defend and protect the *polis*, would embody its courage.[50] The Producers would be characterised by self-restraint in the sense that, while lacking the capacity to be rulers, they would recognise it in those who have it and would acquiesce in being governed by them.[51] Where, then, is the city's justice? We have seen the answer coming for some time, and its arrival is something of an anticlimax. Having sought high and low for justice, Socrates says, here it was all along, rolling around at our feet; we have been looking for it as one sometimes looks absent-mindedly for something that one is holding in one's hand.[52] Justice is that state of affairs which obtains when the members of all three occupational groups work together in harmony because each individual is performing the task to which he or she is best suited by nature.[53] The Guardians rule disinterestedly for the good of the whole city; the other two groups perform their functions under the Guardians' direction, having been schooled by them in placid and unambitious acceptance of their allotted place. Political justice, like justice considered generally, is a matter of limit or measure. It prevails when everyone willingly and unselfishly remains within the boundaries that ensure the efficient functioning of the *polis* as a whole, and hence the wellbeing of all its members.

Socrates gives much more attention to the Guardians than to the other two groups. His treatment of the Producers in particular is very cursory. It is in the Guardians that he is primarily interested. The Guardians, as he portrays them, will be remarkable people. They will be called upon to live exemplary and, one might be forgiven for thinking, ineligible lives: lives from which most of the things usually thought to make life worth living have been removed. Their rule, inasmuch as they rule wisely and for the common good, will be such as to abolish strife and disorder from the city and preserve a contented and enduring condition of harmony. They are depicted as ruling not on the basis of personal wealth or popular choice, but solely on the strength of the special expertise that we shall discuss in due course. All material wealth remains in the hands of the Producers. Political power is conceived, in a way that, with hindsight, seems extraordinary, as being entirely separate from wealth and the use of wealth. The Guardians will have no private property, no family life, no privacy, and no goals apart from that of securing the common good. They will live together like soldiers in a camp. Everything that might lure them away from their natural and proper task of securing the good of the whole community is to be subtracted from their lives.

A consideration of the ideal city, then, has given us an account of political justice in terms of the operational boundaries that hold as between functionally-related individuals and groups. Once again, injustice is not so much wrong as self-defeating. Without justice, the *polis* cannot operate in such a way as to meet the needs of its members; in which case the purpose for which it came into existence in the first place is lost. The more fully justice is present in the *polis*, the more completely will it be able to meet them. When people work together effectively to secure a common good, 'the whole city will grow up into a noble order, and the various groups in it will receive the proportion of happiness that nature assigns to them.'[54] Socrates assumes that the activity of habitual social co-operation will itself foster in those who engage in it a sense of working together for a common purpose. The well-run city is like the human body, in which the whole is aware of the feelings of all the parts.[55]

Individual Justice

Having investigated justice on a large scale—in large print, as it were—we are now in a position to return to our original question. What is justice considered as a quality of the individual soul? The analogy that Socrates invites us to accept between *polis* and individual is not perfect, and has been much criticised. But the comparison is intelligible enough, and, insofar as it is intended to be an analogy only, not really controversial. Again, we must make allowances for the limitations of the dialogue form, and try to arrive at as sympathetic an understanding as we can of what Socrates means.[56]

The human soul, he observes—the human personality—cannot be a unity. Anyone can see this by introspection. Unity cannot be in conflict with itself, yet everybody knows what it is like to feel divided inwardly. We can be simultaneously fascinated and repelled by a horrible sight: we can be 'in two minds' about whether to look or not.[57] The soul, therefore, must have parts, and the feeling of being at odds with oneself arises when the parts are not in agreement. There are, Socrates thinks, three such parts (again, he does not tell us why there are three and only three): the appetitive (ἐπιθυμητικόν: *epithymetikon*), the spirited (θυμοειδής: *thymoeides*) and the rational (λογιστικόν: *logistikon*). 'Spirit,' though customary, is not totally satisfactory as a translation of θυμός (*thymos*), the 'spirit' being the seat of such things as assertiveness, anger, sorrow and courage. 'Emotion' might be preferable; but medieval commentators and translators tend to use the word *voluntas*, 'will,' and this seems to come close to what Socrates usually means. As one might expect in the light of his remarks about political justice, personal justice is the condition that obtains when, within the individual soul, reason governs spirit and appetite in such a way as to secure the effective functioning of the whole self. Personal justice is an equilibrium as between the several parts of our make-up.

It is easy to see how disequilibrium of soul would be bad for the soul's possessor. If an individual's life were to be dominated by appetite without limit or control (which, in effect, is what Callicles and Thrasymachus think is the natural, and hence the good, way to live), it would be a chaotic and frustrated life. If we do not realise this and act accordingly, we cannot live well. Appetite or desire needs to be moderated and directed by reason. A similar observation applies to the spirited faculty. A life of undirected will or purposeless effort would be an incoherent, frustrating, unsatisfied life. Our emotions need to be directed in proper measure towards suitable objects; and, again, this is clearly the task of reason. A useful image is found in Plato's late dialogue called *Phaedrus*. Socrates there likens the relationship between reason, appetite and spirit to that between a charioteer and his two horses.[58] The individual cannot live a happy and successful life without justice, justice being that condition which prevails when the faculties of the soul are acting in a co-ordinated and purposive fashion. We might find it more natural to say that we can live happy and successful lives only insofar as we have a properly integrated character or personality. Again, this is not a matter of opinion or belief. It is presented to us as a self-evident fact of human nature.

But is this not all rather self-centred? Is an account of justice that so emphasises the securing of good consequences for the individual much of an improvement on the Sophist doctrine that self-gratification is everybody's real goal? This type of objection is developed at some length in the *Republic* by the brothers Glaucon and Adeimantus, whose rôle in the dialogue is to continue Thrasymachus's line of argument in a more temperate fashion. The arguments that occur to them are the obvious ones. Why should I not use my reason to co-ordinate my appetites and will in such a way as to get what I want at someone else's expense? Why should I not pretend to be just when it suits me, and grab as much as I can for myself when I can do so without detection or reprisal? If I could become invisible at will, would there still be any point in being just?[59] Stated generally, Socrates's response to questions of this kind is that someone with a properly integrated personality—someone whose wants and impulses are proportionate and not irrational and excessive—would *ipso facto* not *want* to grab as much as he could for himself. The just man would be a serene, happy, well-adjusted individual whose desires would not outstrip his needs. He would have no reason for not spontaneously recognising the moral claims of others and willing their happiness and good as well as his own. Untroubled by greed or ambition or envy, he would be content to play that part in the life of the community for which his temperament suits him. Justice understood as a quality of soul secures the interests of the just person; but it secures the interests of the community of which he is a member also.[60]

The Sovereignty of Philosophy

The upshot of Plato's discussion of political and personal justice is that the good life can be achieved only by just individuals living in a just community, justice in each case being a kind of proportion or measure that is natural rather than conventional. That justice is a matter of *physis* rather than *nomos* is, he holds, an absolute truth, not relative to anything. No one, no matter how plausible or skilled in the art of persuasion, can cause it to be not true. But—and this is the crux—Plato's consistent belief is that most people are not able by their own efforts to achieve personal justice in the complete and proper sense; nor, by the same token, would they be able to create and maintain the kind of community that he regards as essential to full human wellbeing. Certainly, they can acquire beliefs through education and persuasion; and Protagoras is correct in supposing that some beliefs are better—have more beneficial consequences—than others. But most people do not have what it takes to acquire *knowledge* of what is just as distinct from beliefs about it. They cannot achieve such knowledge not, as the Sophists think, because knowledge is itself impossible, but because they lack the right kind of enquiring temperament. They do not have a temperament in which the psychological component of rationality is sovereign over appetite and will. If political stability and tranquillity are to be attained, it follows that people in the main must be taught, not to have knowledge, but to act on the right kind of beliefs. They must be taught to behave *as though* they were just. Their lives and formative experiences must be managed in such a way as to induce in them the same willing acceptance of their place in the social scheme as they would exhibit spontaneously if they were really or endogenously just. Who, then, is capable of performing this educative function? This leads us to the most central of the *Republic's* prescriptions: that 'philosophers' should rule. We must consider in some detail what Socrates's reasons are for holding this view.

Perfect personal justice is found, he thinks, only in people who combine an appropriately rational temperament with a high degree of specialised intellectual attainment. Such people are what he calls φιλόσοφοι (*philosophoi*): literally, 'wisdom-lovers.' They are to be distinguished from 'false wisdom-lovers,' or 'lovers of sight and sounds': people who are content with the mere appearance or superficies of things.[61] True philosophers are those in whom reason is sovereign. They shun all semblance or approximation. They are characterised by a boundless passion for truth. They love and seek knowledge in all its forms: including, of course, knowledge of what is just and right. It is this knowledge or wisdom that, once attained, enables them consistently to maintain the elements of their souls in proper balance and hence to govern their lives in a rational and purposive fashion. Only philosophers have the perfect poise of character that enables them to lead a just life constantly and immovably, without error or incoherence or vacillation.

But the wisdom of the philosopher is more than a merely private or personal quality. The common belief that philosophers are vague and impractical creatures is a mistake.[62] Properly understood, philosophy has a supreme political and social value. In actually-existing

States, instability and strife are as common as they are because most people neither know nor are able to know the difference between the just and the unjust. They have only the kind of opinion or belief about which disagreement is all too frequent. Such beliefs are moreover capable of being moulded and changed by the skilled orator. This, as we have seen, is why Plato thinks that democracies are so prone to being hijacked by demagogues and rabble-rousers. Philosophers, by contrast, inasmuch as they *know* the truth about what is good and right and just, are equipped not only to govern their own lives but to shape and guide the lives of others also. They are equipped to teach others to conduct themselves justly even though those others do not really know what justice is, and so to create and sustain a community that is just as a whole. In the ideal society of Kallipolis, the Guardians would be philosophers. As perfectly just men and women[63] they would be able to dedicate themselves to making the community good and just without being deflected by personal goals and ambitions. A central part of what they would do would be to imbue those under them not with knowledge, certainly, but with true rather than false opinions as to how they should behave. A vital part, perhaps the most vital part, of governing is the activity of education.

But if philosophical knowledge is the secret of both personal happiness and political stability, we need to be clear as to precisely what kind of thing such knowledge is. In particular, we need to know how it is to be distinguished from the opinion or belief with which 'lovers of sights and sounds' content themselves. Plato's opponents, we stress again, are people who believe that there is no such thing as knowledge. However much we may take for granted for practical purposes, we cannot, Gorgias thinks, *know* even that anything exists. However much we may agree about how to conduct our lives, there are no moral certainties. 'Whatever seems right and praiseworthy to a particular city *is* right and praiseworthy to it,' Protagoras says, 'for as long as it holds it to be so.' The Sophists consider that we occupy a world in which there can be *only* opinion, and that the art of politics must consist in manipulating the behaviour of others—possibly, though not necessarily, to self-serving and tyrannical ends—through the techniques of persuasion. This view, insofar as it has a philosophical basis, arises, we have suggested, out of the apparent failure of contemporary science or philosophy to yield incontrovertible truth about

Plato: The Sovereignty of Philosophy

the world. Given that Plato wishes to say that knowledge is indeed possible, getting beyond this scepticism and its practical consequences is the main problem with which his moral epistemology has to contend. It is at this point that we encounter one of the most important and perplexing parts of Plato's thought: his Theory of Forms, often also called his Theory of Ideas.[64]

In developing this doctrine, Plato is revisiting some of the philosophical questions at which we glanced in the previous chapter. What is the nature of change? How can the world as we experience it have a coherent identity yet undergo constant transformation? Must there not be some stable reality underlying the ambiguous world of sensory experience? He is continuing the speculations of those philosophers who had wanted to pass through the veil of appearances and explicate what they believed to be the subsistent reality behind it.[65] In particular, his project is to explore and revise the relation between the intellectual reality that Parmenides had postulated and the world with which plain folk are acquainted. Why he should regard such an exploration as important is easy to infer from what we said in the previous chapter. The Eleatic philosophy of Being apparently forces upon us the conclusion that the empirical world is an illusion. Eyes and ears tell us that it is real, while reason denies its reality. But this leads at once to the inference that philosophy has nothing to contribute to our practical lives and that we live in a world in which no action can be based on demonstrable truth. For Plato, then, the question is this: How can we account for the relation between appearance and reality while avoiding the subjectivism and ethical relativism that he regards as having such pernicious consequences?

His approach to this question, insofar as we need concern ourselves with it, can be clarified by an example. Any example would do; but let us for the purposes of illustration take the case of dogs. In the world of normal sense-perception we come across dogs of all shapes and sizes. There are Irish Wolfhounds; Great Danes; Spaniels; Dachshunds; Pekingeses; Chihuahuas. But is there not something remarkable about the fact that all these names are somehow names of the same kind of thing? A Great Dane and a Chihuahua could hardly differ more completely in appearance. Yet somehow, in spite of this degree of diversity, we are able to recognise that all dogs are dogs. We are able to know that they share some sort of collective or class identity, and we do not need to have this identity explained to us. How can this be? How is such recognition possible? Must it not be because we have in our minds, however dimly or subconsciously, a picture, an 'idea,' of the 'real' thing, against which to measure the many divergent or approximate representations of it that we encounter in the world of sight? Must there not be, so to speak, a 'dogness' in which actual or particular dogs 'participate' and by virtue of which we can recognise them as belonging to the same class? And must it not also be true that if we could grasp this 'dogness' fully and clearly, we should then understand the true nature of that which we now apprehend only vaguely, partially and under a number of different aspects? This example may or may not commend itself, but it suffices to give an indication of what Plato is driving at. Diogenes Laertius reports the following conversation between Plato and Diogenes of Sinope, the famous Cynic philosopher:

> When Plato was talking about ideas and using the words 'tableness' and 'cupness,' [Diogenes] said: 'I can see a table and a cup, O Plato; but I can't see what you call "tableness" and "cupness".' 'That,' replied Plato, 'is easy to explain. You have eyes with which you see the table and the cup; but you do not have the intellect with which you might apprehend tableness and cupness.'[66]

(Diogenes seems to have gone to Plato's lectures largely for the sake of poking fun at Plato. Plato's reply perhaps gives a hint of the relations between the two.)

Plato, or at least the later Plato, believes that such ideas as 'tableness' and 'cupness' are actual metaphysical entities. He believes that 'universals,' as they have come to be called, subsist eternally in a changeless realm beyond the sensible world: a realm that intellect, though not sensation, is capable, through the proper kind of education, of entering and understanding. The world of sense perception is indeed not the 'real' world. Each specific example of something that we encounter in the world of sight—every table, every cup, every dog—is only one of many instances of the single idea or form of itself (εἶδος: *eidos*). To put the same point the other way around, each such form is the παράδειγμα (*paradeigma*), the 'paradigm' or 'pattern,' of which the particular instances are only imperfect copies. This is why the world of sight contains the pluralities and ambiguities that it does;

it is why things change and pass away; it is why the same thing can seem so different to different people. There are so many different tables and cups and dogs because each of them resembles, but none of them *is*, the eternal table or cup or dog. The false philosopher, the lover of sights and sounds, is not aware of this distinction. He does not see the difference between appearance and reality. He believes that the many particular instances of things *are* the reality; which is why he is so inclined, and so able, to flit from one evanescent experience to another. That there must *be* a true and stable reality is clear from the fact that we have opinions at all. Our opinions, Socrates remarks (in a clear echo of Parmenides) must be about something rather than nothing.[67] But it is only to the true philosopher that this reality is known; it is only the true philosopher who apprehends the pure ideas that lie behind and inform the realm of appearance. And it is this knowledge, as distinct from the opinions or beliefs of the false philosopher, that establishes him as authentic. True philosophers, Socrates says, 'are lovers of the vision of the truth.'[68]

How does all this relate to the governance of the ideal *polis*? The point, of course, is that what is true of cupness and tableness and dogness is true also of such things as justice and the just. It is here, when we come to nouns and adjectives expressive of moral value, that the trouble usually starts. No one is normally bothered about whether cups are really cups or tables really tables. But we are often bothered considerably about whether a given act is really right or really just. If there simply is no 'really right' or 'really just,' we are left with the conclusion of Protagoras, with all its troublesome consequences: that what we call 'right' is right only because, and only for as long as, people agree or are persuaded that it is. Why, then, according to Plato, are our notions of what is good and right and just so ambiguous? Why are disputes so frequent and hard to resolve? Not, as the Sophists think, because one opinion is ultimately no more true or false than any other; not because we have no reason apart from persuasion or coercion for doing one thing rather than another: but because our conceptions of justice 'participate' in the *idea* of justice only imperfectly. The opinions that people have about justice are only approximations or reflections. They do not embody justice itself; and this is why the holders of such opinions are so prone to difference and dissent. The truly just individual, and hence the best ruler, will be the philosopher: the individual who has realised that the veil of appearance or opinion is only a veil, and whose mind has reached through it and grasped the true nature of justice. Differences of opinion about justice are not incorrigible, as the Sophists suppose; but only the philosopher can correct them.

In the *Republic*, the complex and protracted processes by which philosopher-rulers might be produced are described in detail.[69] Education in the ideal *polis* would be provided by the State, as it is in Sparta. It would not be entrusted to private and possibly irresponsible teachers; a tilt, we may suppose, at the Sophists. The proposed curriculum is lengthy and exhaustive, and common, it seems, to males and females. It is designed to produce in those who experience it a comprehensive state of physical and moral health, and anything that might induce unwholesome states of mind is excluded. Art and literature are to be carefully censored. There is to be no sad or voluptuous music, for fear of encouraging self-indulgent attitudes; nor are there to be disgraceful stories about the gods.[70] At first, everyone participates in the educational system equally, and each derives from it as much benefit as he or she is capable of. It begins in childhood with a grounding in the liberal arts ('liberal arts'—all those things pertaining to the Muses—is what Plato means by μουσῐκή (*mousiké*); *mousike* is not 'music' in our sense). It includes a large element of physical training (γυμναστική: *gymnastiké*), especially of such a kind as will produce redoubtable warriors to populate the ranks of the Auxiliaries. Then come pure and applied mathematics. Individuals take up their rôle in the *polis* at whatever point is appropriate to their temperament and accomplishments as revealed during the course of their education. The most gifted students progress from mathematics to dialectic: the study of pure ideas, divested of any connection with the world of sight, through the constant practice and analysis of deductive argument. It is at this point in the educational process that the mind of the philosopher is formed and the rulers of the future are produced.

The point of Plato's educational system, insofar as it is intended to produce philosophers, is to lead the student's mind progressively away from the world of sensible particulars and accustom it by degrees to a world of pure abstraction. The study of dialectic as Plato describes it is

Plato: The Sovereignty of Philosophy

> the discovery of reality by the unaided light of reason, without the assistance of the senses, persisting until [the student] grasps the nature of the Good itself, and so finds that he has reached the limits of the intelligible world.[71]

As they come to the end of their educational journey, the emergent Guardians will

> raise the soul's eye to the universal light that illuminates all things. They will see there the ultimate Good, the pattern upon which they are to order the *polis* and the lives of individuals and the remainder of their own lives also.[72]

The essence of this educational process is summed up in Plato's parable of the cave: surely one of the best-known passages in the whole of philosophical literature.[73] We are to imagine a group of people who are prisoners in a cave or subterranean chamber. We are to suppose that they have been prisoners from childhood, and have known nothing but the interior of the cave. They are bound fast, in such a way that they can look only at the wall in front of them. Behind them a fire is burning. In front of the fire but behind the backs of the prisoners, objects are being carried back and forth. The shadows of the objects are cast by the fire on the wall of the cave in front of the prisoners. Because they have never seen anything else, the prisoners believe in these shadows as reality. Who are the unidentified jailers who carry the objects to and fro? Plato does not tell us; but it is not fanciful to suppose that they are the orators, the demagogues, who mislead people by encouraging them to believe in the shadows of falsehood and illusion.[74] Eventually, one of the prisoners manages to break free from his bonds. He 'drags himself up' what is described as 'a rugged, difficult, uphill path'[75]—the path of education—to the outside world. In the outside world, the sun is shining. It is his emergence into the sunlight that completes his escape from the world of shadows. At first, the light hurts his eyes and everything is new and strange and confusing. Then, as he becomes accustomed to the sun's brightness, he beholds reality for the first time. He realises—partially at first, but with increasing clarity—that every part of his experience hitherto has been a delusion. On Plato's account of it, education in its most complete realisation is the soul's progress from an original condition of seeing only semblances or images (εἰκᾰσία: *eikasia*) to one of full intelligence (νόησις: *noesis*). It is an ascent from the visible to the intellectual world. Plato's imagery invites us to understand it as an arduous journey culminating in a kind of enlightenment. At the completion of his or her education, the individual sees reality as it were bathed in the light of the sun.

Unfortunately, but perhaps inevitably, the nature of this enlightenment is not made wholly clear. What is the symbolic purpose of the sun in the parable of the cave? This is a large and difficult question upon which we can only touch.[76] The sun stands for what Plato calls the Idea of the Good: the 'Good itself,' the 'ultimate Good' to which the soul's eye is at last raised. The Idea of the Good represents the terminus of the mind's journey, the end-point of all intellectual development. It is the most inscrutable of Plato's doctrines, and the one to which he attaches the highest importance; but the treatment that he gives to it in the *Republic* is mysterious and has no clarifying counterpart in his other dialogues. This difficulty is intrinsic; it does not arise from any failure of Plato to explain himself. He himself knows that, because what he is trying to describe is, in effect, a direct personal revelation, it is impossible for words to convey his meaning fully. The only way to apprehend the Idea of the Good is to see it for oneself. When he speaks of it, it is notable that Plato's language takes on a markedly religious character.

> I think that in the world of knowledge the Idea of the Good appears last of all, and is seen only with effort; although, when seen, is understood to be the universal author of all things beautiful and right, the parent of light and lord of light in the visible world, and the immediate and supreme source of reason and truth in the intellectual; and that this is the power upon which whoever would act wisely either in public or in private life must have his eye fixed.[77]

He tells us also, in terms that can only remind us of Parmenides, that all other, lesser, ideas receive from the Idea of the Good 'not only their power of being known...but also...their being and reality; yet the Good is not Being, but lies far beyond it in dignity and power.'[78] As one might expect, the Christian Platonists of later centuries found no difficulty in identifying the Idea of the Good with God.

What can we say about Plato's Idea of the Good by way of synopsis? First, it seems to be in some unspecified sense the 'author' or creator of all other ideas. If perceptible things exist only as manifestations of ideas, the ideas themselves apparently exist only as manifestations of the Idea of the Good. Second, knowledge of the Good is the highest accomplishment of human wisdom, inasmuch as such knowledge is what enables us fully to understand everything else. It is in the 'light' of the Good that all other ideas become clear. It is 'the immediate and supreme source of reason and truth' from which other ideas derive 'their power of being known.' It is 'the universal light that illuminates all things.' Third, and for us most important, the Idea of the Good furnishes the philosopher with the surest foundation of his *practical* conduct: a 'power,' a 'pattern.' It enables him to recognise other ideas—justice, rightness and so on—in all their visible manifestations, and to act accordingly. Just as the sun enables the eye to see, so the Idea of the Good enables the mind to know. Those who perceive it are empowered by it to understand fully, and therefore to judge, evaluate and act truly, in directing 'the *polis* and the lives of individuals, and the remainder of their own lives also.'

The philosopher, then, is distinguished by knowledge of the truth. Above all, he is distinguished by knowledge of the mysterious and transforming Idea of the Good. In the nature of the case, knowledge of this kind is the province of those who combine outstanding intellectual gifts with the right kind of disposition: we may take it that this motif in Plato is a riposte to the Sophists' belief that *areté* can be taught to anyone who will pay a suitable fee. The escaped prisoner, when he returns to the cave, does not set about *releasing* the other prisoners. When he begins to tell them about the outside world, they respond to him with ridicule and hostility. The instruction that the philosopher can impart to ordinary people is only approximate and incomplete, and they, indeed, are reluctant to hear him at all. They are reluctant to believe that their world of shadows is not reality.[79] But the philosopher himself has knowledge of the standard of perfection by which the *polis* ought to be guided. 'His eyes are turned to contemplate fixed and immutable realities, a realm in which no injustice is done or suffered, but all is reason and order.'[80]

We note this phrase 'fixed and immutable realities.' Philosophical knowledge is the formula for which Plato was seeking: the formula for stability and order transcending uncertainty and strife. The philosopher himself is the only truly just individual; but with patience and reason the philosopher can educate others in justice—in civic virtue—to the level that each is capable of achieving, and can enable everyone to participate in the Good in proportion to his or her natural capacity. Philosophers must be the Guardians of the ideal city.[81] The best form of government, the ideal form of government, is ἀριστοκρᾶτία (*aristokratia*), 'rule by the best.' It is an aristocracy of those who, because they have their souls fixed on the Idea of the Good, are equipped to ground all their practical decisions, and to educate those subject to them, in wisdom and goodness, thereby securing the wellbeing of the entire body politic. The extended philosophical conversation of the *Republic* has an ultimate purpose different from and broader than its ostensible one. It is not a discussion of the nature of justice so much as the general articulation of an ethical theory of politics: a theory that identifies the *polis* as the natural milieu of human beings and specifies the good of the whole community as the true and natural purpose of government.

Three Standard Criticisms

It is hardly controversial to say that the *Republic* is an impressive and enduring contribution to the study of political morality. In terms of its influence and canonical authority, it has far transcended its original purpose. The extent of its influence needs no elaboration; but it has attracted considerable criticism also, and by no means all such criticism is misplaced. Broadly speaking, it has been subject to adverse comment of three kinds.

First, and perhaps most fundamentally, the *Republic* fails to achieve its object of refutation. What Plato offers is a deductive or 'pure' theory of politics. It is a theory spun out of his own, or Socrates's own, mind. It lacks precisely what it most needs: an incontrovertible link with everyday reality. Plato's method is deductive of necessity, in the sense that no inductive argument could possibly penetrate the scepticism of his opponents. But Plato is mistaken in his assumption that he can in this way answer the radical Sophists' assertions about what the world of human affairs is 'really' like. When all is said and done, Plato has not actually *proved* anything; we have not got beyond the 'man is the measure' principle after all. This is the chief weakness of his political theory: that, insofar as it depends upon the notion of an imaginary *polis* governed by individuals who are 'philosophers' in the sense that Plato specifies, it is a utopian fantasy with no more claim to be thought true than any other fantasy would have. Plato thinks that he is refuting, rather than merely contradicting, relativism and amoralism in politics; but, in the final analysis, the *Republic* turns out to be only a vastly elaborate counter-assertion after all. Ironically, having regard to the position to which it is professedly hostile, it is an exercise not in proof but in persuasion.

Second, the direct link that Plato wishes to postulate between philosophical knowledge and political effectiveness—between theory and practice—strikes one as naïve and unconvincing. Parmenides had in effect made philosophy useless by isolating Being as the only thing capable of being known. The older Sophists responded by observing that we cannot know even that. The result is an account of practical life as purely pragmatic: as uninformed by any principle apart from, for the 'radical' Sophists, the general conclusion or assumption that might is right. Plato believes himself to have spanned the chasm that divides the Parmenidean intellectual realm from the world of sight in which we are called upon to act. He thinks that he has rehabilitated philosophy as a practical enquiry and discovered in it a universal antidote for political disorder. But it is hard to see that the process of philosophical education that he describes might furnish those who undergo it with the supreme governing skills that he attributes to his philosopher-rulers. Philosophical knowledge is knowledge of ideas. Philosophers know what things 'really' are. But in what sense is such knowledge practical? Knowing what a table *is* does not equip one to be an efficient carpenter. It is not obvious that practical efficacy lies in the apprehension of abstract ideas.

Third, Plato's language ultimately produces more difficulties than it solves. The Idea of the Good is of supreme importance to his argument, yet we can only guess at what he means by it, and we are left with no clue as to how it might be put into practice. We are told how it may be found, but we are not told what it is, nor are we told how it could be formulated into rules that anyone might follow. As we have said, it might be urged in Plato's defence that the true meaning of the Idea of the Good, as of any experience of enlightenment or intuition, is not communicable through speech. But this is an unfortunate plea to have to enter on behalf of someone who has undertaken to develop a rational argument against the specific claims of an opponent.

Plato as a Natural Law Theorist

These are weighty criticisms. They are criticisms of which Plato's pupil Aristotle was very much aware. They have a bearing on the character of Aristotle's thought that we shall try to bring out in the next chapter. Leaving these criticisms aside for the time being, what can we make of the statement with which we began the previous chapter: that in the *Republic* we have the earliest extant western attempt to develop a philosophical theory of natural law? We are now in a position to amplify this statement in terms of a number of general themes that a study of the *Republic* reveals.

(a) Plato's enterprise is to assert the primacy of *physis* over *nomos*. He insists, against the conventionalism of the Sophists, that the *polis* is more than an artificial device invented for the purposes of domination or control. It is a natural community. It is natural because it arises from needs intrinsic to human nature: economic needs in the first instance, but moral and social needs also.

(b) Those who complain about the authoritarianism and elitism of Plato's system overlook the fact that the ideal *polis* presupposes a fundamental moral equality. It is not ordered to the good of the gifted few, nor is it meant to secure the interests of a powerful or influential group. Its purpose is to bring about the good and happy life for all, in proportion to their capacity to enjoy it. Individuals differ, and this difference has a bearing upon the question of who should rule. But the differences are differences of ability rather than birth. The ideal *polis* will be stratified by its educational system; but the system itself is open to all, regardless of birth or gender, and it will produce inequalities only in that it will assign to individuals the rôles that most suit their aptitudes. Such inequalities are intended to fulfil, not oppress.

(c) Justice is a universal rational standard. It is the measure according to which political life can be so regulated as to achieve the conditions most consistent with the needs and capacities of those who live it. It is not 'the interest of the stronger party,' nor is it true that any one opinion about justice is as good as any other. 'Being just,' understood as identifying and remaining within the limits that make goal-directed activity possible, is a natural necessity inasmuch as, without justice, life cannot be conducted successfully. This is true whether justice be considered at a personal or a political level. It is true that only a few gifted individuals will be able to understand its nature in every aspect. They will see it bathed in the light of the Good, and this is what will enable them to embody it fully in the life of the community. But the fact that survives Plato's 'elitism' is that the basis of justice is not tradition, positive law, revelation or might, but reason: the reason with which human beings are equipped by nature.

(d) Against the radical individualism exemplified in the *Republic* by Thrasymachus and in the *Gorgias* by Callicles, Plato offers a co-operative rather than a competitive theory of human nature. Human beings are not driven only by an unquenchable thirst for power and self-gratification. They are able, under wise government, to co-operate in developing and maintaining a community directed to a common good. Granted that the members of the community will share in its good in different ways, it is nonetheless an integrated commonwealth of individuals working together to achieve a collective purpose. Thrasymachus and Callicles to the contrary notwithstanding, human beings are not naturally at war with one another.

Some commentators have in fairly recent times thought it right to deplore Plato's mistrust of democracy. They deprecate his lack of belief in the capacity of ordinary human beings to organise their lives without paternalistic supervision. They complain that Plato's Guardians are totalitarian rulers who, on the strength of the esoteric knowledge to which they lay claim, control the lives of those subject to them, and do so, moreover, by methods as disreputable as those for which Plato is so ready to reproach the Sophists. Plato's ideal State is a 'closed society.' It is authoritarian and elitist. The individual is swallowed up in the whole. There is no room for argument or enterprise or ambition or personal development. The philosopher who returns to the cave tries to explain what he has seen to those who are still prisoners, but he does not set them free. The kind of knowledge that Plato values is not used to make people free, but only to create the kind of unfreedom that he regards as benign.[82]

It is difficult for the twenty-first century reader not to sympathise with objections of this kind. Nonetheless, they do not deserve to be taken seriously. For one thing, they take no account of context. Those who urge them introduce strictures imported from a world simply different from the one to which the *Republic* is addressed. It is pointless to censure Plato for not having had the kind of values and opinions that modern liberals applaud. For another, such criticisms do not attend to what Plato's intentions actually are. On the one hand, it is certainly his view that only a few people will have the talent and inclination to become rulers, and that the unenlightened should follow the leadership of the wise. It is also true that, as far as Plato is concerned, the Guardians will, where necessary, use myth, persuasion, and deception as devices for governing the commonwealth. They will lie and mislead when they have to.[83] They will secretly fix the ballots that assign mating partners in order to bring about the best combinations.[84] They will perpetuate the 'noble lie' that the gods have made men of gold, silver and bronze and that each should know his place.[85] But, on the other hand, Plato is clear in his insistence that these things will be done not for the sake of the rulers themselves—not in 'the interest of the stronger party'—but in order to achieve a good that is collective, long-term and natural. The Guardians will do such things because they have to shape into a semblance of justice those who are not equipped with the intellectual and personal resources to be just in their own right. The Guardians themselves will be men and women of supreme goodness of intention. They will lead lives of austerity and disinterest; they will deploy their formidable resources of intellect for the wellbeing of the community over which they preside; they will strive to see to it that those subject to them live happy and complete lives within the limits of what is possible for them. Within its own terms, there could hardly be a more moral account of government. This fact survives any disinclination that one might now feel to subscribe to its prescriptions in detail.

Chapter 3

Aristotle: The Ethical Necessity of Politics

ARISTOTLE (384–322 BCE) was a member of Plato's Academy from 367 BCE until Plato's death in 347 BCE, first as a student, then as a teacher.¹ Plato was absent on his ill-fated visits to Syracuse for longish periods during Aristotle's early years at the Academy; but there is every reason to suppose that Aristotle studied Plato's works closely and that his sometimes sharply critical standpoint is the result of considered reflection.² In this chapter, we shall mention in particular two important respects in which he diverges from Plato's philosophy as represented in the *Republic*. It is a traditional belief that, when Plato died, Aristotle expected to succeed him as head of the Academy. The position went instead to Plato's nephew Speusippus, of whom Diogenes Laertius says that 'he followed Plato's teaching faithfully, but was not like him in character; he was quick to anger and easily distracted by pleasures.'³ Speusippus, it seems, was not an admirable person, nor was he particularly distinguished as a philosopher; but, unlike Aristotle, he was a native of Athens, and it may be that his preferment was due partly to this.⁴ It may, however, also reflect the fact that Aristotle's opinions had already begun to deviate from Plato's to a significant extent.⁵ Aristotle left the Academy,⁶ evidently in some dudgeon, and spent three years at Assos in Asia Minor as a guest of the king, Hermeas, whose niece he married. It was during this period that he developed, in collaboration with his friend Theophrastus, the interest in natural science, especially biology, that was to be such a formative influence on his thought. In 343 BCE he accepted a position at the court of King Philip of Macedon as tutor to his son, the future Alexander the Great, then a lad of thirteen.⁷ Aristotle returned to Athens in 335 BCE and opened his own school, the Lyceum. His family's

Macedonian connections made him less than popular with Athenian patriots after Alexander's death in 323 BCE, and he again left the city, apparently in fear of his life. In the following year he died at Chalcis on the island of Euboea.[8]

Aristotle's political philosophy is at once similar to and unlike that of Plato. Like Plato, though with less overt hostility, he dislikes the intellectual practices and beliefs associated with the Sophists.[9] He too is on the side of *physis* as distinct from *nomos*; he wishes to make out a case for the *polis* as a natural rather than an artificial, and as a moral rather than an instrumental, community. He too is concerned with rationality, stability and the attainment of a calm and steady happiness. But he develops his views in ways that are more rooted in practicality and more 'scientific' than Plato's, and which reflect important differences of principle as between the two philosophers. Aristotle is to a substantial extent a revisionist.[10] He is aware of the shortcomings of Plato's political thought and of the extent to which its usefulness is limited by its fantastic and unfeasible qualities, and he dissociates himself explicitly from some of the more far-fetched aspects of Plato's political prescription.[11] Aristotle is responsible for one of the most frequently quoted aphorisms of political thought: 'Man is by nature (φύσει: 'is by *physis*') a political animal. Whoever is outside the *polis* is either greater than human or less than human.'[12] A correctly organised *polis* does not merely make a contribution to the good life of those who dwell in it; it is an ethical necessity. The living of life is a moral enterprise that can be accomplished successfully only under the conditions that a well-constituted *polis* furnishes, and the proper form of political life is to be read off from ethical requirements that are necessary and natural. Plato had thought these things too; but Aristotle departs fundamentally from Plato in his account of what a well-constituted *polis* would be. His *Politics* is largely devoted to a technical analysis of the ways in which political orders are and may be organised. The important ethical presuppositions that inform this analysis are to be found in the *Nicomachean Ethics*.[13]

Aristotle: Teleology and Human Nature

Aristotle's general view of the world is of the kind known as *teleological*. It is a view—more correctly, a methodology—latent in Plato;[14] but

Aristotle seems to have developed it fully during his time at Assos. It is an aspect of his 'scientific' preoccupation with the analysis and classification of natural entities. Everything in the world is, he holds, capable of being analysed with reference to four 'causes': a material cause, a formal cause, an efficient cause and a final cause.[15] This use of the word αἰτιά (*aitia*), 'cause,' is superficially unfamiliar ('explanatory feature' might be a better way of expressing what *aitia* means in this context);[16] but Aristotle's meaning is not difficult to grasp. The 'material' cause of anything is what it is made of (bronze, for example); its 'formal' cause is the form or pattern or structure that it exhibits (a statue of Pericles); its 'efficient' cause is its cause in the usual English sense: the agent or force that 'effects' it or causes it to be what it is (the sculptor); its 'final' cause or τέλος (*telos*) is the 'end' of its existence in the sense that we must now amplify.

Although the word *telos* is usually rendered into English as 'end' or 'purpose,' neither of these translations is satisfactory except within a limited range of cases. We must be clear about exactly what Aristotle means before we can make any progress with his ethics. Everything, he says, has a natural *telos*, an 'end,' peculiar to itself. 'Nature makes nothing to no purpose.'[17] By this, he does not mean only that everything has a 'purpose' in the way that it is the purpose of a knife to cut or of a pen to write. Such purposes are included in the idea of teleology, but they do not exhaust it. Things that are not artefacts, which have not been made to do something, also have *teloi* in the sense of having an 'end' state: a condition of full or final development towards which it is their nature to unfold. The idea of nature is inseparable from that of *telos*. 'What each thing is when its coming into being is complete, be it a human being or a horse or a household, we call the nature of that thing.'[18] A more exact English equivalent of *telos* might be 'natural completion.' To use the commonplace illustration, the *telos* of an acorn is an oak tree. The process whereby anything accomplishes its *telos*—whereby, in Aristotelian language, it moves from potentiality to actuality—is its ἔργον (*ergon*), the 'work' or 'task' peculiar to it. The intrinsic power or faculty that it has to engage in and complete this work is its δύναμις (*dynamis*). Finally, what we mean when we call a thing ἀγαθόν (*agathon*), 'good,' is that it has achieved its *telos* fully or successfully. A good pen is a pen that writes well; but a good oak-tree is a well-grown and healthy specimen of its kind, and so on. The doctrine is not without difficulties, but these need not detain us.[19]

Aristotle's four 'causes' furnish answers to the questions that one might most obviously want to ask about an object of scientific investigation: What is it made of? What form does it take? What has caused it to be as it is? and What is it 'for'?—in the general sense that we have outlined: What is the completion of its nature, and therefore its good? It will be seen at once that teleological analysis has a dual function in Aristotelian methodology. It is a means of both description and evaluation. To identify the *telos* of something is simultaneously to identify its good. Aristotle adopts the nominalist understanding of the relation between 'nature' and 'good' that we saw in Callicles and Thrasymachus, though to very different effect. The most completely actualised nature of something is what the word 'good' *means* in relation to that thing.

Aristotle's initial interest in teleology as a method of analysis was as a natural scientist. In what sense can the same method be applied to the human science of ethics? The point, of course, is that 'man' does not stand apart from nature. He is as much amenable to causal analysis as any other part of the natural world. He has a material cause (flesh), a formal cause (he is a featherless biped), an efficient cause (parents) and a final cause. His final cause, like that of the oak tree, is to be a fully developed or fully realised specimen of his kind. His end, in other words, is to fulfil the function proper to what he is by living well or completely. What, in precise terms, does this mean? The final cause of man, Aristotle tells us, is the achievement of a condition of εὐδαιμονία (*eudaimonia*).[20] This is another term that has not been well served by its translators. We shall adopt the customary practice of translating *eudaimonia* by the English word 'happiness,' but only because it is useful to have a one-word translation. 'Happiness' in its modern English acceptation means a good deal less than Aristotle does by *eudaimonia*. The word is a compound of εὖ (*eu*), 'well,' and δαίμων (*daimon*), 'spirit' or 'genius.' Originally, *eudaimonia* probably contained the idea of being presided over or protected by a beneficent spirit: Socrates used to say that he was inspired to philosophise by his personal *daimon*.[21] In the Greek of Aristotle's time, *eudaimonia* seems, in everyday usage, to have meant no more than 'prosperity' or 'good fortune.'[22] In Aristotle, it becomes a *terminus technicus* with a distinctive meaning of its own. It denotes an active state of lifelong wellbeing or flourishing considered as the ethical goal of human activity. For the sake of convenience, we shall from now on use the word 'happiness' without further explanation; but this breadth of meaning should be kept always in view.

How do we know that 'happiness' is man's end-state or completion? We know it because we know both that we desire happiness, and that we do not desire it for the sake of anything else. A moment's reflection is enough to show that happiness possesses intrinsic value. If someone asks us why we want any of the things that people usually want—pleasure, money, power, glory—we might say that we want these things because they will make us happy, or because we think they will. But if anyone asks why we want to be happy, we do not answer in terms of some further objective lying beyond happiness. Indeed, we *could* not do so unless we were using the word 'happiness' in a wholly eccentric sense. We can only reply that we want to be happy just because we do: we want to be happy for the sake of being happy. Happiness, therefore, is the 'end' in the uncomplicated sense of there being no further desideratum to which it is a means. Subject to qualifications that we shall mention in due course, it is the 'end' common to every member of the human race.

> The best good is something complete (τέλειον: *teleion*). Now happiness seems to be 'complete' in a more unrestricted sense than anything else is, since we always choose it because of itself, never because of something else. Honour, pleasure, wisdom and every virtue we certainly choose for themselves, for we would choose each of these things even if it had no further result. But we also choose them for the sake of happiness, supposing that through them we shall be happy. Happiness, however, is that which no one chooses for the sake of something else or for any other reason at all.[23]

Happiness, moreover, is only properly such when it is continuous throughout life, 'for one swallow does not make a spring, nor does one day; nor, again, does a single day or a short time make anyone blessed and happy.'[24] In Aristotle's axiology, happiness is by definition related to quantity or duration because it has reference to the whole of life. Happiness is a life well lived, but life cannot be well lived sporadically. Indeed, we cannot really say that a man's life has been 'happy' until it is over: until it can as it were be evaluated as a finished product.

In what way, by what *ergon*, are we to actualise this end, and hence this good, in our lives? It is clear that *eudaimonia* considered as the 'purpose' or meaning of human life cannot consist in such things as growth and nutrition. It cannot consist in the biological processes of being alive, for plants are alive: 'being alive' is not a property exclusive to human beings. Nor can it consist in being alive and sentient, for in that case we should have no *telos* separate from that of the beasts. It must, Aristotle thinks, consist in the deployment of a faculty or power, a *dynamis*, which is 'peculiar' (ἴδιον: *idion*) to us in the sense that man and only man has it.[25] A process of elimination produces the conclusion that this faculty is *reason*. It is the capacity that no other creature has to engage in connected and purposive thought; thought that is, moreover, expressed through the capacity for speech, which enables us literally to 'tell' right from wrong.[26] Aristotle stipulates also that the attainment of *eudaimonia* must be a matter of rational *activity*. It must lie in the use of reason rather than in the possession of it. We do not call a musician a musician because he owns, but because he plays, an instrument. Nor can it lie in the *mere* use of reason. We do not call someone a good harpist because he plays the harp, but because he plays it well; so too, we shall not call someone a good man unless he uses his reason well: unless he uses it 'according to virtue.' What Aristotle means by 'according to virtue' is a little more complex than one might initially suppose; but we shall come to this shortly. The 'point' of human life is to achieve happiness by means of rational activity according to virtue. This is the 'end'—not, strictly speaking, the 'purpose,' but the completion—prescribed for us by our nature.

> We take it that the *ergon* of man is a certain kind of life, and that this life consists in those activities and actions of the soul that require [the *dynamis* of] reason. The function of the outstanding man, therefore, is to do such things excellently and well. And since each function is completed well when its completion expresses the proper virtue, the human good turns out to consist in rational activity according to virtue; and if there are more virtues than one, the good man will express the best and most complete virtue.[27]

We need to pause for a moment over the word 'virtue.' Again, the Greek word is the useful but often confusingly porous *areté*. The

Aristotle: The Ethical Necessity of Politics

Sophists had used the term to mean 'prowess' or 'practical effectiveness.' Aristotle uses it to mean two different but related things. He speaks of moral virtues, which are virtues in what we might call the ordinary sense. They are the excellences of character by which someone is identified as good or righteous.[28] But he speaks also of another class of virtues: the intellectual or 'dianoetic' virtues. The dianoetic virtues are not moral dispositions or kinds of righteous activity; they are faculties of the rational soul.[29] They are the mental capacities through which—'by virtue of which'—we are able to reason in particular ways. Aristotle identifies three main intellectual virtues: σοφία (*sophia*), φρόνησις (*phronesis*) and τέχνη (*techné*).[30] Thanks to difficulties arising from the composite nature of the *Nicomachean Ethics*, his analysis is not entirely easy to unravel; this is an issue about which there has been a good deal of scholarly discussion. One is inclined to suspect that Aristotle developed two versions of ethics, and that the editor of the *Nicomachean Ethics* has tried to conflate the two. But this is a discussion from which we must prescind.[31] On the whole, the most convincing interpretation of Aristotle's thought as we have it is that happiness is accomplished in different ways, or at different levels, through the deployment of two kinds of intellectual virtue, each having an objective of its own.

On the one hand, happiness in the fullest and most complete sense is found in pure intellectual activity: in the disinterested pursuit of philosophical knowledge.[32] It is here that Plato's influence on Aristotle is most plainly seen; though, as we shall see, Aristotle differs from Plato in his understanding of what the objects of philosophical knowledge are. Such pure intellectual activity requires the exercise of the intellectual virtue called *sophia*. We have noted already some of the senses that this versatile word can bear.[33] In Aristotle, it means something like 'theoretical' or 'abstract' rationality. It is the form of rationality peculiar to scientific or philosophical investigation. *Sophia* finds its expression in demonstrative or syllogistic reasoning.[34] This is the form of reasoning devoted to elucidating the logical implications of first principles either established inductively, as generalisations from sense experience, or known by the faculty of intuition that Aristotle calls νοῦς (*nous*). Inasmuch it deals with logical inference, the connections that demonstrative reasoning establishes are permanent or eternal. Demonstrative reasoning has nothing to do with contingent matters, nor does it produce statements that are true only for the time being or in a few cases. It will be seen, therefore—and this is a point to which we shall presently return—that demonstrative or theoretical reasoning is in no sense instrumental: it has no practical objective or outcome. It is the activity of philosophical thought pure and simple, divested of any connection with the material world. It is for this reason that Aristotle assigns so great a value to it. To practise such reasoning, he holds, is to possess happiness in the highest form of which we are capable. To be engaged in abstract contemplation is to be removed from all change, uncertainty and vicissitude, and therefore to be absolved from anxiety. Like Plato, Aristotle assigns supreme importance to that which can lift the mind away from the worrying contingencies of 'ordinary' experience. The philosopher, insofar as he is a philosopher, is without want and without pain, rapt as the gods are in the calm and desireless contemplation of the eternal and changeless. So understood, the philosophical life is a life greater than human; it is semi-divine. 'The human activity that most resembles the activity of the gods will most of all have the character of happiness.'[35]

On the other hand, the happiness that is realised through philosophical contemplation cannot, precisely because it is so sublime, be the normal condition of anyone's life. We should strive after it as diligently as we can, with that part of us that is godlike: 'we must do all we can...to live according to the best thing in us.'[36] But we are not gods; we are bodies as well as minds. No one can live in a state of pure abstraction permanently and to the exclusion of everyday activity; some people do not have the aptitude for philosophy at all. Are we to say that so exclusive or restrictive a form of happiness is the only sort of happiness? Clearly, since we want to discover a happiness capable of being achieved by mankind in general and throughout life as a whole, this would be unsatisfactory. We need to look for a kind of happiness that is, so to speak, a little more mundane or everyday.

It is here that the moral virtues come in. Most of Aristotle's attention in the *Nicomachean Ethics* is devoted to a consideration of moral virtue rather than to the happiness of contemplation. The text of the *Nicomachean Ethics* gives the impression that the highest form of happiness is brought in rather as an afterthought. Certainly it is our highest good, but the science of ethics needs to devote itself to the requirements of life in all its aspects. For most of the time, Aristotle thinks, we find 'happiness'—contentment, wellbeing—not in abstract reasoning conducted for its own sake, but in the making of rational moral choices. We achieve it through the consistent practice of good or honourable behaviour in everyday life. This statement is not at all at odds with the view that the life of philosophy is the sublimest happiness of all. Indeed, Aristotle believes that a life of moral virtue is a prerequisite of contemplation, for it is not to be supposed that anyone can engage in contemplation fully who is not a morally virtuous man. 'But in a secondary degree, life according to the other kind of virtue'—that is, moral virtue—'is happy; for activity according to this is suitable to our human condition.'[37] It is suitable to our condition insofar as it is corporeal and human rather than intellectual and divine. 'Secondary' or everyday happiness, then, consists in the practice of the moral virtues, the moral virtues being such things as courage, temperance, generosity and justice.

In what particular kinds of activity does the practice of these virtues consist? It is in this connection that Aristotle proposes his famous doctrine of the mean.[38] This doctrine is expressed in the definition of morally virtuous activity as

> a habit of choice lying in a mean, relative to ourselves, determined according to a rational principle in the way that a man of practical wisdom would determine it...between two vices, the one of excess and the other of defect.[39]

It is worth remarking that, in its inception, the mean is a Platonic rather than an Aristotelian doctrine. The notion of the mean as a standard of moral activity embodies something like the principle that we encountered in Plato's exploration of justice in the *Republic*: that all activity is made possible by identifying the limits within which it has to be conducted if it is to be conducted successfully.[40] We are reminded also of Plato's statement in the *Philebus* that all good things in life belong to the category of the mixed or intermediate.[41] The doctrine of the mean is not without difficulties, as Aristotle himself understands; but it is easy enough to grasp as a general principle. To behave courageously is to avoid both the foolish courting of danger and the timorous shirking of it: these are the extremes of excess and defect. Someone who lives according to the virtue of temperance does not suppress his natural appetites altogether, nor does he wallow in them swinishly. He enjoys what is enjoyable in the right measure and at the right time. Generosity lies at a suitable point between meanness and reckless liberality. Justice is more complex and can be considered under several aspects.[42] Broadly speaking, however, Aristotle's account of justice is of justice as fairness or proportionality. Justice, whether personal or political, involves acting in such a way, or organising public affairs in such a way, as to ensure that no one has, nor is required to undergo, either more or less than is appropriate in the circumstances.

The individual whose capacity for moral action is fully developed will at all times act rationally and with moderation. Aristotle's moral paragon will be 'great of soul': mature, calm, broad-minded, judicious and above small feelings.[43] He will take a proper pride in his reputation and abstain from false modesty; he will despise whoever deserves to be despised and honour those who are worthy of honour; he will be readier to give than to receive, since to receive is to acknowledge inferiority; he will speak and walk with dignity; he will express his opinions frankly and without fear. The happiness that his behaviour gives him will come from the fact that it originates in the conscious deliberation that it is his nature as a rational creature to perform. Some have thought Aristotle's moral philosophy bourgeois and provincial and his 'great-souled' man something of a prig; but this is to read him superficially.[44] The excellent individual is not smug or pompous. He is a stable, self-consciously developed moral being, satisfied that his life is everything that human life can and should be.

An important part of Aristotle's definition of the mean is the phrase 'relative to ourselves.' What he means by this is 'relative to the kind of person we are and to the position in which we find ourselves at a given time.' The practice of the moral virtues is a matter of acting appropriately rather than according to predetermined patterns. It is a matter of doing what is suitable to person, time and place while avoiding extremes. Ethics is not an exact science, and it is a mistake to look to it for the kind of certainty that mathematics can furnish.[45] The specific and appropriate manifestations of courage, temperance, and so on, will be different at different times and in different circumstances, and will be subject to the judgment of the agent: 'fine and just actions...admit of numerous differences and variations.'[46] One cannot prescribe hard and fast rules of moral behaviour in advance. Sometimes it will be appropriate to be intensely pleased or intensely angry. What the doctrine of the mean prescribes is the avoidance not of intense feeling or strenuous action, but of responses that are excessive or deficient in the sense of not well adapted to their circumstances. Even negative emotions can be good under suitable conditions: 'The man who is angry for the right reason and with the right people and in the right way and at the right moment and for the right length of time, is to be praised.'[47]

The practice of moral virtue brings into play an intellectual virtue of its own. This virtue is different from the *sophia* that we deploy when reasoning abstractly. In order to identify the mean that marks the path of moral virtue one needs to be 'a man of practical wisdom': a *phronimos*, one able to make use of *phronesis*. *Phronesis* is the intellectual virtue that we deploy when we debate not about the logical implications of premisses, but about what to do in a given situation. Unlike *sophia*, it is an instrumental kind of reasoning. Whereas *sophia* proceeds by means of the demonstrative syllogism, *phronesis* makes use of what Aristotle calls the 'practical' syllogism.[48] *Phronesis* is the 'rational principle' according to which moral choices are made. Both moral reasoning and theoretical reasoning are deductive; but the aim of practical reasoning is not universally valid knowledge, but action of a practically or morally beneficial kind.[49] *Phronesis* does not identify our moral goals for us. These are given by our natural disposition to seek the mean, and this disposition is developed in us as a capacity for effective behaviour not by reason or deliberation, but by training and habit (see pp. 79–80). But *phronesis* specifies how the individual should act in given circumstances if he is to achieve his moral objectives. 'Virtue [i.e. moral virtue] makes us aim at the right mark, and [the intellectual virtue of] *phronesis* makes us adopt the right means.'[50]

Our 'end,' then, is *eudaimonia*, happiness: flourishing or wellbeing. We accomplish that end by living well throughout life as a whole, and living well is a matter of rational activity performed 'according to virtue': directed, that is, by the right means towards proper ends. Supreme happiness is found in abstract contemplation by means of the intellectual virtue of *sophia*, without the hindrance of any mundane or material concern; but this is hardly an attainable goal for life considered at large. For ordinary purposes, happiness is realised through the deliberate and consistent practice of moral virtue, calling upon the intellectual virtue of *phronesis* to guide us in our specific acts. Aristotle's exposition of these points lacks clarity in certain respects, but his general position is not as difficult to understand as it is sometimes made out to be.[51]

The Polis *as an Ethical Necessity*

Teleology, we recall, is a method of analysis in terms of nature. The end that man has is the end given by his nature as a rational being. We recall also that 'man is by nature a political animal.' What is the relation between our natural end as moral creatures and our natural existence as political ones?[52] As Plato does in his discussion of the origins of political association, Aristotle begins with the truism that everyone needs access to material resources that depend upon a division of labour. No individual can by his own efforts provide himself with all that is necessary if he is to live, let alone flourish. This is a fact of human nature. All forms of human association and co-operation are therefore natural insofar as they meet a particular level of material need. The household is natural; so is the village, which is a collection of households; so is the *polis*, which may be regarded as a union of villages (we remember the *synoikismoi* from which the *poleis* first arose). But it is the *polis* that is the most completely sufficient, and hence the most completely natural, community. It is 'prior in the order of nature to the family and the individual,' even though it comes after them in time.[53] What Aristotle means by 'prior in the order of nature' is that, unlike less developed or more partial forms of association, the *polis* enables all the needs of our nature to be met in their entirety.

In saying this, he has in mind not only economic needs, but also the full range of moral needs that we have as rational beings. 'The *polis* comes into being so that men may live; it remains in being so that they may live well.'[54] Aristotle's understanding of the connection between ethics and politics can be amplified by way of three statements. First, the *polis* equips its citizens with the economic or material prerequisites of morality. Clearly, economic needs must be met before moral needs can be attended to. Neither the supremely happy life of contemplation nor the life of rational choice that Aristotle identifies with 'ordinary' happiness can be lived in conditions of want. The ethically good life requires a certain level of good fortune and material prosperity. The former does not lie within anyone's control; we are all to some extent at the mercy of chance. But the latter can be provided by the kind of conditions that the *polis* makes possible. Aristotle has the usual intellectual's prejudices against luxury. His remarks remind us of Socrates's preference for the 'first' or 'healthy' city. Too plentiful a supply of external goods is bad for us, Aristotle says. Excessive wealth forms in us habits of laziness and self-importance; we do not need to rule the earth and sea to be happy.[55] We should, he thinks, engage in economic activity only to the extent necessary to meet our needs. But a sufficient level of prosperity is necessary if we are to live well in the moral sense. We cannot engage in pursuits suitable to rational creatures if we are distracted by care; we cannot live well unless we have health and leisure; we cannot be generous unless we have the means with which to be generous, or just unless we have the means to pay our debts.[56] The processes of production, distribution and support that the *polis* makes possible therefore have moral as well as economic dimensions. Indeed, material comfort is worth having at all only as a precondition of moral fulfilment.

Second, the *polis* provides the formative intellectual conditions upon which the cultivation and realisation of moral excellence depend. The capacity to be moral is a natural one, but moral behaviour itself is not innate. 'We are equipped by nature to acquire the virtues, but we achieve them only by practice.'[57] What Aristotle means by this is that, on the one hand, the 'mean' commends itself to us by intuition. We can see by the light of nature that to deviate in the direction of excess or defect is to destroy the very virtue at which we are aiming. The mean as such is a natural standard of virtue; it does not depend upon convention or opinion. On the other hand, the ability actually to make correct choices in relation to it is something that we have to acquire.[58] For Aristotle, education in moral as distinct from intellectual virtue is a matter of developing habitual modes of behaviour through training and repetition. It is by *doing* virtuous acts that we learn to be virtuous, just as it is by practising music that we become accomplished musicians.⁵⁹ The word 'ethics,' he points out, is derived from ἔθος: *ethos*, 'habit' or 'practice.' This emphasis on habit has two important aspects. One is that Aristotle conceives the process of becoming a moral agent as being somewhat like that of serving an apprenticeship. We cultivate and develop the intellectual virtue of *phronesis* by associating with and imitating those who have it already. If our fellow citizens are good, we learn from their example how to take an effective and responsible share in the common life, just as we might learn a craft from a skilled artisan. It is by such emulation that we become accomplished in the practice of deliberating and acting correctly.⁶⁰ Moral development is in this sense a matter of socialisation. The second aspect is the importance that Aristotle attaches to law as an influence upon moral training. He takes it for granted that law can make those subject to it genuinely good, as distinct from merely inducing conformity. It is an important function of legislation, and an objective that the legislator must keep always in mind, to encourage citizens to acquire good habits.⁶¹ Law can contribute to our moral formation by requiring us to act well until we come to take pleasure in doing so spontaneously. This is why Aristotle says that 'Man, when perfected, is the best of all creatures, but when isolated from law and justice he is the worst of all.'⁶² As the other side of the same coin, bad laws—laws not intended to secure, or which fail to secure, the good of the community as a whole—will make men bad; and under bad laws, a moral paradox arises. The virtue of the good citizen— of someone who obeys the laws—will be at odds with the virtue of the good man. The virtue of the good man is always the same; but the virtue of the good citizen will differ according to the constitution under which he lives. The individual who lives under a tyrant will be a good citizen (will, that is, be good considered from the point of view of the tyrant) not if he displays judiciousness, moderation and rationality, but if he is docile and afraid. The good citizen of an oligarchy will be one devoted to personal gain rather than to the common weal. Such citizens, inasmuch as they are not good men, will not be able to teach one another the art of moral judgment. The moral paradox produced by bad laws will therefore be a socially destructive one also. An integral part of the purpose of political association will be lost.

Third, life as part of a political community provides us not only with material security and an education in how to conduct ourselves well, but also with broader social conditions inseparable from our ethical good. Because it is not in our nature to be solitary, it is not in our nature either to find satisfaction or happiness solely in ourselves and our own interests. We take pleasure in and achieve fulfilment through co-operating and interacting with other human beings. In its everyday, attainable sense, our happiness will not be complete unless it is involved to some extent with the happiness of others:

> The complete good is thought to be self sufficient; but by 'self sufficient' we do not mean 'sufficient for a man considered by himself'—for one who lives a life of solitude—but also for parents, children, wife and, in general, for friends and fellow citizens, since man is born for citizenship.[63]

Aristotle does not suppose that human beings are natural altruists who can be expected to put the good of others before their own; nor does he think that our interest in the welfare of others can or should be limitless. What he means is that, because we are the kind of creatures we are, the good of others can make an important contribution to our own good. This aspect of things is clearly brought out in the long discussion of friendship in Books 8 and 9 of the *Nicomachean Ethics*. We derive satisfaction from the concern that we feel for our friends and from the shared activities that friendship or companionship makes possible. We feel what Jeremy Bentham calls the pleasures of benevolence. Friendship takes a number of forms, not all of them disinterested; but the love of friends for their own sake is one of the highest pleasures that life affords. On the other hand, if we take no interest in the welfare and happiness of our friends and fellow citizens, we cut ourselves off from relationships of shared concern and trust that are necessary to the fulfilment of our natural capacities as social beings. If we were to live the sort of life that the radical Sophists recommend—a life given over wholly to self-gratification or self-aggrandisement at the expense of others or in disregard of them—we should be denying ourselves important opportunities for happiness. The relation of citizens to one another is analogous to—perhaps it is more than analogous to—the relation of friendship. Also, since the moral virtues are pre-eminently social virtues, it is clear that moral virtue cannot be practised alone: one cannot be generous or just without other people to be generous or just to.

The *polis* as Aristotle depicts it is therefore the most natural form of association in that it meets all the needs, both moral and material, which attach to the natures of those who occupy it. Since all citizens have the same needs, the *polis* is the property of them all equally; its purpose is the happiness not of individuals or minorities or the strong, but of everyone. 'The common advantage brings them all together insofar as they each attain the noble life. This above all is the end for all, both in common and separately.'[64] The well-organised city is a community rather than a mere aggregation. It is related to its citizens in the way that the body is related to its members. It we are cut off from the society of our fellows we are deprived of moral purpose. We lose our authenticity as human beings in the way that a hand severed from the body is longer in the full sense a hand.

> If the hand or foot were removed from the body, it would no longer be a hand or foot at all, except perhaps in the loose sense in which one might talk of a hand carved out of stone. In such a case it will be ruined, no longer having the *ergon* and *dynamis* by reason of which it is what it is.[65]

Again, this is more than analogy. We are defined as human beings by the organic relations that exist between us and the whole of which we are parts. There are no non-political or non-social men. Those who can thrive without the *polis* are either greater than human or less than human. They are either gods or beasts.

Aristotle and 'Political Science'

Because, properly understood, the city is an all-sufficient community in the way that we have described, the question of how to organise and govern it is clearly of the highest importance. *Sub specie humanitatis*, the study of politics is the 'master science.' It is the form of enquiry by which all other studies bearing on human happiness—economics, strategy, rhetoric and so forth—are directed. Political orders are, in a certain sense, works of art. They need to be created and maintained by prudence or statecraft. But they need to be created and maintained in such a way as to ensure that they answer to their natural purpose. Political science is the study of the common good: 'the end of this science...must be the good for man.'[66]

Aristotle regards the study of politics not primarily as a deductive or logical science but as the systematic practical investigation of human association in its various forms. This fact is an important part of our understanding both of Aristotle himself and of the ways in which he differs from Plato. His enquiry into the good that political life can secure is inseparable from a highly empirical approach to the questions and problems of political organisation. Aristotle is not interested in the notion of an 'ideal' State in the way that Plato is. He does not think it worthwhile to invent a single perfect constitution supposed to be suitable for all communities and in all circumstances. Aristotle's chief criticism of Ideal State theories—he discusses Plato (with reference to the *Republic* and the *Laws*), Phaleas of Chalcedon and Hippodamus of Miletus[67]—is on grounds of their failure to engage with real needs and possibilities. Even when he depicts a commonwealth that is 'ideal' in the sense of being the best imaginable in terms of size, geography, population and constitution, he insists that 'none of these things should be impossible.'[68] To call Aristotle a 'political scientist' is, having regard to what this expression has come to mean, more than a little misleading; but his treatment of politics is historical, comparative and practical in a way that Plato's is not.

Aristotle's empirical approach is often identified as the great strength of his political theory, counterbalancing the fancifulness and impracticability of Plato's utopianism. One might at first sight account for this difference in terms of the audiences at which the two philosophers are aiming. Unlike the *Republic*, Aristotle's *Politics* and *Nicomachean Ethics* are not intended as replies to opponents who deny that true general principles can be produced by the investigation of facts. To that extent, appeal to actual states of affairs is open to Aristotle in a way that it was not open to Plato. This may be true in a certain sense, but it is not the real point. Much more important is the fact that Aristotle's departure from Plato's methodology reflects one of the two major philosophical differences between himself and Plato to which we referred at the beginning of this chapter. It is essential to understand this difference clearly.

The difference in question is that Aristotle does not believe in ideas or 'universals' as having the kind of separate metaphysical existence that Plato attributes to them. Aristotle's reasons for thinking as he does are compelling, though they are not completely original. In the Academy of Aristotle's time, Plato's Theory of Ideas was already 'undergoing frank and lively criticism.'[69] This is a point to which commentators on Aristotle have not always given sufficient weight. Plato's late dialogue called *Parmenides* is enough to show that the Master himself eventually came to have second thoughts about the philosophical conclusions formed earlier in his career. As part of this process of 'frank and lively criticism' Aristotle gave the Theory of Ideas careful consideration, and formulated, though he did not entirely invent, a number of serious difficulties.[70] His analysis is complex and technical. The following list of his misgivings will give some idea of their scope, though the numerical order in which we present them is only a matter of convenience; it does not reflect Aristotle's diffuse arguments in the *Metaphysics* and elsewhere.

1. Why should we take it for granted, as Plato does, that things are as they are only because they are copies or representations of something else? Such an assumption is not self-evident; nor is it supported by ordinary experience. 'Anything can either be or become like something else without being copied from it.'[71] To introduce paradigmatic ideas into an account of why things are as they are is to double, for no good reason, what needs to be accounted for. The Theory of Ideas infringes the principle that would later be called Ockham's Razor: that entities are not to be multiplied beyond what is necessary for the purposes of explanation.
2. It seems clear that while objects can exist without a given quality (objects are not necessarily cups or dogs), the opposite is not true ('cupness' and 'dogness' cannot exist without cups and dogs). But if this is so, then the causal relation between universals and particulars is surely the reverse of what Plato thinks it is. The meaning of an adjective is dependent upon the meaning of a proper name, not the other way around: we know 'dogness' because we know dogs, not vice versa.
3. If the ideas are eternal and changeless, as Plato teaches, they cannot enable us to account for the phenomena of change and extinction that we meet with in the perceptible world; yet this is a large part of what Plato wants them to do.
4. Logically, a given object must 'participate' either in the whole of its idea or a part of it. If in the whole, this is the same as saying

that each object has an idea to itself, in which case there is not one idea for each class of objects; if in a part, then the ideas are not the indivisible unities that Plato thinks they are.

5. Socrates is a man, but is he not also an animal and a biped? It seems plain, in other words, that he must be a 'copy' not of one, but of several ideas, in which case, again, it cannot be true that there is one idea answering to every type of perceptible object.
6. Plato's ideas, as universals, are wholly different in kind from the concrete particulars given in perception. On his account of them, they occupy an intelligible realm completely removed from the 'world of sight.' But how can an object 'participate' in something else when that something else is a separate entity existing in its own transcendent world?
7. Plato thinks that (say) men are recognisable as men because each man resembles the ideal man. But is not the ideal man himself a man? The logic of the argument therefore requires us now to postulate a still more ideal man: a 'third' man that both the 'ordinary' man and the first ideal man will resemble. But as soon as we postulate this third man, the same difficulty recurs, and so on, *ad infinitum*. We find ourselves involved in an infinite regress that again sabotages the idea that each class of perceptible objects corresponds to a single idea.

We have stated these criticisms only briefly and crudely. For our purposes, there is no need to do more. But it is clear that all this amounts to a fundamental critique of the Platonic 'ideal' world to which reason is supposed to afford us access. In view of these and other objections, we are in Aristotle's view warranted in abandoning the Theory of Ideas as a mode of explanation. Usually, Aristotle is polite about Plato and reluctant to criticise him. The study of ethics, he says, has been made more difficult than we should like because respected friends have introduced the ideas.[72] Sometimes he is not so polite. 'Goodbye to the ideas, then: they are only idle talk.'[73] Aristotle agrees that the particular members of a given class share a quality universal to them all. It is hardly possible to deny this. If we did, we should not be able to use the idea of 'class' at all. But he does not think that this universal quality has a separate existence of its own in a metaphysical realm. Plato had supposed that, in order to achieve an understanding that is complete and real, we have to leave the perceptible world behind and embrace with our minds the supersensible world of ideas. Aristotle, by contrast, believes that Plato's 'world of sight' *is* the real world. Universals exist in, and only in, particular cases. General truths about beauty, justice and so forth are to be discovered not by turning away from particular beautiful objects and just actions, but by experiencing and comparing them. Plato's language of 'participation' is, at best, metaphorical. 'To say that the ideas are patterns and that other things participate in them is to use empty words and poetical images.'[74] Our task, if we wish to arrive at the truth, is not to reach beyond 'our' world in order to apprehend the world of ideas. We must attend to the world of sight itself. We must establish the general principles that make sense of that world by investigating the concrete and accessible facts of it. This is true whether the subject of our investigation is biology, physics, aesthetics or politics. 'The Good' is not a mysterious unity existing in the sunlit world outside the cave. As we saw earlier, the 'good' of anything—including the *polis*—is a quality specific to the thing to which it belongs. It is to be discovered by analysing the thing in terms of the causes that make it what it is, and by identifying the *telos* that it is its nature to achieve. The success or failure of the thing in question is to be assessed simply in terms of the effectiveness with which it does or does not achieve it.

It is this difference of philosophical outlook that accounts for the general preoccupation with taxonomy that is present in Aristotle's work as a natural scientist. With regard to the *Politics*, it accounts for his interest in the comparison and classification of constitutional forms. The 'good for man' is not, for Aristotle, the ideal and recondite good of the *Republic*, mediated to ordinary people through the wisdom of an elite. It is the good of rational happiness achievable by all citizens who enjoy suitable economic, educative and social circumstances. As such, it is immediately contingent upon the values and influences that a given constitution embodies and transmits. The moral foundations of politics are to be sought not in a metaphysical world, but in this one. The analysis of actual constitutions is therefore of central importance to political prescription, just as the analysis of actual (rather than abstract or theoretical or ideal) physiques and levels of fitness is important to the trainer of athletes.

Aristotle defines a constitution as 'the organisation of the *polis* with respect to its offices generally, but especially with respect to that office which is sovereign over all matters.'[75] As we have noted, he does not wish to argue, in the way that Plato does, for one ideal constitution from which every other is necessarily a decline. He knows that, in practice, States have devised many different ways of organising themselves and that we have to deal with what exists rather than with what ought to exist. He knows also that even the worst arrangements can be improved, and that what is best for one *polis* may not suit another in different cultural and material circumstances. The form of government suitable to a particular people will depend on the needs, temperament and situation of that people. These conclusions are the result of a determinedly comparative approach. Aristotle is said to have made studies of the constitutions of 158 Greek cities and to have written, or supervised the writing, of treatises on them; although only one of these treatises, on *The Constitution of Athens*, is extant.

The most general conclusion to which the process of comparison leads him is that constitutional types may be grouped into three categories: rule by one, rule by a few and rule by many.[76] In the *Politics*, Aristotle deals at length and in detail with these three forms and their possible gradations and permutations. To a large extent, he is concerned in this discussion with technical questions of stability and change. With considerable impartiality, he recommends ways in which even bad or dysfunctional constitutions can be made more stable.[77] The stability of a constitution is, he thinks, secured by balancing elements of 'fewness' and 'manyness' in such a way as to ensure that as few people as possible are excluded or alienated. Generally speaking, the more moderate and broadly based a constitution is, the less prone to disruption it will be. Similarly, 'pure' forms of constitution will always have instability built into them. This inherent instability arises from the fact that they will invariably contain disaffected and hostile groups. Oligarchies will antagonise the poor, who are numerous; democracies will antagonise the rich, who are few but influential. Thus, oligarchies can make themselves more secure by admitting as many people as possible to a share of political power, even if it is only a token share. Democracies can protect themselves by pursuing moderate policies with regard to the redistribution of wealth and by placating the wealthy with dignified and expensive offices. The most stable and enduring form of constitution will be one in which political power rests with a large middle class. It will be a government of neither the wealthy few nor the propertyless many, but somewhere between the two. The members of the middle class are not wealthy enough to be resented by others, but they are sufficiently well off not to want to dispossess the rich. This is the political expression of Aristotle's doctrine of the mean.[78]

But, as we might expect, given the intimate and necessary connections that he draws between politics and ethics, Aristotle's interest in constitutions is not purely analytic and taxonomic. He is concerned with constitutions not only as organisational, but also, and primarily, as moral phenomena. To that extent, the designation 'political scientist,' with its implication of value-freedom, does not belong to him. The *moral quality* of a constitution, considered as something apart from stability and longevity, is, he thinks, not a matter of structure but of intentionality. It is a matter of the *good* at which the ruler or the ruling group aims. Any kind of constitution is capable of being good or bad, regardless of its institutional arrangements. According to Aristotle's classification, aristocracy and monarchy are good constitutions, oligarchy and tyranny are bad or 'perverted' ones; yet aristocracy and oligarchy both involve rule by the few. Outwardly, with respect to the visible distribution of power, they look the same. But aristocracy is rule by the best men for the good of all, whereas oligarchy is rule by a wealthy minority for its own good. Similarly, monarchy and tyranny are both rule by one; but a monarch rules for the good of all, and a tyrant for his own good.[79] The subjects of a tyrant are effectively slaves, allowed to have no purposes that are not subordinated to those of their master. What Aristotle calls 'polity' at *Politics* 1279^{a}37 is rule by the many for the common good; its bad counterpart, democracy, is, in effect, mob rule: rule by the many for the good of the many.[80] Good constitutions answer to the true nature of constitutions by securing the good—the happiness—of all their citizens; or, more correctly, by providing conditions that enable them to secure happiness for themselves. Bad or degenerate constitutions fail to do so because they secure the good of a part or group only.

Notwithstanding Aristotle's 'scientific' interest in political forms and dynamics, then, he, like Plato, believes that politics is ultimately worthwhile as a mode of human experience only insofar as political arrangements are ordered not to a narrow or sectional good, but to the real and lifelong interests of those affected by them. Genuine monarchies and aristocracies are rare. It may happen that an individual appears who is of such outstanding personal excellence—who is so clearly superior by nature—that it is obviously right to hand over responsibility for government to him.[81] But such individuals are seldom found; also, there is no guarantee that a monarch's successor will have the admirable qualities of his predecessor. Plato himself had recognised, in Book 8 of the *Republic*, that even the rule of philosophers might gradually degenerate into tyranny. Love of justice may turn imperceptibly into love of honour or wealth. In the ordinary way, Aristotle thinks, the rule of good laws is to be preferred to the rule of men. Law not only forms good habits in us; it also provides an impersonal standard free from the prejudice, malice and deterioration to which individual judgment is subject. But the best judges of what good law is are those who will have to live under it, just as the best judges of the food at a banquet are those who eat it. The best laws are produced by the deliberation, and upheld by the willing acceptance, of the citizens whose laws they are. Though he is prepared to regard any constitutional form as good if it aims at the good of the community, Aristotle considers that the best attainable political association will be a mixed constitution that can achieve stability and the common good through involving as many people as possible in the processes by which law is made and administered.[82] Government at its most natural, and therefore at its best, is the government of equals by equals. No member of the community will be able to do everything at once; nor (*pace* Plato) would it be desirable for any individual to have one rôle only throughout life. No citizen could develop himself in the ways that Aristotle considers desirable other than through a range of public experience. The best kind of *polis* will be large enough to be self-sufficient, yet small enough for everyone to be able to take a share in its affairs at whatever level is suitable to their age and aptitudes. In the best achievable city, all citizens will play a part, and all will learn how to rule and be ruled. The young and vigorous will be soldiers; older and more experienced citizens will belong to the legislative assembly and will elect from their number the officials of the *polis*; the aged will retire from active citizenship into priesthoods.[83]

The idea of full citizen involvement in the life of the community is a vital part of Aristotle's political thought. It is his most obvious legacy to 'modern' conceptions of politics. The ordinary citizen of Plato's Kallipolis would be the passive recipient of the guidance of the wise. His natural rôle would be to accept his just place in the social order as allocated to him by the judgment of the enlightened, and to carry out his appointed duties willingly and with no wish to do anything else. In Aristotelian terms, such an individual is not a citizen, but a subject. For Aristotle, the citizen's rôle is one of positive and effective action. The citizen is defined by his participation in the life of the *polis*, and his development as a human being is achieved through it. It is by devoting their time and efforts to public affairs that citizens live well.

What is it that leads Aristotle to conceive the relation between *polis* and citizen in a way so different from that of Plato? Here we come to the second of our two major philosophical differences between them. For Plato, active politics is the province of the talented and accomplished few. Philosophers should rule because only they are truly just. Contrary to what the Sophists think, there are knowable truths about the just and the good; but only philosophers know them. Their rule will consist largely in directing the ignorant by imparting to them as much of the truth as the ignorant are capable of receiving. For Plato, theoretical and practical reasoning do not differ in kind. The latter is only *sophia* directed as it were downwards, towards the world of sight. But Aristotle makes a categorial distinction between theoretical and practical reasoning: between *sophia* and *phronesis*. On his account of the intellectual virtues, the business of decision-making requires not philosophy, but deliberation and choice. In drawing this distinction, he spots what we mentioned earlier as a major weakness in Plato's moral epistemology: that, even if the Theory of Ideas were true, knowing what something *is* would not of itself enable us to *do* anything. In making this point in the *Eudemian Ethics*, Aristotle is politely but definitely critical of the philosophical agenda of the *Republic*:

> Socrates...set out to investigate the *nature* of courage and justice and so on...He therefore enquired what virtue is, not how or from what it arises...[But] our aim is not to know what justice and courage *are* so much as to *be* courageous and just, in the same way as we wish actually to be healthy and fit rather than simply to find out what it *is* to be healthy and fit. In all these matters, we must try to arrive at certainty by discussion, using perceived facts as evidence and illustration.[84]

Aristotle: The Ethical Necessity of Politics

Ethics, we remember, is not a science capable of yielding intellectual certainties. The world of practical affairs is not universal and necessary, but concrete and contingent. Philosophical reasoning, directed as it is to what is universal and necessary, is therefore not appropriate to practical activity. The rightness and wrongness of our actions will depend not on their conformity to a definition, but on their adaptation to the circumstances in which they apply. Practical activity requires the exercise not of abstract contemplation but of prudence: 'we must try to arrive at certainty by discussion, using perceived facts'—not invisible ideas—'as evidence and illustration.' And prudence, *phronesis*, is something that any rational being in the right material and social circumstances can cultivate. It is a form of rationality best cultivated by practising and deploying it, and the more people who have it—the more people able to contribute a considered opinion—the better. On these grounds, Aristotle rejects Plato's view that ruling is best entrusted to those rare and able individuals who have gazed upon the mystical Idea of the Good understood as the unifying criterion of all value. Aristotle's concept of *phronesis* is bound up with a belief in the practical educability of ordinary citizens. This is a belief that confers a new dignity on the idea of participation by the ordinary citizen in the activities of deliberation and decision-making, and it identifies as the best kind of constitution that which will enable as many people as possible to take, and to realise their human potential through taking, a share in the common life. When citizens are united under a good constitution and ruled by wisely made, impartial laws, and when all can play a part in bringing about the good of the whole community, the virtue of the good man and the virtue of the good citizen will be the same: the moral purpose of the commonwealth will be realised most fully.

Aristotle on Justice and Law

Aristotle's *Nicomachean Ethics*, *Politics* and *Rhetoric* contain a number of scattered remarks about justice and law that it is for our purposes instructive to bring together.[85] These remarks illustrate in particular respects that, for Aristotle, the principles underlying well-conducted political activity are not themselves conventional in origin. In the *Nicomachean Ethics*, he distinguishes between 'absolute' and 'political' justice. The point of the distinction seems to be that 'absolute' justice is not relative to any particular community whereas 'political' justice holds as between 'men who share their lives with a view to achieving self sufficiency.'[86] In connection with political justice itself, he draws another distinction between 'legal' justice, which is 'established by enactment' and which varies from place to place as weights and measures vary from market to market, and 'natural' or 'unwritten' justice, which 'has the same force everywhere, and which is not brought into being by reason of our thinking this or that.'[87] The difference between 'absolute' and 'natural' justice seems to be that 'natural' justice is 'absolute' justice considered as applying between fellow citizens rather than between members of different communities; though it is not obvious why Aristotle thinks the distinction worth making. In the passages to which we have referred, Aristotle tells us nothing about the content of 'absolute' or 'natural' justice; but some idea of what he has in mind can be inferred from several of his other remarks. For example, he argues in the *Politics* that a war conducted against natural slaves—against those who 'though intended by nature to be subject to government refuse to submit'—is 'naturally just.'[88] It is naturally just because waged against them by those who are their natural superiors. In the *Nicomachean Ethics*, he observes that the doctrine of the mean does not apply to certain acts—theft, adultery, murder—because those acts are inherently bad.[89] In the *Rhetoric*, he supplies a long list of things that are equitable or fair as distinct from legal. It is equitable to make allowances for human failings; to attend to the meaning rather than the letter of the law; to consider the intention with which an act was done; to consider an act with reference to the whole of its circumstances rather than a part; to ask not what someone is now, but what he has usually or always been; to think of benefits received rather than benefits conferred or injuries suffered; to be patient in the face of wrongdoing; to settle disputes by discussion rather than force; to be willing to go to arbitration rather than to sue.[90] In the *Politics* Aristotle applies the concept of natural norms to questions of economics. Economic activity is natural, and hence good, insofar as it is ordered to our natural needs. Economic activity for the sake of profit, which involves taking from others rather than making use of natural resources, is unnatural and to be censured. A similar argument applies to the practice of usury. The taking of interest on loans is an unnatural form of acquisition because money is not naturally productive of anything: its nature is to be used only as a medium of exchange.[91] Referring to Plato's prescription in the *Republic* that the property of the Guardians should be held in common, Aristotle observes that private ownership and common use are more in keeping with human nature than common ownership would be. Individuals always quarrel about what belongs to everyone, but have pleasure and pride in their own possessions. People whose characters are formed by good laws will be willing to share their property with others without needing to be compelled to do so.[92]

On the subject of legislation specifically, Aristotle insists that law does not originate in convention. It is the rule of rational principle, *logos*, and not of a person or persons.[93] The enactment and promulgation of law is due to human contrivance; but law is good only if it reflects the ethical end of those who are to live by it: otherwise the rule of law would be no better than the rule of a wild beast.[94] Bad laws produce, and are produced by, communities that fail of their natural purpose. Legislation is a process not of making laws but of discovering them: of deriving particular conclusions from general moral principles by 'practical wisdom and reason.'[95] Laws of various kinds stand differently in relation to an absolute standard. Some laws are merely enacted, others are well-enacted in the sense of being the best laws for those to whom they apply; others again are good from the point of view of anyone anywhere.[96] Positive law is only necessary at all because men are imperfect beings. It is because they are subject to caprice and impulse that they need externally imposed rules and sanctions. But moral goodness—the internally imposed and rational goodness of the *phronimos*—stands above positive law. It is, indeed, that which positive laws ought to express. If a man 'utterly superior in goodness' were to appear, no positive law need or could bind him:

> Such a man would be as it were a god among men ... There is no law that can govern such exceptional men, for they are a law in their own right.[97]

It has often been suggested that Aristotle may here be speaking with Alexander the Great in mind. This may be so; but one suspects also that he is remembering Plato's comment in the *Laws*: that if a perfect and incorruptible ruler were to be found, no writ could run against him because

> no law or command is superior to knowledge itself. It is therefore not right for reason to be subordinate to or bound by anything else. If it is really to answer to its name and be free in its very self, it must be master of all things.[98]

Perhaps the readiest illustration of Aristotle's view of the ultimately non-conventional character of what is right is provided by his remarks about equity or arbitration (ἐπιείκεια: *epieikeia*): the kind of judgment that goes behind the letter of the law to its spirit or true meaning. For ordinary purposes, it is expedient that laws should be drafted widely, so that they can take account of as many cases as possible. But the price of this convenience is that the law does not always fit specific cases. No law takes account of extenuating circumstances; no law is of itself able to identify the cases to which it should not apply or in which it should not be enforced strictly; nor can the legislator make provision for every case, because he cannot foresee every contingency. Those who apply the law therefore need some way of adjusting or fine-tuning it. A law forbidding people to stick knives into other people, taken literally, makes the practice of surgery unlawful. It is plain that this is not what the legislator intended; but by reason of what is it plain? If a man strikes another while wearing a ring, is this an assault with a weapon? Clearly not. Such a one

> is guilty of a criminal act according to the written words of the law; but he is innocent really, and it is equity that declares him to be so.[99]

In such cases, equity is necessary 'to fill a gap left in the law itself.'[100] Equity is not simply another kind of positive law, nor even a form of legal justice. As Aristotle says,

> That which is equitable is just, and better than one kind of justice [i.e. than legal justice, insofar as legal justice has failed to meet the case], though not better than absolute justice...The nature of the equitable is to correct the law wherever the law is deficient by reason of its generality.[101]

This is an idea that we shall encounter again in Chapter 4, when we come to look at Roman law. Equity is an unchanging standard of reasonableness or humanity or fairness lying behind positive law and enabling it to be interpreted according to what is naturally just.

Aristotle's view of the fundamentally natural character of justice is best summed up in his own words from the *Rhetoric*. However much legal variation there may be as between time and place, he says,

> there really exists...a natural form of the just and unjust that is common to all men, even where there is no community or agreement to bind them together. It is this form that Antigone evidently has in mind in Sophocles's play, when she says that it was a just act to bury her brother Polynices in spite of Creon's decree forbidding it. Just, she means, in the sense of naturally just.[102]

Beneath all our legal arrangements lie ethical necessities that do not change or vary, and that no one can repeal.

Four Standard Criticisms

Like Plato, Aristotle has been much reproached for certain aspects of his political and social thought. Four criticisms in particular are levelled at him. First, like Plato, though in different ways, he is elitist. Despite the importance that he attaches to political participation as a means of realising the potential of human nature, his notion of citizenship is a highly restricted one. Citizenship requires leisure for the thought and discussion by which prudent counsel is produced. But the business of earning one's living and providing the *polis* with essential goods and services is time-consuming. Farmers, manual workers and those who engage in commerce are therefore excluded from citizenship. So are μέτοικοι (*metoikoi*), resident aliens, because they have no stake in the community. So are slaves, for the reason that we shall mention in a moment. The good *polis*, as Aristotle sees it, is one that makes possible a life of humane, deliberate, rational conduct for as many as possible of the free, prosperous, adult, native-born males who dwell in it, but not for everyone. The leisured, cultivated life of the citizen is pleasant, but it is purchased by the efforts of great numbers of farmers, slaves, artisans and foreign immigrants, all of whom are excluded from its benefits.[103] If *eudaimonia* is bound up with citizenship, large numbers of those who live within the territorial boundaries of the *polis* will not be able to enjoy it.

Second—and it is this for which he has been most frequently censured—Aristotle believes that some human beings are naturally slaves. This belief is related to the emphasis that he places upon the use of reason in achieving the end proper to man. There are some people, he says, whom nature has fitted physically for heavy toil, but in whom the capacity for reason is not present, except, perhaps, to the extent that they are able to perceive themselves as belonging to a master. Such individuals are not capable of functioning as autonomous moral agents. They cannot deliberate; they cannot aspire to a fully human life. They are, Aristotle says (though he offers nothing that we might recognise as evidence) like living implements. Their *telos*, like that of any implement, is to serve the end of their master, and they are not capable of achieving any end independent of his.[104]

Third, Aristotle holds that women, though not devoid of reason, have it in a less developed form than men do and are therefore naturally subject to the rule of men. 'The male is by nature more capable of leadership than the female, unless he is constituted in some way contrary to nature.'[105] Women are able to do things like manage a household under the supervision of the male head of the household, but the faculty of independent judgment and deliberation is not present in them. They too are excluded from citizenship and consigned to a subordinate and silent rôle. It follows that the parents of female children should bring them up to be good and dutiful wives.[106]

Fourth, Aristotle is what would now be called racist. Greeks are best. Northern Europeans have much spirit but they lack intelligence and skill. They are ἀπολίτευτα (*apoliteuta*): unpolitical, uncivilised, and incorrigibly so. They are incapable of the relationships of mutuality and moral improvement that the *polis* makes possible for the cultivated Greek. They are not able either to organise themselves or rule anyone else. Asiatics, on the other hand, have intelligence and skill but no spirit, which is why they can only be ruled and enslaved. Only Greeks, who live between these two groups—this is as it were a geographical version of the doctrine of the mean—have the right combination of intelligence and spirit, and only they are capable of maintaining a political community of free men. United politically, the Greeks would be able to rule the world.[107] Aristotle's belief that some people are genetically superior to others also influences his view of marriage. He believes, as Plato does, that sexual unions should be regulated by the State in such a way as to make sure that the children produced have the best possible characteristics.[108]

What are we to make of these apparent blots on Aristotle's copybook? First, what we said in the case of Plato applies equally to Aristotle. It is pointless to read back into a political theorist of the fourth century BCE the likes and dislikes of subsequent ages. Aristotle, as much as anyone else, has the prejudices and beliefs of his time. As much as anyone else does, he tries, no doubt without conscious humbug, to find arguments to support them. These are biographical and historical facts and, as such, are not deplorable. Second, it should be pointed out that the relationships that Aristotle conceives as subsisting between master and slave and man and woman are not abusive; nor is the relationship of master to slave wholly exploitative. The slave has no purposes of his own, but he derives benefit from his master, at least if his master is the kind of man that Aristotle thinks a citizen should be; the woman derives benefit from her relationship with her husband. These relationships are beneficial precisely because natural. It is good for both women and slaves to be subject to the government of their natural superiors: the slave to a natural master, the woman to the 'constitutional' government[109] of an equal, but one more apt at leading and deliberating than she. It would be harmful to them if they were ruled in any other way, or if they were left to their own devices.[110] Whether or not anybody in fact has a 'natural superior' is not really the point here.

In sum, Aristotle, like Plato, offers a highly moral account of political association: an account that may largely be regarded as a constructive and self-conscious attempt to improve on that of his teacher. Human groupings do not cease to be natural and spontaneous when they pass beyond the biological nexus of the family or household. All co-operative human groupings are natural; but the city-State, the *polis*, is the highest of such groupings. It is identified as such not merely because it furnishes an organisational basis for the division of labour and the exchange of goods and services, but because it provides for the whole range of our needs, material, educational, social and moral. The *polis* is the milieu within which rational beings can achieve the kind of life, the *eudaimon* life, which it is appropriate for rational beings to lead. The good of the State cannot be considered other than in relation to the good of the individuals in it, even if many of those individuals are not admitted to the full status of citizenship.

Aristotle as a Natural Law Theorist

What general conclusions can be inferred from Aristotle's political theory that enable us to locate him within the history of the natural law tradition? As we did in the case of Plato, it will be convenient to deal with this question by listing a number of interrelated points.

(a) For Aristotle, the existence of morality does not depend upon enactment or will. Good laws can reinforce it in us and create the conditions under which it can flourish; but law does not create it, nor could legislation or agreement abolish it. On the contrary: law derives its rationale precisely from this morality, as expressed most obviously in principles of equity or fairness. Aristotle's moral and political philosophy is subject to what we should regard as major limitations: a presumption of Greek superiority and an account of citizenship that restricts the capacity for moral activity to adult, free, native-born males of independent means. But these qualifications are not structurally essential to his argument. If we disregard them as extraneous prejudices, we are left with a substantial residue. There is an ethical end, *eudaimonia*, which is the point or meaning of life not in Athens or Crete or Sparta, but of human life as such. It is the end that human beings have as humans rather than as citizens of a particular State. It is prescribed by the inherent rationality of those whose end it is. In its everyday and most attainable sense, *eudaimonia* is realisable through moral choice and action. We accomplish it by following a standard, the mean, which is intuitive. The need to develop our capacity to act according to the mean determines the kind of socialisation most appropriate to us. *Eudaimonia* is a natural good, and the purpose of political life is to make its achievement possible.

(b) Like Plato, Aristotle regards political existence not as conventional, but as a natural and self-sufficient form of association through which the requirements, both material and moral, of citizens are met. The well-constituted *polis* is a work of art inasmuch as its creation and maintenance require the application of ingenuity; but such ingenuity itself derives its rationale from

Aristotle: The Ethical Necessity of Politics

needs that are intrinsic to mankind.

(c) For Aristotle, as for Plato, the anthropological assumptions of the radical Sophists are false. Men are not rampant individualists dominated to the exclusion of virtually all else by their own wants and drives. 'Man is by nature a political animal.' He is an instinctive co-operator able, under the right conditions, to work with others to secure a shared happiness. The task of political science is therefore to identify what the right conditions are and to bring them into being in a stable, enduring, self-sustaining community.

(d) The *polis* exists, or ought to exist, to secure the good of the whole citizen body rather than the interests of a ruler or a dominant group. Again, this principle owes everything to nature and nothing to convention. All citizens—granted that Aristotle's idea of citizenship is a narrow one—are united by their common identity as rational creatures. This common identity amounts to a moral equality. All are entitled to the moral and material benefits that the *polis* can provide. Aristotle is much more tolerant of political diversity than Plato is. He recognises that there can be many different constitutional forms and that no one of them has an absolute claim to moral excellence. But at the highest level of generality it is not true that 'Whatever seems right and praiseworthy to a particular city *is* right and praiseworthy to it, for as long as it holds it to be so.' The common good is a critical standard against which the adequacy of any existing constitution can be measured.

(e) Aristotle gives a far broader and more flexible account than Plato does of the prescriptive rôle of reason in ethics and politics. Aristotle's recognition of the character of instrumental as distinct from philosophical reasoning—his awareness of the difference between theory and practice—is vital in this regard. To his mind, all citizens, not just those who have survived a gruelling course of specialist education, are capable of cultivating the intellectual virtue of *phronesis* through which effective practical judgments can be made and their true nature as rational beings realised.

In classical antiquity as we have considered it, we discover two clear and competing conceptions of politics and of the relation between politics and morality. It is usual to characterise these conceptions in terms of the ideas of *physis* and *nomos*, nature and convention. The Sophists, on the side of *nomos*, inaugurate a moral relativism that Plato and Aristotle find unacceptable. The 'radical' Sophists insist that all kinds of political order apart from the rule of the tyrant are artificial. Natural justice is the glorious freedom of the *Übermensch*. Legal justice is an expedient devised by the weak to restrain the strong, or used by the strong to milk the weak, or brought about by the agreement of those who, unable to dominate others, wish to protect themselves from the will to power assumed to be characteristic of humanity at large. This is the picture that Plato gives of the radical Sophist view of politics. He regards their uncompromising realism as stemming from the moral scepticism of their more moderate elders. It arises from the conviction that there are no absolute or universal principles of morality. Plato and Aristotle, on the side of *physis*, develop an account of the *polis* as a natural community whose meaning and function cannot be considered apart from the happiness or wellbeing of those whose community it is. Plato's purpose in the *Republic* is to repudiate ethical relativism and political amoralism by offering a version of politics that is universal and philosophical in that it appeals not to myth or custom or tradition, but to rational and systematic argument about the purposes of human existence and the nature of morality. But Plato compromises his political theory by presenting it in terms of an ideal city which, as he readily admits, is probably unrealisable, and by relying so heavily on an account of the nature, power and rôle of esoteric knowledge which, in the final analysis, is credible only to the believer. We have suggested that, as a means of answering Sophist scepticism, Plato's method is understandable but misconceived. By comparison, Aristotle's enterprise is to develop an account of political association as natural and ethically necessary but to ground that account squarely in the 'real' world of the Greek *polis* and its possible constitutional forms. He locates the bases of morality not in a transcendent 'other' world, but in the world that ordinary people know. In doing so, he abandons much of what is questionable, unreal and far-fetched in Plato, in favour of his own empirical, practicable and moderate analyses and recommendations; although, undeniably, he sacrifices a great deal of Plato's imaginative and aesthetic breadth of vision.

Chapter 4

Stoicism: Equality, Cosmopolitanism and the Law of Right Reason

BETWEEN THEM, Plato and Aristotle furnish what historians of political thought have come to regard as 'the' classical doctrine of the State: of the *polis* as a community ordered to a common and rational good. They seek order and stability above all. They seek them, however, not as instrumentalities, but as the preconditions of human self-realisation. In doing so, they give an account of politics as an activity founded upon something more than agreement, might or the art of persuasion. The principles according to which civic life ought to be conducted are natural in the sense of universal and accessible to reason: even if only, in Plato's case, to highly-trained and sophisticated reason or, in Aristotle's, to reason as practised by the leisured incumbents of a status from which most of the city's occupants are excluded. Yet despite their commitment to moral standards supposed to be universal, the political thought of Plato and Aristotle is fundamentally parochial in character. It deals almost exclusively with the small, self-contained political community and its domestic peace.

Given the background of change and strife against which they worked, this can only strike one as remarkable.[1] Plato grew up during the Peloponnesian War, but he takes little interest in questions of war and peace between States. Where he is interested (as at *Republic* 422A–423A and 470A–471C), what he says is, on the face of it, hardly consistent with his belief in eternal principles of justice. His major preoccupation is with internal conflict and its remedy. Aristotle's career as a philosopher coincided exactly with the transformation of the Greek world into the Macedonian Empire. Athens herself became part of that empire after the battle of Chaeronea in 336 BCE. Aristotle was connected by family and professional ties with the Macedonian royal household, and he outlived Alexander the Great by a year. His remark at *Politics* 1327ᵇ30 that, united under a single regime, the Greeks could rule the world, is possibly a nod in the direction of Macedon; yet he, like Plato, is largely unconcerned with matters of 'international' politics. Again, his interest is in internal politics and the associated questions of *stasis*, stability and change.² One is left with the impression that, for all their intellectual vigour, the Academy and the Lyceum must on the whole have been extraordinarily inward-looking with respect to the affairs of the wider world. But we turn now to new and broader currents of philosophy associated with developments in that world during and after Aristotle's lifetime.

Philosophies of Distress

The career of Alexander the Great began in 336 BCE with the assassination of Philip of Macedon.³ Though only twenty at the time, Alexander was already a soldier of experience and distinction; he had held his first military command at the age of sixteen. There is some suspicion that, impatient for supremacy, he had a hand in his father's death. By the time he himself died, in June 323 BCE, he had by strategic and administrative genius created an empire extending throughout Asia Minor, Syria, Egypt, Babylonia, Persia, Samarcand and into India. The great Persian Empire, so long a threat to Greece, was destroyed in three battles: at the Granicus River in 334 BCE, at Issus in 333 BCE and at Gaugamela in 331 BCE. The achievement of Alexander was short-lived. His empire was too large and heterogeneous to survive without a presiding genius of extraordinary capacity. No sooner was Alexander dead than his former generals embarked on prolonged dynastic squabbles over its division. By 281 BCE, the empire was divided into three large territorial States, and in the second century BCE fell into subjugation to Rome. But the creation of the Hellenistic Empire exposed 'classical' Greece to a flood of new experiences. Alexander was an enthusiastic apostle of Hellenism. Under his auspices, the Greek language and Greek ideas and institutions spread throughout the known world. But the influences associated with his conquests did not run all in one direction. Alexander pursued a policy of friendship and assimilation with the peoples whom he conquered. It would have been impossible to maintain, even for a short time, an empire of some 22 million square miles without their co-operation. Near Eastern families sent their children to Athens to be educated. Soldiers of all races mingled in his armies. He managed to reconcile alien religions with the traditional belief-systems of Greece, inventing what was effectively a new religion with himself as god-king at the head of its pantheon. Greek culture, one might say, became increasingly 'barbarian' as 'barbarian' culture became increasingly Hellenised. Commerce, facilitated by a common currency, was the vehicle of new ideas: much more so than during the period that we considered in Chapter 1. Colonisation and intermarriage wore down traditional Greek prejudices about barbarians and their inferiority. These reciprocities made it both possible and necessary for the Greeks to look beyond the relatively narrow loyalties of the *polis* and to think for the first time about mankind as a whole. At the same time, the empire's large, complex and centralised systems of administration began to erode the autonomy of the *polis*. Conditions in the new world of Alexander tended to undermine both the city-State's traditional values of independence and self-sufficiency, and its vices of narrow patriotism, cultural insularity and xenophobia. Those who thought about such things at all were now required to think anew about the meaning and limits of citizenship and its duties.

This is, of course, a sketch. It would be a mistake to exaggerate the rapidity with which the *polis* declined. It would certainly be wrong to suppose that Alexander 'destroyed the *polis*' or that the Hellenistic Empire occasioned its 'demise.'[4] Alexander founded many new cities (seventy of them called Alexandria). After the dismemberment of the empire by the διάδοχοι (*diadochoi*)—the generals who succeeded Alexander—the city-State remained the primary form of social organisation. Athens continued to be the centre of intellectual life for many years, only gradually being overtaken by Alexandria in Egypt. It would be an error also to make too much of the immediate effects of Hellenisation on the lives of ordinary people. Even in the new empire, communication was relatively slow and difficult, and habituated ways of life were hardly to be swept away overnight. But in the moral schools that emerged roughly contemporaneously with Aristotle's lifetime we observe certain definite alterations in the terms of reference of moral and political discussion. In their main features, these alterations have always been understood as the response of intellectuals to the contemporary transformation of social and political experience, and there is no reason to dispute this understanding. The teachings of these schools, like those of the Sophists, suggest a sense of rapid change and the passing of traditional orthodoxies. On the whole, they are to be read as philosophies of distress: philosophies intended to afford a refuge to their adherents from the disintegration of familiar certainties. This may not be the whole story, but undoubtedly it is an important part of it.[5]

These moral schools—so called because their tendency is to subordinate all other branches of philosophy to ethics—are Cynicism, Epicureanism, Scepticism and Stoicism.[6] Their literary remains are, again, scanty. As in the case of presocratic philosophy, it is necessary to retrieve as much of their teaching as we can from sources that are often problematical. Of some individuals, well respected in their day, we have only second-hand or even third-hand knowledge. Stoicism is by far the best documented of the post-Aristotelian moral schools, and it is with Stoicism and its influence that we are concerned in this chapter. Before we come to the Stoics, however, we shall by way of contrast and comparison look briefly at Cynicism, Epicureanism and Scepticism. On the one hand, these schools represent something of a dead end from our point of view. They articulate an anti-politics characteristic of much Hellenistic philosophy, though the fact that they do so is, of course, itself significant as a feature of the history of political thought. They give an account of human nature and its relation to the world, but that account is mostly one from which the political dimensions of experience are excluded. On the other hand, a glance at them is necessary to give a properly rounded picture of the philosophical environment from within which the ethical and political doctrines of Stoicism took their departure.

Cynicism is the oldest of the four schools.[7] It was founded in Athens by Antisthenes (ca 445–360 BCE), one of the followers of Socrates. In origin, it predates the Macedonian empire, but it survived well into the second century CE. The ethical doctrines of Cynicism were at an early stage appropriated by the Stoics and elaborated by them into a separate system, and it is as a parent of Stoicism that Cynicism is chiefly interesting.[8] The ethical end to which the Cynic aspires is individual αὐτάρκεια (*autarkeia*), self-sufficiency or self-containment. Aristotle had used the same term in relation to the self-sufficiency of the *polis*; but to the Cynics it means something different. The wise man as defined by the Cynics will dissociate himself from all externals. He will consciously relinquish everything capable of being lost, thereby escaping the pain of loss. He will train himself to desire no more than the minimum necessary to sustain existence; he will cultivate indifference to misfortune; he will renounce everything that is conventional, and take no part in public life. He will, indeed, hold politics in contempt. The only law to which he is subject is his own virtue—*areté* again: a virtue worth more than all the wealth of men.[9] Here we find yet another meaning of *areté*. 'Virtue' is now conceived not as a practical accomplishment or a repertoire of personal excellences, but as detachment from unnecessary desire. The goal of life, the *telos* or meaning of human existence, is the attainment of a tranquil state of mind: a condition of being from which dependence upon anything artificial and transient is abolished. To be free from desire is to be free from fear. Antisthenes and his immediate followers affected a simplicity and lack of social polish about which Aristotle is rather superior.[10] The Cynic Crates (ca 365–285 BCE) gave away a large fortune and, accompanied by his wife, embarked on a life of poverty as a wandering philosopher. The famous Diogenes of Sinope (ca 400–325 BCE), regarded by some as the real founder of Cynicism, made a point of outrageous behaviour in defiance of convention.[11] The Cynic, it was said, chooses to live like a dog (κύων: *cyon*); though one suspects that this is a pun,[12] in the way that the Dominicans (*Dominicanes*) of the Spanish Inquisition were called 'dogs of the Lord' (*Domini canes*). The name of the school is more likely to come from the gymnasium outside Athens called Cynosarges, where Antisthenes taught.[13]

Epicureanism represents a somewhat different stream of Hellenistic ethics, but still an anti-political one.[14] It is a philosophy of psychological and ethical hedonism. Human beings both do and should seek pleasure as the only good and avoid pain as the only evil, pleasure and pain being synonymous with satisfied and unsatisfied desire. The school's founder, Epicurus (341–270 BCE), was a native of Samos who settled in Athens in about 306 BCE. Unlike the radical Sophists, he does not extrapolate any kind of *Realpolitik* from his hedonism. On the contrary: like the Cynics, Epicurus and his disciples advocated withdrawal from the world, though they eschewed the ostentatious asceticism favoured by Crates and Diogenes. Epicurus is a materialist. His physics resembles, and may or may not be related to, the earlier attempt by Democritus of Abdera (460–371 BCE) to account for the universe in atomistic terms. The world consists of minute particles or atoms of matter in motion.[15] There are two kinds of pleasure: 'kinetic' pleasures, or pleasures of motion, and 'katastematic' pleasures: static pleasures or pleasures of rest. The former are associated with stimuli that excite the atoms of which we are composed; the latter with those that have the reverse effect. The pleasure of eating, for instance, is a kinetic pleasure; the feeling of just having eaten neither too much nor too little is a pleasure of rest. Kinetic pleasures are never entirely free from pain: for as long as we are eating, some part of the desire to eat is still with us. Static pleasures are pleasures from which all desire, and therefore all pain, is absent. These are the pleasures that we ought to cultivate in order to secure the greatest amount of happiness. The most eligible pleasures are pleasures of the mind: the conversation of like-minded companions, a justified sense of our own moral excellence, the enjoyment of beautiful things. Pleasures of the mind are higher than bodily pleasures (though this is a curious distinction for a materialist to make) because they lie more within our control. For Epicurus (contrary to the supposition that has attached such an unfavourable connotation to his name), the best life is one not of bodily indulgence, but of imperturbable *autarkeia* from which the pain of desire is as far as possible absent. Strolling in a garden with friends and a diet of bread and water with some cheese as an occasional treat: these things sum up the Epicurean ethical ideal. Political arrangements are conventional. They are the devices by which individuals secure themselves against the interference of others, and they arise, much as they had for Callicles and Glaucon, not by nature but from agreement. The cares of public life will, however, inevitably detract from one's pleasure, and the wise man will abstain from politics, as he will from children and family life. Epicureanism is hostile to common superstitions and beliefs, which produce much mischief. People worry that life will be disrupted by the intervention of the gods; but this fear is groundless. The gods exist, but they are perfect. Because they are perfect, they have no unfulfilled desires, and because they have no unfulfilled desires they have no reason to interfere in the world of men. Nor is there any need to fear the pains of the afterlife, because there is no afterlife. When we die, our atoms disperse, and we are extinguished quite. The observation that, if pleasure is the good and death the end, death is to be dreaded because it means the end of all pleasure, does not occur to Epicurus. It does not occur to him because what he values is not really pleasure, but the absence of desire.

Pyrrho of Elis (ca 360–272 BCE), the founder of Scepticism, was a soldier in Alexander's army who retired to a life of teaching and contemplation. If he produced anything in writing, nothing of it survives. What we know of him we know only through Sextus Empiricus, and Sextus Empiricus relies on the possibly faulty account of a philosopher called Anesidemus, whose own writings are not extant either.[16] The Greek verb σκέπτομαι (*skeptomai*) means 'to speculate' or 'to consider' rather than 'to doubt,' but Scepticism was from the first a sceptical philosophy in the familiar sense. Pyrrho seems to have held views resembling, and not representing much of an advance on, those of the Sophists. Nothing can be known with certainty; every argument has two sides, and the wise man will suspend judgment on all questions. Since there can be no rational ground for preferring one course of action to another, one must simply conform to the customs of wherever one happens to live. Wisdom lies in the achievement of ἀταραξια (*ataraxia*), peace of mind, by freeing oneself from all passion and choice. Since all things are equally true, or equally false, passion and choice are delusions. The starting-point of Scepticism, Sextus Empiricus tells us, is 'the hope of achieving freedom from disturbance.'[17] Scepticism existed in a number of forms during its history. It became as it were the official philosophy of the Platonic Academy when Arcesilaus of Pitane (315–240 BCE) became its head. Arcesilaus is an exponent of probabilism: since nothing is certain, probability is our only guide to action. His successor Carneades (214–129 BCE) caused something of a stir in Rome in 154 BCE by giving two public lectures on justice on successive days, in the second of which he contradicted everything that he had said in the first: this by way of demonstrating that there are no immutable moral principles. Evidently the feat was similar to the kind of exercise practised by Protagoras (see p. 18). Carneades apparently believed that men are motivated only by prudence and self-interest. Legal justice is for him the same kind of fiction or rationalisation as it was for Callicles and Thrasymachus.[18]

One is inclined to think it likely to the point of probability that the beliefs of the Cynics and Epicureans reflect an acquaintance, however imperfect, with the teaching of the Buddha. A similar remark applies to the most characteristic ethical doctrines of Stoicism. What makes us miserable is desire; the antidote to all pain is the extinction of desire.[19] If a Buddhist influence is present here—and it is not, as far as one can tell, possible to document this supposition—it is a remarkable instance of the cross-fertilisations effected by Alexander's conquests. Cynicism, Epicureanism and Scepticism are, however, of interest to us mainly for the purposes of context and contrast. They illustrate a good deal of the intellectual climate associated with the rise of the Hellenistic empire; it is reasonable to suppose that their exponents are responding to the anxieties and complexities of modern life. But the Cynics and Epicureans do so by the simple expedient of withdrawing from them altogether and seeking in philosophy a purely private consolation. Their account of morality has almost nothing to do with politics. Philosophy as they practise it involves a conscious repudiation of the civic values that had been so important to Plato and Aristotle. Individuals are responsible for their own salvation, and the equation of self-realisation with membership of a community seems to have vanished. Beyond stressing its undesirability from the point of view of anyone who wishes to escape care, the Cynics and Epicureans have little or nothing to say about public life. Scepticism only reasserts the epistemological doubts of the Sophists, combined, at least in the case of Carneades, with the realism of Callicles and Thrasymachus. Wisdom, it seems, is self interest. If your ship founders and you find someone floating on a plank, you are a fool if you do not grab the plank for yourself and let him drown.[20]

But the types of Hellenistic philosophy that we have so far outlined throw into relief the essential features of the fourth of the post-Aristotelian moral schools, Stoicism. The social circumstances in which Stoicism originated are the same, as is its primary desire to avoid suffering through *autarkeia* or self-mastery; but the view taken by its exponents of the relation between philosophy and practical life is very different from those of the Cynics, Epicureans and Sceptics. It is in respect of this difference that the Stoics are important to us. Historians of political thought have always assigned a special significance to Stoicism in terms of its place in the history of the natural law tradition, though the nature of its influence is often misinterpreted. We therefore need to analyse it as fully as we can. In particular, we must attend to four interrelated themes: 'life according to nature,' natural equality, the law of nature, and cosmopolitanism. We shall deal also to some extent with the influence of Stoicism on the development of Roman law.

Stoicism: 'Life According to Nature'

The history of Stoicism is most conveniently treated as having three phases.[21] In about 300 BCE, Zeno of Citium (332–265 BCE) began to teach in the Στοὰ Ποικίλη (*Stoa Poikile*), the 'Decorated Porch' in the centre of Athens. This is the 'Stoa' from which the school takes its name. Zeno was a pupil of the Cynic Crates, and his philosophy, as far as we have knowledge of it, was mostly a systematised version of Cynicism. His immediate successor was Cleanthes of Assos (331-232 BCE), whose interests lay mainly in physics and theology. In about 230 BCE, the teachings of Zeno and Cleanthes were revised and clarified by Chrysippus of Soli (280–208 BCE), to such effect that Chrysippus was from early times regarded as the founder of Stoicism as a school independent of Cynicism. Diogenes Laertius reports the saying that, without Chrysippus, there would have been no Stoicism, though Chrysippus himself made no such claim.[22] Zeno, Cleanthes and Chrysippus are the most prominent figures of the 'Old Stoa.' A second phase, usually called the 'Middle Stoa' and distinguished by the introduction of Platonic and Aristotelian doctrines, emerged during the second and first centuries BCE, under the tutelage of Panaetius of Rhodes (185–110 BCE) and Posidonius of Apamaea (135–50 BCE).[23] In about 140 BCE, Panaetius struck up a friendship with the distinguished Roman Scipio Africanus Minor; and it was chiefly due to Panaetius's contact with Scipio's cultivated circle of acquaintance in Rome that Roman intellectual society was introduced to Stoicism. As we shall see, the influence of Stoicism on Roman thought was considerable, despite the pronounced hostility of some conservative figures in Rome to philosophy.[24] The 'Late' or 'Roman' Stoa created through the influence of Panaetius and Posidonius developed the practical side of Stoic ethics especially, and placed particular emphasis on statesmanship and law. Its luminaries include Lucius Annaeus Seneca (5 BCE–65 CE), the released but crippled slave Epictetus of Hierapolis (55–135 CE), and Marcus Aurelius Antoninus Pius, emperor of Rome from 161 to 180 CE.[25] Marcus Aurelius is the only individual in the west—with the possible exception of Lenin—to have conformed at all closely to Plato's specification that philosophers should rule; though his *Meditations* indicate that he found rulership a burden sometimes barely supportable.[26] In connection with the Roman Stoa, we mention also Marcus Tullius Cicero (106–43 BCE), the first two books of whose treatise *De officiis* are acknowledged by their author to have been inspired by Panaetius's work *On Duty*. The backhanded compliment of St Augustine, that Cicero was 'a distinguished man and by way of being a philosopher,'[27] is not unfair. Cicero is not an adherent of any one school of philosophy; his written works show an eclectic and not always profound acquaintance with Platonism, Epicureanism, Scepticism and Stoicism. But his strength lies in the art of paraphrase and synthesis. It is to him that we owe much of our knowledge of the version of Stoicism that commended itself to cultivated Romans at around the time of the birth of Christ.

This brief description is enough to show that the Stoics, considered generally, compose a very broad church. In view of this, it is probably better to describe Stoicism as a whole, as distinct from any of its particular manifestations, as a tendency of thought rather than as a school of philosophy. During a history spanning some five hundred years, Stoic conceptions inevitably underwent shifts of attitude and emphasis, many of which are far more complex than could be addressed in a single chapter. Mainly, however, these shifts occurred in relation to logic and physics. To this extent, we can disregard most of them. As with the other post-Aristotelian moral schools, Stoicism intentionally subordinated the other branches of philosophical enquiry to ethics; and, in its main features, the ethical thought of Stoicism is remarkably coherent throughout the period that we have outlined. There are some minor variations, but mostly they are of a kind that we need not consider.

To the Stoics, the only thing that has intrinsic value is *areté*; and *areté* is almost invariably defined by them as 'life according to nature.' This is an expression borrowed from the Cynics, especially as represented by Diogenes of Sinope, and it remained a central feature of Stoic ethics throughout its history. In its later evolutions, Stoicism, and especially Roman Stoicism, tended to be much less interested in physics than in the direction of practical life; but in the 'Old' Stoa, the idea of 'life according to nature' is related intimately to a cosmology reminiscent of those developed by the presocratic scientists. The particular influence of Heraclitus is clear; nor is it accidental: the earliest Stoics held Heraclitus in high esteem, and looked to him as a kind of intellectual father.[28] No doubt they had the advantage of a more complete knowledge of Heraclitus's philosophy than is available to us.

The world according to the Old Stoa is a vast integrated system of causes and effects.[29] It is permeated throughout by a rational principle, a *logos*. As to its *Urstoff*, it is composed of material fire that does not vary in quantity, and which is divided internally into an active and a passive part. The Stoics are materialists, but they are not atheists. The active part of fire is identified with God, who is Himself identified with the *logos*; and it is God who causes particular objects to come into being by acting creatively upon the passive part. The remark is attributed to Zeno by the Christian apologist Tertullian that God permeates the world in the way that honey flows through a honeycomb.[30] Fire as such is eternal and without form; but it is capable of being moulded like wax into innumerable individual forms, and it contains within itself the seeds—the λόγοι σπερματικοί: *logoi spermatikoi*—of everything that will come to be. This, incidentally, is an account of the relation between matter and form that was later to appeal to St Augustine.[31] The process of cosmic change is seen, in a manner long familiar to Greek science, as one of coming to be and passing away. The elements that emerge from the primal fire and become distinct both from it and from one another are separated by their relative densities. In the course of coming to be and passing away, part of the elemental fire becomes rarefied into air. The air in turn becomes water; part of the water becomes earth; and part of it becomes air again which, being once more rarefied into fire, returns to God whence it came. All things exist in a state of flux. Marcus Aurelius recalls one of the most familiar images of Heraclitus, comparing the sequence of phenomena to the flowing of a river.[32] Coherence and purpose in the creative activity of the universe is sustained by the presence within it of τόνος (*tonos*): tension. The word differs from Heraclitus's *eris*, strife, but the meaning seems the same.[33]

The Stoics are determinists. Everything in the universe happens according to necessary causes (we are reminded of Anaximander's reported comment (see p. 4) that 'the first origin of existing things is what existing things eventually fall back into "according to necessity'").³⁴ These causes are prescribed by the unchanging purposes of God's providence (πρόνοια: *pronoia*). Nothing, therefore, can be other than it is. The history of the world is the history of Divine providence working itself out infallibly. Divine providence does not, however, work itself out once only. The Old Stoics maintain that our present universe is only one of a succession of universes. It will eventually give place to another, which will in turn be succeeded by another, and so on, in an infinite series of cosmic cycles or περίοδοι (*periodoi*). Again, the idea possibly comes from Anaximander.³⁵ This process of succession is eternal. The series of cycles in which the universe is replicated has no beginning, and will have no end. At the end of each *periodos*, everything that has come into being collapses into the eternal fire in a universal world-conflagration. A new universe then arises from the dissolution of the old, and the process of coming-to-be and passing-away begins again. On the one hand, the periodic conflagration of the world is not a destructive or terminal event; it is an occasion of renewal. On the other, nothing that comes about is ever really new. The events that occur in each *periodos* have already occurred in each of its predecessors. The idea seems to be that, whereas the cycle of creation and destruction is eternal, the number of things that can happen in any one *periodos* is finite, and the end of a *periodos* comes when all the combinations of events that can occur in it have been exhausted. Therefore, everything that happens must happen over and over again, *ad infinitum*. The Stoic view of the world does not admit of progress or historical development in any final sense. What is happening now is only a reprise of what has happened on innumerable occasions before, and the same events will be repeated into the endless future. The whole process operates according to a vast and all-embracing causal nexus called Fate (Ειμαρμένη: *Heimarmene*), from which nothing that has occurred, is occurring or will occur is exempt:

> Fate is the chain of causality of existing things, or the *logos* according to which they are arranged.³⁶
>
> [Fate is] the power that moves matter, operating always in the same way and according to identical rules. It is one and the same with providence and nature.³⁷

We live, apparently, in a world that just is as it is, inevitably, unchangeably and eternally.[38]

Why did the earliest Stoics think as they did about the nature of the physical world? Why did they adopt the cosmology that they did rather than any other? All ancient cosmologies raise these questions, and it is impossible to answer them other than by surmise.[39] At all events, it is clear that they regard the meaning of life as being bound up not with the *polis* but with the world, the universe. This, for the reasons we have mentioned, is hardly surprising; but they show much more respect for the scientific endeavours of earlier generations than the Epicureans and Sceptics do, and a fuller understanding of them than the Cynics had. The Stoics are not mere imitators, as has sometimes been supposed; but they were content to construct a cosmology based for the most part on presocratic models, with special attention given to the Heraclitean *logos*. In doing so, they make explicit something that, in what we have of his writings, is only hinted at by Heraclitus: that the *logos* of the universe is in some sense a human *logos* too (see pp. 6–7). Man himself is a component of the material cosmos. 'Our own natures,' Chrysippus says, 'are part of the nature of the universe.'[40] Mankind is therefore subject to the same inexorable causal laws as everything else. There is, however, a crucial difference between man and the inanimate world. The difference, again, is the faculty of reason. Man contains within himself a spark, a fragment, of the Divine rationality or *logos* of the universe. The essential attribute of human nature is derived from the active principle of the universe and is an integral part of it. Man, alone of all created things, has self-consciousness and the capacity for rational activity. He is not an uncomprehending automaton in a causally determined universe. Inasmuch as rationality is a part of the human composition, some things are within our power, while others are not.[41] Broadly speaking, the things that lie within our power are three.

First, we are equipped to understand the nature of reality and our own condition as part of it. Again, Stoicism looks beyond the frontiers of the *polis* to the cosmos. We are able to grasp the fact that the cosmos is a system of necessary causes to which we ourselves are subject. All ethical reflection, Chrysippus suggests, must be based on an awareness that everything in the universe is perfectly appropriate.[42] Second, our understanding of the natural order and our place in it enables us to emancipate ourselves from the emotions that so often cause men to suffer. It equips us to accept that whatever happens to us happens because it must. So equipped, we can still only undergo what we would have had to undergo in any case; but we can undergo it willingly and with understanding. We cannot control our external circumstances, but we can control completely the state of mind in which we respond to them: we can live 'according to nature' rather than at odds with nature. Our situation, Zeno and Chrysippus remark, is like that of a dog tied to the back of a cart. When the cart moves, we have to move with it. Whether we move willingly or unwillingly is up to us.[43] It may be that my crops will flourish and the harvest be good; it may be that they will be destroyed by a storm and I shall be ruined. In either case, necessary causes are at work. The wise man will act on the principle that, since the world cannot be other than it is, it is pointless to allow oneself to experience either hope or fear in relation to the things that occur in it. By so acting, he will achieve what Zeno and Chrysippus call a 'smoothly-flowing life':[44] a state of spiritual peace or emotionlessness (ἀπάθεια: *apatheia*, or εὐθυμία: *euthymia*) as distinct from the usual human disposition of futile rebellion. This deliberate acceptance of necessity is what is meant by 'life according to nature.' As Diogenes Laertius reports, though with scant regard for chronology:

> Zeno was the first to define the end as 'life according to nature'...He was followed in this by Cleanthes in his work *On Pleasure*; by Posidonius, and by Hecato in his work *On Ends*. Chrysippus too, in the first book of his work *On Ends*, says that to live virtuously is to live in accordance with the actual course of nature...the end may therefore be defined as life...in accordance not only with our own human nature, but also with the nature of the universe itself.[45]

Perhaps the most aphoristic expression of the Stoic ideal of calm resignation is to be found in the following sayings of Seneca and Epictetus respectively:

> I do not obey God; rather, I agree with Him. I go with Him not because I must, but with my soul.[46]
>
> I have placed my impulses under obedience to God. If it is His will that I should catch a fever or that I should obtain something, then it is my will too. If He does not wish it, nor do I.[47]

The *locus classicus* of Stoic fortitude in the face of suffering is surely Tacitus's account of the death of Seneca at the order of the Emperor Nero in 65 CE. Calmly and without fear or anger, he bade farewell to his friends, comforted his wife, opened his veins, and died.[48]

The third thing that lies within our power as rational creatures is the capacity to make wise or informed choices. How can this be, if the universe is a system of necessary causes? The answer to this question is highly complex, and to compress it into a handful of sentences is to ignore a great deal of debate and ambiguity.[49] To put it rather simply, the Stoics are determinists, but they are for the most part compatibilists or 'soft' determinists. The universe is indeed a system of necessary causes, but this fact does not exclude the possibility of free choice. There is no effect that does not have a cause, but there is a distinction between 'basic' and 'proximate' causes; and proximate causes lie within the field of what is open to us. A drum will of necessity roll down a slope if there is a proximate cause: that is, if somebody pushes it; but it is not necessary that anybody will push it.[50] If I jump out of the window, I shall fall to the ground. The fall will happen as the effect of a necessary cause, but the jump will be a 'proximate' cause, and it is up to me whether to jump or not. I shall of necessity die; but I can choose whether or not to kill myself: and so on. Nor is the fact that there are proximate causes at odds with the premiss that everything happens of necessity. If I choose not to jump, I will of necessity not fall; if I choose not to roll the drum, it will of necessity not move. This is a simplification of a difficult topic; but these illustrations, unexamined as they are, are enough for our purposes.

Given that choice is possible, then, what will guide the choices of the wise? First and foremost, the wise individual will realise that such choices as are open to him are not, properly speaking, choices as between good and evil. Since the universe is absolutely necessitated—since everything in it is regulated according to Divine providence—nothing is good or evil *sub specie aeternitatis*. More strictly, since Divine providence is assumed to be beneficent, nothing is of itself evil. As Chrysippus says:

> Even the evil that occurs in terrible disasters has a *logos* of its own; for it too occurs in a manner consistent with universal reason, and so has a kind of usefulness in relation to the whole.[51]

For the Stoics, as for the Sophists, 'good' and 'evil' as we commonly use the terms are names. They have meaning only from the restricted standpoint of whoever employs them. To a certain degree, the Stoics are emotivists in ethics: 'good' and 'evil' are the labels that ordinary, unenlightened individuals attach to the objects of their approval and disapproval. By contrast, the wise man knows that nothing is good or evil, or at any rate that nothing is evil, absolutely. In any set of circumstances, however, certain things will be more expedient than others. They will be not goods, but advantages: προηγμένα (*proegmena*), or, in the Latin literature, variously *producta, promota, praecipua, praelata, praeposita* and *commoda*. Such things will be, not better, but more suitable than others to the circumstances in question. By the same token, certain things will be inexpedient or disadvantageous: ἀποπροηγμένα (*apoproegmena*), or *remota, reiecta* and *incommoda*. When Cicero reports this distinction as made by Zeno and Posidonius, he does so in terms of advantageous things being *secundum naturam* and disadvantageous things being *contra naturam*.[52] Strictly speaking, this is a false distinction. In a necessitated world, nothing is *contra naturam* of itself. Only the attitude of mind that we bring to the world can be *contra naturam*.

The distinction between *proegmena* and *apoproegmena* reminds us of the view of the Sophists that, though no choice can be based on truth, some choices are better than others for practical purposes and should be promoted. The Stoic sage acts appropriately or 'according to duty' (καθήκον: *kathekon*) when he correctly recognises the distinction between *proegmena* and *apoproegmena* and, having identified the course most advantageous to the situation in which he happens to be, follows it. This is what it is to employ right reason: 'to act rationally in the choice of natural advantages.'[53] The correct attitude to things advantageous is to accept them as such, and to act in ways that may be expected to bring them about. Similarly, the wise man will as far as possible act so as to avoid those things that are disadvantageous in the circumstances. The wise man is one who has entirely conquered irrational passion and cultivated a sublime detachment from the hopes and fears that ordinarily trouble mankind. This is 'life according to nature.' His choices between advantageous and disadvantageous things will be completely rational ones, serene and unswayed by personal or emotional considerations. Nor will he experience distress if he fails to achieve what is advantageous, for he will understand that his failure was due to causes beyond his control. If he has to accept things that are disadvantageous, he will do so in a spirit of calmness and self-possession. As Seneca puts it:

> It is not within the power of anyone to have whatever he wants; but it is within his power not to want what he does not have, and to make use positively of whatever comes his way.[54]

Obvious examples of things that might be *proegmena* are life, health and wealth; equally obvious examples of things that might be the reverse are illness, death and poverty. When we come to less straightforward distinctions, there is, as one might expect, little unanimity among the Stoics; nor is there much agreement over exactly how much in the way of advantages a virtuous man needs. In broad terms, however, the point is clear enough.

As we have so far considered it, Stoic philosophy appears to have not much to say about politics or public activity. There seems little to distinguish it from the other post-Aristotelian moral schools. Beneath their elaborate cosmology, the Stoics subscribe to the same minimal axiology as the Cynics do. Nothing has intrinsic value apart from the virtue of the wise man, and the virtue of the wise man consists in *apatheia*: not 'apathy' in the familiar sense of depression and unmotivatedness, but an imperturbable acceptance of necessity. The purpose or 'end' of life is not happiness achieved through participation in the life of a community. It is escape from suffering, and the way to escape from suffering is to understand the nature of the world and extinguish the pointless desire for things to be different from what they must be. All choices are choices not between good and evil, but only between the expedient and the inexpedient. Ultimately, we cannot control our fate.

Human Equality, Right Reason and Cosmopolitanism

On the face of it, all this seems to add up to a seriously restricted theory of action. We come now, however, to the implications that the Stoics understood their philosophy as having for social and political experience. The main bridge connecting Stoicism as an individual *ars vitae* to Stoicism as a social and political theory is the concept of human equality. All men are equal by nature. Sometimes what is meant is that all *persons* are equal by nature, though one cannot attribute gender-neutrality to the Stoics as a consistent principle. The natural equality of mankind is a theme present at all stages of the history of Stoicism, elaborated by successive thinkers into a philosophical account of human relationships and their governing principles. It is related, in ways that we shall try to make clear, to the doctrines of determinism and 'life according to nature.' Like those doctrines, its origin is no doubt to be understood in relation to the dissolution of established social and cultural differences at the time of Alexander. In Stoic writing considered generally, the doctrine of equality has four distinct but related aspects that we shall consider in turn.

First, a new and formidable departure is the Stoic conviction that an individual's material circumstances are irrelevant to his moral status. Members of the human race differ with respect to their external condition. Some are Greeks, some are barbarians, some are slaves, some are free. But the significance traditionally attached to these differences, insofar as it excludes some members of the human race from consideration, is mistaken. That it is mistaken is clear in the light of two characteristics common to all men. These characteristics are sufficient to identify a common human essence lying behind outward disparities. All men, regardless of their immediate origin and dwelling-place, live in the same necessitated universe. All are subject to the same causal laws: the human predicament is the same for all. In addition, all men are rational; all contain part of the Divine *logos* of the universe. All are therefore capable of understanding their predicament and of acting in ways suitable to it; all, at least potentially, have the capacity to live 'according to nature.'[55] *Pace* Aristotle, therefore, all men are the same in morally relevant respects, regardless of conventional inequalities or accidents of birth and location: 'all men are brothers and kinsmen by nature, since all are sons of God.'[56] Cicero expresses this idea succinctly in his dialogue *De legibus*:

> No single thing so exactly resembles anything else as we ourselves resemble each other. Indeed, if bad habits and false beliefs did not corrupt weaker minds and lead them along the paths of their own inclinations, all men would be as much like other men as each man is like himself...For

those creatures who have received from nature the gift of reason have also received right reason. Therefore they have received the gift of law, which is right reason applied to command and prohibition.[57]

What Cicero means by 'the gift of law' is something to which we shall return a little later.

Second, not only are all men equal; they are able also to recognise this equality in one another and respond to it. All have a natural capacity to identify with their fellows that is, in principle, unlimited. In relation to this capacity the Greek Stoics adopt as a technical term the word οἰκείωσις (*oikeiosis*).[58] In its usual, non-technical sense, *oikeiosis* means something like 'appropriation.' In Stoic ethics, it denotes an innate feeling of affinity: a desire to make something one's own, or a perception of what is akin to oneself. At birth and during childhood, this feeling does not go beyond the boundaries of the self. It is the will to self-preservation, the uncomplicated self-love, with which everyone is born; and, in this primary sense, animals have *oikeiosis* also.[59] But by the time they reach the age of fourteen or so, human beings have begun to display an inclination towards social development that animals lack.[60] As part of this development, their *oikeiosis* extends progressively outwards to embrace more and more of their fellows. *Oikeiosis* never ceases to be a kind of self-love or self-identity, but it manifests itself as an increasingly complex involvement with others as an aspect of how we define ourselves. The second-century Alexandrian Stoic Hierocles (fl. ca 120 CE), whose treatise on ethics survives as a number of sizeable fragments, invites us to imagine man as standing in the middle of a series of concentric circles containing, first, immediate family, then more distant relations, then friends, acquaintances and so on. Social development is depicted as a process of expanding the inmost circle outwards so as to include an ever larger number of others within it.[61] In practice, most people's *oikeiosis* does not extend beyond their immediate 'circle' of family and friends. But there is in principle no reason why its expansion should stop short of the whole human race. The key to its complete realisation is the full acknowledgement of human equality as a fact of nature. As soon as we recognise that all human beings are in essential respects the same as ourselves, our *oikeiosis* will by its very nature grow so as to include the whole of mankind within the scope of our affection and concern.

Everyone in the world will become part of our own family. More correctly, perhaps, everyone in the world will become inseparable from our own self-image. We are by nature social creatures, as Aristotle had recognised; but there is no reason why our instinct to identify with our fellows should be restricted by the territorial boundaries of the State to which we belong. The human family excludes no one.

Third, the natural kinship of all human beings and their capacity to apprehend it implies that there is a universal standard of conduct applicable to all men: a standard prescribing how members of the human family should relate to one another. This standard the Stoics consistently refer to as a 'law of nature' or a 'law of right reason.' In the literature of early Stoicism, the 'law of nature' is treated in a general sense, as a universal *logos* governing all matter. In later Stoicism, and especially in the Roman Stoa, it is treated specifically as a moral law. In this latter and dominant sense it is 'law' inasmuch as reason recognises it and as it were commands us to act on it. Law, Cicero says, is *insita in natura*: 'implanted in nature.' Because of the similarity of all members of the human race, everyone who lives 'according to nature'—that is, with a correct understanding of the nature of things—can know it and recognise it as the source of justice.[62] Inasmuch as it is a principle of reason, it is not relative to place or time, nor can anyone be exempt from it. This idea of a 'law of nature' or 'right reason' is one of the oldest and most persistent themes of Stoic ethics. Diogenes Laertius says of Zeno, Cleanthes, Posidonius, Hecato and Chrysippus that they understand a life of virtue as being

> one in which we refrain from everything that is forbidden by the law that is common to all things: that is, by right reason, which pervades everything and which is identical with God, the Lord and Ruler of all.[63]

Perhaps we are justified in regarding the phrase 'common to all things' as an intentional echo of Heraclitus's principle that 'one ought to follow what is common to all' (see p. 7). Of the many formulations of the Stoic doctrine of natural law in its later form, probably the best known is the one put into the mouth of the protagonist Gaius Laelius in Cicero's dialogue *De republica*:

> There really is a law—right reason in accordance with nature—that applies universally, and which is unchanging and eternal. It summons to

duty by its commands, and by its prohibitions it deters from wrongdoing...It is never right to countermand this law by legislation, nor is it right to restrict its operation; and to abolish it entirely is impossible. Neither the Senate nor the people can absolve us from its obligations, and we need not look beyond ourselves for an expounder or interpreter of it. Nor will there be one law for Rome and another for Athens; nor one for now and another for the future. Rather, there will be one eternal and unchangeable law, valid for all nations and all times.[64]

This passage repays analysis in some detail. The law of nature is a law of 'the highest reason.' It is accessible to the individual *qua* rational creature: if we want an expounder or interpreter of it, we need not look beyond ourselves. It reflects the rational order of the cosmos: it is 'right reason in accordance with nature.' It is a prescriptive law: it commands, forbids and obliges. It is the same always, everywhere and forever: there will not be 'one law for Rome and another for Athens,' but 'one eternal and unchangeable law.' It is not created, nor can it be abolished: 'Neither the Senate nor the people can absolve us from its obligations.' We shall consider the obligations that the law of nature imposes on us shortly.

Fourth, each individual is in a sense simultaneously a member of two communities. On the one hand, he is a citizen of the State into which he was born. At this point, it is as well to be clear that the Stoics do not disesteem citizenship as such. Though Stoicism originated in Cynicism, the Stoics do not follow the Cynics in teaching that the wise man will despise the ordinary amenities and institutions of organised life. They do not suggest that political life is in itself unnatural or undesirable. Cicero attributes to them the view that 'by nature we have been bound together and united for civic association.'[65] Chrysippus's lost work *On Law* apparently began with an Aristotelian echo: the statement that man is by nature a social animal. As such, he is amenable to being governed by laws prescribing what he ought and ought not to do.[66] Both Zeno and Chrysippus are said to have written treatises on the State, and many of the Greek Stoics were involved in the public life of their own communities. Zeno, Chrysippus and Panaetius regard active and effective participation in public life as a positive duty, and this attitude to practical conduct is particularly seen in the Roman Stoa, for whose members the practice of statesmanship is the highest calling that the wise man can follow. Of all the relationships that we have, Cicero says, 'none is more serious, and none dearer, than that which we have with the commonwealth.'[67] We owe more gratitude to the commonwealth for the benefits that it bestows on us, he remarks, than we do even to our parents.[68]

But, on the other hand, the moral horizons of mankind are not circumscribed by the boundaries of this State or that, nor by ties of family, tribe or race. Running alongside Stoic exhortations to be loyal to one's own commonwealth, we find the view that, in addition to his citizenship of Athens or Rome, each man belongs to another and wider community. The universality of the moral faculty of reason identifies us all as fellow-citizens of a universal or world-State—a *polis* co-extensive with the *cosmos* itself: a *cosmopolis.* There is a brotherhood of man over and above the fellowship of citizens. This cosmopolitanism is no doubt another feature of Stoic thought that derived its initial impulse from the broadened social perspectives of the Hellenistic age; but it is a theme characteristic of Stoicism during all phases of its history. As Chrysippus puts it:

> Just as the word *polis* is used in two senses, to mean both a place to live and the entire State and its citizen body, so is the whole universe a kind of *polis*, including gods and men, in which the gods rule and the men obey. Men and gods are able to have such relations with one another because both are possessors of reason. This is law by nature, and it is for this that all things have come into being.[69]

More than two hundred years after Chrysippus, the Roman Stoic Seneca expresses the same idea in similar terms:

> Let us understand that there are two communities: the one, which is truly great and truly common, embracing both gods and men, in which we look neither to this corner nor that, but measure the boundaries of our commonwealth by the sun; the other, that to which we have been assigned by accident of birth.[70]

So too, Marcus Aurelius, in the second century CE, develops the following sequence of reasoning:

> If our intellectual part is common, then reason, by possessing which we are rational creatures, is common also. If this is so, the reason that commands us what to do and what not to do is common also. If this is so,

there is a common law. If this is so, we are fellow-citizens. If this is so, we are members of some political community. And if this is so, the world is a kind of commonwealth. For to what other political community will anyone say that every member of the human race belongs?[71]

The universal community in which all men are brethren is united not by ties of blood or culture, but by reason or intelligence.[72] 'My nature is rational and social,' Marcus Aurelius says. 'As Antoninus, my city and country is Rome; as a man, it is the world.'[73]

Inasmuch as we belong to two different communities, we are simultaneously subject to two kinds of law. As belonging to a particular State, we are subject to the enacted law of that State. As belonging the cosmopolis we are subject to the 'common law' of nature: to the law that governs us as rational creatures rather than as citizens. But the two kinds of law are not to be conceived as entirely separate. The law of nature, because it is common to all men, ought to be reflected in the particular laws of the States in which individuals dwell. It provides us with a criterion by which we can distinguish between good and bad positive law and to which the wise statesman can look for guidance in framing the law of the commonwealth. Good law is law in harmony with the eternal law of reason. The legislator of whose law this is not true is not a statesman, but a tyrant; and the tyrant, Cicero assures us, is more beast than human.[74] He is a malignant growth needing to be cut out of the body politic.[75] The implication, clearly, is that the law of nature can be appealed to as a justification for civic disobedience and, ultimately, for getting rid of a tyrannical ruler.

What does the law of reason or the law of nature prescribe? As Marcus Aurelius expresses it, it requires that we behave towards one another 'according to the natural law of fellowship, with benevolence and justice.'[76] The law of nature is the law of eternal and unvarying justice. It enjoins us to treat everyone according to their merits and deserts; it forbids arbitrariness, tyranny and respect of persons. It teaches us that, since everyone else is like ourselves, we should extend to all human beings the same equitable treatment as we should wish to receive were we they, and that we should do so regardless of who they are or where they come from.

> Out of all the subject matter of philosophical discussion, there surely emerges nothing of greater significance than the realisation that we are

born for justice, and that right is based not on human opinion, but upon nature.[77]

Justice, says Cicero, is 'a disposition of mind which, having regard to the common good, gives to each his due.'[78] No one is excluded from justice on the basis of rank or condition. It is true in practice that what is due to each will be not be uniform. Justice is not a matter of treating everyone in the same way, but of treating everyone fairly, having regard to his circumstances. Moreover, despite Cicero's suggestion that the law of nature might justify the removal of a tyrant, none of the Stoics is really interested in what we have come to think of as the 'radical' implications of natural law arguments. They do not find it uncomfortable to believe in equality under the law of nature while accepting the real and obvious inequalities of everyday life. Distinctions between slave and free, Greek and non-Greek are real; nor are they to be deplored, still less challenged or overthrown. But such inequalities are superventions upon an underlying equality of human value. They may be convenient or serviceable, but they do not define the moral nature of man. What is due to the master may be different from what is due to the slave; but something is due to everyone. Each is entitled to expect fair treatment relative to his condition, and each has a correlative obligation to extend such treatment to others. What the law of nature teaches, and what the wise man will understand, is that no human being is beneath consideration. In ideal conditions, indeed, all would live in common, without any social or economic discrimination at all. Seneca, paraphrasing Posidonius, casts this ideal into the form of a myth: the myth of the Golden Age of man. There was once a happy and innocent time, before the invention of politics and private property, when the world was held in common for the enjoyment of all, communities were governed by the wise for the good of all, and all were equal in fact as well as in nature.[79]

Stoicism and Roman Law

Despite the continuity of the main ethical themes of Stoicism, there is a major difference of outlook as between the Greek and Roman Stoics. For the most part, the Roman Stoics were lawyers, statesmen and orators rather than philosophers. On the whole, they valued the practical

Stoicism: Equality, Cosmopolitanism and Right Reason 125

life above the contemplative. We have mentioned already a certain tendency on the part of Roman public figures to be hostile towards abstract thought, and even the most philosophically-minded Romans did not add much to the Greek traditions that they admired. It is not unfair to say that their philosophical interests were sometimes rather shallow, reflecting not much more than a fashionable admiration for things Greek. The Greek Stoics did not despise or abstain from political activity; but they tended to consider politics primarily under the aspect of philosophical generalisations. Their Roman admirers were more interested in discovering immediate practical applications for Stoic doctrines. The Roman Stoics occupied a political culture that had for many centuries accorded great value to selfless devotion to the State, to the importance of legal order, and to the prize of *gloria*, renown, awaiting a life of distinguished public service. Roman statesmen had moreover been obliged from an early stage in Rome's history to confront an intractable problem of territorial expansion: that of how to reconcile and unify different peoples with widely divergent interests and beliefs. They found it easy to make connections between the Stoic doctrine of the law of nature and the definition and practice of law in the ordinary sense. It is to this relationship between Stoicism and the development of Roman law that we shall devote the remainder of this chapter.

The codification of the whole accumulated body of Roman Law undertaken under the auspices of the Christian emperor Justinian (527–565) is the culmination of a lengthy and intricate development.[80] This development extends far back into the history of republican Rome: to the appearance, in about 450 BCE, of the earliest known written Roman law, the Twelve Tables. Justinian's was not the earliest attempt to bring a universal legal order to the administration of an increasingly extensive empire. The work that he sponsored between 529 and 534 was itself largely based on three earlier legal compilations: the *Codex Gregorianus* and the *Codex Hermogenianus*, which had been assembled from the imperial archives in about 294 CE and 334 CE respectively; and the *Codex Theodosianus*, made by a commission appointed by the emperor Theodosius II in 438.[81] But there has never been any doubt as to the supreme importance of the Justinianic codification, from the point of view of an understanding of both the history of Roman jurisprudence and the development of European legal and political thought and institutions.[82] Justinian's work was everywhere taken to be the statement of Roman law in its definitive form. As such, it was studied (albeit often in the form of summaries and commentaries) throughout the Middle Ages. This came to be especially true after the foundation, in about 1088, of the celebrated law school at Bologna, to which students came in their thousands from all countries of Europe.[83] As Professor Ullmann puts it, 'to say that [the Justinianic] codification became one of the most formative agencies in Europe would be no overstatement. The general principles relating to justice, to the concept of law, the division of law, its enforcement, and so on, became central to the medieval conception of law...And the *Code* of Justinian was later, when it came to be the subject of scientific treatment in the medieval universities, one of the main sources of the doctrines relating to government.'[84]

The Justinianic codification, now known as the *Corpus iuris civilis*,[85] consists of three parts: the *Codex*, the *Digesta* (also called the *Pandectae*) and the *Institutiones*. The *Codex* and the *Digesta* are compilations of the two branches of written law recognised by the Roman legal tradition: the imperial constitutions (*placita*) and the opinions of eminent legal authorities (*rēsponsa prudentium*). The *Institutiones* is primarily a handbook for the use of law students. It is addressed to *cupidae legum iuventuti*, though it was given full legal standing and force by Justinian. The *leges* or *constitutiones novellae* which have long been printed as part of the *Corpus iuris civilis* are not, in fact, an integral part of it. Justinian had intended that his many legislative innovations should from time to time be incorporated into a series of revised editions of the *Codex*, but this plan was never carried into effect.

In the *Corpus iuris civilis*, there is no direct attribution of any legal doctrine to the Stoics or to any other philosophical school. But is not unreasonable to suppose that Roman lawyers, as members of the city's intellectual elite, began to come into contact with fashionable Stoic ideas in the second century BCE. Quintus Mucius Scaevola, who is said by the jurist Pomponius to have been the first to produce a codification of the law (in eighteen volumes), was a member of the 'Scipionic circle,' a pupil of Panaetius and a minor luminary of the Roman Stoa.[86] More generally, the treatment of natural law and of the concept of equality in the *Corpus* is conducted in a spirit and language that is unmistakably that of Stoicism. 'There can,' it has been observed, 'be no question that the earliest attempts at systematic jurisprudence were made by men strongly influenced by Stoicism,'[87] and there is no reason to quarrel with this assertion.

In the *Corpus iuris civilis*, the *ius naturale*, the unwritten, rational law of nature, takes its place alongside two other divisions of law: *ius civile* and *ius gentium*. It will be as well to describe these two divisions briefly. *Ius civile*, 'civil' law, is the law of the *civitas* itself. Initially, though a broader definition presently emerged, *ius civile* was the law of the city of Rome, noted for its extraordinary harshness and inflexibility. It was the law applying to Roman citizens specifically, whether they actually lived in Rome or not. It was by appeal to the *ius civile* that the Apostle Paul was able to ask for and receive special treatment as a Roman citizen.[88] *Ius civile* was interpreted and expanded according to need by the *ius honorarium*: the body of case law expressing the decisions of the jurisdictional magistrates of Rome, the *praetor urbanus* and the *curule aediles*. But Rome's territorial expansion and the growth of commerce produced at an early stage a need for a body of law capable of applying to those who were not Roman citizens. As early as the third century BCE, we note the appearance of a special magistrate, the *praetor peregrinus* or *praetor inter peregrinos*, whose function was to settle disputes arising either between non-citizens living within Rome's jurisdiction, or between foreigners and Roman citizens. The body of positive law to which such settlements gave rise came to be known as the *ius gentium*, the 'law of nations' or 'law of peoples.'

It should be pointed out that the *ius gentium* is not what a modern writer would mean by the expression 'International Law.' The provisions of the *ius gentium* are not primarily contained in treaties or agreements regulating relations between States. Such regulations might from time to time be treated as though they were part of the *ius gentium*. We find the phrase used frequently in this way by historians (especially Livy) when speaking of the sanctity of treaty relations or the immunity of ambassadors. Technically, however, 'International Law' falls under a heading of its own in Roman jurisprudence: the *ius fetiale*. *Ius gentium* itself is a different and wider concept. As a corpus of law, it developed in the light of the realisation that a large number of legal relationships and institutions were regarded by other nations in much the same way as they were at Rome. On the basis of experience, Roman legal practitioners concluded that certain obligations arise from principles that are everywhere considered as binding. The *ius gentium* therefore emerged as a collection of laws and principles believed on the strength of such experience to be present in all particular legal systems. Hence the following definitions:

> The *ius gentium* is that law which the human race as such observes.[89]
>
> All peoples who are governed by law and custom observe laws that are partly their own and partly common to all mankind.[90]
>
> The *ius gentium*...is common to the whole human race...From the *ius gentium* come almost all contracts, such as sale, hire, business associations, deposit, loan and innumerable others.[91]

It seems clear that the *ius gentium* was the initial point of contact between Roman jurisprudence and the Stoic natural law theory. The *ius gentium* was established as component of Roman jurisprudence well before the introduction of Stoic ideas into Rome. But the coming of Stoicism, conjoined with the fact that certain legal principles were already known or believed to command universal acceptance, began to raise in the minds of Roman jurists an obvious question. Does not the existence of the *ius gentium* suggest that, at the heart of all diversity and change, there is a core of law that is taught to mankind by a rationality in which all peoples share? At least partly in response to this question, the Roman idea of *ius gentium* and the Stoic conception of a law of nature or right reason began to come together in a confluence that we see represented clearly in the *Corpus iuris civilis*.

The confluence is not entirely seamless. In some few passages of the *Corpus*, we find the relation between *ius gentium* and *naturalis ratio*, natural reason, stated in a way that seems to imply that *ius gentium* and *ius naturale* are simply interchangeable terms. The second-century jurist Gaius[92] says:

> Those laws which each people has given to itself are called *ius civile*, since they are peculiar to each city. That which *naturalis ratio* dictates to all men...is called *ius gentium*, since it is the law practised by the whole of mankind.[93]

The same jurist in another place asserts that the *ius gentium* is as old as the human race itself, and has been taught to mankind by *naturalis ratio*.[94] A similar definition is given in Justinian's *Institutiones*:

> What *naturalis ratio* has established among all men is observed equally by all peoples, and is called *ius gentium*.[95]

But this apparently straightforward identification is not consistently maintained. The third-century jurist Domitius Ulpianus[96] distinguishes between *ius gentium* and *ius naturale* in the following terms:

> Private law is of three kinds. It may be gathered from the precepts of nature, from those of nations, or from those of the city. *Ius naturale* is that which nature has taught to all animals. As such, it is not confined to the human race only…From this law come the conjunction of male and female that we call marriage, and the procreation and rearing of children. The *ius gentium* is that law which mankind observes; and it is easy to see that this law differs from the natural law inasmuch as the one belongs to all animals while the other is peculiar to man.[97]

According to this somewhat unclear passage, it seems that the *ius gentium* is part of a broader law that 'nature has taught to all animals.' It is that portion of the natural law that applies peculiarly to man. In other passages again, certain provisions of the *ius gentium*, pertaining to slavery, the separation of States, the foundation of kingdoms, the division of property, are said to be not part of the *ius naturale*, or are even identified as being at variance with it. The *ius gentium* is a universal system of law observed by mankind, but some of its formulae are at odds with the natural principle that all men are equal. It contains provisions for war, captivity and servitude *quae sunt iuri naturali contrariae*: 'that are *contrary to* the natural law.'[98] It appears that the jurists of the third century wish, at least partly on this ground, to differentiate the *ius gentium* from the *ius naturale*, whereas there is a tendency in the second century to regard the two as coextensive, or at least not to make the distinction explicit. But the general point is clear. Some parts of the *ius gentium* are not part of the *ius naturale*, and the *ius naturale* contains provisions that are not reproduced in the *ius gentium*; but there is a large area of common ground. The two are not identical, but to the extent that the *ius gentium* consists of laws that commend themselves to all peoples without infringing the principle of natural equality, it is informed by the *ius naturale*.

Considered apart from the other divisions of law, *ius naturale* as depicted in the *Corpus iuris civilis* consists of certain broad and unwritten principles that are immutable and applicable everywhere and at all times.

> The laws of nature, which are observed by all peoples equally, remain always firm and immutable, constituted as they are by Divine providence.[99]

Positive law should embody justice, but positive law and justice are not the same. Justice is not conventional: it is prior to positive law, not created by it. It is a rational principle; as rational, it is natural; as natural, it is universal, imposing certain moral minima on all peoples everywhere. It is

> a constant and perpetual willingness to give every man his due. The law teaches us to live honestly, to do injustice no one, and to give to each what is due to him. Law is a knowledge of things human and Divine, the science of the just and unjust.[100]

The attribution of the laws of nature to *divina providentia*—Divine providence, now, in a Christian sense, but a providence that reminds us of the Stoic *pronoia*—is meant to indicate that they represent permanent principles of justice and humanity that should be taken as the formative standard for civic law. All men everywhere should be treated equally by the law; all should be dealt with honestly and fairly; all should receive their due; no one should suffer injustice.

To reduce all this to a succinct statement: Roman jurisprudence enabled the hitherto philosophical idea of the 'law' of nature to become a legal reality. As Professor D'Entrèves remarks, 'The first great achievement of natural law lies in the legal field proper, in the foundation, that is, of a system of laws of universal validity.'[101] What were the practical implications of the doctrine of *ius naturale*? With Roman law, as with Stoic philosophy, it is difficult to make general statements about a tradition spanning hundreds of years. Broadly speaking, however, *ius naturale* came to be regarded as a standard of *aequitas*, equity or fairness: as a resource by which the interpretation and application of positive law might be regulated with an eye to what is reasonable as distinct from literal. The idea here is the same as the *epieikeia* that we saw in Aristotle: that the legally just can and should be corrected and refined in the light of the naturally just (see pp. 92–95). It is important not to claim too much or to be led into anachronism. No Roman jurist ever suggested that *ius naturale* might be used to overturn or invalidate positive law; nor is it suggested that *ius naturale* confers 'natural rights' on anyone. *Ius naturale* is no more a radical doctrine to the Romans than to the Greeks, nor is it a doctrine of individualism. The suggestion of some older historians that there is a simple continuity between the Roman *ius naturale* and seventeenth- and eighteenth-century doctrines of natural rights is a serious over-simplification.[102] *Ius naturale* was, however, increasingly used by the magistrates to mitigate the proverbial harshness and inflexibility of the *ius civile* by appeal to considerations of reasonableness and humanity. In this humanising sense, it was applied by the courts as a regulative standard in relation to such things as the conduct of trials, the interpretation of contracts, family law and the law of succession. Also, *ius naturale* provided a vehicle for gradual social and legal reform. The extension by successive edicts of both the *ius civile* and the *ius gentium* came to be perceived by the jurists of the second and third centuries as a process of ameliorating existing law by the restoration of principles supposed to have governed mankind in a primitive state of nature.[103] It was appealed to as a means of reducing the absolute control of the *paterfamilias* over the belongings and persons of his children; of increasing the control of married women over their property; of protecting slaves against cruel and arbitrary treatment, and of increasing the opportunities open to them for manumission.

In Roman law, then, *ius naturale* is conceived as a rational standard of equity and humanity lying behind and guiding the administration and reform of positive law. The *ius gentium* provided a seedbed in which the pre-existing idea of such a standard was able to take root readily in Roman legal thought. The existence of the *ius gentium*, though *ius gentium* is not coextensive with *ius naturale*, is evidence for the existence of principles of justice that present themselves to the reason of all peoples. Alongside, and as part of, its transformation from a philosophical into a juridical conception, the idea of natural justice also established itself as a constitutive feature of the imperial ideology of Rome. In introducing Greek ideas into Roman society, Panaetius and Posidonius found themselves up against an Old Guard of establishment figures who regarded philosophy with hostility and suspicion. Both Panaetius and Posidonius took pains to adapt Stoic abstractions to the Roman taste for the practical. They were on close terms with Roman public figures—Posidonius was a friend and confidant of Pompey—and they found it easy to mould Stoic cosmopolitanism into a seductive justification of Rome's expansion. This justification was developed in deliberate opposition to the opinions that had made the Sceptic Carneades so opprobrious in Rome: that there is no natural justice, and that Roman imperialism is based on mere expediency and the power of the stronger. In his continuation of the history of Polybius, Posidonius promoted the idea that Rome has world domination as her manifest destiny: domination not for her own good, however, but in the interests of the material, moral and intellectual welfare of those dominated.[104] Dominion is the right of the better, not the stronger. Rome's historic mission is to create an empire institutionalising the brotherhood of man: an empire assimilating all races into a community of peace and justice ruled by a universal law.

This kind of justification came especially into its own after the settlement of Augustus in 31 CE. The Augustan settlement brought to an end the century of civil war begun by the assassination of Tiberius Gracchus in 133 BCE. No doubt as part of a general atmosphere of optimism and relief, it was accompanied by a good deal of triumphalist revision of history. The conception of the empire that we find in the literature of the Augustan period is instructive. By restoring the ancient virtues of the republic, Augustus had made the achievement of Rome's destiny possible. Fate or the gods have assigned to Rome from the beginning the task of pacifying mankind and presiding over a world-wide commonwealth of peace and justice. 'These are your arts,' Anchises, father of Aeneas, tells the Romans: 'to protect the vanquished and subdue the proud.'[105] The Roman people are *rerum domini*, 'lords of the world,' granted *imperium sine fine*: an 'empire without end.' When Jupiter surveys the world from his seat on the Capitol, Ovid declares, he can see no land that is not under Roman rule.[106] It was now easy to perceive the Roman Empire as the legal and administrative incarnation of the Stoic cosmopolis. By the fourth century, the belief that Rome had united the world into a coherent civilization, the empire of *Romania*, had become a part of Roman official culture.[107] This belief in the unity, reality and moral mission of *Romania* was able to persist into the fifth century despite the steady decline in the real fortunes and security of the empire.[108] *Ius naturale* is an important part, perhaps the crucial part, of what enabled such a belief to make sense. Rome's sway is not a matter of hegemony or armed might merely. Her rôle in history is to transfigure the world by bringing to its peoples true and eternal principles of justice and right reason.

Summary: *The Stoic Doctrine of Natural Law*

As we have in previous chapters, let us conclude this one with a few paragraphs by way of summary and orientation.

(a) Plato and Aristotle had grounded morality in reason: in nature rather than convention; but both, though from different perspectives, had believed or assumed that the majority of people are unable to exercise the faculty of reason fully. To Plato, moral and political prescription in the light of reason is the province of the gifted individual who has reached the end of a protracted course of intellectual preparation. It is a skill of the most refined and sophisticated kind, to which people in the main cannot aspire. Aristotle had thought that most human beings will be too preoccupied with daily cares to engage in calm deliberation, that some people are only partially rational, and that natural slaves are incapable of reasoning at all. In Stoicism, by contrast, all men are rational creatures. In early Stoicism, this doctrine is bound up with a complex cosmology that looks back to the presocratics. This cosmology, distracting as it may initially seem, is not irrelevant to our purposes. It establishes from the outset a principle that Stoicism was never to relinquish: that human beings are intrinsically a part of nature rather than apart from it. They are bound up with its order and implicated in its universal system of causes. All men moreover have the potential to understand their place in the natural order and make appropriate ethical judgments. Not everyone is wise, but everyone, high or low, rich or poor, Greek or foreigner, has the capacity to become wise. It is reason that enables us to live according to nature. For the older Stoics, living according to nature involves calm resignation in the face of what cannot be changed, and dispassionate choices as between advantageous and disadvantageous things where choice is open to us. In later Stoicism, human reason came increasingly to be understood as an inherent capacity to apprehend and follow an unwritten moral law implanted by nature or God into our minds.

(b) All men are moral equals; to at least some of the Stoics, despite their use of gender-specific language, all human beings are. The fact that we all occupy the same causally-determined universe and that we have the capacity for rational choice, creates a natural condition of kinship, of fellow citizenship of the cosmopolis. *Oikeiosis* is the capacity that enables us to be aware of this kinship and to act consistently with it. External differences exist; nor do the Stoics deplore them. Men are citizens of this State or that; some are slaves, some are free. These distinctions are not objectionable as such, but they are only conventional distinctions, superimposed upon a condition of natural equality. Ultimately, the human condition is the same for all. The parochialism and chauvinism that we notice in Plato and Aristotle have—initially, no doubt, under the impetus of rapid political and social transformation—given place to an account of humanity rather like that in the preamble to the Universal Declaration of Human rights of 1948: each individual is part of 'the family of mankind.'

(c) In view of this natural equality, the law of right reason, the law of nature, prescribes that we should treat all men as fairly or equitably as we should wish to be treated ourselves. '[W]e are born for justice, and…right is based not upon human opinion, but upon nature…For no single thing so exactly resembles anything else as we ourselves resemble one another.' Accidental or conventional distinctions aside, 'all men [are] as much like other men as any one man is like himself.' Justice is giving to each what is due to each, without favour or discrimination and with no regard to superficial differences.

(d) Thanks to the transmission of Stoicism from Greece to Rome and its consequent influence upon Roman jurisprudence, the idea of universal moral principles became, in the *Corpus iuris civilis*, for the first time a legal as distinct from a philosophical doctrine. 'The importance of the Roman Stoics is that they incorporated Greek philosophical ideas about a Universal Moral Order into the traditional legal ideas of Rome, providing a unifying principle for the empire in the community of reason and reasonableness.'[109] Roman

Stoicism, integrated into Roman law, enabled the idea of a cosmopolis to become a military, administrative and political reality. The enormous authority that Roman law acquired during the second and third centuries of the Christian era made it one of the most influential vehicles by which the ethical conceptions of classical antiquity were transmitted to the political culture of the Latin world. Through the medium of Roman law, the Stoic themes of natural equality and fairness were to play an important part in shaping the legal conceptions of western Europe.

We began this chapter with a short survey of Hellenistic philosophy. By way of scene-setting, we noted that Stoicism, Cynicism, Epicureanism and Scepticism all began as responses to a profound transformation in the contemporary intellectual environment. This is the view taken by most students of the post-Aristotelian moral schools and, in broad terms, we see no reason to dissent from it. It is perhaps not too quixotic to suggest that Hellenistic philosophy expresses a kind of late-classical postmodernism. But Stoicism is interesting to us, in a way that the other Hellenistic schools are not, for one pre-eminent reason: that out of its search for individual peace of mind emerged not an anti-politics, but a positive and influential way of engaging with questions of political morality.

It is necessary to be clear as to the precise meaning of this statement. Contrary to what has so often been supposed, the most important feature of Stoicism is not that it establishes 'right reason' as a tool by which our institutions and practices can be appraised and modified. Plato and Aristotle had already postulated reason as a criterion of political judgment, albeit in a fashion somewhat vitiated by conceptions of rationality that are in practice restrictive and inegalitarian. But Plato and Aristotle had limited themselves to a consideration of the classical *polis* and its constitutional arrangements. Their political thought is almost entirely devoid of what we should now call an international dimension. The Stoics, on the other hand, are the inventors of cosmopolitanism. It is in this respect above all that Stoicism is innovative as a political philosophy. It imports a new element into the moral logic of politics: a genuine and consistent theory of natural equality. This element creates the possibility of rational moral judgment not only with respect to domestic political relations, but with respect also to relations in the wider world. It is not inevitable and obvious after all that the only 'law' that can hold as between discrete communities is the law of natural necessity: the law to which the Athenian emissaries to Melos appealed. What the Stoics propose is a universal justice that transcends territorial boundaries: 'one eternal and unchangeable law, valid for all nations and all times.' Under this eternal and unchangeable law, all are equal, and all are entitled to fair and humane treatment. This is a new and immensely fruitful departure. However indirectly, it is an ancestor of our modern rhetoric of international ethics: of 'human rights.'

From our point of view, then, the historical importance of the Stoics does not lie in the fact that they originated a theory of universal political morality. Quite clearly, they did not. It lies in the fact that, in their hands, that theory transcended the relatively narrow perspective of the classical *polis* and the prejudices and mental habits associated with it. As Plato did in relation to the Sophists, Stoicism in its origin represents an attempt to re-think political morality in the face of rapidly and radically changing conditions. It is, in effect, an incipient theory of international relations. Subsequently, it proved congenial to the cosmopolis of the Roman Empire, which in turn became its vehicle. Also, quite apart from its impact on the development of Roman law, Stoicism was one of the dominant western philosophies of the early Christian centuries, and that it had a considerable impact on the formation of Christian ethical doctrines is indubitable. It is the coming of Christianity and its interaction with classical moral and political thought that we must now begin to consider.

Chapter 5

The Transvaluation of Classical Anthropology

THE CHRISTIAN faith began as a Jewish heresy, but a resolutely evangelical one. Its votaries were at an early stage forced to reflect on their relationship not only with Judaism but with the gentile world that they sought to transform.[1] For many years, that relationship was a difficult and perilous one. Until the conversion of the emperor Constantine in 312, the Christians were a despised minority within the Roman Empire, regarded by the pagan establishment with suspicion and hostility and periodically subjected to persecution. Not until the late fourth century was the Church granted full official recognition, by the Christian emperor Theodosius I (379–395). But Christianity during the first four centuries gradually fashioned itself into an intellectual presence within the empire independent of both Judaism and the official cultus of Rome.[2] As it did so, it came especially into contact with two thriving traditions of thought: Stoicism and Neoplatonism, the revision of Plato's teachings especially associated with the Alexandrian philosopher Plotinus (205–270 CE). It was in a context largely shaped by these traditions that the Church began to develop her own social and philosophical doctrines. Partly out of a temperamental desire for order and partly for the sake of persuading their pagan adversaries, Christian intellectuals soon began to investigate the possibility of an accommodation between their beliefs and the philosophical climate in which they found themselves. In some respects, the processes by which this accommodation was reached were straightforward. In one respect, however, they came up against an enormous obstacle; and it is with this obstacle that we are here chiefly concerned. In this chapter and the next, we shall consider these processes of accommodation in as much detail as is practicable, with reference especially to the writings of St Augustine of Hippo (354–430). We shall do so in order to discover something of how classical natural law ideas were on the one hand incorporated into a Christian view of the human condition and, on the other, modified by it. Both aspects of the matter, incorporation and modification, are of importance to an understanding of medieval conceptions of the relation between politics and morality.

Christianity and Classical Philosophy

By way of ground-clearing, let us dispose of a common misconception: that emergent Christianity was radically at odds with the culture of pagan antiquity or stood entirely apart from it.[3] Some early Christians do express an unqualified hostility to the aspirations and achievements of secular philosophy. This hostility is nowhere more implacable than in the writings of the third-century apologist Tertullian (ca 160–225), active in the Church at Carthage during the persecution of 202–211 under Septimius Severus.[4] 'What,' he asks rhetorically,

> has Jerusalem to do with Athens or the Church with the Academy or the Christian with the unbeliever? Our principles come from the Porch of Solomon [i.e. not from the *stoa* of the Stoics], who taught that the Lord is to be sought in simplicity of heart. I have no use, therefore, for a Stoic or Platonist or dialectical Christianity. Since the coming of Christ, we have no need of speculation; since receiving the Gospel, we have no need of scholarship.[5]

Tertullian is a disjunctive thinker, of a kind not, after all, uncommon among the religiously disposed. Though obviously learned in Stoicism, he regarded his conversion to Christianity as cancelling out all previous influences and as obliging him to condemn the heathen world and its works *tout court*. Few, it has been remarked, 'had so learned an acquaintance with heathenism, and could expose its follies with a more bitter sarcasm…or whip its wickedness with a heavier lash.'[6] Tertullian regards the political, religious and moral establishment of the Roman Empire as the Church's enemy, and he directs against that establishment every resource of condemnation and invective. If any document could be guaranteed to provoke suppression of the Church by the authorities, Tertullian's *Apologeticus* surely is that document. Nor is this unintentional. Tertullian represents the small but vocal wing of the early Church whose members went out of their way to court persecution and martyrdom as the true end of the faithful;[7] and he is certainly not alone in his repudiation of the pagan world and its accomplishments. The early Church did not lack those who saw it as their duty to turn their backs on that world, or even to escape from it as quickly and spectacularly as possible.[8]

It is, however, possible to make more of this tendency than is warranted by its currency and duration. Clearly, the exaggerated taste for martyrdom belongs to the period before Constantine's Edict of Toleration of 313: the edict that brought the era of the persecutions to an end. It seems also to have been characteristic of enthusiastic minorities whose members exhibited a fascination with death and relics that one might feel inclined to call morbid. From the time of the first persecution under the emperor Nero in 65, the sufferings of the martyrs were reported in minute and awful detail and fragments of their bodies collected and venerated. We may take it, however, that Christians in general had no great wish to emulate the martyrs.[9] The inclination towards extreme suspicion and exclusivism was mainly the province of radical and anti-intellectual minorities such as the Montanists of Phrygia and the Donatists of North Africa.[10] These minorities exhibit the world-renouncing tendencies typical of chiliastic religious movements everywhere.[11] The picture is different if we consider what, for want of a better term, may be called 'mainstream' Christianity during the first four centuries. The Eastern Fathers—Theophilus of Antioch (ca 120–190), Clement of Alexandria (d. 215), Origen (185–254), Gregory Nazianzenus (ca 325–389), Basil of Caesarea (ca 330–379), Gregory of Nyssa (ca 335–394)—develop a response to the Greek understanding of humanity and nature that, while not one of uncritical admiration, is positive, constructive and sympathetic. We have mentioned already the obvious compatibilities between Platonist metaphysics and Christian theology (see p. 60). It would be hard to find a more sensitive Christian response to Neoplatonism than that of Gregory of Nyssa, whose 'whole doctrine of unity is a wonderful and successful example of the use of Plotinian philosophy in the service of Christian theology.'[12] It is notable too that Irenaeus of Lyons (ca 125–202),

Athenagoras (134–190), Minucius Felix (fl. ca 160), Origen, Clement of Alexandria, Lactantius (ca 240–320), Basil of Caesarea, St Ambrose (339–397) and St Augustine all give serious and intelligent consideration to the anthropological, ethical and cosmological themes of Stoicism.[13] The most influential and impressive Christian authors were disposed to think that God has allowed some of His wisdom to as it were leak into the minds even of those denied the full benefit of revelation. We cannot discuss these matters in detail, nor shall we mention most of these names again. For the sake of completeness, however, we must observe that those who exerted the most enduring influence upon the Christian world-view were for the most part at home in, even if not completely at ease with, the world of secular philosophy. In general, they were ready to see it as a resource and to make use of it insofar as its doctrines were not positively at odds with the requirements of Christian belief.

These preliminaries bring us to the particular question of the Christian reception of the natural law doctrine. It was evident from the outset that Christianity, Neoplatonism and Stoicism occupied a large area of common territory in this regard. The conception of an invisible sublime world lying above our own; of the universe as a moral order, ruled by a Divine reason that pervades it 'as honey runs through a honeycomb';[14] of the universal brotherhood of mankind as children of God; of the ethical irrelevance of conventional social distinctions; of the importance of reciprocal justice, generosity and goodwill; of the natural freedom and equality of all men: these motifs are as much endogenous to Christianity as they are to pagan ethics. The Stoic idea of an original Golden Age of equality and common ownership inevitably struck a chord with Christians familiar with the Biblical story of Eden and the Fall. Also, the world in which the Christians lived was a world governed by Roman law and understood in terms of a definite ideology of natural justice. Christian evangelists were from the earliest times aware of this common territory and made attempts to colonise secular thought—especially Stoicism, but to a large extent Neoplatonism also—in support of the Christian gospel. Two New Testament passages come especially to mind. First, there is the opening paragraph (it is usually called the 'prologue') of the Gospel according to St John, which we may assume to have taken its final form at around the end of the first century:

> In the beginning was the *logos*, and the *logos* was with God, and God and the *logos* were one. The *logos* was with God from the beginning. All things came into being through Him [i.e. through the *logos*], and nothing was made without Him. In Him was life, and that life was the light of man.[15]

The protean term *logos* was to become one of the definitive words in the technical vocabulary of Christology. It is customary to translate it, in this New Testament occurrence, as 'word.' This is in no sense a mistranslation; but, as we have seen, *logos* as a philosophical term has a depth of meaning far in excess of this. The *logos* makes its appearance in the prologue of the Fourth Gospel as a term evidently thought to require no explanation or gloss. In part, it may have been included, with a gentile audience in mind, as a *captatio benevolentiae*: a 'recommendation of the Gospel to those [gentile readers] who have approached it through metaphysics rather than through history.'[16] But it would not have been unfamiliar to Jewish readers either. The term had entered the vocabulary of liberal Judaism during the intertestamental period,[17] especially through the writings of Philo Judaeus, who, more than anyone, had promoted the cross-fertilisation of Jewish and Hellenistic cultures.[18] The Johannine *logos* is fundamentally the same immanent, cosmic-Divine potency introduced into cosmological thought by Heraclitus and elaborated by the Stoics. It signifies, as Rudolf Bultmann puts it, 'a mode of Divine manifestation, or a divine law.'[19] When we come to John 1:14, the parallel with the Stoic *logos* cosmology is no longer so clear. At this point, the term ceases to be the name of a concept or of an immanent Divine power, and becomes appropriated as one of the proper names of God the Son. But it is clear enough that the author or redactor of the Fourth Gospel has selected a point of departure that poises the Gospel towards an audience already at home with the Stoic family of ideas.[20]

The second passage in question occurs as part of the account given in the Acts of the Apostles of St Paul's sermon on the Hill of the Areopagus to the people of Athens:

> Men of Athens: I see that you are by way of being a god-fearing people.[21] On my way here, I took note of your objects of religion. In particular, I came across an altar bearing the inscription: 'To an Unknown God.' I now reveal to you Who it is that you worship without knowing Him...The God Who created the world and everything in it, and Who is Lord of heaven

and earth, does not dwell in shrines made by human hands. It is not because He has need of anything that He accepts the services of men. For it is He Himself Who is the giver of life, breath and everything else. He created the whole of mankind from a single origin, to populate the whole face of the earth. He determined the phases of their history and the limits of their territory. They were to search for God and, perhaps, to find and touch Him. Indeed, He is very close to us all, for in Him we live and move and have our being. As some of your own poets have also said, 'We too are His children.'[22]

The address of which this passage is a part 'became the symbol of Christian theology in the environment of Greek culture.'[23] It was, we are told by the narrator of the Acts, addressed to an audience containing 'some of the Epicurean and Stoic philosophers' who had given St Paul such a mixed reception at Athens.[24] The 'poets' mentioned in connection with the words 'we too are His children' are the Stoics Aratus of Chios (a younger contemporary and pupil of Zeno of Citium) and Cleanthes of Assos. The phrase occurs verbatim in Aratus's long poem called *Phaenomena*,[25] and something close to it appears in Cleanthes's 'Hymn to Zeus.'[26] It is interesting to compare the above passage from the Acts with the following extract from Aratus's poem (there seems little point in trying to translate it into verse):

> Let us begin with God, Whose name is always upon the lips of men. All the streets, all the places where men gather, the sea and its harbours, are full of God. We all have need of God always, for we too are His children...He it was Who placed signs in the heavens and marked out the stars, and appointed the stars to be the chief guides for mankind of the seasons of the year, that all things might grow without fail.[27]

It has been suggested that the phrase 'in Him we live and move and have our being' at Acts 17:28 is also a pagan literary allusion, taken from the semi-mythical Cretan poet Epimenides of Knossos.[28] The question is surprisingly intricate; but it seems more likely that these words, if not original to St Paul, also come from a Stoic source. It is not possible to verify this suggestion by any independent evidence, but in the context it is a plausible conjecture.[29]

On the face of it, both St Paul and the author of the Fourth Gospel are sufficiently imbued with Stoic thought and its literary expression to be able to speak without effort in a language intelligible to an educated pagan audience. To say this is, of course, to leave aside the numerous questions posed by the complexities of New Testament criticism. It would require great simplicity of heart to suppose that in the Acts of the Apostles we have the *ipsissima verba* of St Paul, made up on the spur of the moment, or that the Fourth Gospel flowed directly from the hand of the Beloved Disciple. But this is not the point. The passages that we have quoted indicate as clearly as may be that a parallel between Stoic and Christian ideas was perceived as early as the first Christian century, by the compilers of the New Testament. It is this perception that is significant, regardless of the processes by which that compilation may have been effected.

In a similar vein, we observe the frequent occurrence in the New Testament of the ideas of natural equality and cosmopolitanism, and the corresponding emphasis given to the ethical non-relevance of distinctions between Jew and gentile, just as the Stoics had emphasised the irrelevance of the distinction between Greek and barbarian.

> And I tell you that many shall come from the east and west, and shall take their seats in the kingdom of heaven alongside Abraham and Isaac and Jacob [i.e. alongside the Jewish people].[30]
>
> There is neither Jew nor Greek nor slave nor free man; for you are all one in Jesus Christ. Whether we be Jews or gentiles, slaves or free, we are all baptized into a single body.[31]

It would of course be a mistake to read every such passage in the New Testament as if it were evidence of a direct Stoic influence upon the Christian gospel. Apart from anything else, the message of Christ was from the first understood primarily as fulfilling the prophecy of Isaiah: that the Messiah would establish righteousness and justice for all mankind and bring the knowledge of God to the whole world. To this extent, Christian cosmopolitanism has an origin quite separate from that of the Stoics. But we can hardly fail to be struck by the degree of shared ground to which these resemblances point; nor should we underestimate the degree to which Hellenism had already contributed to the erosion of the traditional exclusivity of the Jews. The syncretic influence of Hellenism was greatly opposed in St Paul's time by the more conservative elements of Palestinian Judaism; but it was precisely against those conservative elements that the universalism of the Christian faith was first preached.³²

It would, moreover, be difficult not to see the influence of Stoicism in the following passage from the Epistle to the Romans:

> With God, there is no respect of persons. As many as have sinned outside the Law [i.e. the Law of Moses] shall also perish outside the Law; and as many as have sinned within the Law shall be judged within the Law. For it is not those who hear the Law who are justified before God, but those who act on it. And when the gentiles, who do not have the Law, nonetheless do by nature the things that the Law enjoins, then, not having the Law, they are a law in themselves. They show that the requirements of the Law are written into their hearts, and that their conscience and thoughts testify to them, accusing them and exonerating them accordingly.³³

By way of what Karl Barth somewhat oddly called this 'obscure and provocative piece of information,'³⁴ St Paul incorporates into his theology of salvation the principle that it is possible 'by nature and in the natural order [to] do the law.'³⁵ It may be, as the Apostle goes on to explain in the next chapter, that men are in fact inveterate sinners without exception: 'there is no one who does good; no, not one.'³⁶ This, indeed, is the fly in the ointment, and we shall return to it in due course. But his point is that, potentially, the capacity for righteous conduct is not the exclusive preserve of men as Jews: as recipients of the Torah, the Mosaic Law. It is the common property of men as men: as men having 'the requirements of the Law...written into their hearts.' Thus, against the isolationism of the Jewish-Christian community at Rome, it is said of the gentiles that 'in their God-created natural disposition they are a law in themselves.'³⁷

Where does St Paul's acquaintance with Stoicism come from?³⁸ It is reasonable to suppose that he acquired it from the Hellenistic culture of his native city of Tarsus in Cilicia and through contact with the educated 'Hellenising' Jews whose acquaintance he would no doubt have made during his work as a teacher of the Law in Jerusalem. It may be that, in the passage from Romans just quoted, he has in mind Philo Judaeus's description of the Patriarchs (who, since they lived before Moses, had no access to the written Law) as being in themselves 'laws endowed with life and reason.'³⁹ But the exact nature of St Paul's philosophical education is something about which we can only guess. From our point of view, the issue is not really worth pursuing. Whatever the immediate antecedents of the passage from Romans may be, what is important to us is that there should be, in the New Testament itself, such a clear affirmation of the idea of a law of nature 'written into [the] hearts' of mankind: existing, that is, independently of positive law.

This affirmation, fed by streams of secular philosophy to which, as we have indicated, they were on the whole not averse, was to be developed through the writings of the Fathers into an integral part of the moral philosophy of the Church. The number of possible illustrations is large, and we here present only a selection. The Christians, says Origen, have come to realise that the law of nature is the same as the law of God.[40] Tertullian, for all his hostility to sources apart from Divine revelation, accepts that it is through nature that God first teaches us the truth. Whatever nature teaches, God teaches; nature is the master, the soul is the pupil.[41] Lactantius, examining Zeno's principle of 'life according to nature,' at first complains that the principle is excessively vague, but concedes at last that man is born for virtue and that it is good for him to follow his own nature.[42] 'Let us imitate nature,' says St Ambrose. 'Conformity with nature provides us with a pattern of discipline and a standard of right conduct.'[43] Precise and consistent specifications of this pattern are given by St Ambrose, Ambrosiaster (ca 350), St Hilary of Poitiers (315–367), St Isidore of Seville (560–636), St Jerome (347–419), Lactantius, Minucius Felix. The law of nature is written by God into the hearts of men; it instructs us to do good and avoid evil; not to injure another, not to steal, not to defraud, not to commit perjury, not to undermine the institution of marriage. All men are by nature equal; the world is the common property of mankind, and private property has come into being by convention only, or because of human greed.[44] Holy Scripture teaches these things too, but the Scriptures were given to men precisely because they could not or would not obey the law of nature.

> Law is twofold: natural and written. The natural law is in the heart and the written law on tables. First of all, nature herself teaches us to do what is good; afterwards came that Law which was given though Moses.[45]

The Patristic conception of the relation between the natural law and the Law of Moses is important, and we shall come back to it in the next chapter (see pp. 198–200). The authorities whom we have mentioned are usually, though not always, writing with an eye to St Paul, often by way of direct comment on Romans 2:11–15. The Pauline notion of a law written into the heart of mankind has become a common coin. But they unmistakably use the language of the philosophers also and, in Isidore's case, of the Roman lawyers. We cannot with precision estimate the extent of Isidore's knowledge of Roman jurisprudence; but in his *Etymologiae* he reproduces the distinction that we find in the *Corpus iuris civilis* between three kinds of law. *Ius autem*, he says, *naturale est aut civile aut gentium*: 'law is either natural or civil or of nations.' Evidently with Ulpianus and the *Institutiones* in mind (see p. 129), he then proposes the following definition of *ius naturale*:

> The natural law is common to all nations, in that it is everywhere held by instinct of nature, not by any enactment: with respect, for example, to the coming together of man and woman, the begetting and rearing of children, the possession of all things in common and the one liberty of all men, the acquisition of those things taken from the sky, earth and sea; also the restitution of an article given in trust or money loaned, and the repelling of force with force. For this, or whatever is similar to this, is never considered unjust, but is natural and equitable.[46]

But there is little virtue in a mere catalogue. We must now attempt a more detailed account of the Patristic interpretation of the natural law doctrine and try to estimate the impact of that interpretation upon the doctrine's subsequent history. We shall do this by looking specifically at the moral and political ideas of St Augustine of Hippo.[47]

St Augustine and the Reception of Natural Law

Why should we confine ourselves to Augustine when so many other Patristic figures accept and operate with the idea of a natural law? We do so partly for reasons of space; but there are more substantial reasons also. First, in Augustine we find a synthesis and expansion of everything in Patristic writing that is of relevance to us. In this sense, he may be taken as representative. Second, his doctrines were overwhelmingly the most decisive influence on western philosophical ideas in general, and on moral and political ideas in particular, between the fifth and the thirteenth centuries. What is of special importance to us is the way in which he modifies the classical natural law doctrine in the light of the anthropology forced upon him by the tenets of the Christian faith. He is the first Christian author to grasp this nettle firmly: to tackle this 'enormous obstacle,' as we called it at the beginning of this chapter. It is with this process of modification—this transvaluation of classical anthropology—that we shall be concerned for the remainder of this chapter and in the one following.

Let us deal first with the most unproblematical ways in which Augustine takes over the idea of natural law. His understanding of it may be described as a composite of Stoicism, Neoplatonism and elements suggested by the Christian Scriptures and his Patristic forebears. His attitude to pagan philosophy is in material respects captious and unfair. He has little Greek, and much of his knowledge of Greek philosophy comes to him second-hand, especially through Cicero; but he is probably the most educated in philosophy of all the western Fathers. Philosophically, he is first and foremost a Neoplatonist.[48] In some moods, he considers the Platonists to be the only philosophers worth arguing with;[49] but in practice, and as one might expect, he is not unsympathetic to Stoicism and the Patristic adaptations of it that he knew. To his mind, the philosophical traditions to which he had access entirely support the Biblical truth that certain moral precepts are intrinsic to the nature of things; and such precepts are, in principle, intelligible to us (the force of the phrase 'in principle' will become clear as we go along). The universe is the handiwork of a Creator Who 'saw everything that He had made, and, behold, it was very good.'[50] God has designed nature as a whole to be a model for our emulation. He has set everything in its proper place and established such relations between things as are fitting to their nature. In an echo of Plato, Augustine refers to the moral truths that the universe contains by way of an analogy with light. The rules of conduct that moral reflection discloses are, he tells us, *lumina virtutum*: lights that shed moral illumination upon the mind, in the same way that theoretical reflection sheds scientific illumination. Collectively, these lights comprise the law of nature; and our immediate awareness of this law is called *conscientia*.[51] Augustine reiterates the suggestion found in St Ambrose, Ambrosiaster and St Jerome, that the law of nature has been inscribed upon the hearts of men by God, but that the Law of Moses and of the Gospel was given because mankind was not able to obey the law of nature without the reinforcement of a codified or written law.⁵² Stated at its most general, the law of nature contains a single precept, in which all lower-order principles of conduct are implicit: that we should treat others as we should wish to be treated by them. If men were able to act on this principle consistently, the world would be a place of peace and harmony. Augustine's most detailed statement along these lines may with profit be quoted at length.

> To all men, as to an audience consisting of the whole human race, the Truth cries: 'If truly indeed you speak justice, judge right things, you sons of men.'⁵³ For is it not an easy thing to speak of justice even to the unjust man? What man, if asked about justice when his own interests are not at stake, would not easily be able to tell you what is just? This is because the hand of our Maker has written the truth into our very hearts: 'That which you do not wish to have done to yourself, do not do to another.'⁵⁴ Even before the Law [of Moses] was given no one was permitted to be ignorant of this truth, so that there might be some standard by which even those to whom the Law was not given could be judged. But lest men should complain that something was lacking to them, that which they did not read in their heart has been written on tablets. For it was not that they did not have it written, but that they would not read it...There has been placed before their eyes that which they would [in any case] be compelled to see in their conscience...Who has taught you that you do not want other men to make advances to your wife? Who has taught you that you do not want to have someone rob you? Who has taught you that you do not want to suffer injustice?...Come, if you do not want to suffer these things yourself, are you the only man? Do you not live in the society of the human race? He who is made together with you is your companion; and all men have been made in the image of God,⁵⁵ even though they wear away what He has formed by their earthly desires...For you declare that there is evil in that which you do not wish to suffer; and this is something that you are constrained to know by an inward law written into your very heart.⁵⁶

Echoing Minucius Felix, Lactantius, Ambrosiaster and St Ambrose,⁵⁷ Augustine applies a Christianised doctrine of the law of nature to the institutions of slavery and private property. Parallels with Stoicism are especially clear in his remarks on these subjects. Slavery exists, and Augustine has no desire to challenge it. In many respects, it is a source of good: it is one of the ways in which God orders and controls human affairs in a disordered world. But the relation of master and slave is conventional, not natural. As such, it is not ultimately important. Masters and slaves, though differentiated by human law, are equal by nature; they are children who acknowledge a common Father. Slaves should be dutiful servants, but their masters should treat them with respect and consideration. They should not regard them as items of property to be bought and sold; above all, they should take thought for their salvation.[58] The institution of private property, too, is a creation of human law. The love of possessions is an aspect of human greed. Because it distracts us from God it is a source of danger to our souls. Property laws are necessary to prevent the quarrels that would arise if the expropriation of natural resources were unregulated. By nature, however, the world is the common property of all. Property laws are convenient and beneficial, but no one has a natural title to any part of the world, and no one should be shut out from its resources by those who have claimed them as their own. Moreover, private property is only justified when it is directed towards righteous ends. The authorities of the State may rightly confiscate the possessions of those who put them to sinful uses:[59] this is a doctrine that the papal publicists of the 'high' Middle Ages were glad to find in Augustine (see pp. 205–206). As to warfare: human nature being what it is, war is inevitable and invariably horrible. It is to be avoided at all costs, and he who does this through diplomacy is more worthy of praise than the bravest warrior. But when war cannot be averted, there are principles of justice that should govern its conduct. For Augustine, as for Cicero,[60] there is a natural difference between just and unjust war. The difference is 'natural' inasmuch as the principles that constitute it hold as between parties who acknowledge no common sovereign. Unjust wars are unjustified in the sense of unprovoked; they spring from cruelty, avarice, imperial ambition. A just war is one fought in self-defence, or to right a manifest wrong, or in obedience to God's will. It should not be actuated by hatred, greed or the desire for revenge. Soldiers who obey the orders of their superiors incur no blame, but they must banish from their minds all private and ulterior motives. Those who wage war should as far as possible act in a spirit of loving correction, and they should not exact reprisals upon the defeated. The victor should do whatever is possible to secure a fair and enduring peace. The considerations that distinguish just from unjust warfare depend not upon revelation or authority, but upon reasoned reflection pure and simple.[61]

Clearly enough, these are in essential respects standard natural law doctrines, present in, or inferable from, the literature of pagan ethics. For the most part, they are confirmed by Scripture and the earlier Fathers. But in the process of adapting such doctrines to a detailed Christian theory of politics, Augustine comes to grips with a difficulty of which his predecessors, from St Paul onwards, had been aware, but which no earlier Christian author had really confronted. God 'saw everything that He had made, and, behold, it was very good.' His original creative intention was that human activity within, and as part of, the natural order should be righteous activity. But God's creative intention alone does not ensure that righteous activity will actually take place. It is at this point that the crucial difference between pagan and Christian psychology or anthropology makes itself felt. Plato, Aristotle, and the Greek and Roman Stoics had all taken for granted both human rationality—the faculty by which mankind is able to perceive and interpret the principles of nature—and also an inherent righteousness of will that equips us to carry such principles into effect. They had assumed that part of what it is to be human is to possess a capacity, granted that the capacity needs to be educated and developed, both to identify and accomplish ethical ends. But Christians cannot make such assumptions. They cannot, because the Christian faith requires us to believe that human nature is above all *fallen* nature. Moral activity will occur spontaneously only if the agents whose activity it is have an intellect and a will that is healthy: that is 'rightly ordered,' as St Augustine so often expresses it. But rightly ordered is exactly what the human intellect and will in their present condition are not. We are sinners; we have an inveterate predilection for unrighteousness. What are we to make of this difficulty and its impact on any attempt to integrate classical moral philosophy into Christianity? It is to this question that we must now attend.

Nature, Sin and Grace

Broadly speaking, there are three master keys to our understanding of Augustine's thought on the subject of human nature and its moral condition. The first, and certainly not the least important, is the account of his own early life with which he provides us in the *Confessions*. One's heart aches for the complex and tortured character that this essay in spiritual autobiography reveals. The experiences of his youth and conversion—more accurately, perhaps, his later review of those experiences—created in Augustine a profound and distressing sense of sin. The *Confessions* contains a minute examination of the disgraceful life that he thinks himself to have led as a young man, particularly in regard to sexual lapses.[62] Everyone has heard of the prayer that he attributes to himself as a 'wretched youth': *Domine, da mihi castitatem et continentiam, sed noli modo*;[63] 'O Lord, give me chastity and restraint, but not yet.' To anyone who tries to look at the matter objectively, Augustine's preoccupation with his own failings seems disproportionate. If he incurs the reproach of the modern reader, it is for an act that he himself considers virtuous: the abandonment of the woman with whom he had lived for upwards of ten years and with whom he had a son, Deodatus.[64] This apart, he does not seem to have done anything very dreadful; but he is invincibly persuaded of his own wickedness: persuaded to the point, one sometimes thinks, of self-indulgence. Sexual misbehaviour aside, the most trivial delinquencies cause him endless retrospective anguish. Seven chapters of the *Confessions* are filled with self-condemnation over the pointless theft, when a lad of sixteen, of some pears from a neighbour's tree.[65] The very fact that the theft was pointless is what troubles Augustine most. 'I stole them simply for the sake of stealing them; when I had stolen them, I threw them away. My only pleasure in them was my own sin.'[66] Personal reflections of this kind raised general questions in Augustine's mind. Why are human beings so much inclined to do wrong purely for the sake of it? Why are we so much in love with the means of our own destruction? Even babies in their mothers' arms are full of selfish demands. If they do no harm, this is only because they lack strength. 'The innocence of the infant lies in the weakness of his body, not in the infant mind.'[67]

At an early stage of his development as a Christian, and for psychological reasons at which it is not difficult to guess, Augustine's sense of personal sin and unworthiness broadened out into a picture of the plight of mankind as a whole. The mature Augustine is convinced of the moral destitution of even ordinary men and women and of each individual's inability to overcome, or even really to understand, his or her own wicked propensities. Augustine's thinking on social and political matters depends almost entirely upon his conviction as to the wholly sinful nature, not of this person or that, but of the human race as such. This conviction is of such importance to every department of his thought that, as a preliminary to matters strictly political, we must devote some time to an examination of it.[68]

Insofar as it has a theoretical basis as distinct from a personal or psychological one, Augustine's beliefs about the moral predicament of mankind are grounded in his understanding, mediated through St Paul, of the Biblical narrative of the Fall. Perhaps his interpretation of Scripture is really a rationalisation of his own feelings about himself; but this, for our purposes, is neither here nor there. It is his interpretation of the story of Adam and Eve that gives us our second master key.

For Augustine, the Scriptural account of the Fall is not myth, but history. It is a factual chronicle of the origin of every earthly evil. When God created Adam, He placed him in the Garden of Eden and appointed the rest of the natural order to serve him. Seeing that it is not good for man to be alone, He made Eve to be Adam's companion and helper. The life of our first parents in the Garden was happy, self-sufficient and free of care. All their needs were supplied without toil. They were exempt from old age and bodily infirmity. They would have been able to produce offspring without the pangs of childbirth or the shame of lust: a point to which the sex-fearing Augustine devotes much attention. Eventually they would have passed over from earth to heaven without suffering death.[69]

> The love of the pair for God and for one another was undisturbed, and they lived in a faithful and sincere fellowship that brought great gladness to them, for what they loved was always at hand for their enjoyment. There was a tranquil avoidance of sin; and, for as long as this continued, no evil of any kind intruded.[70]

One condition only was imposed on them. 'Of every tree of the garden thou mayest freely eat; but of the tree of the knowledge of good and evil, thou shalt not eat of it: for in the day that thou eatest thereof, thou shalt surely die.'[71] With this small exception, their life was one of untrammelled freedom. But it was possible for them to fall from this blessed state. They were made sinless, but they had the capacity to sin: latent as yet, but present nonetheless.

It is here that we begin to perceive the barrier that stands between

Christian moral theory and the main traditions of classical ethics: the apparent denaturing of mankind by sin. Augustine is fully alive to the questions that Christian anthropology raises for secular moral philosophy, and he is at pains to deal with them. If the first human beings were the good creation of a good God, why did they not remain good forever? The philosophical problem of evil, of which this question is an aspect, preyed very much on Augustine's mind during his formative years.[72] On the face of it, as he points out, the existence of evil appears to show that God, inasmuch as He either permits it or cannot prevent it, is either not good or not almighty.[73] The answer to this conundrum at which he eventually arrived is firmly rooted in his Neoplatonist background. We can account for the 'existence' of evil by observing that, correctly understood, evil *has* no existence. More strictly, it has no positive existence. What we call evil in any particular instance is only a relative lack or privation of good.[74] Evil is moreover always relative to some pre-existing good. Clearly so: for anything to be evil, it must first exist, and insofar as it exists, it is the work of God, and to that extent good. The only absolute evil is nothingness or non-existence: the complete non-existence of good. For Augustine, nature is not evil; rather, it is necessarily or intrinsically imperfect.

> Because...the Creator of all natures is supremely good, all natures are themselves good. But because they are not, like their Creator, supremely and immutably good, their good may be diminished and increased.[75]

Adam and Eve were good; but neither they nor any other creature could have that perfection of being which, in the nature of things, belongs to God alone. But anything that does not have God's perfection of being is to that extent separate from Him, and this separation, inasmuch as it exists at all, is capable of becoming wider. To Augustine's mind, created things, because they are imperfect, have a kind of gravitational tendency to fall away from God towards that which is lower. This way of putting it is very characteristic of him, though why he thinks as he does is never made entirely clear.[76] The tendency of the natural order is to deteriorate. Every creature tends, under the weight of its own imperfection, to descend towards nothingness or negation. But God does not allow even His fallen creation to become entirely evil; He does not, that is, allow it to pass out of existence altogether. In

His mercy He keeps the fallen angels and men in being, making use of them, as is His way, to bring good out of evil.[77]

Moreover, the will with which Adam and Eve were created was a free will. It was a will capable of falling away from God, but not bound to do so. Free will was a necessary ingredient of man's nature as a moral being, created to love God and take delight in doing His will. It was a necessary ingredient because, had Adam and Eve been made without it, they would have been automata merely, unable to choose to act well, and therefore unable to achieve the purposes for which God intended them.[78] Inasmuch as they were free, the possibility of choosing *not* to sin was open to them. But Eve, tempted by the serpent, tempted Adam in turn, and he succumbed also. Both sinned equally—God paid no attention to Adam's paltry attempt to blame his wife—and both sinned by their own free choice. The sin of our first parents lay not in the mere eating of a piece of fruit. It lay behind the act itself, in their intentional disobedience of the Divine will. The seed of this disregard, the internal factor that made their will evil, was the inflated self-esteem that Augustine regards as so invariable and destructive a feature of human psychology. He calls it by various names: pride, self-love, exaltation. 'You cannot attribute the cause of any human fault to God; for the cause of all human offences is pride.'[79] Eating the forbidden fruit made Adam and Eve conscious of their own 'nakedness'—their own inferiority—and resentful of it. They wished to be more than they were; they wished to become like gods themselves. Impelled by this proud desire, they allowed love of God to be displaced from their hearts by love of self. Their sin, Augustine insists, was all the more terrible, and all the more deserving of punishment, because it would have been so easy to avoid. So little was asked of Adam and Eve, yet still they put their own miserable wants before their duty to the God to Whom they owed everything. As a punishment, they were expelled from the Garden. They were made subject to all the tribulations of this life, and, after this life, to damnation in the material flames of hell, where it is their lot to suffer alongside the fallen angels with whom they share the punishment of rebellion.[80]

But the Original Sin has consequences extending far beyond those visited upon our first parents. It is here that the bridge between the Original Sin and the social and political implications of that sin begins to appear. There are two such consequences in particular. First, Augustine insists that all the offspring of Adam and Eve—even newborn infants[81]—are sharers or participants in their guilt. All the descendants of the first two human beings are, he thinks, born into the world bearing the guilt of the Original Sin. They are therefore just as much worthy of damnation as Adam and Eve themselves were. The sinful condition of humanity is, literally, radical. 'The whole mass of the human race is condemned; for he who at first gave entrance to sin has been punished with all his posterity who were in him as in a root.'[82] Augustine seems to think that sin has in an actual sense tainted the physical stuff of which we are made. We are all vessels fashioned from the same lump of clay: this imagery is, of course, borrowed from St Paul.[83] The impurities introduced into that lump at the beginning are therefore now present in us all. 'Nothing else could be born of [Adam and Eve] than that which they themselves had been.'[84] Second, Augustine holds that the Original Sin has somehow made man incapable of *willing* rightly. Adam and Eve, by making unrighteous use of the will by which they might have chosen to love God before self, damaged it or impaired it in some way; and, again, all their offspring have inherited it from them in this damaged condition. As descendants and heirs, they could succeed only to what their parents had actually possessed. For this reason, Augustine thinks, human beings in general have become incapable of not sinning: of not being actuated by the same self-love that actuated Adam and Eve. It is not that mankind no longer has free will. We can choose still; but we can choose only in the sense of selecting from among the many possible sins which ones actually to commit. Our sins spring from our damaged intentionality. Everything that we do is sinful not because of what the act is, but because of why we do it: because we are invariably motivated by love of self rather than by love of God. By our own unaided efforts, we cannot choose non-sin. We are caught in an insoluble paradox. The very act of trying to redeem ourselves by abstaining from sin would be a selfish act.[85]

Once again, Augustine's account of the Fall and its consequences is at odds with some of the most fundamental assumptions and doctrines of classical moral philosophy. The problems that it encounters are numerous and, on the face of it, obvious. How can anyone bear the guilt of a wrongful act committed by his most distant ancestor or, indeed, by anyone at all except himself? How can someone who has not yet done anything be guilty of anything: how, in other words, is it possible to be born guilty? Why should it be supposed that a single lapse, however regrettable, permanently altered Adam and Eve's capacity to will righteously? Granted that all human beings have the same physical origin, why should this *moral* alteration have become a general human impairment: a *damnosa haereditas* passed down from generation to generation? Augustine is not unaware of these objections. He knows quite well, for example, that, in ordinary circumstances, it is senseless to ascribe either guilt or merit to acts other than those freely willed by those whose acts they are.[86] But when it comes to the doctrine of Original Sin and its implications, he accepts the evidence of Scripture with implicit faith. This is in keeping with his customary attitude to Scripture and to knowledge in general. Holy Scripture contains everything that is necessary to salvation. If the Scriptures do not provide answers to certain difficult questions, this must be because it is not necessary to salvation for us to know those answers. God has not chosen to reveal the whole of His purpose to us. That which we cannot know we must accept on trust.

It seems, in a word, that faith ultimately trumps reason. In that case, however, does not the classical idea of an autonomous *naturalis ratio* evaporate? How are we to reconcile the primacy of religious authority with the traditional aspirations of philosophy? Is such a reconciliation possible, or must the faithful simply abandon philosophy as mistaken or even impious? Augustine himself believes that philosophy is a possible and fruitful enterprise. In this respect, he departs from the anti-intellectualism of some of his forebears in African Christianity, as represented especially by Tertullian. Faith does not simply cancel out philosophy or render it pointless; but, Augustine insists, we must correctly understand the order in which faith and philosophy stand to each other. His account of this standing, briefly put, is as follows. Reasoning can accomplish much. It can clarify the truth for us, and reveal the relations that constitute the wholeness of truth insofar as that wholeness is accessible to mortals. But reasoning necessarily proceeds from premises that are not themselves established by reason. What we know and how we can know it depends upon the way in which our beliefs train or condition our intellect. We cannot know anything, and therefore we cannot reason about anything, unless we have a correct apprehension of the reality that our knowledge purports to be knowledge of: there can be no epistemology without a prior ontology. But a correct apprehension of reality can come about only through an act of belief. Reason itself, because consequent upon such an apprehension, cannot effect it. If our beliefs are true beliefs, the conclusions that reason infers from them will be valid; if not, not. Augustine therefore habitually accords a logical priority to faith over reason. He postulates faith as a necessary precondition of true understanding, of 'right reason.'[87]

If we reformulate it in secular language, Augustine's position is not philosophically unfamiliar. His argument is, in effect, that all knowledge must in the final analysis rest upon principles that are *a priori*. We need, therefore, to be clear about what those principles are. If his attitude seems odd and exasperating, this is because, with a disregard for categorial distinctions that the modern reader observes as a matter of course, it is so much entangled with his religious preferences. It is also, one might add, to a great extent a matter of temperament. Augustine speaks as one for whom the mere display of intellect did nothing to satisfy—indeed, only intensified—his longing for spiritual certainty. 'These,' he says in the *Confessions*, referring to the astrological doctrines of the Manichaeans that had attracted him as a young man, 'were the dishes in which, when I was starving for Thee, they served up to me the sun and moon!'[88] He is intolerant of those philosophers who delude other people and themselves by seeking to discover through reason what only faith can teach;[89] and he knows that faith enjoins many beliefs that seem contrary to reason. That God is good and that He has created the natural order in the way revealed by the Scriptures: these are the first principles of all understanding. But God has chosen to hide much from us, and we may not question His wisdom or His justice in doing so.

One of the most fertile sources of ignorance and error, then, is that we have access only partially to the Divine mind and the ineffable breadth of its intentions. Realising our own limitations is the beginning of philosophical wisdom. Because our understanding is so incomplete when compared to the omniscience of God, we cannot hope to understand the nature of reality other than by taking as our starting-point what God tells us. Nothing is hidden from His sight. He is not subject to the limitations by which things are concealed from us.

Our minds, by contrast, can work only within historically determinate circumstances. We cannot see the future, nor can we grasp how everything in the universe works together according to the Divine plan. Unlike ourselves, God does not exist within time. He is the Creator of time. He dwells outside it in a changeless eternity, from the vantage-point of which His vision takes in the whole of what we call past, present and future in a single and all-encompassing glance.[90] He can neither forget anything past nor be taken unawares by anything that is to come, because, for Him, there is no 'past' and no 'to come,' no 'then' or 'yet.' These categories have meaning only from the restricted viewpoint of the creatures whom He has made.

What does reflection upon the Divine omniscience tell us about the present condition of humanity? One implication of it is that God knew from the beginning that Adam would sin. It must be understood, however, that this fact does not reduce or qualify Adam's free will, nor does it mitigate his guilt. In his critique of Cicero's *De divinatione* at *De civitate Dei* 5:9–10, and in his discussion of the same question at *De libero arbitrio* 3:1:1–3:4:11, Augustine explains at length that the Divine foreknowledge is not the *cause* of Adam's sin. Cicero denies the existence of fate because he thinks that, if there is fate, there can be no free will. Augustine addresses a Christian version of the same problem. Some think that, if God foreknows what we will do, and if His foreknowledge by definition cannot err, then we must necessarily do what He has foreknown, and that our wills therefore are not free. But Augustine's answer to this difficulty is simple (though he does not always express it simply): God in His omniscience foreknows what we will freely will.[91] Adam was created with freedom to choose for himself, and it was therefore always possible that he would *not* sin. But God knew from all eternity that he would in fact do so, and would thereby bring damnation on himself and all his posterity. God foreknew the entry of sin into the world, but did not will it.

From all eternity, however, God resolved that the loss inflicted upon His creation by the Fall, though immense, would not be total. In a world made by a good God, total evil is impossible. It is here that a glimmer of light begins to shine on the scene of damage and loss that Augustine has so far depicted. Considered with respect to his unassisted will, man is morally helpless. He is not able to save himself by anything that his own efforts might accomplish. He cannot perform any act that might undo the damage wrought by Adam and Eve. He cannot do so because he cannot make any choice that is not actuated by selfishness or self-love, however heavily disguised. But it is God's will that a remnant of the human race—only a small remnant, Augustine insists[92]—should be saved from the general collapse. He has chosen to effect this rescue by restoring moral freedom to some men through the gift of His grace: by repairing their damaged wills and so reinstating in them the capacity for righteous—that is, selfless—choice. The restoration is not complete. Even those whom God has chosen to redeem have to struggle against temptation for as long as they remain on earth. It is necessary for them constantly to wage war, as Augustine likes to express it (once more echoing St Paul),[93] against their own sinful inclinations.[94] It is only in heaven that the souls of the redeemed will be free from every sinful impulse. Then, their wills will be as incapable of willing what is wrong as our wills are at present incapable of willing our own misery.[95] But the grace of God restores at least the possibility of righteous conduct on earth to those who receive it. Those to whom grace is given can break free, even if not completely and not without effort, from the tyranny of self-love under which the rest of us labour.

It must be understood that this grace cannot be earned or deserved by anyone who receives it.[96] No one of Adam's descendants, as such, is either less or more depraved than any other. The grace of God is precisely a grace: an unmerited gift, conferred upon a few chosen, predestined, members of the human race. These members thereby become the Elect, capable of salvation in a world otherwise full of condemned and helpless sinners. Grace is the necessary condition of all virtue. It is 'prevenient': every good work that we do follows from and is a result of it, and no good work can precede its bestowal.[97]

> God's mercy calls us, but not as rewarding the merits of faith: the merits of faith follow His calling; they do not precede it...Unless, therefore, the mercy of God in calling precedes, no one can even believe and so begin to be justified and to receive the power to do good works.[98]

We do not know why the number of the Elect is so small (Augustine at one point suggests that it corresponds to the number of the fallen angels);[99] nor do we know why God has predestined some rather than others, or a few rather than all, to be the recipients of His grace. Again, there are difficulties here that mankind does not have the intellectual resources to solve.[100] We know only, and we know it only by faith, that the great majority of the human race is reprobate, and that only a minority is endowed with the grace that enables those who belong to it to be truly virtuous. Damnation and salvation are different aspects of God's goodness. Damnation shows His justice, salvation His mercy.

The fact that Augustine devoted so much attention to a close analysis of grace and predestination is due mainly, even if not entirely, to his encounters with the heresy known as Pelagianism, so named after its supposed founder, the British monk Pelagius.[101] The Pelagian controversy is our third master key. Augustine was deeply involved in it from 411 until his death in 430. To it he contributed a number of long letters and several treatises regarded as authoritative expositions of the Catholic doctrine of grace.[102] Pelagianism may with good reason be described as the most subversive heresy yet faced—perhaps ever to be faced—by the Catholic Church. Its rise and widespread acceptance confronted her with a theological crisis of major proportions. In effect, Pelagianism is an attempt to deal with a problem that we have already mentioned: how can God impute to us the sin of another? This question is, perhaps, the most vulnerable link in the whole chain of Christian reasoning. Pelagianism deals with it simply by declining to accept that God does impute to us the sin of another. Broadly speaking, it teaches that Adam's sin harmed only himself; that his guilt has not been transmitted to all his posterity; that we do not inherit physical or spiritual death from him; that we can act rightly by our own moral efforts; and that we can make ourselves acceptable to God by so doing. According to the Pelagians, man is able to accomplish his own salvation. It is tempting to see a definite Stoic influence in the documentary sources of Pelagianism. For Pelagius, the Christian resembles the Stoic sage. He is an individual able to understand his predicament in the world and redeem himself by effort of his own will. Pelagius himself by all accounts lived a life of exemplary uprightness and asceticism; even Augustine is happy to call him *vir sanctus*: a saintly man.[103]

But the Pelagian belief—and, by extension, any version of the classical belief—in human self-perfectibility is contrary to the teaching of

Scripture and the Church. 'As in Adam all die,' St Paul teaches, 'even so in Christ shall all be made alive.'[104] If we could be virtuous, and hence saved, without Divine assistance, why was it necessary for God to become man? If the Pelagian understanding of Original Sin is correct, what does Christ's death atone for, and why do we need the Divine grace that comes to us through the Church? To the orthodox, the meaning of the Incarnation is inseparable from the necessity of redemption. To the Pelagians, Christ's life and death have set us an example by which we may be nerved in our efforts to surmount human weakness, but Christ is not our Redeemer.[105] Pelagianism therefore cuts at the root of the Christian faith and Christian ecclesiology. Not only does it negate the doctrine of the Atonement; also, it renders the Church's existence, insofar as the Church is conceived as the community of grace on earth, largely meaningless. The project of defeating its exponents was one that Augustine saw as having supreme importance. 'You introduce a race of men,' he says, 'who are able to please God by the law of nature without the faith of Christ. This is the main reason why the Church of Christ detests you.'[106] But it seems that, in opposing Pelagianism, Augustine is, after all, opposing the whole conception of a rationally-accessible natural law.

The Two Cities

At the same time as he was evolving his views on damnation, grace and predestination, Augustine was developing the comprehensive account of world history expressed in his celebrated image of the two Cities: the City of God and the Earthly City—the *civitas Dei* and the *civitas terrena*. The idea is, of course, most often associated with the work usually regarded as Augustine's masterpiece, *De civitate Dei*, begun (though it soon passed beyond its original purpose) as a defence of the Christian faith against pagan criticism after the sack of Rome in 410. But we know that the conceit was in his mind well before he began to write that enormous work in 413, and we run across the same theme and imagery in a number of other places. He tells us in his *De Genesi ad litteram*, the literal commentary on the Book of Genesis composed some time before he began *De civitate Dei*, that he is proposing to write a book on the nature of the two 'cities' brought into being by the fall of the angels.[107]

The terminology, intentionally biblical in inspiration and resonance—'Glorious things are spoken of thee, O City of God,' says the Psalmist[108]—has the potential to mislead, and Augustine's use of it is not always without ambiguity. Viewed broadly, however, his meaning is not in doubt. The two 'Cities' look very like Christianised expressions of Stoic cosmopolitanism: a cosmopolitanism lifted onto a spiritual plain and interpreted in terms of a Platonist 'other' world. The Cities are not temporal institutions or entities. They do not exist in any determinate place or at any particular time. They are the two all-embracing categories—'camps,' Fr Coplestone not infelicitously calls them[109]—into which God's rational creation has been divided by sin throughout the world's history. Thus, the City of God is not what some of Augustine's medieval admirers took it to be. It is not a metaphor for the institutional Church, the Church Militant on earth. It is the *communio sanctorum*: the society of grace, the entire community, past and present, of those who love God unfeignedly. The City of God is the Church, but it is the Church in the widest sense. Its citizens are those who live 'according to God.' They are of three kinds: those angels who remained loyal to God and who dwell with Him forever; those of the Elect who have already died and whose souls now await the resurrection of the body in heaven; and those of the Elect who are for the time being alive on earth. This last category Augustine often calls the *civitas Dei peregrina*, the pilgrim City of God. The City of God has an earthly contingent, but this contingent is only a small, and temporarily exiled, fraction of its total membership.

In the same way, the Earthly City, though most plainly instantiated in the great pagan empires—Assyria, Babylon, Rome[110]—is not any one earthly State, nor all of them taken together; although, once again, Augustine's language is not always free from ambiguity. The Earthly City is the community, the 'camp,' of all those, past and present, in whose hearts love of self predominates over love of God. Sometimes Augustine calls it the *Civitas diaboli*: the Diabolic City, the City of the Devil. It is the society of those to whom, in the Divine economy, the gift of grace has not been given. The Earthly City lives 'according to man,' not 'according to God.'[111] Again, its population consists of three groups: the fallen angels; those of the reprobate who have died and now share the punishment of hell with those angels; and those of the reprobate who are for the time being alive on earth. Without departing from Augustine's meaning, we might suggest that the two Cities have potential or future memberships also: the souls, uncreated as yet, of those who, whether Elect or reprobate, will be born during that portion of history remaining before the final judgment.

The two Cities, then, are not 'cities' in the ordinary sense. They are what one might call moral categories. They are supernatural communities whose existence spans the whole of history from the Creation down to the time of Christ's Second Coming. They are united, as every community can be said to be united,[112] by what their members love: by the goals and values to which they are collectively committed. The City of God is united by love of God and the earthly by love of self.[113] Their supernatural populations are already separate; their respective dwelling places are heaven and hell. But the earthly members of the two Cities are for the time being indistinguishable. 'The two Cities,' Augustine says, 'are mingled together from the beginning down to the end.'[114] He regards this as a fact of considerable significance, and makes frequent reference to it. Every created soul belongs to one or other of the two Cities, but we cannot, he insists, tell by outward appearance who belongs to which. Appearances, indeed, can be misleading. Many of those now alive who might seem to be among the saved are not, and many who might seem to be among the damned will be saved. 'Few share in the inheritance of God, while many participate in its outward signs.'[115] Earthly status and outward exhibitions of piety are no guides. Since the coming of Christ, no one can be saved who is not a member of the earthly Church;[116] but the earthly Church is also full of hypocrites and time-servers. Augustine does not doubt that many who are members of the visible Church in appearance are in truth members of the Earthly City.

> There are some...who hold the office of shepherds so that they may tend the flock of Christ; but there are others who occupy that office so that they may enjoy temporal honours and the advantages of this world.[117]

In this world, in this time of pilgrimage, the members of the two Cities inhabit the same States. They exist together, mingled like wheat and chaff on the threshing-floor. For the time being, the redeemed share the earth's resources with the unregenerate, and all undergo the tribulations of this life together. Indeed, the righteous often seem to endure a greater share of tribulation than the unrighteous.[118] The Cities will be visibly and finally divided only at the end of history, when Christ will return to judge the living and the dead. Then, the wheat will be separated from the chaff, the sheep from the goats, and the two Cities will each 'receive its own end, of which there is no end.'[119]

Augustine's doctrine of the two Cities is inseparably associated with a Christian perception of history. One cannot properly call it a 'philosophy' of history, because it is really no more than an acceptance of the narrative and prophecies of the Bible; but it is presented explicitly as a rebuttal of the Stoic theory of eternal recurrence.[120] Much of *De civitate Dei* is 'a presentation of Christianity in the form of Biblical history from Genesis to Revelation. Beginning with the Creation and the Fall it unfolds God's plan of salvation through Christ as revealed in Scripture.'[121] For Augustine, history is a linear development; it is a progressive 'salvation history.'[122] In the light of the sack of Rome and similar calamities, he was inclined to believe that the end of the historical process could not be far away. Like many contemporary Christians, he regarded these things as tokens or portents of the approaching end.[123] 'According to his favourite sixfold division of history,'[124] Professor Markus observes,[125] 'the world was now in its old age.' Human history, Augustine thinks, is not, as the Stoic philosophers suggest, an endless cyclical re-enactment of the same events of creation and destruction; nor is it the chronicle of the exploits of Rome or any other empire. It is the gradual unfolding, in accordance with God's will, of the respective destinies of the two Cities from the beginning of the world to the end. History is not working towards some end or culmination *in* this world. The true destination of mankind, whether it be damnation or salvation, does not lie within history, but beyond it.

Augustine and the Law of Nature: a Preliminary Observation

We began this chapter with some account of the Biblical and Patristic reception of natural law ideas. Our focus then shifted exclusively to St Augustine: partly, as we said, for reasons of space, but mainly in recognition of Augustine's authoritativeness and his great influence upon subsequent thought. It is not strictly true, but as a generalisation it is as true as makes no difference, that in Augustine we have the earliest Christian political philosopher. It is in his reflections about human nature, society and political life that we first encounter on any scale the interaction so characteristic of the Middle Ages between political theory and Christian doctrine. What have the theological matters that we have outlined in this chapter to do with the natural law tradition as a theory of political morality? A good deal yet remains to be said; but we can at least give an interim answer to this question.

On the one hand, in much of what he says Augustine subscribes straightforwardly to a version of natural law. He acknowledges a rational principle which, expressed at its broadest, teaches us to treat others as we should wish to be treated by them. His understanding of this principle involves elements derived not from Scripture alone, but from Platonism, Stoicism and the interpretations of those traditions effected by the earlier Fathers, especially the western Fathers. On the other hand, in much of what he says Augustine repudiates the very conclusion that the natural law doctrine supports. He holds that our moral good cannot be achieved by 'natural,' that is, by unaided, reason. We shall in due course come to the synthesis that was eventually to be constructed out of these two antithetical statements: the synthesis that has been called 'Political Augustinianism.' For the time being, let us summarise the conclusions to which the Augustinian doctrines of sin, predestination and grace most immediately point.

The most far-reaching of these conclusions is that political activity cannot, as such, have the ethical significance attributed to it by the main stream of classical thought from Plato onwards. For Augustine, the political community cannot be a moral community in the way that it was for the Greeks. The Greek theorists as we have considered them take it for granted that certain ethical goals are prescribed for us by nature, and that we are in some sense equipped by nature to make free and rational choices with respect to those goals. We can, of course, choose ill rather than well. Our choices can be supported by mistaken opinions and false values; we can be deflected from the truth by rhetoric or misled by greed or short-sightedness. But at least we can choose, and by choosing rightly we can make the good life available to ourselves. Moreover, right choice is educated choice. It is made possible for us by the way in which our minds and wills are formed by association with other rational creatures like ourselves. Redemption lies in our capacity to make use of the moral opportunities furnished by a life shared with our fellow citizens. Man is by nature a political animal whose good lies in this world and is connected intimately with the life of citizenship: citizenship either of a literal *polis* or of a cosmopolis embracing all who have learnt to perceive in one another an equality of rational capacity and moral worth.

For Augustine, however, moral choice in the full sense is open to us, if it is open at all, not through natural reason cultivated by education and social interaction, but through the prevenient grace of God. This grace is given to some but withheld from most, according to a Divine economy that we cannot fathom. The children of Adam and Eve whom God has chosen to redeem are members of the City of God; those whom He has rejected are members of the Earthly City. Those who are not blessed with Divine grace are morally powerless. They have been disempowered by the sin of their first parents. They cannot by their own exertions achieve any good whatsoever. Only his membership of the City of God or the Earthly City has reference, for good or ill, to the ethical life of the individual. The idea of two great communities to which the entire human race belongs owes a good deal to Greek and Roman Stoicism, even if Augustine's inspiration and terminology are largely or primarily Biblical. Each of the Cities is, as we have suggested, a kind of cosmopolis. But the ends to which the two Cities are ordered pertain entirely to a world beyond the present one; nor can anyone choose which of the Cities to belong to. Human rationality does not create them; nor, strictly speaking, can anyone be said to participate in them. Their members are not 'citizens' in any way that would have made sense to Plato, Aristotle or the Stoics. Man's final end, whether it be good or bad, is not to be found in this world, and cannot be achieved in this life.

In short, the Christian message as Augustine presents it appears to have invalidated a large part of the understanding of politics and morality exemplified in the ethical philosophy of classical antiquity. In view of this, how are we to account for the origin and purposes of the State, and what can we say about political life with respect to its moral character? These are the questions with which we must deal in the next chapter.

Chapter 6

The Augustinian Conception of Politics

ST AUGUSTINE wrote no single treatise on politics, but he has a great deal to say about States and the motives by which political behaviour is driven. His was not a cloistered existence. His activity as a bishop and controversialist had a large public dimension. His political remarks are to be found not only in his many treatises, but also in numerous letters written to the Roman officials with whom he was on corresponding terms. Having regard to the diversity of its sources, his understanding of the State and its functions is most usefully considered under three aspects. These aspects reflect his own threefold characterisation: a characterisation that is never made explicit, but which may be regarded as a matrix informing his political and social thought as a whole. As we might expect, all three parts of this matrix are centred upon the idea of sin. They illustrate in detail the various implications of the Fall for political life and international relations. The State has arisen, he thinks, first, as a consequence and an expression of sin; second, as a mechanism for ameliorating the material damage arising from the behaviour of fallen men; third, as a disciplinary order: an order by which sinners are punished and the righteous prepared for their supernatural reward. We assign a numerical order to these aspects only as a matter of convenience. In reality they interact. Augustine resorts to them, or to combinations of them, at will, according to the particular point he is making at the time; but we shall as far as possible look at them separately. As part of our discussion of the first, we shall consider Augustine's response to some of the moral and ideological doctrines of imperial Rome to which we referred in the latter part of Chapter 4. We shall look also at his remarks on war and political obligation, and we shall conclude this chapter by giving some account of his influence on arguments about political morality down to the thirteenth century.

St Augustine's Theory of the State

Augustine's social philosophy begins with a Christian version of a classical commonplace: that human beings are not by nature solitary.[1] When He created the world, God could have made many individual men, just as He made many individual beasts. In fact, He made one man only, forming him from the dust of the earth. He then created the whole of the human race from that one man. His intention in doing this was that men and women should be drawn together not by superficial resemblance only, but by a tie of actual biological kinship.[2] The original husband-and-wife relationship of Adam and Eve, presently extended to take in their children as well, is the origin of a universal bond. Man was created to love God, but he was created to love his fellows also, and to regard them all as members of the same family. This is a notion that unmistakably resembles the Stoic doctrine of *oikeiosis*.

> There is no one in the entire human family, even those by whom our love is not reciprocated, towards whom kindly affection is not due by reason of the bond of shared humanity.[3]

Also, as we have noted, God equipped the human family with a law of nature: a law of conscience inscribed on the heart, instructing its members not to do to others what they would not want others to do to them. Had human beings not damaged the righteous will with which they were created, they would have been able to live together in peace and co-operation by the light of nature alone. There would have been no need of coercive government. Governments would not have arisen because the psychological forces that generate and sustain political activity would have been absent. No one would have wanted or needed to exercise power over anyone else; no one would have stood in fear, or been the subject, of anyone else.[4]

For Augustine, therefore, human beings, though naturally social, are not naturally political. Here again arises an important distinction and contrast. For Aristotle, we recall, there is no essential difference between the social and the political. Ethics and politics merge into a general theory of what it is to live well. Man is political by nature: we are born to govern and be governed, and our good emerges through and within the processes and relationships of governed life. Anyone of whom this is not true is either greater than human or less than human, and to that extent falls outside the consideration of political science. For Augustine, on the other hand, relationships of subordination and superordination—political relationships—were not part of God's original creative intention. The propensity to engage in such relationships is not, as it was for Aristotle, a definiendum of human nature. God's plan in creating mankind was that men should be equal and ungoverned save by Him in Whose image they were made. He gave to Adam 'dominion over the fish of the sea, and over the fowl of the air, and over every living thing that moveth upon the earth';[5] but

> He did not intend that his rational creature, made in His own image, should have dominion over anything but the non-rational creation: not man over man, but man over the beasts. And this is why the righteous men of the earliest times were made herders of cattle rather than kings of men; for God intended to teach us by this what the relative position of His creatures is, and what the desert of sin.[6]

We are made in the image of God insofar as we are rational. Like the Stoics, Augustine holds that our natural condition is one suitable to creatures who share the property of reason. It is one of equality and common possession of the earth. Political arrangements have become overlaid on that condition by convention merely.

Augustine offers a distinctive account of how this state of affairs has come about and of why it continues. A theme to which he resorts often is the way in which the state of things in the modern world is foreshadowed and symbolised in the Old Testament. The fabric of history, understood in the light of revelation, is a coherent whole in which the same lessons are repeated continuously. From the Old Testament we learn that the first city of all, called Enoch, was founded by Cain, a man driven by envy and resentment to slay his own brother.[7] The Roman commonwealth too originated in fratricide. Romulus murdered Remus in order to seize for himself all the glory of founding Rome: a fine example of the standards that rule the hearts of earthly heroes. The coincidence is Divinely intended. The foundations of Cain and Romulus illustrate, each according to its own symbolism, the sinfulness and strife that lie at the heart of political association.[8] Had the Fall not occurred, the State and its mechanisms of coercion, oppression and control would not have come into being. There would have been no place for them in a world of harmonious and innocent relationships conducted under the law of nature. But since the coming of sin, and because of the coming of sin, most human beings have been in the grip of destructive impulses and passions. They are envious, aggressive and vindictive; they are full of selfish pride; they love glory and praise; they long for material riches. Each is above all consumed by what Augustine calls *libido dominandi*: the lust for mastery, the desire to dominate others. This desire, Augustine says, has its origin in 'a wholly intolerable pride' that refuses to accept that all men are equal: a pride that refuses to accept that the natural state of things is right.[9]

The State is an obvious and enduring manifestation of the vainglory typical of fallen men. It was established because of man's lust for power. Most of its wars are fought either to oppose or gratify such lust. It has always existed largely to acquire and preserve those things that human beings desire only because they are sinful and greedy (though the satisfaction that they derive from these things is itself hollow and short-lived. Even in our greatest moments of triumph, we have to reflect that no triumph can last for ever).[10] The law of nature, though still present in our hearts, is ineffective as a guide to conduct for as long as it remains unassisted by grace. Our conscience still troubles us, but conscience is not strong enough to restrain our self-centred impulses and biases. On the contrary, it is precisely a bad conscience that makes us try to lose ourselves in self-destructive pleasures. A man's sense of guilt, Augustine remarks, will drive him out of himself as effectively as smoke or a flood will drive him out of his house.[11] Even though the law of nature has been reinforced, first by the Law of Moses and then by the Gospel, men largely disregard it. Mankind loves the very things that are most productive of strife. As Augustine says repeatedly, the Earthly City is divided against itself.[12] It is divided against itself because there

The Augustinian Conception of Politics

can be no unity where the one God is not faithfully worshipped.

It might be objected that Augustine's account of human motivation and association is falsified, at least in some degree, by the examples of magnanimity celebrated by Roman history. The annals of Rome are full of individuals who are by the most obvious standards of judgment admirable. How else might one regard Marcus Regulus, who went back to certain death at the hands of his enemies rather than incur dishonour, or Lucius Valerius and Quintius Cincinnatus, proud and self-reliant citizens who served the commonwealth faithfully and despised all thought of gain? Here, surely, are people who did conduct themselves well by the light of nature; and Augustine is not without a certain admiration for them.[13] Mistaken as they were in what they desired and loved, these are men who, in some ways, are a salutary example to the Christian. If Gaius Mucius burnt off his own right hand to show an aggressor what the men of Rome were made of, what right has the Christian to complain if he is called upon to offer up even his whole body for the sake of the kingdom of heaven? If Torquatus sacrificed his son to preserve military discipline, what sacrifice is too great for the disciple of Christ? Augustine on more than one occasion suggests that God has allowed the Roman State to achieve greatness in order to furnish the Christian people with such examples as these.[14] But in the final analysis it is an error to regard such deeds as truly virtuous. Despite the concessions that he is prepared to make, Augustine ultimately regards the apparent altruism of pagan heroes either as self-interested because actuated by pride or the desire for glory, or as vitiated by the wish to placate false gods.

The State, then, is both a result of sin and an expression of sin. Like sickness, death and the other miseries of this world, it is an outcome or product of the Fall. It is a result of the alteration wrought in human nature and on the human will by the self-love of Adam and Eve. The State is not, as it had been for Plato and Aristotle, a natural part of human life or a natural forum for the development and expression of human character and potential. It is an unnatural supervention upon the created order. It has been called into being by the fact that man's naturally sociable and co-operative disposition has been denatured and turned inwards by sin. Even those heroes of Rome's past whose exploits are usually regarded as examples of astonishing fortitude and courage have been inspired by a selfish longing for renown or by misguided loyalty to gods and institutions that are not worthy of devotion.

Inevitably, it is Rome and her empire that Augustine usually has in mind when talking about politics. His political consciousness was formed entirely by Roman governmental mechanisms, viewed and criticised from a Biblical perspective. Many of his most pungent comments about the moral quality of earthly association are directed against the pagan commonwealth of Rome, and it is in relation to Rome that his general view of the State is most fully developed. We must therefore give some attention to his appraisal of Rome's political self-image.[15]

By Augustine's day, the transformation of pagan into Christian Rome was in outward respects complete. Toleration had been granted to Christianity by the emperor Constantine in 313, as one of the gestures accompanying his own conversion. After 380, Christianity was established as the official religion of the Roman Empire, and the cults of paganism finally abolished.[16] But 'official' is, of course, not the same thing as 'universally accepted.' The old order was not swept away overnight. Augustine encourages us to regard the former religion of Rome as a crude and absurd idolatry; but there is no reason to doubt that it was associated with powerful feelings of devotion and cultural identity. Such feelings were not obliterated by the formal proscription of pagan worship; predictably enough, they were in some ways strengthened by it. In some quarters the abandonment of Rome's traditional pantheon and the heritage attached to it was regarded as an unpardonable betrayal. When, in 410, Rome was entered and sacked by Alaric and the Visigoths, a pronounced current of opinion, especially in aristocratic circles, attributed this calamity to Rome's having forsaken her ancient gods; forsaken them, indeed, in favour of a God hostile to the martial virtues so long prized by the Romans: a God Who enjoins upon His votaries meekness and rewards submission. Augustine tells us that it was in response to this opinion—in opposition to those who 'began to blaspheme against the true God more fiercely and bitterly than ever'[17]—that he began to write *De civitate Dei*: a work that was to grow into a comprehensive critique of the whole literary, religious, political and military heritage of pagan Rome. In developing this critique (a critique based, to an extent not always realised, on the earlier writings of Tertullian and Lactantius), Augustine's purpose is to deconstruct Rome's traditional claim—a claim that had been part of her ideological heritage for three centuries and more—to a place of unique importance in the history of the world.

We have outlined something of this claim already (see pp. 131–133). We have seen that it involved an account of Rome's destiny reflecting to no small extent the political and moral doctrines of Stoicism. But Augustine has his own version of Rome's history and significance, worked out in *De civitate Dei* in a spirit of detailed confutation. Rome certainly is an important agent of world history. God appointed her from the beginning to be an instrument of His will. That is why she has enjoyed so remarkable a degree of material success. But it is certainly not her destiny to create a world-civilisation of justice and universal moral order. To the cosmopolitan ideology of *Romania* insofar as that ideology is a pagan one, Augustine's response is thorough and radical. It extends even to the assertion that, considered in terms of moral authenticity, the very existence of the commonwealth of Rome—her existence as a commonwealth in the true, the moral, sense—is a kind of illusion. His reasoning on this point illustrates to perfection the way in which religion, morals and politics interact in his mind. One of the most deplorable aspects of Rome's heritage, he insists, has been her devotion to the worthless and wicked gods who have deluded her citizens into worshipping them. These 'gods' are not gods. They are impure demons. That they are is clear from the ways in which they wish to be worshipped. The true God asks of His children only the sacrifice of a broken and contrite heart; the gods of Rome want circuses and degrading rites and filthy stage-plays. The pagan gods betray those who worship them. Under their tutelage the Roman commonwealth underwent an inexorable moral decline, as even her own historians admit. They are also futile nonentities, undeserving of worship and unworthy even of appeasement. Long before the coming of Christ, Rome suffered calamities from which her gods were powerless to extricate her. They stood helplessly by while she sustained a succession of disasters: pestilence, military defeats, civil wars.[18] Her persistent commitment to these gods is, Augustine thinks, enough in itself to show that there never was a true Roman commonwealth. That commonwealth existed in a sense; but it existed only in the way that a painted representation of something might exist.[19] Rome was never a *real* commonwealth. She was never a real commonwealth because, he says, true justice was never present in her.

We need to consider this question of justice carefully. It is an important aspect of Augustine's political thought and a persistent source of disagreement among those who study it.[20] In advancing his argument that the Roman commonwealth never really existed, Augustine is trying to discredit the moral culture of imperial Rome by turning against it the words of one of republican Rome's most admired intellectual figures, Marcus Tullius Cicero. Augustine develops his point by way of a commentary, begun at *De civitate Dei* 2:21 and resumed several years later at *De civitate Dei* 19:21, on Cicero's discussion of the Roman commonwealth in his dialogue *De republica*. As part of this discussion Cicero says, or causes the protagonist Scipio Africanus Minor to say, that a commonwealth cannot exist unless justice (*iustitia*) is present in it; and we remember that, for Cicero, justice is *natural* justice. A commonwealth, a *res publica*, belongs to those whose commonwealth it is. It is the property of a people, a *res populi*: literally, a 'people thing.' But a *populus*, a people, is something more than an indiscriminate multitude. It is a unity, a moral community in true classical fashion. It is an association brought together by its members' consensus on matters of justice or right (*ius*) and by a common interest. It follows that a multitude not united by a shared conception of justice, of what is *ius*, is not a *populus*, and so cannot form a commonwealth in the required sense. Justice, therefore, is of the essence of a commonwealth. But in that case, Augustine observes, Rome herself was never a commonwealth. For what is justice? According to Cicero, we recall, justice is that virtue which gives to each his due. How, then, can the Roman State be just when throughout its history its people have worshipped false and wicked gods by disgraceful means? Withholding from the true God the worship proper to Him is clearly not a case of giving to each his due.[21] On this view, then, Rome never really embodied justice, and so, using Cicero's own definitions, she was never a true commonwealth. Part of what this revaluation of the traditional Roman self-image implies—and is, of course, intended to imply—is that the sack of Rome was not a disaster after all. Everything that the Romans have achieved has been done 'for the sake of a merely human glory.'[22] If Rome has been sacked, that is no great loss. It is no great loss because Rome never offered men anything that is of eternal value to them.

In place of Cicero's definition of a commonwealth, Augustine proposes one of his own. Suppose, he says, that, instead of defining a commonwealth as the property of a people held together by a common agreement as to what is right, we say that it is the property of a people held together by a common agreement as to the objects of their love.[23] The idea of shared love, of a mutual commitment to something, as a unifying influence is very characteristic of Augustine. We have seen already that the two Cities are constituted by two kinds of love (see pp. 162–163). This emphasis on love as a social force possibly owes something to Plato's analysis, in Book 8 of the *Republic*, of constitutional deterioration in terms of changes in what the city's rulers value and adopt as their priorities. The analogy that Augustine draws at one point—somewhat disingenuously, given his measureless contempt for the theatre—is with the collective identity exhibited by a crowd of playgoers: by, as one might say, a fan-club. 'In the theatres...if a man loves a particular actor, he also loves those who love him too: not for their own sakes, but for the sake of him whom they all admire in common.'[24] You can, he says, easily discover the moral quality of any group of people. You have only to look at what they love. It is this that makes them more than a mob; it is this that gives them their identity and purpose as a *populus*. According to this alternative definition—we may fairly call it a theory of identity—the Roman commonwealth was a commonwealth of sorts, united by its members' devotion to false gods and earthly goods: but an unworthy commonwealth clearly, as is every human grouping that derives its cohesion from a commitment to unworthy objects. According to the same reasoning, the only commonwealth really worthy of the name is the City of God: the eternal commonwealth of those bound together by their shared love of the true God.

Augustine holds that what is true of Rome is, by extension and implication, true of all States:

> But it must be understood that what I say of the Roman people and commonwealth I think and say also of the Athenians or any Greek State, of the

Egyptians, of the early Assyrian Babylon, and of every other nation, great or small, that has had a public government.[25]

Why is this truth such a general one? The answer lies in the ideas of grace and predestination. The reprobate, we remember, outnumber the Elect at all phases of the world's history since the Fall. It is to be assumed therefore that all States—including, we must stress, States that now have a Christian government—contain a majority of persons who are excluded from salvation. Most of the citizens of any political order will at the same time be denizens of the Earthly City rather than members of the City of God. But such people *ipso facto* cannot be just or righteous. They are not subject to the true God. The soul that is not subject to the true God cannot govern the body rightly; the reason cannot rule the vices. A multitude containing such people therefore cannot be a *populus* in the sense that Cicero intends. It cannot be a moral community united by agreement as to what is right. It follows that such a multitude cannot comprise a State or commonwealth that is strictly speaking just.

In this connection, we must take account of the striking and much-discussed passage at *De civitate Dei* 4:4, where Augustine tells us that, 'justice removed,' earthly kingdoms differ from bands of robbers only in point of size and immunity from consequences. He borrows an illustration from Book 3 of Cicero's *De republica*:

> It was a pointed and true answer that a pirate whom he had seized made to Alexander the Great. When the king asked him what he meant by infesting the sea, the pirate replied with defiance: 'The same as you do when you infest the whole world; but because I do it with a little ship I am called a robber, and because you do it with a great fleet, you are an emperor.'

The attitude of the defiant pirate inevitably reminds us of the radical Sophists and of Thucydides's report of the Melian debate. Might is right; weakness is the only wrong; the only difference between an emperor and a pirate is that the emperor is in a position strong enough to be able to ignore all opposition.

Is it Augustine's view, then, that this world's political institutions simply do not enact anything of the kind that classical philosophy had called justice? If we take *De civitate Dei* 4:4 in conjunction with

De civitate Dei 19:21, and if we read both in the light of Augustine's general principle that every human association contains an unequal mixture of Elect and reprobate, it certainly looks as though he thinks that the justice to which States lay claim is only a genteel disguise for organised banditry: a position not dissimilar to that of Callicles and Thrasymachus. But this is not quite what he means. It has to be admitted that his remarks about the justice of States are not entirely consistent; nor, as is so often true of Augustine, are they without ambiguity. Looking at the matter broadly, however, it is possible to infer from them a largely coherent position that may be summarised as follows. No earthly State is just in the fullest or most proper sense of the term. No State embodies an undisturbed and perfect harmony grounded in the love and worship of God, which is what true justice, *vera iustitia*, is.[26] But to the extent that they make possible for their citizens a comparatively safe and orderly existence in a world disordered and made dangerous by sin, States can at least achieve an *approximation* of justice. We may call this approximate justice earthly or temporal or human justice, as distinct from *vera iustitia*. Such merely temporal justice consists in the maintenance of a secure and well-ordered environment for men to conduct the external aspects of life in. The point—the distinction between earthly justice and true justice—is unmistakably a Platonist one. *True* justice, Augustine insists—perfect justice, ideal justice—is laid up in heaven. It is to be found only 'in that commonwealth whose Founder and Ruler is Christ.'[27] What he means by this is that it is to be found only in the City of God, the commonwealth of God's Elect, united and transfigured by love of God. It is not that, when contrasted with true justice, earthly justice is somehow 'false' justice. Rather, it is incomplete or imperfect justice. It resembles *vera iustitia* in the way that a picture of something resembles the thing itself. Justice is certainly possible on earth in this limited or incomplete sense. As far as it goes, it is a kind of good, and, as such, it is to be regarded as a gift from God. It is moreover undeniable that this kind of justice was brought to a high degree of realisation by Rome. This achievement, Augustine thinks, is an important part of her Divinely-intended rôle in history, and in this 'more feasible' sense Rome was, according to Cicero's definition, indeed a commonwealth *of a kind*.[28] But even the best earthly justice—granted that it exists, and that earthly rulers are not just brigands too powerful to bring to book—is only a semblance of the real thing. Thanks to the added factors of sin and grace, it is far less like the real thing for Augustine than it was for Plato. For Augustine, philosophers cannot be saviours. Moreover, Augustine considers that even earthly or temporal justice is not *essential* to the State. It is not, as Cicero had supposed, part of the definition of the State. Tyrannies are in the nature of the case unjust; but, as we shall see, they are valid and authoritative political orders nonetheless, and we must regard ourselves as bound to obey them in all but the single limiting case that we shall consider later.

Medieval political controversialists were fond of citing the Augustinian maxim that there can be no true justice except 'in that commonwealth whose Founder and Ruler is Christ.' They tended to do so in the apparent belief that Augustine had meant that only those States governed by Christian rulers are capable of being just. This belief lent impetus to—it was, indeed, adopted mainly for the sake of—an argument about which we shall have something to say in the final section of this chapter: that the institutional Church is the earthly repository and custodian of justice. It supported the view that the only just rule is that of the Christian prince who acknowledges himself to hold his power at the Church's pleasure and for the Church's purposes.[29] But, seductive as this interpretation is from a certain point of view, it is not what Augustine means. To his mind, *true* justice cannot find expression *anywhere* on earth. It cannot find expression in any State, Christian or otherwise; nor, however, can it find expression in the Church. We have seen already that it cannot, and why it cannot, find expression in the State. But it cannot find expression in the Church either, because, as we have also seen, the Church, like the State, contains a mixture of Elect and reprobate. The earthly Church is no more a true 'commonwealth,' a true *res publica*, than the secular State is. The mere submission of its rulers to the will of the Church therefore cannot suffice to make the State a moral community of the classical kind. Augustine believes that Christian rulers can achieve a better version of justice—a less approximate version, so to speak—than pagan ones can. Christian rulers will set a good example to their subjects; they will also 'serve the Lord with fear' by making their material and coercive resources available to the Church.[30] But the function of even the Christian State is to preside over a multitude that is not a moral community, not a *populus*, because many—probably the great majority—of its members are not true lovers of God. In all actually existing States, even those governed by dutiful and faithful Christians, the saved and the lost are thrown together indistinguishably. No earthly State, therefore, no matter how 'just' it may be in the sense of effectively policing its citizens' exterior lives, can be truly or fully just. There can be true justice only among those who belong not to this State or that, nor to the merely institutional Church, but to the City of God conceived as the whole community of grace: to the Divine and eternal cosmopolis. True justice will therefore be realised fully only after this world ends, when that City's pilgrim contingent, finally divested of impure associations, enters upon its eternal inheritance.

In sum, then: the State is a consequence of sin. It is rooted in sin and associated with sin. It originated in the sinful, self-loving urge to dominate; it institutionalises the impulses of envy, aggression and acquisition that are part and parcel of our fallen nature. The claim of Rome, or of any other State, to embody more than an approximate and instrumental kind of justice is false. Granted, Rome has shown herself to be an efficient controller of human behaviour, and has in this sense contrived to secure justice of a kind. To that extent, she has served a Divine purpose. But true justice can exist only among those united by commitment to the true God: which is the same as saying that true justice cannot exist in any earthly association as such. The State is not a moral community. It is not a *polis* of the kind made familiar to us by Plato and Aristotle, nor is the Roman Empire a cosmopolis in the Stoic sense.

We come next to the second aspect of Augustine's understanding of the State. This is an aspect upon which we have already begun to touch in what we have said about approximate or earthly justice. The State is a result of sin and an expression of sin. But it is also and simultaneously one of the agencies by which the external and practical effects of sin are ameliorated.[31] Earthly justice is flawed and incomplete, but justice flawed and incomplete is better than no justice at all. To the extent that it is capable of providing at least some degree of order and security, the State has a positive contribution to make to human life. Again, this not a moral contribution, but it is a significant instrumental one. God has permitted the State to come into existence as a means of imposing restraints upon man's self-destructive capacities. It 'coerces even sinners into the bond of its earthly peace.'[32]

Even pagan States therefore have a part to play in securing the peace and order that all men want and need. It is for the sake of such peace that wars are waged. Without earthly peace, even robbers cannot live. Certainly, this peace is not true peace. True peace, *vera pax*, is like *vera iustitia*. It has the character of a platonic 'idea,' capable of being enacted on earth only in the most incomplete and defective way. True peace is found only in heaven because true peace depends upon the kind of relationships that cannot exist in a fallen world. True peace is 'the perfectly ordered and harmonious enjoyment of God and of one another in God.'[33] Its essence is the absence of strife, whereas earthly peace, which has to encompass within itself those who are irremediably estranged from God, can consist only in the suppression or containment of strife. Earthly peace is therefore a transient and unstable state of things. On the whole, it is achieved and maintained by violence and fear. It is often desired only so that ignoble ends may be pursued without hindrance. But it is still peace of a kind, and, as such, it is a kind of good.[34] It brings back a measure of order to a world imperilled by the aspects of human behaviour that sin has brought into the ascendant. In this way, it brings benefit to Christians and non-Christians alike; for while the two Cities are intermingled on earth, the Elect also make use of the resources and advantages of this life.[35]

It seems to have been Dr A.J. Carlyle who initiated the habit of saying that Augustine depicts the State as a 'remedy' for sin.[36] This way of putting it is not exceptionable if its limitations are understood. But we must be quite clear that the State and its laws and instrumentalities are 'remedial' only in a temporal and restricted sense. There is only one true and perfect remedy for sin. That remedy is not politics, not natural reason, not the law of nature, but the grace of God mediated to the world through Christ. The State is an external regimen only. It cannot make us good. For the most part, it creates only the conditions that make it possible for us to sin in peace. It coerces us into observing its laws by threatening us with unpleasant consequences if we break them. But 'no one is good through fear of punishment; only through love of righteousness.'[37]

The Augustinian Conception of Politics 181

The State exists to secure outward conformity to those standards of behaviour that make life on earth tolerable, but it can do no more than this.

> What...does the temporal law bid us do? Does it have any purpose other than that men should possess those things that can be called 'ours' for the time being, and to which they cling so greedily, in such a way that peace and human society may be preserved insofar as they can be preserved in such matters?[38]

Christian States have the further advantage of providing the kind of order that facilitates the work of the Church. But the State as such, even the Christian State, has no bearing whatsoever on our inner lives. It can only reduce the immediate and material harm that arises from the depredations of the unrighteous. To this extent, it reflects once again the mercy of God in not forsaking His creation. If the State did not exist, men, actuated as they mostly are by selfish individualism, would destroy one another in their endless struggle to possess what they covet. Attachment to possessions endangers our souls, and the State can do nothing about this. But unrestricted competition for possessions would endanger our bodies, and this danger, at least, can be minimised by positive law and its enforcement.

Third: according to Augustine, the State is not only an institutionalisation of sin and a device for minimising the material damage that sinful men do. It is also a kind of large-scale *ordo poenitentiae*. It is one of the disciplines that God has imposed upon mankind. It is disciplinary in a twofold sense. It exists to punish the wicked; it exists also to subject the patience of the righteous to wholesome trial. How we respond to such discipline will depend on what kind of people we are:

> For as the same fire causes gold to shine brightly and straw to smoke, and under the same flail the chaff is beaten small while the grain is purified; and as the lees are not mixed with the oil even though the same force is applied to both in the press, so the same violence of affliction proves, purges and clarifies the good, but damns, ruins and exterminates the wicked.[39]

Voicing what was to become a commonplace of medieval political thought, Augustine insists that *all* political power comes from God, regardless of whether the rulers upon whom it has been bestowed are good or bad. The sentiment is, of course, Pauline in inspiration. It reflects the Apostle's dictum that 'the powers that be are ordained of God.'[40] In the form of the Divine Right doctrine, it was to play a part in political theory down to the seventeenth century. On the one hand, Augustine believes that no law can be just even in his limited and earthly sense of the term unless it reflects the 'eternal law.' By this, he seems to mean both the revealed law of God and the rationally obvious principles of equity that classical philosophy had regarded as a law of nature (and see p. 192). But, unlike Cicero, he does not make justice or righteousness part of his definition of the State. Augustine insists that even tyrants derive their power from above. They hold it rightly even though they do not use it rightly. God gave power not only to the gentle Vespasii but to the monstrous Nero also.[41] Why did He do this? Because wicked rulers are numbered among the instruments of Divine punishment and trial. If we find ourselves under the dominion of a tyrant, this is no more than our sinful condition deserves. If we are virtuous, earthly adversity serves to test and refine us and make us worthier of an eternal reward.

But it is not only tyrants who are appointed to discipline us. Even under the most mild and beneficent rulers, the State is a punitive order. The fairest of judges, because they cannot know what is in men's hearts, have to resort to torture to get at the truth. Also, the distribution of pain and punishment is not always consistent with desert. Judges sometimes condemn the innocent while the guilty go free.[42] Even the non-tyrannical State is, for Augustine, symbolised by its most fearsome officials and its most terrible acts:

> Surely it is not in vain that we have the institution of the power of kings; the judge's right to inflict the penalty of death;...the executioner's hooks; the soldier's weapons...All these things have their methods, their causes, their reasons, their uses. For as long as they are feared, the wicked are coerced and the good live more peacefully in the midst of the wicked.[43]

Elsewhere, he asks:

> What is more terrible than the hangman? What is more cruel and ferocious than his mind? Yet he occupies a necessary place among the laws

themselves, and he is inserted into the order of the well-governed city. He himself is hurtful in his mind; yet, by the appointment of another, he is the penalty of evildoers.[44]

The State in general must secure its purposes not through reason and the fostering of spontaneous co-operation, but through force and fear, threatened and actual. The State is not natural, but conventional. It is intrinsically punitive because it is through violence and the fear of violence that human behaviour is most effectively held in check. The selfish impulses of fallen man are so strong that his behaviour can be controlled only by drastic and terrifying means.

War and Peace

Augustine is much more alive than the thinkers whom we have previously considered to the international dimensions of politics. He has a great deal to say about war; nor is it surprising that he should be so much preoccupied with it. He is steeped in Old Testament imagery of strife and battle. Throughout *De civitate Dei*, he is engaged in a critique of an imperialist culture that prided itself on its military prowess. He lived, moreover, in a world in which it must have been easy to regard war as an ordinary part of life. His lifetime coincided with the invasion of the Roman Empire by the barbarian tribes from the north. The Visigoths crossed the Danube in 376 and in 378 destroyed a Roman army at Adrianople. In 410, under their king Alaric I, they sacked Rome. The Vandals crossed the Rhine frontier into Gaul in 406–407; they were in Africa by 430; at the time of Augustine's death, they were attacking Hippo itself. According to his earliest biographer:

> They destroyed whatever they could reach...they spared neither sex nor age nor even the priests and ministers of God, nor the ornaments and vessels of the churches, nor the buildings...In the midst of these calamities he would console himself with the words of a certain sage who said, 'No great man will think it a matter of importance when wood and stone falls and mortals die.'[45]

As we saw in the previous chapter (see p. 149), Augustine acknowledges that there is a difference between just and unjust warfare. Nonetheless, he believes that the majority of the wars fought by men are anything but just. War in some form or other is, he holds, the ordinary condition of mankind; and, in this connection, as in the case of the State, he thinks in terms of three interacting levels of explanation. War is a consequence of sin; paradoxically, it is also a means of limiting the damage arising from sin; and it is an instrument of the Divine discipline by which mankind is punished and tested.

First and foremost, it is plain that war arises out of the sinful condition of humanity. Men are so much driven by the desire for mastery, praise and glory that they invariably seek to subdue others to their will. When they are not fighting with the people of other nations, they turn against their own people. The lust for mastery 'disturbs and consumes the human race with frightful ills.'[46] So much, in practice, for the idea of a 'human family.' All men and all States are always actually or potentially at war with one another. These generalisations are borne out by numerous examples from history. The records of Rome are full not only of foreign wars, provoked and unprovoked,[47] but of civil strife also.[48] The world has been at war since the earliest days of recorded history.[49] Men, impelled by greed, ambition and hatred, have always striven to overcome one another, and there will be no end to war for as long as this world lasts.[50]

> There are wars among the nations for kingship; there are wars among sects: among Jews, pagans, Christians, heretics, with some contending on the side of truth and some on that of falsehood. This is not yet fulfilled, then: 'He maketh wars to cease unto the end of the earth.'[51] But there is no doubt that it will be fulfilled.[52]

There is no doubt that it will be fulfilled; but only when the history of the world is over.

There is, however, a positive side to the equation. All men desire peace; wars are waged precisely in order to secure it;[53] it is largely by violence and the fear of violence that peace is maintained in the world.[54] As we know, earthly peace is not true peace. It is tenuous and easily lost, and we typically desire it for selfish reasons and use it for selfish ends. Those who seek true peace on earth are looking in the wrong place. 'There is no peace in this life. What we are seeking on earth has been promised in heaven; what we are seeking in this world has been promised in the world to come.'[55] But earthly peace is at least a kind of good, and it is often through war that we secure it.[56] It is in this sense, albeit a limited sense, that war can be regarded as one of the palliatives that God has provided for our condition. The expansion of the Roman Empire, though so often driven by self-serving motives, has unquestionably brought benefits to mankind. Rome's conquest of other nations has imposed a degree of order on the world.[57] Her feats of arms have created and maintained as much justice as men are capable of, and the exploits of her great men, though worldly and self-centred in motive, have not been completely negative in outcome.[58]

Augustine moreover takes the view that war can have a strengthening effect on the characters of those whom it forces to defend themselves; or, at any rate, that it can preserve their morals from too swift a decline. His tendency is to regard the earliest Romans not as good, but at least as less bad than other pagans. In some moods, he is prepared to believe that, though misguided, they were good-hearted. The great men of Rome exemplified a kind of civic virtue which, though not true virtue, is still virtue of a sort, and their addiction to fame and glory, though a vice, is by no means the worst of vices.[59] For as long as Rome lived under the threat of invasion by Carthage, the Romans were noted for their probity, austerity and courage.[60] As soon as the Carthaginian menace had been overcome, their morals began to go downhill. Rome's military successes were in a certain sense her downfall. They removed the fear of outside aggression and laid before her the enervating riches of conquest. Her achievement of military supremacy was therefore accompanied by the corresponding slide into decadence that her own chroniclers noted and deplored.

Also, warfare, like the other tribulations to which this world is subject, has a kind of disciplinary function. The suffering and injustice of war serve not only to punish the wicked, but to test the faith of the righteous and train them in fortitude. The punitive aspect of war is only too obvious. Foreign wars give rise to atrocious suffering, much of it avoidable if men would only restrain their love of glory.[61] Civil war is one of the worst evils than can befall mankind.[62] The punishment that war metes out is indiscriminate. Not all men suffer equally as a result of it; the innocent often suffer more than the guilty do. Granted that there can be such a thing as a just cause, victory does not always go to it. But war is part of the penal condition under which we live. At the individual level, it brings suffering even to the righteous. On a larger scale, history records the appalling tragedies of Cannae or Saguntum.[63] The case of the Saguntines, who during the second Carthaginian War put themselves collectively to death rather than betray their alliance with Rome, is another of those instances of pagan heroism for which Augustine cannot quite conceal his admiration. The Saguntines faced a choice between terrible death and dishonoured survival. The fact that war can create such dilemmas is part of its punitive quality.

Augustine is glad to note that the coming of Christianity has in some measure reduced the human cost of war. In a lengthy discussion of the sack of Rome, he applauds the relative leniency with which the Visigoths, who were Christians, albeit Arians, treated their captives.[64] They did not molest Christians who had taken shelter in the churches; indeed, they encouraged them to take shelter there. Their behaviour compared favourably with the traditional practices of military conquerors. For this, as for all benefits, we have to thank the mercy of God.[65] If just war is possible at all, it is Christians who will wage it. But an apparent difficulty for the Christian lies in the fact that we are so strongly enjoined by the Scriptures to eschew conflict: not to resist evil, to requite evil with good, to love our enemies and pray for those who hate us. Even where war is just, how can the Christian soldier reconcile the demands of his profession with his duty as a Christian not to harm his fellow men? This had been a dilemma of long standing in the Church, particularly since so many of the earliest converts to Christianity were soldiers. It was still topical in Augustine's day. To older generations of teachers—Clement of Alexandria, Tertullian, Lactantius, Origen—no such reconciliation is possible.[66] According to this older view, the Christian should decline to act in any capacity that might implicate him in bloodshed,[67] and this opinion was supported by a repertoire of distinguished examples. St Maximilian of Tebessa was martyred under the emperor Diocletian because, having been conscripted as a soldier, he refused to fight.[68] St Martin of Tours, taunted with cowardice, offered to stand naked and unarmed in the front line of battle.[69] The prayers of the Christians, Origen had said, can accomplish more than the swords of the legions.[70] But in 314 the Council of Arles under the Christian emperor Constantine had condemned soldiers who declined to fight because of religious scruples. Augustine, always disposed to try to reconcile the duties of Christian life with the requirements of the established order, is at some pains to rehabilitate military service from the Christian point of view.

How is this rehabilitation to be effected? Augustine's procedure is to appeal to a distinction, not disreputable in itself, between what an agent does and the intention with which he does it. Military service is not objectionable as such. King David was a mighty warrior; John the Baptist did not tell those soldiers who came to him for advice to give up being soldiers; Christ Himself thought well of the centurion who acknowledged Him.[71] One's profession or occupation does not, so to speak, use up the whole of one's personality; there is a valid distinction between public and private personae. This distinction is such that we are not necessarily required to take personal responsibility for acts of a public or official nature. When a soldier acts in his professional capacity, without allowing the motives and intentions that might belong to him as a private citizen to spill over into his public rôle, no blame attaches to him as an individual. If he sheds blood without passion or personal involvement but simply in the course of duty, he is as it were an instrument in the hands of his commander. It is the superior who commands him who bears the moral responsibility. The soldier's duty is to obey the orders given to him without question or reflection.[72]

What, with hindsight, are we to make of Augustine's attempt to disentangle military service from considerations of blame? His argument is certainly not without difficulties. It is perhaps pertinent to note, with an eye to the twentieth-century categories of human rights, war crimes, crimes against humanity, and so forth, that it is one that has come to be thought peculiarly obnoxious. This is an issue that we must postpone to our second volume, but it is as well to mention it here. Consider the trial of Adolf Eichmann, charged under the law of Israel with 'crimes against the Jewish people' and 'crimes against humanity.'[73] According to Hannah Arendt, in her book *Eichmann in Jerusalem*, Eichmann was an 'ordinary' individual. He was 'not sinister,' not anti-Semitic, not actuated by hatred or the desire for vengeance, not 'perverted, sadistic, and obsessed with killing...neither feebleminded nor cynical, and perfectly capable of telling right from wrong.'[74] The impression that Arendt's account conveys is of a pale and minor bureaucrat. Eichmann's defence was that he had committed no crime under the law to which he was subject at the time, that his duty had been to obey orders meticulously and with zeal, and that no alternatives were open to him. On the face of it, this is a defence that an Augustinian attitude to duty and public service would have to endorse, or at least regard as admissible. The soldier who, with no motive of his own, commits 'atrocities' under orders is relieved of moral complicity in them.

Political Obligation

Given, then, that political relations are what Augustine says they are—negative, penal, coercive, ego-driven, infected with war and strife—can such relations possess any moral dimension at all? Is government no more than the reign of force, or is there a sense in which we can be said to 'owe' obedience to it? Augustine in fact has a very strict doctrine of obligation; but it should be understood that this doctrine not a theory of 'political obligation' as that expression is usually understood. On the one hand, he believes that most people's relationship with the State is to be accounted for in terms of simple self-love. Most citizens obey their governors not from any sense of duty, but either out of fear of what would happen to them if they did not, or in order to secure the rewards—riches, office and, above all, renown—that come to those who serve their country well. The relationship that such people have with those who govern them is prudential or self-interested or both. Rightly or wrongly, Augustine has no more to say about it than that. Christians, on the other hand, must recognise a genuine obligation to obey the government and uphold the institutions of society; but this obligation is not political, but religious. It does not depend upon, nor does it express, a moral relationship subsisting between governor and governed. The Christian is morally set apart from human institutions. Strictly speaking, such institutions have no reference to him. 'Those who cling to the eternal law with a good will do not need the temporal law,' Augustine says, whereas 'upon unhappy men the temporal law is imposed.'[75] It is the Christian's duty to submit to government not because government as such has any claim on him, but because it is God's will that we should submit even to the rule of the cruel and wicked.

> Although we are called to that kingdom in which there will be no power of the former kind [i.e. no temporal power], nonetheless, while we are here in the midst of our pilgrimage, and until we arrive at that age when every principality and power shall pass away, let us endure our condition for the sake of maintaining that very order of human affairs, doing nothing falsely, *and by that fact in itself obeying not so much men as the God Who has commanded us.*[76]

God has turned the State to good use.[77] It is bound up inextricably with sin; the conditions of life with which it presents us are to be endured rather than enjoyed: but its existence and operation are in accordance with God's plan for the world. In keeping with His general policy of bringing good out of evil, He allows earthly rulers to have power over others, thereby using even flawed institutions to create for mankind a tolerable degree of peace and order. The Christian must recognise this aspect of the Divine plan and faithfully conform to it, even if the ruler under whom he finds himself is cruel and ungodly. No earthly ruler has any reason to complain about the standards of citizenship that the Christian religion enjoins. On the contrary:

> Let those who say that the doctrine of Christ is inimical to the welfare of the commonwealth therefore give us an army composed of such men as the doctrine of Christ commands soldiers to be. Let them give us such subjects, such husbands, such wives, such parents, such children, such masters, such servants, such kings, such judges, indeed even such taxpayers and tax gatherers as the Christian religion has taught that men should be, and then let them dare to say that it is inimical to the welfare of the commonwealth. On the contrary, let them no longer hesitate to confess that this doctrine, if it were obeyed, would contribute greatly to the health of the commonwealth.[78]

Inasmuch as the model Christian is also the model citizen, the kings of the earth have persecuted the Christians without cause.[79] But what makes the Christian a model citizen is his sense of obligation not to the kings of the earth, but to the God Who has empowered those kings.

As one might expect, there is a limiting case. Although we are normally obliged to obey the State as a matter of religious duty, we have an equally binding obligation, and an obligation of the same kind, to *dis*obey it if its demands run counter to what God requires. Even here, however, we must be clear as to just how limited and precise Augustine's 'theory' of disobedience is. His thinking on this issue harks back to the days of pre-Christian Rome. During the years when the Church was persecuted by the Roman authorities, Christians were from time to time invited to demonstrate their loyalty to Rome by making a formal gesture of submission to Rome's official religion. In return for such a gesture they would be issued with a certificate, a *libellus*, exempting them from further persecution. Such an act of submission might involve offering incense before a statue of Jupiter, or participating in a rite of sacrifice. At all events, it involved violation of the first two Commandments, and hence could only be construed as a repudiation of the faith.[80] If those to whom we are subject were to require us to do something of this kind, what should be our response? The question had become almost completely academic by Augustine's day; but, as to the principle, he counsels what, and only what, we should now call civil disobedience or passive resistance. In such a predicament, he says, we should confidently follow the example of the martyrs.[81] What do the conditions of this life matter after all, provided only that we are not forced to betray our faith? Death is only death, and its pangs are far exceeded by the rewards of the righteous.[82] If we are commanded to do something in violation of the known will of God, we should decline to comply, politely and with an explanation, and willingly suffer the consequences. No matter how wicked or oppressive our ruler or his acts, rebellion, active resistance or even disrespectful defiance cannot be justified. Augustine's terminology is unequivocal. Where religious duty is at stake, we may courteously refuse: we may disregard commands that are in this sense unlawful;[83] but never does he suggest that we may or should do more, and in no other case may we do even that.

As to the question of Christian obligation, then, Augustine recognises the distinction between political and tyrannical rule that Plato and Aristotle had recognised, but he accords no general significance to it in terms of its bearing on our obligation as subjects. It has no such significance because our obligation as subjects does not depend on the moral merits or demerits of those to whom we are subject. The power that rulers wield comes to them from above. It descends

The Augustinian Conception of Politics

from God.[84] It does not proceed upwards from their subjects, and no one may prescribe or limit the use of a power that he has not conferred. Christians may not regard themselves as entitled to question the ruler whom God has appointed, even if that ruler is a despot. We say again that Augustine is clear in his insistence that bad rulers are not merely a misfortune, but the agents of our deserved punishment. If the emperor harms or persecutes us, he does not on that account cease to be our rightful ruler. Justice and injustice have no bearing on the legitimacy of government. Even in the most adverse circumstances, our willing support is due to 'the manners, laws and institutions whereby earthly peace is secured and maintained.'[85] If the emperor commands us to worship false gods, we must decline to obey: not, however, because we do not acknowledge his authority, but because both he and we are bound to defer to an authority higher than his.

> Consider, now, those who are above you...Let them enjoin nothing against anyone who is above themselves, and let them be obeyed...So, then, if the emperor commands one thing and God another, what do you think? Pay me tribute; submit yourself to me in obedience. Right. Not in the temple of an idol, though: He forbids it in the temple of an idol. Who forbids it? A greater power. Excuse me, then: you threaten prison; He threatens hell.[86]

> Julian[87] was an unbelieving emperor: an apostate, a wicked man, an idolater. There were Christian soldiers in the service of the unbelieving emperor. When they came to the cause of Christ, they acknowledged Him alone Who is in heaven. If at any time the emperor said to them, 'Worship idols,' or 'Offer incense,' they put God before him. Nevertheless, whenever he said to them, 'Form a line of battle,' or 'March against this people or that,' they obeyed at once. They distinguished their eternal Lord from their temporal lord; yet, for the sake of their eternal Lord, they were obedient to their temporal lord also.[88]

The Christian's behaviour in both giving and withholding obedience to the State and its officials is governed by no other principle than his allegiance to God. Both obedience and refusal arise out of an obligation that is not political, but religious.

This consideration of Augustine's theory of obligation highlights for us the clear and important sense in which he is a legal positivist. To his mind, with the single exception that we have mentioned, we are rightfully subject even to tyrants. Human law derives its obligatory force not from its content—not from its conformity to reason or nature—but from the fact that it is the command of the sovereign whom God has set over us. We give special emphasis to this point because there has been a tendency to misrepresent Augustine quite seriously with respect to it. The misrepresentation arises especially in relation to the following paragraph from the dialogue *De libero arbitrio*, written in Rome in about 388:

> There is nothing just or proper in the temporal law that men have not derived [i.e. apart from what men have derived] from the eternal law. For if [a] people...has conferred honours justly at one time and unjustly at another, the difference in each case pertains to the temporal sphere, but the judgment as to justice and injustice is derived from the eternal sphere, where it is abidingly just that a responsible people should confer honours and a fickle people should not...To put into words as briefly as I can the idea of the eternal law as being impressed upon our minds, I should say this: that it is just for all things to be perfectly in order.[89]

As we noted earlier (see p. 182), we can take the phrase 'eternal law' as being at least partly co-extensive with what Augustine elsewhere calls the law of nature. Such variation of expression is not uncommon; not until the time of St Thomas Aquinas do we find an explicit differentiation being made between eternal law and natural law (see Chapter 7). On the strength of this passage from *De libero arbitrio*, the opinion has been attributed to Augustine that a law not in conformity with the eternal law 'is a formulation that is simply null and void, incapable of prescribing an obligation or commanding obedience,' and that 'an unjust law is not a law, and the citizen must refuse to obey it.' In view of Augustine's repeated statements to the exact contrary of this, one can only regard such an interpretation as astonishing.[90] Nor is there any need to save the appearances by suggesting that *De libero arbitrio* is an early work that does not reflect Augustine's mature opinion. What he means in the passage just quoted is that there is a difference between good laws and bad laws and that it is the 'eternal' law that enables us to recognise the difference. What he does *not* mean, and what he nowhere says, is that bad laws are not laws and that citizens can rightly disregard them.[91] Nowhere in Augustine's writings is there any inconsistency as to the relation between positive law and the law of nature, or the 'eternal law.' It is understandable that the modern reader might find his language misleading: *In illa tempore, nihil esse iustum et legitimum quod non ex hac aeterna sibi homines derivaverint.* We have rendered *legitimum* in this sentence as 'proper,' which is a perfectly acceptable translation. But if it is translated as 'legitimate,' and since it is impossible, given the normal English meaning of the word, for us to conceive of an illegitimate law, it seems to follow that Augustine is telling us that laws not in conformity with the eternal law are not laws. We must stress, however, that he does not mean anything of the kind. For Augustine, we can recognise tyrants and bad laws as such, and it is through our rational apprehension of a higher law, a natural or 'eternal' law, that we are able to do so. But this recognition does not relieve us of the obligation that we have under all ordinary circumstances to obey them. The laws of this world do not depend for their validity upon their moral content. To suppose otherwise is a serious and fundamental misunderstanding of Augustine's view of the character of law.[92]

Augustine and the Natural Law Tradition

The task of summarising Augustine's political theory is exceptionally difficult. The main complication is that, strictly speaking, he is not a 'political theorist' at all. As we remarked at the beginning of this chapter, he wrote no political treatise. His concerns are the theological, pastoral and devotional ones of a Christian intellectual and bishop. Everything else in his writing is subordinated to those concerns. His political, social and historical 'thought' has to be extracted or reconstructed from a great variety of written works, none of which is primarily political in intent. These works include essays in theology and biblical exegesis, letters, sermons, controversial exchanges, philosophical treatises and catechetical manuals. In the nature of the case, such a reconstruction cannot be entirely satisfactory. One cannot 'reconstruct' what was never constructed in the first place, and the kind of synthesis undertaken in this chapter and the previous one inevitably makes Augustine look more systematic than he is.

With this reservation, is it possible to make a synopsis of Augustine's political thought in two or three paragraphs? From our point of view, the salient fact that emerges from our discussion is the divergence of that thought from the 'mainstream' of classical political writing as we have surveyed it. Augustine is self-consciously heir to a rich and intricate tradition of ancient philosophy. He is a Christian Neoplatonist *par excellence*. Moreover, he understands and is in many ways sympathetic to Stoic ethics. The two Cities are recognisably Stoic *cosmopoleis*. The idea of mankind as a family united by the bond of human kinship owes much, even though clearly not everything, to the Stoic notion of *oikeiosis*. Yet the contrast between his and the 'classical' estimate of the value and ends of political life could hardly be sharper. At the centre of Augustine's conception of political life lie two constitutive ideas. One is the impairment of our relationship with God by sin. The other is the conviction that this impairment has consequences for every aspect of man's individual and collective life. It is in the light of this conviction that Augustine so largely departs from the kind of political morality that we described in our second, third and fourth chapters. It is also in the light of it that he so comprehensively dismisses the traditional moral and political claims of Rome. Man's nature has become so disordered by the sin of his first parents that he is born both guilty and incapable of not living a sinful, unhappy, destructive life. The only thing that can rescue him from this moral disempowerment is the grace of God, bestowed undeservedly and given only to a minority of the human race. He cannot achieve any good whatsoever without this grace: not by political participation, not through education, not through rational reflection, not through military accomplishment. All reason, all achievement, all courage, all fortitude are mere expressions of egoism and self-love unless and until they are transfigured by the grace of God.

Man's ethical good is therefore related not to any earthly citizenship or engagement, but to his membership of the company of the Elect: the City of God. This membership, this citizenship, comes to him from a source lying entirely beyond the present world. The political arrangements that arise in this world do so not by a process of natural growth, not because they provide a milieu that is natural to human beings, but because they are the outcome of sin. Without sin, they would not have arisen at all. They embody or exemplify sin; they are permitted to exist by God in order to provide a remedy of sorts for sin's immediate effects; and they operate as one of the ways in which man is punished and tested during this life. They are products and features of our fallen condition, and the Christian's duty is to live in the presence of them with fortitude and hope. Until this world ends, the two Cities are mixed indistinguishably in every earthly State. They are mixed indistinguishably even in the earthly Church. Many have been drawn to the Church by sordid motives, and we cannot by outward appearance tell who is truly a Christian and who is not. The righteous man on earth is a member of the pilgrim City of God. His life is a journey through a world of trial and uncertainty and false values: a world in which he is ultimately a stranger.

Augustine's response to traditional political assumptions and claims may properly be described as radical, but it transcends what one might call normal radicalism. As Professor Markus puts it: 'The complexity and poise of his final estimate of politics stems from his conviction that the quest for perfection and happiness through politics is doomed. The archetypal society, where alone true human fulfilment can be found, is the society of the angels and saints in heaven: not a *polis*.'[93] Augustine's critique goes beyond any historical possibility. His project is not that of drawing attention to weaknesses and inadequacies in our political arrangements with a view to recommending their abolition or improvement in the light of natural principles of justice. He does not emulate the classical practice of delineating an ideal State, or a best possible State. He does not do so because, to his mind, all States are imperfect of necessity. They are the expedients whereby an imperfect world is regulated. They can provide justice of a kind; they can produce peace of a kind. But even the best earthly versions of justice and peace are not true justice and peace, and even tyrannical government, from which justice is absent by definition, has its part to play in God's plan. If true justice could exist on earth, the light of nature alone would be enough to guide us. It is precisely the impossibility of accomplishing true justice on earth that makes the State necessary. True justice and peace exist only in heaven. They will be realised only when this world's history is at an end. Members of the *civitas Dei peregrina*, the pilgrim City of God, cannot know them until their pilgrimage is over.

How, in the light of all this, are we to locate Augustine within the natural law tradition? The important points that emerge from this chapter and the previous one are as follows.

(a) On the one hand, Augustine exemplifies, and presents in its most fully elaborated form, the Patristic reception of classical natural law theory. His version of that theory, like that of the earlier Fathers, combines Christian, Platonist and Stoic themes. There is a law of nature, an 'eternal law.' That law is, in St Paul's phrase, written into our hearts by the Creator. It is available to us through reason and conscience insofar as we are made in God's image: insofar, that is, as we are rational creatures. We are capable of apprehending the difference between *vera iustitia* and *vera pax* — true and eternal justice and peace — and the serviceable but incomplete forms of justice and peace that manifest themselves in the temporal world. By nature, all men are members of the same family and the world's resources are the common property of all. Private property, slavery and so forth are conventional merely. They are useful and necessary institutions, but they mask an underlying equality. The most general principle of the law of nature is that we should treat others as we should wish to be treated ourselves. The implications of this principle are specified in detail by the written Law of Moses and of the Gospel, and all positive law ought to reflect it: though, we stress again, Augustine does *not* believe that positive law which fails to reflect it is not law or not obligatory.

(b) On the other hand, there is as it were a barrier between the law of nature and what Augustine regards as the typical behaviour of human beings. That barrier arises from the vitiation of our reason and will by the Fall. The barrier is in a certain sense transparent; but it is a barrier nonetheless. It is transparent because we are able to see the natural law from our position within a fallen world, but we cannot consistently follow it. As rational creatures, we can understand our obligations to others; we can be troubled in conscience. For the most part, however, our actions are distinguished by a self-love that makes each man the enemy of every other. Human beings as they now are are rampant individualists, mostly incapable of altruism or sustained cooperation. The only thing that can penetrate the barrier is the grace of God; but the grace of God is given to a few only, and even they, though capable of righteous action by nature—'by nature' because the effect of grace is to restore the nature impaired by sin—have always to fight against their base impulses, their lower selves. The justice and peace attainable in this world are, and can only be, pallid and incomplete representations of their heavenly exemplars.

(c) Augustine's thought therefore combines natural law thinking with what one might call a reluctant political realism. There is a human family, united by a natural bond; but, in practice, the selfishness and narrow vision of fallen man estranges members of that family from one another. The impulse of *oikeiosis* is thwarted by the countervailing impulse of egoism: by the self-love that impels the competition and conflict by which the world is disfigured. Augustine regards this as a truth of experience. In this respect, as in several others, he reminds us of the radical Sophists. If you examine the history of the world, you see the same thing, everywhere and always. Domestically and internationally, war and struggle are the normal condition of human affairs. Human beings engage in ceaseless efforts to achieve mastery and security for themselves at the expense of others. This is the reality with which we have to live. There is a distinction between just and unjust war, but the need for such a distinction arises only because even those capable of righteous action are forced to repulse the aggression and punish the wrongdoing of those who are not. War is not without its positive features: it can be a means of peace, order and discipline; but all war is horrible. The human predicament is a tragic one. In this world, even the good have to do evil. The Christian soldier must smite those whom he is obliged to love, and does not necessarily incur blame in doing so. Often, he must swallow his conscience and obey the orders of wicked superiors.

(d) There is something recognisably modern about Augustine's thought as we have summarised it.[94] At its heart, though never fully explored by Augustine, is the same Platonist logic that, divested of religious dress, informs the international political devices invented in the twentieth century to sustain the ideology of human rights. On the one hand, there is a universal political morality capable of being known. On the other, that morality is routinely disregarded. The proper conduct of human affairs therefore requires a power strong enough to be able to enforce a respectable approximation of it upon the recalcitrant. Might is not right, but right without might cannot prevail. This chain of reasoning implies that those who understand the true nature of righteous conduct have a duty to take charge of the behaviour of those who do not or who, through malice or weakness of will, do not conform themselves to it. The importance of this logic in the modern world is something that we shall have to consider in our second volume. Within an older, Christian, setting—within the kind of moral environment exemplified in the European Middle Ages—it has certain clear implications for relations between 'Church' and 'State,'[95] and it is to some account of those implications that we must for the time being attend.

Natural Law and 'Political Augustinianism'

In the course of several centuries, the institution customarily referred to as the 'medieval Church'—the Church of Rome, the papal Church, by which the politics of the Middle Ages was so much shaped—evolved into a complex corporation with laws, courts and procedures of her own.[96] The corporate form of the 'high' medieval Church reflects the fact that the Roman Empire within which she had emerged was itself such a corporation. She developed a legal, an administrative and a doctrinal system reflecting both a strongly juridical cast of mind and, in many ways, the pre-existing structures of Roman law and governance. As a part of this process, she adopted a doctrine of natural law that followed closely the formulations of the *Corpus iuris civilis*. She did so, however, with two important differences. These differences may be illustrated by passages taken from the *Decretum* of Gratian (ca 1139): the most comprehensive and authoritative of the several attempts made during the twelfth century to bring together within a single compass the Church's growing body of canon law.[97]

The first difference is the way in which, in the *Decretum*, the Roman law doctrine of *ius naturale* is formally taken over by and subordinated to the influence of the Fathers. On the one hand, the Fathers in the main have no specialised knowledge of, nor interest

The Augustinian Conception of Politics

in, Roman jurisprudence. Their treatment of natural law is philosophical and theological, and they attempt no reconciliation with legal thought as such. On the other hand, we discover in the *Decretum* exactly the same technical division of law as we found in the *Institutiones* of Justinian—*ius aut naturale est aut civile aut gentium*[98]—but with a significant modification.

> The human race is governed in two ways: by natural law and by custom.[99] The law of nature is that which is contained in the Law and the Gospel [i.e. in the Old and New Testaments]. It commands that each should do to others what he would have done to himself; it forbids him to do to anyone else what he would not have done to himself. Thus, Christ says in the Gospel: 'Whatever you wish men to do to you, do the same to them; for this is the Law and the prophets.'[100] As Isidore says at *Etymologiae* 5:1: 'All laws are either Divine or human. Divine laws come from nature, and human laws from custom. This is why the two differ, for different peoples are responsive to different laws.'[101]

By the middle of the twelfth century, then, we find the canon law of the Church stipulating that *ius Divinum*, Divine law, and the Roman jurists' *ius naturale* are simply one and the same thing. The *Decretum* does not suggest that the law of nature owes it *origin* to Biblical revelation. The natural law continues to be understood as primarily a law of reason: it 'came into being with the creation of man as a rational creature and does not vary with time, but remains immutable.'[102] But the *Decretum* explicitly incorporates into its account of natural law the Patristic doctrine that *ius naturae est quod in lege et evangelio continetur*: 'the law of nature is that which is contained in the Law and the Gospel'; and this principle is reiterated and confirmed by the most influential twelfth- and thirteenth-century commentators on the *Decretum*: Paucapalea, Rufinus, Stephen of Tournai, Damasus.[103] In the *Decretum* and its glossators we find that the classical doctrine of natural law, as transmitted from its Greek origins through Roman Stoicism and the *Corpus iuris civilis*, has collapsed completely into the Patristic doctrine that equates the natural law with what is taught in the Scriptures. The law of nature teaches us to do good and avoid evil. It commands what is beneficial, forbids what is harmful, and recommends what is expedient. It requires us to do to others what we would wish to have done to ourselves. It was given to us by God at the Creation, and admits of no variation.[104] But because our ability to perceive and act on the law of nature has been so much weakened by sin, it has been formulated and reaffirmed first in the Law of Moses, then in the Gospel of Christ. Everything that the natural law prescribes is contained in the Old and New Testaments.[105] This direct and formal identification of natural law with Divine law is of the highest importance.

The second of our two differences may be illustrated by the following passages from the *Decretum*:

> The natural law takes precedence in point of dignity over custom and legislation. Anything accepted as custom or incorporated into legislation that is contrary to the natural law is to be considered null and void [*vana et irrita sunt habenda*].[106]

> Nothing is commanded by the law of nature except what God wills. Nothing is prohibited by it unless it is prohibited by God; and there is nothing in the canonical Scriptures that is not also found in the Divine law, which is itself consistent with nature. It is clear, therefore, that whatever can be shown to be contrary to the Divine will or to the canonical Scriptures or to the Divine law is also opposed to the natural law. Thus, when something is identified as part of the Divine will or the canonical Scriptures or the Divine law, it is thereby also identified as part of the natural law. Thus, any legislation, whether secular or ecclesiastical, that is shown to be contrary to nature must be decisively rejected [*penitus sunt excludendae*].[107]

This is another departure of great significance. No previous exponent of the natural law doctrine had seriously or consistently supposed that appeal to it might justify disobedience or rebellion or the overthrow of positive law. Plato and Aristotle had observed that political orders must conform to certain natural criteria if they are to answer to their purpose, but they had not suggested that the law of nature should function as a radical critique of existing institutions. To the Stoics, the law of nature is the law that the wise man will follow, but, with the possible exception of Cicero (see p. 123), there is no suggestion that it should in practice overrule the law of the State. In Roman jurisprudence, *ius naturale* came to be employed as a principle of equity whereby existing law might be modified as necessary and interpreted fairly and humanely; and we saw a similar principle at work earlier in Aristotle. According to Augustine, whose thought

The Augustinian Conception of Politics

may be taken as an inclusive formulation of the Patristic doctrine of natural law, we must obey even the exactions of tyrants. Augustine, as we have emphasised, is a legal positivist. We may challenge the powers that be if and only if they require us to betray our faith. In all other cases, we must comply with laws that we may perfectly well recognise as unjust under the 'eternal' law but which bind us nonetheless. In the *Decretum*, however, we find it stated as a principle that *any* legislation contrary to the natural law 'is to be considered null and void' and 'must be decisively rejected.' *Vana et irrita* is, literally, 'empty and laughable'; but it would be difficult to quarrel with 'null and void' as a translation. The principle is reiterated in comprehensive language by commentators on the *Decretum*.

> Any custom or constitution contrary to the law of nature with respect to command and prohibition must be judged *vana et irrita*, for the Lord said 'I am the Truth'; He did not say, 'I am custom or constitution.'[108]
>
> Whatever there may be in the laws of the emperors, in the writings of authorities or in the examples of the saints that is contrary to the natural law: all these things are to be held as *vana et irrita*.[109]

Here, in short, we have a doctrine of natural law that not only equates the natural law with the will of God as revealed in the Scriptures, but which also states in plain terms that any custom or constitution not in conformity with the natural law is 'empty,' 'vain,' 'laughable,' 'null and void,' and accordingly is to be 'decisively rejected.' A weighty question therefore arises: who is to decide when the natural law has been infringed, and who is to prescribe what ought to be done about it?

Between the fifth and the thirteenth centuries, a definite and influential body of opinion emerged in answer to this question. For the most part in response to confrontations with secular rulers over the differentiation of 'Church' and 'State,' the western Church formulated what may be called a thoroughgoing ideology of ecclesiastical supremacy: an ideology that, at its highest level of development, amounts to a theory of international government. It is appropriate to call this ideology 'political Augustinianism'[110] because, even where Augustine is not cited directly, it depends unmistakably upon political and social ideas contained in his writings, or capable of being extrapolated from them. As always, generalisation is difficult. Broadly speaking, however, 'political Augustinianism' in its most characteristic medieval form rests upon the following propositions:

(a) Secular politics is in the nature of the case a sordid and unworthy business. As Augustine makes clear, the governments of this world would not have come into being at all were it not for the sin of Adam and Eve. The powers that be are ordained of God, but they are ordained only to contain and punish the destructive behaviour of fallen humanity. Moreover, they are themselves characteristically motivated by selfish ambition and the love of mastery. In a long letter written in March 1081 to Hermann, Bishop of Metz, Pope Gregory VII repeats in trenchant terms the Augustinian principle that, of itself, kingship is an expression of avarice and pride.

> Who does not know that kings and princes derive their origin from men ignorant of God, who have raised themselves up above their fellows by pride, robbery, treachery, murder—in short, by every kind of crime—at the instigation of the devil?[111]

(b) 'Happiness' in anything like the Aristotelian sense—the realisation of human ethical potentialities—is simply not possible in this world. Earthly life is no more than a sorrowful journey towards the joys of the next world. To pursue happiness by material means is a delusion, and the right thinking individual will repudiate such means. No temporal institution, therefore, can have any value at all unless what it does is ordered to goals pertaining to the world to come; and, thanks to the pervasive and denaturing effects of sin, nothing can be ordered to the world to come except through the grace of God.

(c) But the grace of God comes into this world only through Christ and, since Christ's Ascension, through the Church that He created to act on His behalf. Inward and invisible grace is now mediated to us through the outward and visible sacraments of the Church, and those sacraments can be performed only under the Church's prescribed form. The mightiest king, Gregory VII observes, will on his deathbed implore the services of the humblest priest; but who in his last moments ever asked the help of an earthly king?[112]

(d) It follows that this world's rulers must regard themselves and their judgments as being entirely subject to the jurisdiction of the Church. Without such willing subjection, they are agents of sin merely. The duty of princes is to take care of those departments of life too squalid for the Church to soil her hands with—war, torture, punishment, suppression—or too trivial to be worthy of her consideration. Princes are, so to speak, appointed to do the humble and dirty work of this world. The eleventh-century pamphleteer Manegold of Lautenbach, in a little tract directed against the imperialist author Wenrich of Trier, goes so far as to suggest that a king who fails to secure the welfare of his subjects should be dismissed as readily as a swineherd who neglects his master's pigs; a rustic image, perhaps, but a revealing one.[113] In discharging their secular duties, princes must submit uncomplainingly to the will of the Church, and they must accept her censure if they go astray. The 'material sword' of princes is in all respects subject to the 'spiritual sword' of the Church. The Church possesses both swords, but she deputes the material sword to a subordinate hand. Since the material sword is hers to depute, it is also hers to remove from those whom she deems unworthy.[114]

(e) The 'two swords' language so commonly used in medieval political literature as a shorthand for distinguishing between spiritual and secular power is more than imagery. There is a literal sense also in which the prince receives a material sword from the hand of the Church: that is, when an actual sword is presented to him by the bishop or archbishop, along with the other symbols of his office, during his coronation. Beneath the pomp and circumstance of the king's crowning there is a political message. From the eighth century onwards, the western Church exploited to the full, albeit not always with complete success, the dramatic possibilities of coronation and anointing as ways of emphasising that the king's authority descends upon him from God through the agency of the Church.[115] Coronation rituals were conscious imitations of Biblical exemplars. Just as Saul was anointed by the prophet Samuel—and, of course, eventually deposed by him[116]—so are the kings and emperors of the present day anointed by bishops, archbishops and popes. The example most often mentioned in this connection is the coronation of the emperor Charlemagne by Pope Leo III on Christmas day 800: the act which, as popes and their publicists so tirelessly insisted, had effected the *translatio imperii*, the 'translation' of imperial authority from Byzantium to the west.

(f) For the most part, those who embrace this ideology of ecclesiastical supremacy use the terms 'Church' and 'pope' virtually as synonyms. The Church is an absolute monarchy with the pope at its head. Scripture gives us clear testimony of this. The pope is the successor of Peter, appointed by God as the 'Rock' upon whom the Church is built. Christ has entrusted to him the keys of the kingdom of Heaven: what he releases on earth is released in heaven; what he binds on earth is bound in heaven.[117] The pope is *vicarius Christi*, the 'vicar' or deputy of Christ. This papal title was introduced by the great thirteenth-century pope Innocent III (1198–1216). But as early as 360 or thereabouts, in an act of great symbolic significance, the emperor Gratian bestowed upon Pope Damasus I a title hitherto held by the Roman emperor and inherited by the pagan emperors from the magistracies of the republic: *Pontifex Maximus*, 'Supreme Pontiff.' The pope is the embodiment of the Church, the Pontiff of pontiffs. His will is the Church's will, and the Church's will is the will of God.

This ecclesiastical, and ultimately papalist, ideology developed not as an abstract principle, but during the course of several acrimonious controversies between the fifth and the fourteenth centuries, as popes and papal publicists strove to assert, first, the Church's independence of secular control and, increasingly, her superiority to all temporal rulers. The most important reference-points in the development of this ideology are the pontificates of Gelasius I (492–496), Gregory VII (1073–1085), Innocent III and Boniface VIII (1294–1303). In the twelfth century, shortly after the great contest over lay investiture between Gregory VII and the emperor Henry IV, we find it articulated for the first time as a definite theory of politics in the *Policraticus* (ca 1159) of the English cleric John of Salisbury.[118] John wants us to think that he is paraphrasing a work of Plutarch called *Institutio Traiani*; but no one else has heard of such a work, and there is no reason to think that it ever existed. John is in fact systematising,

The Augustinian Conception of Politics

with Plutarch invoked to provide classical respectability, ecclesiological views that the Investiture Controversy had brought to the fore, but which come from much older roots. The commonwealth, he says, may be likened to the human body. The prince is its head; the Senate is its heart; officials and soldiers are its hands, and so on. But the soul of the body politic is the Church. The prince receives the 'sword of blood' at the Church's hand, and he must submit to the governance of the Church just as, in the actual body, the head must submit to the governance of the soul. The prince's function is not to make law, but to discover and enact 'the justice of God, Whose justice is eternal justice and Whose law is equity'; and it is interesting to note that John here cites Chrysippus and the Roman jurist Papinian as part of his discussion of law and equity.[119] In performing his function, the prince must submit to the guidance and correction of the Church. The tyrant is now defined not as a ruler who exploits his subjects, but as one who will not bring his laws into line with the Church's interpretations. Perhaps the two come to the same thing, but the mode of expression is significant. Errant princes may be deposed by the Church. Indeed, in sufficiently grave cases she may authorise or condone tyrannicide.

Some forty years after the *Policraticus*, in defence of his own intervention in a major international dispute, Innocent III insisted that the pope may take cognisance of any temporal case whatsoever in which sin is involved,[120] and in this he was sustained by an influential body of canonist commentary.[121] The decretal *Novit* at once became an authority of great weight and influence. By the end of the thirteenth century and in the early decades of the fourteenth, learned publicists—Giles of Rome (1247–1316), Bl. James of Viterbo (ca 1255–1308), Augustinus Triumphus (1243–1328), Alvarus Pelagius (ca 1275–1349)—were writing treatises intended to prove that the pope is the supreme ruler of the whole world, with fullness of power— *plenitudo potestatis*—in temporal and spiritual matters alike.[122] All temporal power is given, and may be removed, by the Church. Princes must submit entirely to the will of the pope, and may be deposed if they fail or refuse to do so. The pope has authority in all temporal matters whatsoever *ratione peccati*, 'by reason of sin,' and resistance to him is itself a mortal sin. All property of whatever kind is held of him subject to good behaviour, and he may, if he thinks fit, confiscate the property of the unrighteous and transfer it to others. If he does not usually do this, this is not because he may not, but because the Church is kind and merciful even to sinners. The pope may adjudicate all disputes, domestic and international; from him there is no appeal; he himself is bound only by the natural law. Nor is his authority confined to the institutional Church. The Spanish Franciscan Alvarus Pelagius, whose *De planctu ecclesiae* was written in about 1332, holds that unbelievers, Jews and Saracens are all as much subject to papal authority as Christians are, *de iure* even if not *de facto*. The pope

> rules and disposes all things; he orders and governs everything as he pleases...He can deprive any person of his right, as it pleases him, for with him his will is right and reason: whatever pleases him has the force of law.[123]

It goes without saying that such grandiloquent claims did not pass without remonstrance. Throughout the recurrent medieval debates about 'Church' and State,' there is an extensive royalist and civilian literature, associated particularly with the kingdom of France, arguing for the independence of secular rulers from the Church. The powers that be are ordained of God; temporal princes are elected directly by God; they are only blessed or confirmed, not appointed, by the Church; they are answerable to God alone in temporal matters, and to the Church only in spiritual ones.[124] But the ecclesiastical case is in general far more impressive than the royalist one. This is due partly to the fact that, down to the thirteenth century, the spokesmen of the Church had on the whole a much more assured and educated grasp of the issues than did those of kings and emperors. More importantly, the argument that princes are subject to the pope only in spiritual matters foundered invariably upon a single rock: the rejoinder that there is absolutely nothing on earth that is not in principle a spiritual matter. Giles of Rome, writing on the papal side during the great conflict of 1296–1303 between Pope Boniface VIII and Philip IV of France, has this to say:

> [S]ince, in a sense, all crimes and all mortal sins can be called spiritual in that they slay our spirit and our soul, it follows that the spiritual power will be able to intervene in disputes involving any temporal questions

> whatsoever if those disputes are brought forward in connection with an allegation of crime. For it rests with the spiritual power to judge every mortal sin and to rebuke every Christian for it. Otherwise, God would not have said, at Matthew 18, 'And if your brother should sin against you, go and rebuke him between yourself and him; and if he will not hear you, take one or two persons with you; and if he will not hear them, tell the Church.' He would not have said this if it did not rest with the Church to rebuke every Christian for every mortal sin. Therefore it is clear that this condition, by reason of which the Church can concern herself with temporal things and by reason of which appeal can be made to the Church on temporal questions, is so broad and ample that it may embrace all temporal disputes whatsoever, since such a dispute can always involve an allegation of crime.[125]

This, within its own terms, is an unanswerable argument. Every dispute over right and wrong is a dispute over sin and non-sin, and no one can deny that the pope is the final earthly judge in matters of sin. The pope alone may interpret for us the Divine law as revealed in the Scriptures. He may do so by virtue of the authority to which, as Peter's successor, he is heir.

But if Divine law and natural law are one and the same, as the canonists insist, it follows that the only correct reading of natural law, the only true version of right reason, is the pope's. Thus 'his will is right and reason; whatever pleases him has the force of law' and, by the same token, whatever displeases him is 'null and void.' By the end of the thirteenth century, we find that the idea of natural law has been to all intents and purposes engulfed by that of Divine law. We find also that it has been pressed into the service of an ambitious theory of papal absolutism. In the final analysis, this theory is Augustinian in origin and spirit, though its exponents often read and expound Augustine with a good deal of wishful thinking.[126] It is, we might say, the medieval culmination of the transvaluation of classical anthropology that Christianity appears to make necessary and over which St Augustine so largely presided. Within the terms of this theory of papal absolutism, the pope has authority to chastise monarchs and even depose them. What this means in practice is that he can dispense subjects from their oath of allegiance; he can command a crusading army to invade the territory of an intransigent prince; he can place the territory of such a prince under papal interdict. In short, he can do anything he likes, and he is responsible for his stewardship of God's sheep only to God. The law of nature, the law of right reason, has become a kind of monopoly; it has become transmuted into the property of the Church. There is no such thing as government, and no such thing as citizenship, considered apart from dutiful submission to her will.

Chapter 7

St Thomas Aquinas: The Recovery of Aristotle and the Rehabilitation of Politics

THE MEDIEVAL transmutation of natural law arguments into arguments about the revealed law of God was, as we have seen, a process driven during several centuries by controversy of a political or quasi-political kind. Down to the end of the thirteenth century, the most effective and substantial work in political theory was done by ecclesiastics wishing to defend and advance the temporal claims of the Church, and especially of the papacy, against the pretensions of kings and emperors. By contrast, St Thomas Aquinas was not a partisan in any political dispute. His philosophy, to the extent that it is controversial at all, is the product of a recondite intellectual battle over the acceptability, from the point of view of Catholic orthodoxy, of the philosophy of Aristotle. He has relatively little, and nothing new, to say on the subject of 'Church' and 'State.' It is not his purpose either to affirm or deny papal or ecclesiastical supremacy in temporals. His position with regard to this thorny issue is vague and, insofar as he states it at all, moderate and unremarkable.[1] His life was one of seclusion and scholarship. His importance to us lies in the contrast between his political thought and the Augustinian tradition that we have described in our two previous chapters. He was at the forefront of an intellectual movement that was substantially to undermine the theoretical foundations of medieval papalism and, more broadly, to contribute to a large-scale redefinition of political activity and political morality.[2] It is with St Thomas's rehabilitation of politics that we shall here be concerned. In particular, we shall examine the reunion of ethics and politics over which he presided to so great a degree, and his development in this context of a doctrine of natural law distinguished by unprecedented comprehensiveness and rigour.

So significant a figure deserves a paragraph of biography. The details of St Thomas's life, and especially of its closing phase, are much distorted by hagiography, but the outlines are clear. Although he abstained from public affairs and sought no worldly advancement, he was not isolated from the activities and outlooks of contemporary politics. He was born in the castle of Roccasecca, near Naples, in 1225.[3] His father, Landulph, was Count of Aquino; Theodora, his mother, Countess of Teano; his family was related to the emperors Henry VI and Frederick II, and to the Kings of Aragon, France and Castile. In adult life, St Thomas was on terms of friendship with Louis IX of France. He began his education in 1230 as an oblate at the Benedictine monastery of Monte Cassino, where his uncle, Landulph Sinibaldi, was abbot. At the age of thirteen, he entered the Benedictine *Studium generale* at Naples. At some point between 1243 and 1245, to the dismay of his ambitious parents, he became a member of the mendicant Dominican order. In 1245 the order sent him to the University of Paris, partly, it seems, to get him away from his family. There, he came under the influence of the Swabian theologian Albertus Magnus. In 1248 he followed Albertus to the new Dominican *Studium generale* at Cologne. Between 1252 and 1256, in preparation for his *licentia docendi*, he compiled his *Scripta super libros sententiarum*, the dissertation on the *Sentences* of Peter Lombard that, by the thirteenth century, had become a standard part of medieval university education. He received his *licentia*—his 'Master's degree'—in 1256, and spent the next eighteen years teaching and studying at Paris, Naples, Orvieto, Viterbo and Rome. His *Summa contra gentiles*, a handbook for missionaries to the Moslems and Jews of Spain and North Africa, was completed at Orvieto in 1264. He began his *magnum opus*, the *Summa theologiae*, at Rome in 1266 and worked on it more or less continuously, with the aid of relays of secretaries, until his constitution failed him seven years later. During a final period at the University of Paris between 1269 and 1272 he found time also to write a dozen commentaries on the works of Aristotle, including the *Nicomachean Ethics* and *Politics*.[4] Not surprisingly, in view of his astonishing workload, his health began to deteriorate in 1273. At Naples in December, he suffered a sudden and debilitating illness, perhaps a stroke. Evidently in a weakened condition he left Naples in February 1274 to attend the second Council of Lyons, to which he and St Bonaventure had been summoned by Pope Gregory X. He died on the journey, at the Cistercian abbey of Fessa Nuova, on 7 March, 1274. *Doctrina ejus*, said Pope John XXII, canonising him in 1323, *non potuit esse sine miraculo*: 'His teaching could not exist without a miracle.'[5]

Christian Aristotelianism: the Reunion of Ethics and Politics

What above all distinguishes St Thomas's philosophy from that of his medieval forebears is the way in which, considered under virtually every aspect, it reflects ideas and habits of thought associated with Aristotle. It is in respect of his Aristotelianism that St Thomas is the most eminent contributor to what may be called an intellectual revolution.[6] In order to understand this revolution, it is necessary to remember that from the fifth down to the late twelfth and early thirteenth centuries, the philosophical work of Aristotle was effectively unknown in the west. *Hiatus valde deflendus*, perhaps, especially from the point of view of political philosophy; but the absence of Aristotle is on almost every front due to the supremacy of Platonism, especially as transmitted through the works of St Augustine,[7] as the philosophical system apparently most congenial to the Christian world-view. The esteem in which St Augustine and his intellectual descendants were held had the effect of closing off other streams of philosophy from the intellectual life of the European Middle Ages. If this is not quite true, it is true enough as a general statement. Aristotle's logical writings, the *Categories* and *De interpretatione*, were known through the sixth-century Latin translations of Boethius (480–525). But most of Aristotle's other works, displaced from Latin curricula by the pre-eminence of Christian Neoplatonism, had been translated from the Greek not into Latin, but into inaccessible Semitic languages: into Syriac at the school of Edessa during the fourth and fifth centuries, and into Arabic during the ninth century, after the establishment of a school of translators at Baghdad. A consequence of this development was that the study of the Aristotelian corpus was for many years the province of Arab commentators, the most distinguished of whom were Avicenna (980–1037) and Averroes (1126–1196). That so many works of Greek science and philosophy became known to the Latin world during the thirteenth century is due to the activity of a handful of scholarly orientalists: Gerard of Cremona (d. 1187), Michael Scotus (d. 1235) Albertus Magnus (d. 1280) and especially William of Moerbeke (d. 1286), who was the first (ca 1260) to make a Latin translation, inelegant but literal, of the *Politics*. These scholars drew freely on the work of their Arab exemplars, particularly Averroes. His western admirers refer to Averroes as 'the Commentator' with the same intention of respect as that with which St Thomas almost always calls Aristotle 'the Philosopher.' The study of Aristotle came in the thirteenth century to be associated especially with the University of Paris, and it was there, under the tutelage of Albertus Magnus, that St Thomas began to be acquainted with him. St Thomas also knew and encouraged William of Moerbeke and worked with him for a short while, probably at Viterbo during 1267–68.

The University of Paris was a prestigious royal foundation, established by Philip Augustus in 1200 and generously endowed by Louis IX.[8] But, like the medieval Universities in general, its activities were subject to the supervision, sometimes heavy-handed, of the ecclesiastical authorities; and the response of the Church to the renewal of interest in Aristotle was one of suspicion and opposition. To some extent, this response reflects a conservative institution's dislike of novelty. It was not, however, without rational foundation. St Bonaventure (1221–1274) in particular is a thorough critic of Aristotle's metaphysics from the standpoint of Catholic orthodoxy. Aristotle had believed that the world is eternal, thereby denying the truth of Creation.[9] His critique of the Platonic theory of ideas (see pp. 83–85) implicitly denied God's knowledge of particulars, and of Divine foreknowledge and providence.[10] Apart from his native unsoundness as a pagan philosopher, the fact that Aristotle had been so much handled by heretics and unbelievers—first by the Nestorian Christians of Edessa and then by Arab commentators—was enough to make him an object of suspicion. Certain of the interpretations of Averroes were especially at odds with the fundamentals of Christianity. The doctrine attributed by Averroes to Aristotle of the numerical identity of the intellect in all men was rejected by the orthodox as being incompatible with the true notion of person and with personal immortality. This was an Averroist error into which the poet Dante was to fall in his little imperialist treatise of ca 1310 called *De monarchia*.[11] As St Bonaven-

St Thomas: The Rehabilitation of Politics

ture observes, it is a doctrine that entails a denial of individual blessedness or punishment after death.[12] But the interpretations of Aristotle that had been developed *in partibus infidelium* found Latin champions nonetheless, notably in Siger of Brabant (1240–1281), Professor of Philosophy at Paris.[13] The result was an angry and protracted controversy. The Church found especially unacceptable the tendency of Christian Averroists to espouse the so-called 'twofold truth' theory: a contrivance intended to make the study of Aristotle according to Arab interpretations compatible with the profession of Christianity. This theory involved a curious and uncomfortable view: that a proposition may at one and the same time be philosophically true and theologically false.[14] Growing ecclesiastical disquiet led, in 1270, to the condemnation of thirteen Aristotelian propositions as heretical by Bishop Étienne Tempier of Paris. This condemnation reiterated earlier condemnations of 1210, 1231 and 1263, which had mostly been ignored. Dispute and ill will continued well after the death of St Thomas in 1274. In January 1277, Pope John XXI asked the Bishop of Paris again to investigate a rumour that error was being taught at the University. Two months later, after what seems to have been a hasty and ill-conducted enquiry,[15] Bishop Tempier extended his condemnation to 219 propositions.[16] Teachers at the University were forbidden on pain of excommunication 'to teach or defend or sustain in any way' (*dogmatizare aut defendere seu sustinere quoquo modo*)[17] the condemned propositions. In the same year, a similar condemnation was issued in England by Archbishop Kilwardby of Canterbury.

St Thomas's scholarly life was therefore passed in an atmosphere of sustained hostility to Aristotle. It is not too much to say that for a teacher to show an interest in Aristotelian philosophy was to invite professional ruin or worse. One can only admire the persistence with which, having no reason to suppose that his arguments would one day come to be thought definitive, St Thomas stuck to the view reflected in the whole of his philosophical output: that nothing in the teaching of Aristotle himself is contrary to the Christian faith. It is possible to retrieve Aristotle's teaching from the erroneous constructions and interpretations of the Arabs. Reduced to its pure form, that teaching can be reconciled with the doctrines of the Church, and this can be done without recourse to the dubious expedient of 'twofold truth.' Aristotle, though he lacked the advantage of Divine revelation, and though his understanding of truth was to that extent defective, had carried intellectual investigation as far as reason can go without Divine assistance. When his conclusions are corrected by the addition of revealed truth, the resulting integration of reason and revelation will be an intellectually complete system. So St Thomas believed. To produce such an integration, and to do so by the kind of minute analysis displayed in the *Summa theologiae*, became his life's work. He, more than anyone else, is responsible for completing what has become known as the 'recovery' of Aristotle: the reinstatement of a purified Aristotelianism to the educational curriculum of the west. St Thomas's project is nothing less than to construct an entirely new synthetic philosophy: a philosophy of Christian Aristotelianism embracing not only ethics and politics but physics, metaphysics and epistemology also, insofar as these disciplines lend themselves to the service of Christian doctrine. It is a measure of his achievement that, for better or worse, this Christian Aristotelianism was to be the centrepiece of Roman Catholic philosophical education down to the second half of the twentieth century.

In examining St Thomas's political ideas, we run up against a difficulty similar to, though less acute than, that which we mentioned in relation to St Augustine. St Thomas is not primarily a political theorist. Many of his remarks on political and social questions arise in connection with, and in subordination to, other philosophical and theological themes. There is no treatise in which his political 'philosophy' is set forth as a whole. As with St Augustine, St Thomas's political and social thought has to be compiled from a range of sources. The longest uninterrupted account of it occurs in the little *speculum principis* known in some manuscript sources as *De regimine principum* (*On the Government of Princes*) and in others as *De regno* (*On Kingship*). St Thomas's authorship of *De regimine principum* has been questioned from time to time; but the preponderance of scholarly opinion favours authenticity.[18] The work, written in about 1267, is short because unfinished. Dedicated *ad regem Cypri*, 'to the king of Cyprus,' it consists of the first part and the first six and a half chapters of the second part of a much longer book, eventually completed by St Thomas's pupil and friend Bartolomeo Fiadoni, also called Tolommeo of Lucca (b. ca 1227).[19] Most of the rest of St Thomas's political thought is found at various locations in the massive *Summa theologiae*, and especially at Ia

IIae 90–108: the section sometimes, though misleadingly, called *Tractatus de legibus*.[20] Other material comes in his commentaries on Aristotle's *Politics* and *Nicomachean Ethics* and in the *Scripta super libros sententiarum* (although this *Jugendwerk* should not necessarily be taken as expressing his settled view). On the one hand, therefore, the reader must again keep in mind that the kind of 'reconstruction' undertaken in this chapter tends to make St Thomas's thought seem more connected than it is. On the other, there are no very serious problems of coherence. When all is said and done, the task of reconstruction is, as it was in the case of St Augustine, largely unproblematical.[21]

As one might expect, St Thomas's Aristotelianism gives a distinctive character to his thinking on politics and morality: a character very different from the Platonist and Augustinian orientations typical of medieval controversy as we have described it. With qualifications arising from the requirements of Christian doctrine, the contrast between St Thomas and St Augustine resembles that which we noted as between Aristotle and Plato (see pp. 85–86). St Thomas is much readier than St Augustine is to look for truth and value, at least of a certain kind, within the world of ordinary experience rather than beyond it. Whereas the kind of 'Augustinian' theory sketched in our two previous chapters had set so much of the tone of political debate in the west from the fifth century down to the thirteenth, in the middle years of the thirteenth century we find St Thomas developing a form of political understanding systematically more humane and optimistic than that associated with St Augustine. St Thomas's thought displays these features because it lacks the insistence, so characteristic of Christian Platonism, on the unworthiness of this world and its ends when measured against the transcendence of the 'other' or supernatural world. Having said this, it should be noted that St Thomas never contradicts St Augustine explicitly. On the contrary, in all departments of philosophy he is careful, sometimes to the point of contrivance and artificiality, to validate his arguments by bringing them into harmony with the Christian authorities of the past. His punctiliousness in this regard no doubt reflects his awareness of the controversial nature of the task of making Aristotle respectable. Nonetheless, the contrast between St Thomas's political and social ideas and those of Augustinian Platonism is real and of the first importance. It is the key to understanding St Thomas's significance in relation to the decline of 'political Augustinianism' in western political thought.

We may begin to bring out this contrast in the following terms. As we have so much emphasised, St Augustine, with his eyes fixed on a realm above and beyond our own, had found the present order of things unnatural and disordered. There are rational standards of goodness and justice, but most people are cut off from them completely, and everyone is cut off from them to some extent, by the defect of will sustained by humanity at the Fall. This world's political arrangements are harsh and coercive; the justice and peace that they create are inauthentic; in our present life, we can expect only pain, trial and war. Like Tertullian, though without Tertullian's repudiation of philosophy, Augustine is a disjunctive thinker. He is more at home with sharp and dramatic divisions than with integration and continuity. To his mind, the individual is aligned either with earth or with heaven, with the natural or the supernatural; and to be allied to the one is to be estranged from the other. We have one true end only. That end does not belong to this world, and the things of this world have no contribution to make to the ethical good of the Elect. Augustine had accepted that the *civitas Dei peregrina* can make use of this world's resources, including its 'peace' and 'justice,' and that such use can be a limited kind of good. But he had insisted as a matter of principle that earthly 'goods' are not real goods. The only true goods lie beyond earthly endeavour, and most individuals are deluded in what they suppose to be valuable. For the most part, Augustine regards the things of this world as an encumbrance and a snare, distracting us from our true purposes and full of spiritual danger.

It is hardly surprising that so complete a discounting of earthly goods by the greatest of the Fathers should have had a negative effect on the Church's perception of the political. More to the point, it is not surprising that Augustine's evaluation of material things should have lent itself so readily to a theory of spiritual, and hence ecclesiastical, supremacy. It is this evaluation that had led Gregory VII, in his letter of 1081 to Hermann of Metz, to assert in so many words that unless their rule is underwritten by ecclesiastical approval, earthly kings are no more than instruments of the devil. St Thomas, by contrast, departs from the ethical and anthropological presuppositions of St Augustine. In so doing, he departs also from the conclusions about the moral quality of earthly life that those presuppositions support. Intellectually, this departure is to be attributed almost wholly to the influence of Aristotle. For St Thomas, there is not a 'Platonist' divide between the sordid things of this world and the sublime things of the world to come. He accepts Aristotle's teleology and the eudaimonist ethic that is a part of it. 'The object of the will,' he says, 'that is, of the human appetite, is that which is universally good, just as the object of the intellect is that which is universally true.'[22] And he sees no reason why Aristotle's teleology should not apply to this world as well as to the next. It is true that man's complete or perfect happiness—his true *finis* or 'end,' the Aristotelian *eudaimonia*—consists in the Beatific Vision of God in heaven.[23] This is a truth of which Aristotle, being without the benefit of revelation, could not be aware. But the fact that our final happiness lies elsewhere than in this world does not, for St Thomas, imply that happiness or wellbeing in this world is merely fraudulent, or that earthly life cannot include morally meaningful acts and relationships. Nor does he hold or assume that most human beings are self-centred moral defectives. Man, he says, in his commentary on the *Nicomachean Ethics*, is 'naturally part of some community by which he is enabled to live well'; and we must be clear about what he means by 'well.' The sharing of life with other human beings is, he thinks, necessary to an individual for two reasons:

> First, it is necessary to provide him with those things without which he cannot conduct this present life at all...But life in a community further enables man to achieve a complete sufficiency of life: that is, *not merely to live, but to live well and to have everything necessary to a complete life*. In this sense, the civic community of which he is a part assists him to obtain not merely the corporeal benefits produced by the many activities of a city, but moral wellbeing also.[24]

It will be seen at once that this statement replicates Aristotle's account of the relation between politics and ethics. Human beings are capable after all of the kind of mutual association and ethical purposes celebrated by Aristotle and identified by Cicero as a constitutive ingredient of a commonwealth. St Thomas finds nothing to quarrel with in the rational and justly ordered world depicted by the Philosopher: a world in which everything has its own end and, related to that end, its own kind of good. He believes in the capacity of ordinary men to make rational, free and responsible choices. He believes also that men are capable of co-operating for the sake of common advantage, and that the goods secured by such co-operation are genuine goods, albeit partial ones. They include intellectual and moral satisfactions as well as material wellbeing. Certainly, the goods of this world can be misused through an inordinate love of them. St Thomas is as much aware as St Augustine is that we live in a sinful world. But there is no *a priori* reason for supposing earthly things to be only regrettable necessities, objects of self-centred lust or worthless copies of heavenly exemplars. As long as we are aware of our ultimate goal and do nothing to compromise it, and as long as we direct all earthly goods towards heavenly ones, we can legitimately pursue earthly wellbeing. Temporal prosperity and happiness, such as they are, are legitimate purposes of which we have no reason to be ashamed. We can identify the goods of this world, estimate them at their true value, and use them responsibly. In this way, earthly things can be intermediate or 'proximate' ends leading us towards our highest and final end, and certainly not obliterated or cancelled out by it.

But because he believes that earthly wellbeing is both possible and desirable, St Thomas accords to the political means by which it is secured a degree of intrinsic worth ruled out by the presuppositions of 'political Augustinianism.' St Thomas several times repeats with approval the 'political animal' maxim of Aristotle's *Politics* (though he does so in a form differing slightly from that given in William of Moerbeke's translation): [25] *Naturale autem est homini ut sit animal sociale et politicum*; literally, 'It is natural to man that he be a social and political animal.'[26] Clearly, this maxim runs counter to the Augustinian insistence that God 'did not intend that His rational creature, made in His own image, should have lordship over anything but the non-rational creation: not man over man, but man over the beasts.' For St Thomas, government is not 'Augustinian' government. It is not a punitive and disciplinary order ordained to do little more than hold the lid on human destructiveness by force and fear. It is capable of achieving genuine justice, understood, in the classical sense that St Augustine had analysed, as rendering to each what is due to each.[27] It is a benign administration suited to the kind of sociable and co-operating creature that man is by nature, and appropriate to his needs. It is able to provide real goods in which all those subject to it can share.

What, in precise terms, are these goods? In describing them, St Thomas follows Aristotle exactly.[28] It is a defining feature of human nature that all men desire, and are capable of achieving, what Aristotle had called *autarkeia*: 'self-sufficiency.' Subject to the modifications required by Christian belief, St Thomas means by 'self-sufficiency' what Aristotle had meant. Within the constraints of our earthly condition, we can secure both material and ethical goods. St Thomas attributes to the human faculty of reason a far greater capacity and autonomy than Augustine does. Man is a rational creature, able by ingenuity to achieve his own purposes insofar as those purposes are temporal rather than supernatural. But it is as obvious to St Thomas as it had been to Aristotle than no individual can furnish himself with everything that is necessary to life. At the material level, we need to co-operate in order to secure the benefits of a division of labour. Co-operation comes naturally to us. We are sinful, weak and fallible, and often led astray by the strength of our own desires; but we are not the helplessly selfish and destructive creatures that Augustine thinks we are. Genuine co-operation, as distinct from forced compliance with an order that manipulates our behaviour through punishment and reward, is possible. But such co-operation needs to be guided and supervised if it is to achieve its ends. Moreover, not only is the individual insufficiently versatile to meet all his material needs unaided. Also, we are in some ways more vulnerable than the beasts, who are better equipped than we are by nature with the means of defence or flight and who are able to know by instinct what is harmful to them. Speech and rationality—the capacity to deliberate, draw conclusions, make choices and achieve shared purposes—are the gifts of God that equip us to compensate for this disadvantage in securing our own safety. We need to organise the means of our livelihood, protection and defence by the application of reason to our situation. But there is almost always more than one way to achieve our purposes. Unco-ordinated effort is likely to be wasted effort. Nothing constructive could be accomplished if each individual were left alone to pursue whatever course of action happened to suggest itself to him. None of these considerations as such has anything to do with our fallen condition. The facts that make it necessary for us to live and work together are facts of human nature as God created it. They did not come into being because of the Fall, and they would have obtained even had the Fall not happened. They are the facts that make it necessary for a community to be knit together by wise leadership and directed to the common good. Wherever there is a multitude with a common good to be attained, there must be some common ruling power. We need to be guided towards our goals by a prudent ruler just as a ship needs to be steered into harbour by a skilful pilot. The chief purpose of government is not suppression and punishment, but the achievement of earthly wellbeing through the rational organisation of collective effort.

Nor, we say again, is earthly wellbeing only a matter of bodily protection and economic satisfaction. St Augustine had insisted that temporal government is an external order only. It is moreover a penal and disciplinary order, to be endured by the Elect and feared, served and placated by the lost. Human law can accomplish no more than the enforcement of outward conformity. It cannot touch us as moral beings because it has no purpose 'other than that men should possess those things that can be called "ours" for the time being, and to which they cling so greedily, in such a way that peace and human society may be preserved insofar as they can be preserved in such matters.' But St Thomas revives an Aristotelian doctrine that adds an important dimension to our understanding of positive law. He holds that the law of a community, by requiring us to conform to its norms, not only controls us but can train us in good habits until those habits become spontaneous and therefore genuinely virtuous. In this way, law can reinforce and develop the 'infused' virtues that we already have by nature because God has implanted them in us.[29]

> [A]cquiring the habit of virtuous action contributes to virtue...And since law is given for the purpose of directing human acts, then, insofar as human acts conduce to virtue, law to that extent makes men good. Hence the Philosopher says in the *Ethics* that 'legislators make men good by habituating them to good works.'[30]

St Thomas also follows Aristotle in believing that an ordered and cooperative life with others can be a source of virtue and happiness in itself, apart from any material benefit associated with it and apart from the direct educative influence of law. Each individual, as a 'social and political animal,' is naturally part of a whole. Our sense of wellbeing cannot be completed other than through conscious participation in the wellbeing of others. In the commonwealth, as in any whole, the good of its parts and the good of the whole are related intimately, and a truly human good cannot be accomplished until individual goods are ordered to the collective good. In St Thomas, therefore, we encounter again the conception of political association that had effectively disappeared in the tradition of Christian political thought inaugurated by St Augustine: an organic conception resembling in all important respects that of the classical *polis*.

> [T]he end for which a community is brought together is to live according to virtue; for men come together so that they may live well in a way that would not be possible for each of them living singly. For the good is life according to virtue, and so the end of human association is a virtuous life.[31]

In this way, the commonwealth is restored to its status as an ethical, rather than a merely instrumental, community: an agency not of control alone, but of individual and collective moral wellbeing and growth.

Government as Natural Condition

For St Thomas, as one might expect, submission to the rule of another is not foreign to our nature as rational creatures. Contrary to what St Augustine had argued, the institution of government is not at odds with the fact that we are made in the image of God. On the one hand, all men are moral equals inasmuch as all have the same ultimate end. With respect to this end, there is no difference between one man and another in the sight of God. On the other, there are, in the realm of means, material senses in which we are not equal. No one need regard these inequalities as regrettable or unnatural. God has created a world of beauty and diversity in which all things work together for a total good that only He can see.[32] Some men are naturally wiser and stronger, and therefore better equipped to govern, than others; and 'if there were one man pre-eminent over others in terms of knowledge and justice, it would be inconsistent [with the idea of moral pre-eminence] if this pre-eminence were not deployed for the benefit of the others.'[33] This, again, is a familiar Aristotelian principle: it is natural and right that we should be subject to our natural superiors. Just as it is natural for material objects to be moved by stronger forces of nature, so is it natural for human beings to be 'moved'—to be induced to act—by the commands of those who are best fitted to lead them.[34] The comparison is perhaps factitious, but the point of it is plain. Differing human capacities are not deformities produced by sin. They reflect differences that would have been present as between individuals even had our first parents not made their fatal concession to temptation. The subjection of inferiors to superiors is part of the Divinely-willed order, and it is God's will that we should obey our natural superiors in all that they may lawfully command.[35] Dominion and rule are expressions of human law; but the Divine law, which is a law of grace, does not abolish human law, which arises from natural reason.[36] Christians must not suppose that their having become Christians exempts them from obedience to the secular powers.[37] Obedience is the virtue which, by its habituating influence, reinforces all the other virtues in us.[38] Of itself, even the distinction between Christians and unbelievers is without political significance. The rule of unbelievers over the faithful, at least where such rule is already established, is legitimate, provided only that it does not involve scandal or danger to the faith.[39] St Augustine had said some very similar things; but, unlike St Augustine, St Thomas holds that the subjection of some men to others would have been necessary and right even had mankind not fallen. The fact that it is right for some to rule and others to be ruled has nothing to do with sin. It has to do with the nature, needs and aptitudes of human beings as such.

Given, then, that government is natural and right and can confer both material and moral goods on us, St Augustine's view, that it does not matter under what form of government someone lives as long as his faith is not endangered, no longer holds. Earthly life is no longer to be seen only as a pilgrimage towards something lying beyond it. Earthly life itself, and hence the means whereby it is organised, is, within limits, a good. It is therefore entirely in keeping with his Christian Aristotelianism that St Thomas should revert to the classical practice of discussing the best form of government. His opinion on this question is nowhere expressed as a single statement. It needs to be pieced together from *De regimine principum* and from several passages in the *Summa*. But the picture to which these sev-

St Thomas: The Rehabilitation of Politics

eral sources contribute is coherent, and, to anyone who knows Aristotle's *Politics*, predictable.

At *De regimine principum* 1:3–4, St Thomas holds that the kind of leadership that the human condition requires is best provided by a king. This preference is consistent with the general medieval inclination towards monarchy, but St Thomas's arguments in favour of it combine Biblical and Aristotelian elements also. What commends kingship, he thinks, is precisely its consonance with nature. Everything in nature originates from unity: the one God is the Creator of all the diversity that we experience. Kingship, because it is government by one, is the most natural, and hence the best, kind of government. The unity and co-operation that peace and prosperity require are most readily achieved by a government that is itself one. The archetype of all government is God's government of the universe, and we see the principle of monarchy exemplified everywhere in the natural order. The body is ruled by the heart; the soul is ruled by reason. St Thomas follows Aristotle in citing the 'king' bee as a typical example of monarchy in nature.[40] Kingship is also the most efficient kind of government, and therefore the form most conducive to the common good. Its efficiency is due to the simple fact that unity cannot be at odds with itself. Under kingship, the power to initiate action and supervise its execution is undivided, and the king is able to act quickly and decisively. By the same reasoning, monarchy perverted into tyranny is the most efficient, and hence the worst, kind of bad government. But monarchy is also the form of government least likely to become perverted. Morally and institutionally, it is the most reliable kind of government because it is not subject to the stresses that arise when power is shared between individuals who will inevitably envy and resent one another:

> For where a number of persons rule and dissension arises, it often happens that one man overcomes the rest and usurps to himself dominion over the whole community...In almost every case of government by many, the outcome has been tyranny, as appears manifestly in the case of the Roman republic.[41]

One suspects that, in saying this, St Thomas has in mind a comparison as between the cities and provinces of his native Italy and the centralised monarchy of France under which he passed so much of his life.

But though he favours strong and efficient kingship, and though this preference is consistent with his having spent so much of his career in Paris, the Capetian capital, St Thomas is by no means a supporter of absolute monarchy.[42] In that part of *De regimine principum* usually attributed to him, the discussion of governmental forms is incomplete. In the *Summa*, he again recommends kingship, but the kingship that he depicts there is a kingship blended with elements of democracy and aristocracy.

> Of the different kinds of rule that the Philosopher discusses at *Politics* 3,[43] the foremost are kingship, in which one man governs according to virtue, and aristocracy, that is, the power of the best men, in which a few govern according to virtue. Hence the best ordering of government in any city or kingdom is achieved when one man is chosen to preside over all according to virtue; when he has under him others who govern according to virtue; and when such government nonetheless belongs to all, both because all are eligible for election to it and because it is elected by all.

Balanced or mixed government of this kind St Thomas calls 'polity,' the Latin word *politia* being a straightforward transliteration of Aristotle's πολῖτεία (*politeia*).[44] Such 'polity' is, St Thomas thinks, the form of government least susceptible to disruption. Its stability is due to the fact that it is

> a benign mixture of kingship, because there is one man who presides; of aristocracy, because it is the rule of several according to virtue; and of democracy, that is, popular power, because the rulers can be elected from the people and it belongs to the people to elect the rulers.[45]

This remark of St Thomas reflects Aristotle's belief in the difference that can be made to the success or failure of a constitution by the subjective perceptions of those who live under it. A government in which different constitutional elements are blended in the manner described will tend to endure because it will be acceptable to all sections of the community. No significant part of the community will have an interest in subverting the government, because no one will feel alienated or excluded from a sense of participation in it.

Despite what some commentators have thought, St Thomas's remarks in the *Summa* about 'mixed' government are not inconsistent with what he says about kingship in *De regimine principum*. There is

St Thomas: The Rehabilitation of Politics 225

no reason to suppose that St Thomas ever intended to advocate unlimited monarchy. At *De regimine principum* 1:7 he says:

> Once the king has been appointed, the government of the kingdom should be so arranged as to remove from the king the opportunity of becoming a tyrant; and, at the same time, his power should be restricted so that he will not easily be able to fall into tyranny. How these things can be done will have to be discussed in subsequent chapters.

He did not write the 'subsequent chapters,' but it is reasonable to conjecture that, had he continued with *De regimine principum*, he would have qualified his preference for monarchy by adding aristocratic and democratic elements as precautions against tyranny, as he does in the *Summa*. To make this addition is in no way at variance with the assertion that kingship is best because one. The 'polity' described in the passage from the *Summa* quoted above combines the advantages of unity with safeguards against its dangers. The king may have elected ministers or advisers 'under him'; he may owe his own original elevation to election; and he may be answerable for his good governance to those who elected him: but executive power still remains in a single pair of hands. What has been added to the idea of kingship is the requirement that it should be used well and responsibly, not that it should be diminished. Incidentally: because of the shift in meaning that the word has undergone, the idea of an elected aristocracy now sounds odd to English ears. It is, of course, necessary to remember that *aristocratia*—again, a transliteration of Aristotle's ἀριστοκρατία— means for St Thomas what it does for Aristotle: 'rule by the best people,' not 'rule by an hereditary nobility.' There is in principle no reason why the 'best' people in this sense should not be popularly elected (though one should add that medieval authors who favour 'popular' election intend something different from what we should now take the expression to mean).[46]

Kingship, in short, is the best type of government. But what St Thomas has in mind is not, now, a kingship appointed, supervised and if necessary censured or deposed by the Church, but an elective kingship, described with an eye to the Aristotelian principle that a mixed constitution is a stable constitution: a strong kingship, indeed, but one moderated and balanced by elements of aristocracy and democracy. This is the best type of government precisely because it is the most natural type, both in terms of its own characteristics and because it is the form best suited to mankind's needs and capacities. There is no suggestion anywhere in St Thomas that secular government is in itself unnatural or a concomitant of sin, or that the rôle of a king is merely to impose order on chaos by force.

Tyranny

As part of his discussion of kingship in *De regimine principum*, and in several places in the *Summa*, St Thomas brings out an important contrast between righteous rule and the phenomenon of tyranny.[47] On the one hand, his thought on this subject is not completely divested of the Augustinian view that tyrants have a part to play in the Divine plan: that their function is to afflict the wicked and tempt the good. If it is simply not possible to escape the clutches of a tyrant, St Thomas says, we ought to regard his depredations as a punishment and pray to God for deliverance. In such a plight, we should remember the words of Job—'He maketh a man who is an hypocrite to rule because of the sins of the people'[48]—and secure Divine aid by abstaining from sin.[49] On the other hand, St Thomas does not think of tyranny only, or even primarily, under the aspect of Divine punishment, and he does not hold, as Augustine had, that the right to disregard a tyrant's commands extends only to those commands that expressly contravene the Divine will. Nor, unlike John of Salisbury, does he display any tendency to define tyranny in terms of the tyrant's unwillingness to submit to the Church's supervision or to acquiesce in her interpretation of the law. Nor does he suggest, as John seems to, that the decision to oppose tyrannical government should come wholly or mainly from the Church, or must be validated by the Church's permission or blessing (see p. 205). For St Thomas, as we have seen, kings and princes exist to do much more than carry out those aspects of government too base or trivial for the hands of the clergy. Their rationale is to secure a common good, a public interest: an interest, moreover, that is secular, as it was not for John of Salisbury, in that its achievement does not depend directly or exhaustively upon the prince's acceptance of ecclesiastical direction. If, therefore, instead of securing such a public interest, the king devotes himself to his own enrichment or aggrandisement—if he becomes a tyrant of the kind described in

Book 3 of Aristotle's *Politics*—he has betrayed the purposes to which God has ordained him. He is not providing the goods that his people may legitimately expect of their government, and so the people have no obligation to obey him. They can, indeed, take action against him—on one occasion St Thomas uses the word *resistere*[50]—in appropriate circumstances. Such action does not suffer from moral ambiguity. Whatever guilt is involved belongs squarely to the tyrant, not to those who resist his tyranny.

> Tyrannical government is not just, because it is ordered not to the common good, but to the private good of the ruler. This is clear from what the Philosopher says at *Politics* 3 and *Ethics* 8. Disruption of such rule therefore does not have the character of sedition...Indeed, it is the tyrant who is guilty of sedition, since he nourishes discord and sedition among his subjects in order to dominate them more securely. For this is tyranny: a form of government directed to the private good of the ruler and the injury of the community.[51]

St Thomas therefore assigns a renewed importance to the distinction between just and unjust or despotic government. Contrary to what St Augustine thinks, the form of government under which an individual lives *does* matter in this life. The relation between ruler and ruled has again become a moral one, and the obligation to obey is no longer collapsed into religious duty. The 'right' of disobedience is not restricted to those circumstances which compromise the subject's religious allegiance, though it does, of course, include those circumstances. Indeed, it now extends even to a right of resistance. In a medieval context, we have to use the word 'right' as it were in inverted commas. No medieval author uses the idea of rights in the explicitly individualist way made familiar by, say, John Locke. But the emergence in the thought of St Thomas of an obligation that is clearly and genuinely *political* in character is a highly significant development.

The question of exactly what action St Thomas thinks the victims of a tyrant may take against him has given rise to a certain amount of puzzlement. Some have thought him incoherent or pusillanimous on the issue. This, however, is an unsubtle appraisal of his various remarks. It would be fairer to say that, to his mind, so delicate a question is not amenable to a general answer. In his early *Scripta super libros sententiarum*, speaking with apparent approval of the assassination of Julius Caesar, he seems to subscribe to a straightforward version of tyrannicide. When the tyranny is extreme and no other course of action is available, 'one who slays a tyrant in order to liberate his fatherland is to be praised and rewarded.'[52] At *De regimine principum* 1:7, he adopts the view that action may be taken against tyrants, but only by those who are in some definite way entitled to do so: either because they have a formal 'kingmaking' role or because they are carrying out the will of an oppressed community. If action is to be taken against tyrants, it must be taken by 'public authority.' St Thomas no doubt puts it in this way because he does not wish to sanction assassins or private wars. Tyrants may not be slain or overthrown on the private judgment of someone who happens not to like the king; those who think otherwise are a source of danger to themselves and everyone else.[53] Again at *De regimine principum* 1:7, and in the *Summa* also, he holds that tyranny of a relatively mild kind ought to be tolerated. He thinks this not, now, because we are to regard tyranny as no more than our just desert, but because prudence always counsels us to strike a balance between advantages and disadvantages. It requires us to perform, as one might now say, a risk-analysis. Action should be taken against a tyrant only where the harm involved in doing so is not greater than the benefits that action might be expected to secure.[54] One should bear in mind especially that a deposed tyrant may be replaced by another and worse one who has learnt from his predecessor's mistakes. St Thomas's cautious remarks about getting rid of tyrants may also be read in conjunction with what he says elsewhere about war and violence: that wars waged to repel aggression or escape oppression, and reasonable force used in self-defence and without malice, are morally justified, but that one must always be vigilant of one's own motives and careful not to do more damage than one averts.[55] Granted that it is too *ad hoc* to be a 'theory,' his position on the question of tyranny is neither inconsistent with itself nor with his general view of how people who are threatened or aggrieved ought to behave; nor, really, does he fudge the issue. His remarks, taken together, add up to a position of cautious conservatism. It is a position that recognises that extreme measures may be justified in extreme cases but should be avoided if at all possible and must, if taken at all, be taken by the proper agencies and with a proper and responsible intention. This moderation is characteristic of St Thomas's thought considered at large. Perhaps he is open to the criticism of having said little that might actually assist the victims of a tyrant. It is, though, important to note that, considerations of expediency aside, he thinks that we do not have a general duty, either moral or religious, to submit to tyranny come what may; nor is it now the Church who is necessarily the sole or chief arbiter—or, indeed, the arbiter at all—of when tyrants may be defied. Once again, politics is re-established as an autonomous field with a morality of its own.

Property

St Thomas's willingness to engage in a positive spirit with the institutions and practices of the secular world is illustrated also by his attitude to private property and his interest in some of its legal and moral minutiae.[56] He does not abandon the belief taken over by the Fathers from the Stoics, that by nature all things are common. Nor does he doubt that property can be put to wrongful uses and that we are prone to avaricious and excessive love of it.[57] Departing once more from the Augustinian view of things, however—though again without overt disagreement—he does not associate the institution of private property merely with greed; nor does he think that it arises only from the need to control the urge of fallen men to grab as much as they can for themselves. He agrees with St Augustine that it is only by human law that we possess what is ours; but he thinks that our possession of private property is justified by reference to practical considerations that are not only innocent, but positively beneficial. Although all things are common by nature, human laws regulating ownership have suggested themselves to men as a matter of convenience. They are, St Thomas tells us, additions to the law of nature, but they do not depart from or contradict it. Even had the Fall not occurred, men would have had to make constructive use of the earth over which they were given dominion. But if there were no private property the earth's resources would not be as well managed as they are when distributed into the care of individuals. Individuals will inevitably be more effective in looking after what belongs to them as individuals than they will be in dealing with what is common to all. 'Human affairs are administered in a more orderly fashion if each man has his own property to take care of; for there would be confusion if each man were to take care of everything.'⁵⁸ This is not because human beings are sinful or irremediably greedy. It is because our view of things is necessarily limited; and, again, this fact of human nature has nothing to do with sin. It is one of the limitations to which we are subject as mortal creatures. Sooner or later, even sinless men would have had to devise ways of managing and distributing the earth's resources efficiently. If there were no laws to make clear who owns and is responsible for what, disagreements would occur more often than they do. The institution of private property therefore has an important contribution to make to earthly wellbeing, and offences against property are sins as well as crimes. It is significant that St Thomas discusses the character of such offences with a degree of detail that no earlier Christian writer had thought it necessary to bestow.

Granted, then, that we can put it to unrighteous uses, St Thomas identifies private property as a positive benefit rather than as an inevitable source of spiritual peril. It should be noted, however, that there is a significant respect in which his account of 'private' property differs from what one may call 'modern' doctrines. For St Thomas, what human laws confer is the right to expropriate property from nature and manage it responsibly. What they do not confer is the kind of unlimited right of acquisition and use that has been so central a part of liberal political theory from the time of Locke onwards. The convention of private ownership cannot overrule the common right to use the world's resources conferred on us by nature. Ownership is therefore to be distinguished from use. As to the latter, a proprietor 'should not hold exterior things as his own, but as common: that is, each should be ready to share them with others in their necessity.'⁵⁹ The distinction between ownership and use upon which St Thomas draws is, again, derived from Aristotle (see p. 93). We are entitled to as much personal property as will enable us to meet our material needs comfortably, but what we have in excess of those needs we owe, as a matter of moral duty, to the poor as alms. St Thomas wisely abstains from trying to specify what level of prosperity we are entitled to claim for ourselves. No doubt this will depend on individual circumstances and cannot be prescribed except in relation to those circumstances. Nonetheless, he holds that the right of private ownership must as a matter of principle defer to an overriding obligation to respect a higher or 'natural' right (remembering again that we must

St Thomas: The Rehabilitation of Politics   231

not attribute to St Thomas a 'modern' theory of rights). Private property exists as a convenience superimposed by human law upon the law of nature; but 'things pertaining to human right cannot take anything away from natural right or Divine right.' St Augustine had stated the same principle, but as an exhortation to generosity and without exploring its implications in any detail (see p. 149). St Thomas, however, derives from it a rather striking practical application: that, in the event of a necessity

> so urgent and clear that [it] must be met at once by whatever means are to hand—for example, if a person is in immediate danger and no other help is available—anyone can then lawfully supply his own need from the property of another by taking it either openly or in secret; nor, properly speaking, does this have the character of theft or robbery...Properly speaking, to take and use another's property secretly in a case of extreme necessity does not have the character of theft, because that which someone takes in order to support his own life becomes his own by reason of that necessity.[60]

Necessity knows no law; or, much more to the point, it knows no human law. In a case of severe material deprivation or peril, the law of nature overrides the normal application of human law. St Thomas is content to leave the actual distribution of surplus property to the conscience of the individual proprietor; but, in a modern guise, his argument would no doubt find expression as an argument in favour of progressive or redistributive taxation: an argument justified in terms of natural needs and natural entitlements.

Law

The distinction that we have just drawn between natural law and human law brings us to the best known and most discussed department of St Thomas's political writing: his analysis and typology of law. This typology is found at *Summa theologiae* Ia IIae 90–108, the so-called *Tractatus de legibus*. It is in developing it that St Thomas is usually held to have made his greatest contribution to legal and political theory; and it is this aspect of his thought that is most directly of interest to us. He distinguishes four types or orders of law: eternal law, natural law, human law and Divine law. As far as his long-term influence is concerned, the most significant part of his analysis is its departure from the Patristic or 'Augustinian' tendency to conflate the natural law with the moral or 'eternal' or 'Divine' law of God as revealed in the Scriptures. This tendency, as we saw, had hardened in the *Decretum Gratiani* into a formal identification (see pp. 198–200). In St Thomas, however, we come across an explicit differentiation of the idea of natural law from that of a Divine or eternal law. The natural law is reinstated to its classical form as a law of reason specifically, independent of revelation. Having been isolated from the other kinds of law, it is then given a philosophical treatment unprecedented, in terms of detail, depth and precision, in Christian or pagan literature.[61]

In some respects, St Thomas's philosophical orientation when dealing with law reminds us more of Plato than of Aristotle. Law in general, he holds, is 'a kind of rule and measure of acts' provided by reason. This is a definition that he proposes several times, with only small variations.[62] What, exactly, does he mean by a 'rule and measure of acts'? His conception of law *simpliciter*—of law in its essence, considered apart from any of its manifestations or expressions—is of a rational pattern after the fashion of Plato's forms or ideas. Any relationship between a superior and an inferior involves, St Thomas suggests, a kind of picture or norm in the mind of the superior: a picture of what the inferior should do or be. Before he sets about making anything, the craftsman will have in his mind an idea, a rational pattern, of what his product will be like. The presence of such patterns in his mind is what enables him to produce actual and concrete versions of ideal but invisible objects. Such patterns are in a manner of speaking the 'laws' that govern his craft; and this account of the matter is, of course, uncomplicated Platonism.[63] In the same way, the ruler is a kind of craftsman in relation to his subjects. The idea that he has in his mind of what his subjects should do, and therefore of what the community over which he presides should be like, is, when formally enacted and promulgated as a command, what we call 'law' in the civic or political sense. Law is thus the 'rule and measure' that governs the acts of subjects. When they act in accordance with it, they 'participate' in it in the way that a table and a cup 'participate' in the ideas of tableness and cupness that carpenters and potters have in their minds. This is what St Thomas means when he says that law is 'in' both ruler and ruled.[64] It is in the intention of the ruler as commanding and in

St Thomas: The Rehabilitation of Politics

the compliance of the ruled as obeying. With these preliminaries in mind, let us consider each of St Thomas's four types of law in turn.

First comes the *lex aeterna*, the eternal law.[65] St Thomas uses this expression much more precisely and consistently than St Augustine does, and to mean something rather different. Because God is the supreme Governor of everything, the rational pattern of the government of the universe that exists in His mind, and which is exemplified in the world as we experience it, is 'law' in the most general or comprehensive sense. This pattern is what St Thomas calls the eternal law. It is 'law' because it is the will of God promulgated as a command to His creation from all eternity, and to it everything is subject without exception. The natural law is part of the eternal law, but it is not coextensive with it, nor is either the natural law or the eternal law exhaustively specified in the Scriptures. The eternal law, St Thomas says, 'is nothing but the rational pattern of the Divine wisdom considered as directing all actions and motions.'[66] In what sense can all things, even material and non-sentient things, be 'subject' to law? It is perhaps helpful to suggest that St Thomas's eternal law is 'law' in the way that, for instance, Newton's 'laws of motion' are laws. The eternal law expresses the regularity of nature; it is the *ordo naturalis*, the 'order' of nature.[67] It does not in the ordinary sense prescribe or enjoin anything, nor can it be disobeyed. It is directive only in a secondary fashion, as one might say that falling objects are 'directed' downwards by the 'law' of gravity. Things are 'subject' to it inasmuch as they are necessitated to act in the ways appropriate to what they are. The world cannot be other than the Divine will wills it to be; nor does the eternal law exist, in the way that prescriptive laws exist, to bring about any unfulfilled purpose. God, as the Supreme End, does not have any unfulfilled purposes.[68] Rather, the eternal law is that through which God impresses their natural characteristics or 'inclinations' on all created things. It is literally 'by dint of' the eternal law that the universe is orderly and predictable.[69] The natural order exhibits a regularity that we are able to apprehend rationally, and from which it departs only when God suspends the normal operation of things to perform a miracle.

Inasmuch as mankind is part of the natural order, it follows that there must be a department or dimension of the eternal law that expresses God's purposes for human beings in particular. This is the *lex naturalis*, the 'natural law,' the 'law of nature.' [70] St Thomas uses the expressions *lex naturalis*, *lex naturae* and *ius naturale* interchangeably, but this is elegant variation and does not affect his meaning. There is a broad sense in which all animals have access to a 'natural' law: the sense, that is, in which every sentient creature is imbued with an inclination to protect and reproduce itself. [71] So considered, the natural law manifests itself as what we may call instinct; and this, we recall, is a principle that goes back to Ulpianus's definition in the *Corpus iuris civilis* (see p. 129). But the natural law in the ethical sense that St Thomas wishes to bring out is something more than the urge to survive and procreate. Because we have reason and free will—because we are able to make and act on rational choices—we are able to participate in the natural law more fully, or in a more sophisticated way, than non-rational creatures can. For St Thomas, as for Aristotle, our rationality is what makes us moral agents. The faculty by which we are able to participate in the natural law is called *synderesis*: an innate principle present in the moral consciousness of every person that directs the agent to good and restrains him from evil. *Synderesis* is to all intents and purposes the same as Augustine's *conscientia*, though St Thomas derives the word *synderesis* from Basil of Caesarea.[72] For human beings, therefore, the natural law is a prescriptive law; it tells us—more correctly, we infer from it—what we ought to do. St Thomas's account of its content is more or less the same as we find in the Fathers. The natural law tells us do what is good and avoid what is evil. It tells us to value and preserve human life, including our own; to beget and rear offspring; to live at peace with our neighbours and to do nothing that might jeopardise that peace.[73] It is 'natural' inasmuch as we are creatures to whom its prescriptions are rationally obvious. These prescriptions are the same at all times and in all places. We do not have to learn about them or have them legislated for us. To all human beings, pagans included, they simply 'stand to reason.'

For St Thomas, then, we are able to discern patterns of right conduct as part of our rational apprehension of the universe and our place in it. Because we are equipped by nature to tell right from wrong, certain invariable standards present themselves to the consciousness of everyone everywhere. But why, in that case, is it necessary also to have positive or statute law: what St Thomas calls *lex humana*, 'human' law? To this question, we remember, St Augustine

St Thomas: The Rehabilitation of Politics 235

had given a clear answer. There is a natural law, written into our hearts by God. This inward law precedes all written law. It tells us not to do what we would not wish to suffer. People cannot, however, be relied upon to follow it. Self-love has so effaced the law of nature from our hearts, or has so undermined our strength of will in relation to it, that we now need coercive laws to repress individual pride and avarice. But St Thomas, again without disagreeing with St Augustine explicitly, gives a quite different account of why we need positive laws. The law of nature, St Thomas insists, is clear to us. Individuals, granted that their 'infused' virtues need to be developed by training in good habits, can not only make use of reason in forming moral judgments; they are able also to act according to those judgments. The problem is not that sin has set up a barrier between us and the natural law, nor is it that our wills are intrinsically too feeble to follow it. Rather, the problem is that the natural law is too general with respect to the requirements of civic life. The natural law prescribes that good is to be done and evil avoided. It does not, however, indicate what 'good' and 'evil' mean at the level of cases. Nor does it furnish the agencies of government with suitable responses to people who do evil; it does not, for instance, show what punishments should be and who should incur them. The need for human laws is created not simply by sin or self-love, but by the gulf that exists between the comprehensiveness of the natural law and the rules necessary to enact its precepts into practice. Human laws, St Thomas says, are particular inferences or 'determinations' derived from the general provisions of the natural law.[74] Legislators arrive at them by the application of reason to the problems of common life and social relations. They are, St Thomas tells us, inferred from the natural law by 'practical reason' in the same deductive fashion as, in scientific or speculative reasoning, we infer particular conclusions from general first principles:

> Just as, in speculative reason, we proceed from indemonstrable principles, naturally known, to the conclusions of the various sciences, such conclusions not being implanted in us by nature but arrived at by effort of reason, so also is it necessary for [practical] human reason to proceed from the precepts of the natural law, as from certain common and indemonstrable principles, to other, more particular, dispositions. And such particular dispositions, discovered by human reason, are called human laws.[75]

The distinction that St Thomas here draws between speculative and practical reasoning is exactly the distinction that Aristotle draws in Book 6 of the *Nicomachean Ethics* between *phronesis* and *sophia*. Practical reason or prudence is the intellectual faculty—the intellectual 'virtue'—that equips the legislator to infer from the 'common and indemonstrable' principles of nature what it is right to require a particular association of citizens to do. Considered as an intellectual activity distinct from theoretical reasoning, practical reasoning is a process that culminates not in truths of reason, but in practical outcomes. Applied to individual moral judgment, it identifies the Aristotelian mean between excess and defect: it specifies the course of action that is appropriate to each case.[76] Applied to legislation, it produces rules precise enough to be applicable to the detailed purposes of government. A human law is therefore the conclusion of a 'practical syllogism': a syllogism that has a principle of the natural law as its major premiss and a particular legislative problem or need as its minor premiss. Hence 'Law is nothing but a certain dictate of practical reason in the ruler who governs a perfect community.'[77] By a 'perfect' community, incidentally, St Thomas means not a faultless community, but a complete or self-sufficient one in the Aristotelian sense.

Some inferences from the natural law are so direct and obvious that they appear in more or less the same form in the positive laws of all peoples. These inferences, St Thomas observes, comprise what Roman jurisprudence calls the *ius gentium*, the 'law of nations.'[78] As the Roman lawyers mostly saw, the *ius gentium* is part of the natural law, but not the whole of it (see pp. 128–129). Other, more particular, 'civil' laws may be peculiar to a given community and, to that extent, separated from the natural law by a longer chain of reasoning. This chain of reasoning may, indeed, be so long that it is sometimes hard to see what the connection between the natural law and a given human law is.[79] But, St Thomas insists, all human law properly so called takes its character as law from the fact that it reflects the general principles discoverable in the natural law. This consideration holds notwithstanding local differences of custom and practice. All human laws are inferences from the natural law, even though some are more immediately and plainly so than others. Positive laws can be altered to suit changing times and they can vary according to the circumstances of the people whose laws they are. Moreover, they can be dispensed from in the name of equity, in order to counteract the injustices that arise when general laws do not fit the circumstances of the case. This is a principle that we encountered both in Aristotle and in Roman jurisprudence. Human laws must accommodate the actual requirements of individuals in interaction with one another; and, as Aristotle saw, these requirements may take different forms according to different needs and preferences. But the principles of the natural law itself cannot be changed and must always be honoured.

> The human will can by common agreement make anything just that does not have in itself anything repugnant to natural justice; and it is in this that positive law has its place...But if something is repugnant in itself to the natural law, it cannot be made just by the human will: for example, if it were enacted that it is lawful to steal or commit adultery.[80]

Also, it is as well to mention again the fact that St Thomas, like Aristotle, believes that being governed—being required by human law to conform outwardly to standards of virtuous conduct—can form habits in us that are genuinely virtuous. Human law not only directs us outwardly; it can also be a positive force in moral education. The difference between good laws and bad laws is therefore more than a matter of convenience or expediency.

In his account of how human law and natural law are related, St Thomas's Christian Aristotelianism once more stands in significant contrast to the 'Augustinian' tradition. On the one hand, St Augustine had consistently held that human laws do not derive their binding force from their content and that, in general, we cannot justify non-compliance on moral or conscientious grounds. In one or two passages, read superficially, he may seem to say that they do and that we can; but this interpretation, as we have tried to show, is a mistake (see pp. 191–193). For Augustine, positive laws derive their obligatory force from the fact, and only from the fact, that they are the commands of the ruler under whom God has seen fit to place us. Laws that do not conform to what Augustine calls the 'eternal' law are bad laws; they are unjust laws: but they are laws nonetheless. Even cruel and unjust laws, granted that they are indeed cruel and unjust in a way that we can apprehend by reason, contribute to the order and security of a world disrupted by sin. Subject to a single limiting case, we are required as a matter of religious duty to obey them. For St

Thomas, on the other hand, the very nature of law—its claim to *be* law—depends upon the righteousness of its content.

> Hence a command has the force of law insofar as it is just. Now in human affairs a thing is said to be just insofar as it is right according to the rule of reason. But the first rule of reason is the law of nature...Hence, every human law has the nature of law insofar as it is derived from the law of nature. But if it is in any respect at odds with the law of nature, it will then no longer be law, but a corruption of law.[81]

From our point of view, this is a distinction of the greatest importance. 'Laws' that are not validly inferred by practical reason from the natural law—laws that are unjust in the sense of oppressing or corrupting the community subject to them or failing to secure its good—are not bad laws. Rather, they are not laws at all; and, because they are not laws, it follows that we cannot be bound to obey them. They infringe the most general natural precept—that good ought to be done and evil avoided—from which law derives its authority. For this reason, they are not laws, but unjustified acts of coercion. An argument therefore arises in relation to law similar to the one that we noted in connection with tyranny.

> Laws may be unjust in two ways. In one way, by being contrary to the human good...[This may come about] either from their end, as when some ruler imposes on his subjects burdensome laws that pertain not to the common good, but rather to his own greed or glory; or from their author, as when someone makes a law that goes beyond the power committed to him; or from their form, as when burdens are imposed unequally upon the community even if they are directed to the common good. Laws of this kind are more acts of violence than laws; because, as Augustine says in the book *De libero arbitrio*, 'a law that is not just seems to be no law at all.' Hence such laws do not bind in the court of conscience, except perhaps to avoid scandal or disturbance...In another way, laws may be unjust by being contrary to the Divine good: for example, the laws of tyrants enjoining idolatry or anything else contrary to the Divine law; and laws of this kind must not be observed in any circumstances, because, as is said at Acts 5:29, 'we ought to obey God rather than man.'[82]

The quotation from Augustine in this passage is unwarranted inasmuch as it is made to bear a construction that Augustine did not intend; but the meaning of the passage is clear enough. St Thomas repeats the principle that we are absolutely bound to disobey laws that contravene the Divine will directly; but our right of disobedience now extends much further than it did for Augustine. Unjust laws 'do not bind in the court of conscience.' We are free to disobey them unless doing so would only make matters worse. When we do so, we are not really 'breaking the law,' because the laws in question are not laws really, even if they are so in form or appearance. Once again, the Augustinian doctrine that we normally have no rights against the existing order is challenged by a new affirmation: that we are entitled to expect the existing order to exhibit a certain moral quality, namely justice, in the absence of which it has no claim to our allegiance.

St Thomas's fourth and final kind of law is *lex divina*, Divine law.[83] The Divine law answers fully to the formal definition of law. It is 'a rule and measure of acts'; it is enacted by God; it is promulgated by Him through the Scriptures; it regulates aspects of our conduct, and hence we 'participate' in it as we do in all law. But St Thomas treats the Divine law as an order separate from both natural and human law. The Divine law is part of the eternal law, but it is that part which is made available to us through revelation *rather than* through reason. It becomes accessible to us through the teachings of Scripture and the Church, but it is no longer presented, in the manner of the Fathers and the *Decretum*, simply as a transcription of the law of nature. Divine law is a separate and self-dependent field of law. Human law must not contravene it, and may, indeed, codify aspects of it; but it is from the natural law rather than the Divine law that the determinations of human law as such are derived. This, as we have emphasised, is a departure of considerable significance. Why do we need the Divine law in addition to the natural and human laws? From a theological perspective, the answer is obvious. On the one hand, human law as St Thomas describes it is no longer a merely external law, to be regarded as binding almost regardless of what it enjoins. It is related to morality in two clear senses. It is only law at all insofar as its provisions reflect the requirements of the natural law; also, it can contribute to our moral formation by reinforcing the practice of virtue in us. But human law has to do with justice in those things that belong to public or external life. On the other hand, our ultimate end, eternal salvation, requires that we be righteous in our private acts and intentions. Because human judges cannot see the heart, this is something that cannot fall directly within the scope of human law. It is possible to observe the letter of human laws scrupulously and yet be inwardly unrighteous: covetous, jealous, lustful, impious. The Divine law is therefore necessary to govern those parts of our conduct that no mortal eye can see and judge. It regulates us with respect to our intentionality; it punishes us insofar as we are sinners as distinct from criminals; it instructs us in those duties that are inward and religious rather than outward and civic.

The legal theory that St Thomas develops, then, is of the kind called 'intellectualist' rather than 'voluntarist.' In strict usage, legislative provisions that depart from, or fail to institutionalise, the natural law are not 'bad' laws. Rather, they do not have the character of law at all. Granted, promulgation and command are important parts of what makes law a practical reality. To this extent, there is a formal or technical sense in which even pernicious laws are 'laws.'[84] Also, it may in a pragmatic sense be 'right' to obey even 'bad' laws in order to avoid the worse consequences that disobedience might produce. This proviso, like St Thomas's similar caveat about resistance to tyrants, reflects an uncontroversial principle of moral theology: that, if we have to choose between evils, we should choose the course likely to produce the least evil. But positive law receives its authority from its content rather than from the command of a legislator. No one who commands or promulgates something against nature makes law in the proper sense. The value and obligatory force of human law depends upon the fact that it expresses an objective and rationally apprehensible good inferred from eternal and invariable moral principles. Nor, we notice again, is it necessarily the province of the Church to define the meaning and application of those principles. The Divine law is now clearly differentiated from the natural law. St Thomas thinks that human law derives the morally important aspects of its character from its conformity to principles of reason inherent in the nature of human beings; and this, in turn, involves a belief—a characteristically Aristotelian belief—in the power of natural reason to make genuine moral judgments. Under the influence of Aristotle, the activities of both legislation and citizenship are given a dignity that, according to the Augustinian mode of understanding, they could not have.

St Thomas and the Natural Law Tradition

How may we sum up those aspects of St Thomas's thought that bear most directly upon the history of the natural law tradition? The following points suggest themselves especially.

(a) It is usual to regard St Thomas's doctrine of natural law as a kind of apotheosis of classical and medieval thinking on the subject. This is a view with which we certainly shall not take issue. The influence of his theory upon subsequent moral and political thought has been immense, even down to the twentieth century.[85] The esteem in which it has been held is in some degree due to St Thomas's adoption as the semi-official philosopher of the Roman Catholic Church. But it is due also to the precision and detail of his treatment, and to its compendiousness in terms of what it brings together. The natural law as St Thomas understands it is a fusion of several discernible elements, all of which we have encountered previously. Philosophically speaking, it is the natural law of the Stoics and Roman lawyers, now formulated in terms of Aristotelian ethics and logic, with accompanying elements of Platonism. It resembles the Patristic or Augustinian doctrine in some respects; but St Thomas's Aristotelianism gives him far more confidence than Augustine had in the moral capacities of reason and will as such: to reason and will considered, insofar as anything can be considered, apart from the influence of grace. The natural law is part of the pattern of the Divine mind in which human beings 'participate' as creatures made in God's image. It is a law of right reason in which are contained the universal moral prescriptions that God has incorporated into the natural order. At its most general, it teaches that good must be done and evil avoided. From this general precept all lower-order principles and rules of conduct follow by a process of inference considered as something quite distinct from Divine revelation.

(b) Under the influence of Aristotle, St Thomas departs from the influential moral pessimism that distinguishes St Augustine's account of social and political experience. In consequence, he departs also from those currents of medieval thought that may be attributed, directly or indirectly, to that pessimism. He understands that man is fallen man. As a Catholic author, it is not open to him to suppose that we can perfect ourselves by our own efforts; nor can he deny that we have a supernatural end available to us only through the operation of Divine grace. But he does not think, as Augustine does, that fallen man is completely denatured man; nor does he think that the ends of this world are to be wholly repudiated by the righteous. Human beings are not inveterately destructive, competitive and selfish. Well directed and well governed, they are capable of co-operation and altruism and of rational deliberation directed to a common purpose. Under the tutelage of Aristotle, St Thomas assigns to earthly life and pursuits a degree of value that Augustine's Christian Platonism could not accommodate, and a corresponding degree of autonomy to secular government. For St Thomas, a kind of human good is capable of being found and realised *in* the world rather than beyond it.

(c) As a corollary of this point, St Thomas does not believe, as so many medieval followers of Augustine believed, that temporal government can be redeemed only by being wholly subordinated to an authority higher than itself. On the one hand, he does not relieve secular government of its duty to seek the spiritual good of those under it. To that extent, he continues to hold that princes are, in the final analysis, responsible to the Church. He believes also, though he does not develop the theme, that rulers who betray the faith may be subject to ecclesiastical punishment or even removal. On the other hand, there is no suggestion in his writings that temporal rulers are only the Church's auxiliaries or swordbearers; nor is it anywhere suggested that the 'material sword' comes to princes through the Church or that their use of it is in a general sense conditional upon ecclesiastical or papal approval.[86] Earthly happiness, though such happiness is not our supreme good, is no longer discounted as worthless or deluded, nor is it beyond the reach of secular reason. The natural law ceases to be identified with the law of God as revealed in Scripture and ecclesiastical interpretations of Scripture. The Divine law directs us to our eternal end; but the natural law, both of itself and when expressed in human law, directs us separately to our earthly end. It directs us to a state of moral and material felicity or wellbeing that has a value, albeit a secondary value, of its own.

St Thomas: The Rehabilitation of Politics 243

(d) Most significant of all, with an eye to the subsequent development of natural law arguments in their most characteristic and persuasive form, is the intellectualism of St Thomas's legal theory. Conformity to the law of nature no longer makes, as for Augustine, the difference between good law and bad law: it makes the difference between law and non-law. Strictly speaking, the question of whether or not we should obey an unjust law does not arise, because there is no such thing as an unjust law. Human law consists of rules derived by a process of practical inference from universal principles of nature and ordered to the common good, having regard to the sociable and political nature of mankind. Human laws that do not answer to this description—laws that are not ordered to the good of those to whom they apply—are simply not laws, except in an empty formal sense, and so have no binding force.

(e) Much more fully and explicitly than ever before, therefore, the natural law is set up as a critical standard. It is the criterion against which actual regimes and laws can be evaluated independently of the judgment of the Church or pope. St Thomas is not a political radical. Indiscriminate rebellion against tyrants is not permitted, nor should we lightly refuse to comply with unjust 'laws.' He appears to think that, in practice, subjects should be prepared to put up with a good deal, for fear of occasioning more hardship and peril through defiance than they would incur by submission. In principle, however, there is such a thing as political as distinct from religious obligation, and the limits of political obligation are defined not primarily by spiritual considerations, but by the common good that governments exist to secure. The principle that we have an ordinary duty to submit even to unjust laws and tyrannical rulers no longer holds. It no longer holds because, for St Thomas, government is not a regrettable necessity brought into being by sin, nor is its function that of punishing the wicked and testing the perseverance of the righteous. It is a source of good. Those subject to it have, in a sense readily intelligible to the modern reader, though not put in quite these terms by St Thomas, a 'right' to expect their government to serve that good. In the same sense, they have a right also to take suitable action if it fails to do so. Individuals are no longer merely subjects. They are citizens in the classical, Aristotelian, sense: rational individuals able to judge, evaluate and participate in the processes by which earthly life is governed and earthly goods acquired.

It is with St Thomas that we must take our leave of the Middle Ages. Given our terms of reference, we have no need to examine the political thought of the period between St Thomas and the Renaissance. For the most part, nothing of interest was added to the natural law tradition for several centuries after St Thomas. When, with hindsight, we measure his theory of natural law against the background of classical and medieval moral philosophy, it looks so modern and so complete mainly because it is part of what we have called an intellectual revolution. St Thomas was responsible—not single-handedly, but certainly pre-eminently—for re-introducing the political and ethical theories of Aristotle to the Latin west and, concomitantly, for moderating the Platonist tendencies that had for so long slanted political theory in an ecclesiological direction. This, in itself, is an achievement of considerable magnitude and long-term importance. As a consequence of his rehabilitation of Aristotle, St Thomas helped to inaugurate a thorough re-evaluation of political activity and participation as worthwhile pursuits apart from any connection with the Church. Although he himself abstains from an extended treatment of questions of 'Church' and 'State,' he made available the intellectual equipment by which his immediate successors—most notably Marsilius of Padua (ca 1275–1343)—were to begin to unravel the long-established interweaving of secular and spiritual themes in European political discourse.[87] We may say that, in this respect, he helped to make modern normative political theory possible. These are, of course, vast generalisations; but they are not unacceptable ones. With St Thomas's Christian Aristotelianism, a recognisably 'classical' doctrine of natural law re-emerges from the theological and ecclesiological complications introduced by Patristic, and especially Augustinian, ideas about politics, morality and religious allegiance. This, at any rate in some sense, marks the starting point of the modern secular natural law doctrines that we are to consider in our second volume.

Chapter 8

Machiavelli: Virtù, Fortune and the Autonomy of Politics

During the course of almost five hundred years, Niccolò Machiavelli has been damned and praised, according to fashion and preference, but seldom ignored. 'No writer, probably, has been so persistently used and abused or so little understood.'[1] In the estimation of some, he is the personification of wickedness; to others, he is a champion of honesty. He has been represented as an exponent of power politics and as a defender of republican values. In fact, and in a way not as paradoxical as it may seem, he is both. If St Thomas's thought is the apotheosis of all that we have said about the tradition of natural law, Machiavelli's presents us with a corresponding apotheosis of political realism. It is chiefly for this reason that he has been so much 'abused' and so much admired. All subsequent attempts to deal with issues of political morality, whether domestic or international, have had to accommodate his astringent and uncompromising account of the realities of political experience. It is to that account that we turn in this final chapter.

Machiavelli's was an active life, full of personal vicissitude and lived at a time of severe political instability. These facts are reflected in almost everything he wrote. Born in Florence on 3 May 1469, he was the second son of Bernardo di Niccolò Machiavelli, a lawyer of some standing, and his wife Bartolommea di Stefano Nelli. Both parents were members of the old Florentine nobility, but the family had fallen on hard times. Machiavelli received an education in the humanities that led him naturally into a public career. He entered the service of the government of the republic of Florence after the fall of the Medici in 1494. Despite the odium that has so often accompanied his name, he was by all accounts a man of great personal probity. In

1498, in the wake of events following the execution of Savonarola, he was appointed to the headship of the Second Chancery. He was entrusted with a number of diplomatic missions: to the Romagna, as envoy to Cesare Borgia (1502), France (1500, 1504; 1510–11), the Holy See (1506) and the Empire (1507–08). Alone of all the major figures whom we have considered, Machiavelli was a career diplomat. His excursions furnished him with many examples later to be incorporated into his political writings. More importantly, perhaps, they gave him a certain outlook that is present in these writings consistently.[2] With the accession of Piero Soderini as *gonfalonier* — chief magistrate for life — of Florence in 1502, Machiavelli became his military adviser and in 1505 was given the task of organising a national defence militia. When, in 1509, Florence dispatched a small army to reconquer the city of Pisa, Machiavelli made a point of leading it himself. In 1511, Pope Julius II formed the Holy League against France, and with the help of the Swiss drove the French out of Italy. Florence lay at the mercy of the pope, and had to submit to his terms, one of which was the restoration of the Medici. The return of the Medici on 1 September 1512, and the consequent fall of the republic, was effectively the end of Machiavelli's public life. For a few weeks he hoped to retain his office under the new regime, but he was dismissed by a decree of 7 November 1512. Accused of conspiring against the Medici, he was imprisoned for a short while and tortured. He retired to the family estate at Sant' Andrea, where he devoted himself to political analysis, military theory and the study of history. He found his enforced retirement depressing and boring,[3] but it was during this time that he produced the works that are most of interest to us: *The Prince* (*Il Principe*), written in about 1513, the much longer *Discourses* (*Discorsi sopra la Prima Deca di Tito Livio*), written between 1513 and 1519, and the *Art of War* (*Dialogo dell'Arte della Guerra*), written in 1519 or 1520.[4] Part of his purpose in writing *The Prince* was to ingratiate himself with Lorenzo de' Medici, to whom it is dedicated; but it was not until 1525 that Machiavelli was recalled to government service by the Medici, and then only in minor capacities. With the restoration of the republic in 1527, Machiavelli was excluded from office once more. He died later in the same year. In his last years he completed a *History of Florence* (*Istorie Fiorentine*), a commentary on the city's historical records commissioned by Cardinal Giulio de' Medici, who had been impressed by *The Prince*. It is in the *History of Florence*, remarkable for its sophisticated account of causal relationships rather than mere chronology, that Machiavelli's ability as a historian is most in evidence.[5]

Machiavelli's Italy

Machiavelli's writings reflect the perspectives and experience of a public servant, a diplomat, a soldier and a historian. What of the intellectual and political setting of his life? On the one hand, it is impossible to exaggerate the long-term influence upon political thought of themes associated with the Thomistic revival of Aristotle: the naturalness of political life; the teleological function of secular society; the notions of the common good and distributive justice; the theory of the mixed constitution.[6] On the other hand, the political complexion of Europe at the end of the fifteenth century and the beginning of the sixteenth was very different from what it had been in St Thomas's day. The medieval idea of a unified *corpus Christianum*, a transnational society ordered to God's purposes, was no longer even a theoretical possibility. Europe was a Europe of nation States, ruled by princes devoted to expansion by military means. England was the England of Henry VII (1485–1509) and Henry VIII (1509–1547). France, recovered from the Hundred Years' War with England (1337–1453), had become a major European power. Maximilian I (1493–1519) was strengthening the Habsburg Empire which, under Charles V (1519–1558), was to be France's great rival. Absolute monarchy had become, or was becoming, the normal form of western European government. As a force in international politics, the Church had all but fallen out of the folds of history. The Conciliar Movement of 1409–1449 had risen and collapsed, its collapse due mostly to the assertiveness and skill of the popes against whose monarchical ideology its efforts had been directed. The Church was still a monarchy presided over by the pope; but the papacy's claim to supremacy in European affairs was effectively a thing of the past. The plausibility of this claim had seeped away during and after the great conflict of 1296–1303 between Philip IV of France and Pope Boniface VIII.[7] The 'Babylonish captivity' of the Church in Avignon from 1305–1377 and the Great Schism of 1378–1414 had gravely undermined the Church's claim to occupy the moral high ground of European life. The Reformation was not far distant.[8]

Machiavelli's Italy was, in the phrase, a geographical expression. She was a military expression also. Machiavelli describes her condition in passionate language. She is 'more enslaved than...the Hebrews, more oppressed than the Persians, and more scattered than the Athenians; without head, without order, beaten, despoiled, divided and overrun.'[9] The feudal principalities and free cities of the Middle Ages had by the end of the fifteenth century coalesced into five larger units: the republics of Venice and Florence, the kingdom of Naples, the duchy of Milan, and the Papal States. These units formed a kind of international system in miniature. From 1494 onwards, northern Italy became the field upon which was waged the conflict between the French king and the Emperor. The independence of the Italian States was to that extent seriously compromised. Concerted action was essential to effective defence; yet the external relations of the States were conducted under conditions that made sustained co-operation impossible. Relations between the States were bedevilled by destructive rivalries. No one of them was powerful enough to impose unity on the others. Outside powers, especially France, played off one Italian State against another in their attempts to gain power in the Italian peninsula. The general policy of the popes was to resist unification in order to retain control of the Papal States. Machiavelli is in this connection particularly unforgiving of the Church:

> It is to the Church of Rome and her priests that we Italians owe...something that will bring us to ruin: the fact that the Church has kept, and continues to keep, our country divided. It is certain that a country can never be united and happy unless it is wholly obedient to one government, whether a republic or a monarchy, as in the case of France and Spain. The only reason why Italy is not in the same condition, and is not governed either by one republic or one monarch, is the Church...The Church is not strong enough to rule all Italy, but nor will she allow any other power to do so; and this is why Italy has never been able to unite under one head but has remained always under a number of princes and lords. This has brought her to a condition of such division and weakness that she has fallen victim not only to mighty barbarians but to whoever has chosen to attack her.[10]

The impression given by Italian politics at the beginning of the sixteenth century is one of self-destructive instability both domestically and internationally. Factional strife within the cities and wars between them produced a succession of able and ruthless adventurer-despots, obliged always to be on their guard against ambitious rivals and influential noble families. The famous Cesare Borgia, Duke of Valencia (ca 1476–1507) is the readiest example, and the example whom Machiavelli finds most interesting. Such despots perforce deprived the citizens of freedom. The political morality that they embraced led inevitably to the aggrandisement of some cities at the expense of others; to the employment of mercenary soldiers, actuated by self-interest rather than patriotism; to conspiracies, assassinations, banishments, imprisonments and cruelties. 'Here is an example,' Machiavelli says, speaking of Cesare Borgia,

> that repays close study and imitation by others. The duke won control of the Romagna. He decided that the territory needed good government and to be subject to princely authority. So he placed Remirro de Orco, a cruel, ruthless man, in charge of it and entrusted him with the greatest powers. Remirro pacified and unified the land. Cesare then decided that there was no further need for this excessive power. To exonerate himself in the minds of the people and win them over, Cesare resolved to show the people that Remirro's cruelties were inflicted by him and not Cesare. One morning, Remirro's body was found cut into two pieces on the piazza at Cesena, with the block and a bloody knife next to it.[11]

When the people discovered the two halves of Remirro, Machiavelli goes on, they were appeased and satisfied. This instance—it occurred in 1501—will show something of the flavour of Italian politics at the time when Machiavelli was an ambitious young public servant embarking on a diplomatic career.

It is against this background of extreme political turbulence and disunity in Italy that we are to read Machiavelli's political writings. He is not interested in questions of Church versus State, or pope versus council. To his mind, these matters no longer have a place on the agenda of political theory. It has been remarked that whereas critics of the papacy such as Marsilius of Padua and Martin Luther scold the Church for being too political, Machiavelli considers that she is not political enough to interest the student of power relations.[12] Bishops and popes, he says—with an irony that does not entirely survive translation—are the only princes who can remain in power regardless of how they act and live.

> These princes have states and do not defend them, subjects and do not govern them; yet their states, though undefended, are never taken from them; nor do their subjects object because they are not governed; nor do they dream of being alienated from the Church, because they cannot be. These principalities alone, then, are secure and happy. But since they are protected by higher causes to which the human mind does not reach, I will abstain from speaking of them; because, since they are maintained and established by God, it would be the act of a presumptuous and arrogant man to discuss them. [13]

Nor is Machiavelli concerned with the doctrines of the Fathers or the teachings of scripture or the principles of natural law. He has no patience with the idea of a universal political morality, and theology is absent from his writings. He is, indeed, consistently hostile to the Christian religion considered as influencing the quality of public life. Quite apart from the fact that contemporary religious figures are a poor advertisement for what they teach, he thinks that a people truly committed to the Christian virtues of meekness and submission would not thrive in the cutthroat world of contemporary affairs.

> Our religion places the greatest happiness in humility, meekness and a contempt for the things of this world...It seems to me that these principles have made people weak, so that they become an easy prey to ill-disposed men who can control them more securely inasmuch as the great body of men are more inclined to endure injuries for the sake of attaining Paradise than to avenge them.[14]

In this passage, Machiavelli reminds us of those Romans who had reproached the Christian faith at the time of the sack of Rome in 410 (see p. 172). The sentiment is the same in both cases. Machiavelli is, in an intelligible sense, a pagan; nor can he forget the great influence that religion has on a people's political culture. What is needed, he thinks, is a religion like that of the ancient Romans: a religion whose votaries are taught that he best serves the gods who serves the State.[15]

Machiavelli is, in a word, an Italian patriot, preoccupied above all with the question of how to establish and maintain a strong State in the face of foreign aggression and domestic disunity. Rousseau is no doubt right in suggesting that, in teaching princes, Machiavelli intended also to teach the people about the nature and dangers of despotism.[16] He realises on the one hand that energetic and ambitious leadership can conjure, even if by drastic means, order and unification out of political fragmentation. On the other, he recognises that such leadership, because it has to rely so heavily on force and suppression, will tend to produce fatal weaknesses in the order over which it presides. This dilemma works itself out in his political writings in two separate but connected ways. In form, though certainly not in content, *The Prince* is a traditional *speculum principis*.[17] In it, Machiavelli's interest is in how one man can maintain his sway over subjects. In the *Discourses*—they are notionally a commentary on the first ten books of Livy's history of Rome—he addresses the question of how a republic can be made to endure and prosper by transmuting the fundamentally selfish vigour of its citizens into civic virtue. The relation between these two works is something that we shall try to clarify in this chapter.

It is for his departure from the logic-chopping of the Middle Ages that Machiavelli is most often congratulated. His method is historical and comparative. 'He who wishes to see what will be must consider what has been.'[18] He considers that it is only by analysing the events of the past that we can understand the present and to some extent control the future. Given what he takes to be the realities of human nature, he thinks it futile to invent imaginary commonwealths intended to teach citizens and rulers how to behave. Such pipe-dreams are seductive in a world full of anxiety; but to indulge in them at the expense of losing touch with how things are is to invite destruction rather than preservation.[19] Machiavelli's works display a penchant for general patterns arrived at by way of real examples and counter-examples, granted that his selection of examples is often tendentious and uncritical. The material that he examines is drawn from history as well as from contemporary affairs. The world as we experience it from our circumscribed viewpoint is one of flux and instability, lacking in comforting certainties;[20] but a sufficiently wide study of history can disclose principles that are at least broadly reliable. This conviction is the corner-stone of Machiavelli's methodology. He looks back, with the interest and approval typical of one educated in the tradition of renaissance humanism, to the illustrations yielded by classical antiquity. The commonwealth of Rome is his chief model, though he never quite succeeds in making convincing comparisons between Roman politics and the conditions of contemporary Italy. His purpose is to consider actual events and conditions, to show how events are shaped by the circumstances in which they occur, to identify their causes, and to lay bare the general principles that underlie human relationships and behaviour. His procedure is, at least roughly, inductive. Machiavelli, like Aristotle—though with the same qualification (see pp. 83; 88)—is a 'political scientist' in a way with which we can easily identify. He is self-consciously so; he regards himself as a kind of political physician, 'treading a path upon which no one else has ever walked.'[21] Ernst Cassirer even suggests that, in terms of his use of inductive method, Machiavelli was to politics what Galileo was to natural science.[22] At the same time, educated as he is in the tradition of classical rhetoric, he is as much a persuader as the Sophists were. His purpose is not merely to describe, but to reach and sway an audience.[23] No doubt part of his purpose is to shock and satirise.[24]

It is not seldom suggested that *The Prince* and the *Discourses*, though written more or less simultaneously, are inconsistent with one another. This suggestion is on the whole associated with the belief that the composition of *The Prince* was a mere act of cynicism on the part of Machiavelli: a convinced republican, but wishing for reasons of personal ambition to truckle to Lorenzo de' Medici. This assessment is not without plausibility; but it is only partially valid.[25] Despite tensions and contradictions, Machiavelli's political thought, when read as a whole, exhibits a high degree of coherence. One of the most useful clues to this coherence is the cyclical theory of constitutional change that he adopts from the Greek author Polybius.[26] Cities begin as principalities. They do not arise by nature; they are created by the manly virtue and enterprise of princes.[27] But manly virtue flourishes best in strenuous and austere conditions. When such conditions give place to soft and luxurious ones, monarchies become elective and ornamental, selfish and decadent, and princes grow demanding and tyrannical. Eventually, the best men—by which Machiavelli means the most forceful, assertive and ambitious men—will rebel against the tyrannical prince. Initially the result will be benign: an aristocracy based on laws ordered to the protection of both private and public interests. But with the passing of the conditions that called them forth, aristocracies deteriorate in turn. They become self-indulgent and inward-looking oligarchies, and when a vigorous individual arises who can command popular support, he is able to turn himself into a prince, and the cycle starts again. Viewed in the context of this theory, *The Prince* and the *Discourses* may be read as analyses of constitutional forms at different stages of the cycle, Machiavelli's purpose in both cases being to understand the conditions of stability and security. Also, both works are informed by a similar and consistent account of human behaviour and motivation.

Nature and Politics

Throughout his political writings, Machiavelli subscribes to a theory of human nature and its impact on history that has been called cynical or pessimistic, but which it is more illuminating to describe as typically realist. In several respects it reminds us of the radical Sophists, Thucydides, St Augustine and Thomas Hobbes. We are right to regard it as a 'theory' rather than as a compendium of misanthropic observations. It is a generalisation extrapolated from Machiavelli's own reading and experiences, and it provides a constant basis for his political analyses and prescriptions. The most important feature of this theory is the presupposition that human nature is stable or immutable. It is the changelessness and predictability of human behaviour that enables us to make timeless generalisations about politics.[28] Although their conduct is always in some degree modified by the conditions under which they live, human beings display the same fundamental characteristics always and everywhere; and these characteristics are not of the kind traditionally admired. 'One can,' Machiavelli says in *The Prince*,

> make this generalisation about men: that they are ungrateful, fickle, liars and deceivers; they shun danger and are greedy for profit; while you treat them well they are yours...but as soon as you are in danger they betray you.[29]

In the *Discourses* he remarks in a similar vein that

> All men are bad, and ready to display their vicious nature whenever they find an opportunity to so do. If their evil disposition remains for the time being concealed, this must be attributed to some unknown reason, and we must assume that it has lacked occasion to show itself; but time, which has been called the father of all truth, does not fail to bring it to light.[30]

Machiavelli's suggestion, in these and similar passages, is not that men are 'bad' only because of some extraneous factor that might be corrected by education or removed by changes in their material circumstances. Nor is his view a religious one, having to do with sin or the Fall. His anthropology is not unlike St Augustine's, but it is completely secular. He uses the language of condemnation—'bad,' 'vicious,' 'evil'—but his purpose is descriptive. Men are vicious because that is what human nature is like; and this, Machiavelli thinks, is a judgment supported by the overwhelming evidence of the past. For him, as for the radical Sophists, it is a truth of experience that the behaviour of mankind is distinguished by an inveterate and aggressive individualism. This 'evil disposition' has its root, he believes, in selfishness or egoism. To borrow the expression that St Augustine had used to make in effect the same point, the behaviour of mankind is driven by self-love. This self-love manifests itself primarily in the desire for self-preservation and security. Then, when security has been achieved and men feel safe, they fall prey to a single-minded devotion to personal power and the glory inseparable from it. Power, for Machiavelli as for the radical Sophists, means freedom to act and live as one chooses. This is one of the main reasons why people value it so highly. Liberty for Machiavelli is 'negative' liberty. One is free to the extent that one is not under the power of anyone else. Even those who will never be in a position to rule others at least wish to have power enough to prevent themselves from coming too completely under the control of others. The world is divided into those who dominate and those who strive not to be dominated; but there is no one who is not striving at all. This is the most basic premiss of Machiavelli's theory of human nature: that there is no one—or at least that experience encourages us to believe that there is no one—who is not striving at all.

Political relations, both within and between States, can therefore never be understood except in terms of such striving. For Machiavelli, as for Augustine, the heart of man can find no rest because desire is incessant. It is this feature of their psychology that makes individuals unreliable, careless of even the most elementary moral standards, and dangerous to one another. While self-love can sometimes make people timid, its usual effect is to make them ferocious. On Machiavelli's account, men are fighting animals. There is a paradox at the heart of the typical human temperament. We want security, but we also like strife and thrive on it. Peace and prosperity always turn out to be boring; when we get what we want, we always find that we want more. This explains why men turn on one another not only when they have to, but whenever they get the chance. 'When men are no longer obliged to fight from necessity,' Machiavelli says,

> they fight from ambition; and this passion is so powerful in the hearts of men that it never leaves them. The reason for this is that nature has created men in such a way that they desire everything, but are unable to attain it. Because desire is thus always greater than the capacity for acquisition, discontent with what they have and dissatisfaction with themselves results.[31]

Such remarks purport to express truths of experience. They are stated as generalisations assumed to be so universally valid that they must govern all our expectations of how political actors will behave. *Nature has created men in such a way that they desire everything*. It is because this natural desire is so constitutive of human behaviour that political experience has always been inseparable from struggle. Nor is such desire confined to the great and mighty. The great and mighty are only those who have for the time being succeeded in achieving what everyone really wants. The wish to dominate others is, Machiavellli says in the *Discourses*, 'so great that it not only governs the mind of those born with the expectation of a throne, but also that of those who have no such expectation at all.'[32]

For Machiavelli, therefore, politics is not, and cannot be, characterised by the kind of co-operation and organic interdependence that Plato and Aristotle assumed to be possible and desirable. The view of human nature as having a natural capacity for altruism and co-operation is mistaken, as is the 'feudal' conception of an unchanging and organic social order.[33] Political society is necessarily a thing of divisions, and cannot be reduced to a single unity of purpose. All men wish to achieve power over their fellows in order to satisfy their own desires, even if those desires extend to nothing more than security for themselves and their families. Men are able to co-operate, but they do so only insofar, and only for as long, as co-operation serves their personal goals. We should take it for granted that, in any particular instance, self-interest will triumph over moral principle and social responsibility. It is humbug for rulers to represent themselves as being dedicated to a common good or public interest. Undoubtedly it is useful humbug. It is always a shrewd move to persuade people that what is happening to them is happening for their own good, and most people are stupid or apathetic enough to be taken in.[34] But, in reality, politics invariably involves struggle of one kind or another, and such struggle is always the self-interested struggle of egocentric individuals. This state of things is intensified by the fact that we live in a world where resources are scarce.[35] There is no natural law; only natural necessity.[36]

It is in a monarchy that political struggle is played out in its most elemental form. Here, the struggle is that of one man, the prince, to dominate everyone else. It is true that the prince's private gratification can have an incidental public utility. Strong princes establish States that, at least in the short run, are strong themselves. The ruthless qualities of a Lorenzo de' Medici are just what is needed to unite Italy in the face of her enemies.[37] But the prince's primary purpose is easily described. It is his own secure tenure and free enjoyment of power. Machiavelli observes moreover that the struggle for power can be studied most effectively, and its complications understood most clearly, in the case of the 'new' prince: the political *arriviste* who has seized power only lately. His position is not buttressed by the normal legitimating factors: ecclesiastical sponsorship, tradition, or the people's veneration for his family. 'A new princely government encounters difficulties,' Machiavelli observes, whereas 'hereditary States, being accustomed to the family of their princes, are maintained with fewer difficulties than new ones.'[38] It is the vulnerability of the new prince, and hence the level of virtuosity that he is called upon to display, that makes his predicament so illustrative of the nature of politics and his success so worthy of congratulation. The established prince who contrives to lose power in conditions where it is so easy not to do so incurs great disgrace. The new prince, by contrast, has to maintain and consolidate his position by his own prowess, and we can only admire the prince who succeeds in doing so. Ostensibly, *The Prince* is a treatise—cynical, satirical, sincere: opinions have always differed—on the conditions and dynamics of princely success.

Machiavelli's recommendations are famously candid. Above all, the prince must make skilful use of force and deceit. In proposing this, Machiavelli is, of course, recommending the kind of behaviour that his most admired predecessors in the canon of political thought had condemned as tyrannical. But because, to his mind, we must believe that man is the creature of his passions, and that those passions are invariably selfish, it is both pointless and unsafe to suppose that subjects can be ruled by obtaining their rational consent or appealing to their better nature or setting them a good example. All men will 'display their vicious nature whenever they find occasion to so do.' There is, in politics, no such thing as an effective appeal to reason. Where there is a choice, individuals will always respond to the dictates of passion rather than to the requirements of reason. It is, therefore, only by manipulating those passions that men can be made to do what one wants them to do.

Machiavelli supposes, again on what he takes to be the basis of experience, that the passions to which men are subject are four: love, hatred, fear and contempt. These passions govern human behaviour in several combinations, though the number of combinations is restricted by the fact that some passions cancel one another out.[39] Love and hatred are mutually exclusive; clearly, it is not possible simultaneously to love and hate someone. Similarly, it is not possible simultaneously to fear and despise someone; fear and contempt are also incompatibles. The compatible pairings are love and fear, love and contempt, hatred and fear, and hatred and contempt. The passions that the prince will most obviously seek to inspire in those under him are the compatibles of love and fear. If men hate and despise their ruler, they cannot be controlled; they will, indeed, be tireless in seeking opportunities to act against him. On the face of it, therefore, love and fear are to be induced, and contempt and hatred avoided. But the very worst thing that can happen to a ruler in seeking to maintain his power is that he be despised. Thus, though love and fear are best, hatred and fear are to be preferred to love and contempt. Any combination with fear will be good from the prince's point of view because it will mean that men can be controlled through their fear. Any combination with contempt, even if that combination is love, is to be avoided because it will deprive the ruler of his power to coerce: fear and contempt are incompatibles. It is desirable but not essential to be loved; but it is essential to be feared, and it is above all essential not to be despised.[40]

Whatever else is desirable, then, the primary secret of power and security is fear. Here again, Machiavelli finds himself at loggerheads with much of the political thought of the past, and with the ideas of many of his contemporaries. Political writers before Machiavelli had often counselled princes to seek to inspire love in their subjects. They had taken it as self-evident that subjects who love their prince will be dutiful and obedient subjects. 'From love,' says St Thomas, 'comes the fact that the kingdoms of good kings are stable; for their subjects do not refuse to expose themselves to any peril whatsoever for their sake.'[41] So far as Machiavelli is concerned, however, the political animal will understand well that all love is really self-love. If he does not strictly know that this is true, he will at all events proceed on the supposition that it is. He will assume that his subjects love him for the favours he can do them, and that they will cease to love him when he is compelled, as he inevitably will be from time to time, to punish them or demand sacrifices of them. Though it is a good thing for the prince to be loved, this is not something over which he has final control. If he relies on love alone, he places himself in the hands of others: a sacrifice of freedom which, to Machiavelli, is the worst mistake he can make. Fear, on the other hand, has the great advantage that it is within the prince's power always to induce it. It is a passion that depends not on the circumstances or gift of its object, but on the coercion that he can deploy and the reprisals that he is in a position to exact.

> Men have less scruple in offending someone who makes himself loved than someone who makes himself feared; for love is fastened by a chain of obligation which, because men are selfish, is broken whenever it serves their purpose; but fear is maintained by a dread of punishment that never fails...[M]en love of their own free will, but they fear at the will of the prince, and...the wise prince must rely on what is within his own power, not on what is in the power of others.[42]

It is better to accept the fear and hatred of your subjects than to risk their contempt by trying to buy their love. Fear is not subject to fortune, and will underwrite the continuance of the prince's power. Love not backed by force can all too easily turn into hatred or the still more dangerous contempt, but fear can stand alone.

What all this means, in plain terms, is that the foundation of the prince's power is armed force and his willingness to use it ruthlessly. Machiavelli says repeatedly that the only arts that the prince need acquire are the military arts. Savonarola had tried to govern Florence by moral force. When the people no longer believed in him, he had no means of compelling their obedience: unarmed prophets never succeed for long.[43] The lesson of Savonarola is one that Machiavelli takes very much to heart. Many of Machiavelli's renaissance contemporaries, and many of his forebears in the history of political thought, had taught that the prince should be a cultivated and humane man: a patron of the arts, godly, wise, learned, and so on. This is one of the ways in which he can make himself loved and admired. To Machiavelli, though, the proper study of the prince is the art of war. This is because, for Machiavelli, political life is itself only a kind of muted or ritualised warfare. In understanding politics in this way, he is thinking along precisely the lines that one might expect a professional diplomat to favour. He finds it easy to suppose that, in quality if not in scale, the relations between a ruler and his subjects are the same as those between sovereign States. To borrow an expression adopted by later political writers, the prince and his subjects are in a state of nature relative to one another. It is as if, to Machiavelli's mind, subjects are perpetually at war with their ruler, just as States are always potentially or actually at war with their neighbours.

The correct general policy of the prince, therefore, is to ensure that there is no one who has sufficient power to challenge him, because, if such persons exist, he must calculate that they will be driven by lust for power to challenge him indeed. As far as domestic politics is concerned, the prince must have always in mind the conviction that any or all of his subjects will harm him if it suits them and if they can do so with impunity. A similar consideration applies in the field of foreign policy or international relations. War between States, Machiavelli thinks, can never be avoided; it can only be postponed. The prince who does not realise this is heading for disaster. If there are neighbouring powers capable of challenging his position, war is inevitable, because neither side can rest secure until the threat from the other is removed. It is always best to attack if one has the advantage or to destroy the other's advantage by diplomacy if not. War should never be postponed to one's own detriment. It is also a great mistake to employ mercenaries, for the prince's security will then depend on people over whom he has no reliable hold. Above all, if the prince is forced to injure others, he should do it in such a way as to eradicate them altogether, or at least he should find some way of permanently depriving them of their power. If he does not do this, their desire for vengeance will augment their natural ambition and they will leave no effort unmade, no stone unturned, to undermine him. 'Men,' Machiavelli says, 'must be caressed or annihilated.'[44] If the prince conquers a free city, he will be well advised to destroy it utterly, because a people accustomed to liberty can never be reconciled to losing it.[45]

Politics and Morality

As we have so far considered it, then, Machiavelli's view of nature, morality and politics is very different from the beliefs and prescriptions of the major political philosophers of the past. It is a far cry from the insistence that the good ruler is also and necessarily a good man; that he will set an example of moral virtue to his subjects; that he will seek to secure the common good rather than his own good; that he will submit to the guidance of the Church or make his laws conform to universal natural principles. It is by reason of his frank departure from the conventional pieties that so many have thought, or professed to think, Machiavelli shocking. To the author of *The Prince*, politics is about getting and keeping power. The important features of political conduct are not its moral aspects but its consequences and strategic effects. Virtue in the usual sense—moral virtue—is neither here nor there. Machiavelli often uses the word virtue, but the primary meaning that he attaches to it is a quasi-technical one. It is a meaning that looks back to the Greek idea of *areté*. It looks back especially to the kind of *areté* that the Sophists claimed to be able to teach (see p. 20). Virtue, to Machiavelli—let us adopt the customary practice of retaining the Italian spelling, *virtù*—is not moral virtue. It is a particular kind of skill or aptitude, combined, of course, with the will to use it.

We can amplify Machiavelli's idea of *virtù* by noting the relation that he conceives as holding as between *virtù* and *fortuna*.[46] There is, he observes, a considerable extent to which human beings live at the mercy of the goddess Fortuna. Half of everything we do is in her hands. The greatest of men—Cesare Borgia is a case in point—can be brought low by sheer bad luck.[47] Experience teaches us also that Fortuna is a fickle goddess. Her favours are not necessarily bestowed upon the righteous. The good do not always prosper; when they do, the bad often prosper too: fortune favoured the pious Scipio, but she favoured the brutal Hannibal also.[48] Life does not run in comfortable grooves; unpredictable and unexpected things happen; we find ourselves in a morally incoherent world in which there is no necessary relation between what we deserve and what we get. And nowhere is this unpredictability and moral incoherence more pronounced than in the political forum. Those who occupy the shifting and unstable world of politics are pre-eminently at the mercy of Fortuna. For them, there is certainly no reliable connection between desert and reward. They do not know from one day to the next what will happen, who is true and who false, how loyalties will change, how the balance of forces will alter, and so forth.

In contrast to the variable and contingent world of practical affairs, however, stands an important fact: that human beings have moral temperaments that are for the most part inflexible and resistant to change. An individual's character and disposition, and therefore his mode of procedure, is usually something fairly fixed and constant. This feature of human psychology is created or reinforced by the kind of education to which most people are exposed. One is not brought up to be truthful or just only sometimes or when it serves one's interests; the moral virtues, as traditionally understood, are virtues that one must deploy consistently. But what is the good of having an inflexible mode of procedure in a world where the necessities under which fortune places one are so shifting and unforeseeable? Always to act in the same way regardless of the predicament in which you find yourself is, Machiavelli insists, a short road to ruin. This is particularly true if you are a prince, and especially a new prince, trying to survive in the volatile and merciless arena of politics.

We can say in a nutshell, then, that, for Machiavelli, *virtù* is that combination of personal qualities, that skill or prowess, which enables an individual to encounter the blows of fortune, however unexpected, and overcome them by whatever means prove necessary. Machiavelli's *virtù* is Roman, not Christian. It is not moral excellence, but energy, indomitable will, courage, ambition, resourcefulness. Above all, it is a kind of versatility or adaptability. Fortuna, he tells us, committing in the process a celebrated piece of political incorrectness, is like a wilful and headstrong woman. A man of energy and vision will cope with her, as he would cope with any wilful and headstrong woman, by beating her into submission.[49] In his encounters with Fortuna, it will not do for the prince to be confined by a rigid moral temperament. He must be able to use both the lion and the fox in him; he must employ every resource of strength and cunning; he must be ready to be both man and beast.[50] When mercy is appropriate, let him be merciful; when it is appropriate for him to be merciless, savage and terrifying, let him be merciless, savage and terrifying. Let him be honest and truthful where necessary; but let him lie and break faith where necessary too.[51]

> One who wishes to make a profession of goodness in everything must inevitably come to grief in the midst so many who are not good. It is therefore necessary for a prince who wishes to maintain himself to learn how to be not-good and to use this knowledge, or not use it, according to the necessity of the case.[52]

It is in politics that we most strikingly confront the irreconcilable plurality of our values. The prince must do whatever circumstances dictate. If those circumstances oblige him to disregard the traditional moral values and Christian ways of behaving, then disregard them he should and must. This may be regrettable—and we should not forget that Machiavelli thinks that it *is* regrettable.[53] But, given that the individual in question wishes to take part in the power-struggle of politics at all, it will be self-defeating for him to act in ways that will increase his chances of losing power, or to omit to act in ways that will increase his chances of keeping it.

Many of Machiavelli's contemporaries held, and many subsequent critics have continued to hold, that he is a teacher of evil. By the early seventeenth century, his name had become a synonym for perfidy and cunning.[54] But it is easy enough to see that Machiavelli does not really counsel wickedness, and that the prince whose picture he paints is not, strictly speaking, a wicked man. Machiavelli does not condemn violence, but nor does he glorify it for its own sake: 'It is the man who uses violence to destroy things who is to be blamed, not the man who uses it to improve them.'[55] He does not repudiate the moral values to which most people subscribe. He is ready to concede that, from the point of view of ordinary morality, necessity requires political actors to do deplorable things. But he understands that a prince who cannot change his mode of procedure to suit changing conditions will not be a prince for long.[56] This is a fact of life; there is no point in rending one's garments about it. Most people cannot deviate from what their character or education predispose them to; or, perhaps, having prospered by walking in one path, they cannot persuade themselves to adopt another. If one could alter one's character and mode of procedure to suit the varying conditions of life, one's fortune would be as much under one's own control as it is possible for it to be. The successful prince, Machiavelli thinks, is a man who can do exactly this. The ability by which he counteracts the fluctuations of fortune is the ability to be infinitely flexible, to bend with the breeze. Everything he does he does because circumstances require it.

We might, therefore, most accurately describe the prince not as wicked or immoral, but as an individual called upon to act in a theatre where genuine morality (as distinct from the sham morality necessary for purposes of disguise) simply has no part to play. Machiavelli, says Benedetto Croce,

> discovered the necessity and the autonomy of politics, of politics which lies beyond moral good and evil...and has its own laws against which it is vain to rebel, nor can politics itself be exorcized or chased out of the world with holy water. This is the idea which pervades Machiavelli's work.[57]

Machiavelli's prince is not good, but nor is he bad. He is neither evil nor the reverse. *Qua* prince, he *has* no moral character; he does not have a fixed habit of mind to act in a certain way. Unlike most people, who do have such a fixed habit, he is able to be completely virtuous or utterly vicious; and he knows how to be both. He is someone who does nothing merely because temperament or moral principle dictates it. The traditional moral virtues are not absolutes to which he adheres through thick and thin. They are modes of action that he can pick up and discard at will.

In analysing Machiavelli's account of the princely character, it should be noticed also that, just as the prince is not the slave of any particular moral disposition, nor is he the slave of his passions. In some respects, indeed, his is an admirable character. The stereotypical villain of classical and medieval political thought, even to those who believe that we are obliged to submit to tyranny, is the tyrant as depicted in Book 8 of Plato's *Republic*. The tyrant is a man out of control; an individual who has surrendered himself to the impulse to try to gratify his every desire, however extravagant. For Plato, the tyrant is a kind of advanced psychopath. Machiavelli's prince, however, even while displaying the kind of behaviour that might normally be described as tyrannical, is certainly not out of control. He is a man of considerable will and strength of character; he is capable of austerity and self-discipline. Just as he can freely set aside any moral scruples he may have, so also can he freely disregard his appetites. Indeed, if he is to avoid incurring the dangerous hatred of his subjects and their still more dangerous contempt, he must be able to ignore his natural desire for gain, luxury, women and so on. If it is true that Machiavelli's prince has none of the traditional moral virtues, it is equally true that he has none of the traditional vices. The demands of morality and the demands of passion are equally irrelevant to him, and he can ignore them at will. At least part of what Machiavelli means by *virtù* is this equal indifference to both moral virtue and vice. The successful prince is the prudent and flexible man who is able to maintain his power and prosper generally by doing whatever the necessities of the time demand of him. In him, the passion for dominion and power is so strong that it overrides all other passions and all moral predispositions or habituated modes of action. In this way, he achieves a reconciliation between *virtù* and fortune.

Republics

Machiavelli's consistent assumptions about human nature and behaviour lead him to conclude that, though power is most easily studied in the principality ruled by a new prince, a republic is a healthier and more successful form of government than an absolute monarchy. Republican government is the subject of the *Discourses*: a work very different from, and much longer than, *The Prince*, but resting upon presuppositions that are in all important respects the same. We return now, then, to a theme mentioned earlier: the unity or coherence of Machiavelli's political thought as represented in *The Prince* and the *Discourses*.

Monarchies and republics, we recall, represent different phases in the process of constitutional change. Machiavelli thinks that republican government is both preferable to monarchy and historically subsequent to it. Republics do not found themselves; unity cannot be created by diversity. States are founded by *virtuosi*, political heroes, who make themselves monarchs.[58] But, in a monarchy, one man has supreme power. One man is in a position to stifle—and, if he is to survive, must stifle—the self-assertive impulses of all those subject to him. Herein lies the chief weakness of monarchical government. Because they focus strife, enmity and envy upon the person of a single individual, monarchies are intrinsically unstable. Moreover, a prince who is answerable to no one is likely to undermine himself by doing foolish things. Even if he does not, there is no guarantee that the prince's successor will be as good a man as his predecessor was. In a republic, by contrast, every individual is in a sense a prince, but in a manner subject to healthy limitations.[59] On the one hand, each is able to develop and deploy his own *virtù* in defence of his security, freedom and property and in pursuit of personal gain and renown. On the other, each is in competition with all others, and no one can act in a way that is completely unrestrained. Machiavelli believes that this kind of individual action tempered by rivalry produces a sort of collective or civic *virtù* that conduces to the stability of the State and therefore to the welfare and safety of all. In a monarchy, he says, only one man is free; in a republic, all are free. Each citizen is able to express his own self-assertive nature as fully as he can, but in ways that allow others to do so also.

It must be understood clearly that Machiavelli's view of human nature is not different as between *The Prince* and the *Discourses*. No moral transformation is effected by the coming of republican government. The collective *virtù* that republics exhibit does not arise out of the kind of friendship or social harmony that Aristotle thinks possible. Men can co-operate with one another; they do so because they know that no individual can match the collective effort of a multitude. But their co-operation is self-interested. Each individual works in harmony with others so far as is necessary to secure his own good, while at the same time competing with others for the things that men value: glory, honour, riches. A republic is likely to be healthier and more successful than a principality not because it is morally purer, but because it furnishes each citizen with both the benefits of cooperation and the opportunity to develop *virtù* by striving to assert himself in an open forum. Republics will be more stable than monarchies, more able to defend themselves, more successful at extending their territories by war: not, however, because they submerge or counteract human self-assertiveness, but because they give more ample scope to it. Public service and love of country are only self-service and self-love viewed under a different aspect. Republican government creates a kind of natural aristocracy. It produces proud, free, indomitable spirits whose vitality and confidence will cause the State to thrive and grow. In republics, as in principalities, political life has something of the nature of muted warfare; but republican government does not break, and does not have to break, the spirits of those subject to it.[60]

Clearly, human nature being what it is, the government of any republic will be confronted by a persistent problem: namely, that of ensuring that the republic does not turn into a tyranny; or at any rate, since constitutional change is cyclical and inevitable, of holding the processes of deterioration at bay. Republics can only be stable and strong if they enable citizens to compete with one another creatively without allowing anyone to acquire so much power that he can subjugate everybody else. There are, Machiavelli thinks, bound to be rivalries within the commonwealth, especially between the aristocratic or commercial élites and the mass of the people. The former will wish to dominate the latter; the latter will wish to remain free. The struggle between the plebs and the Senate in the Roman republic is the case that Machiavelli cites as most instructive.[61] Such conflict is inevitable and ultimately beneficial. 'The multitude is wiser and more constant than the prince.'[62] This is not, however, because there is a 'general' or public will distinct from the aggregate of private wills. Rather, it is because the need constantly to accommodate conflicting private wills produces the force by which good laws are generated.[63] The selfishness of many, who cancel one another out, is likely to do less harm than the unbridled selfishness of one, provided that conflict is kept within bounds by properly designed institutions. Machiavelli realises that actual governmental forms will vary according to the circumstances of the people in question; but the best form of State, he thinks, will be a republic with a mixed constitution like that of the commonwealth of Rome. His reasoning in favour of a mixed constitution is similar to Aristotle's. Such a constitution is best because most able to keep competing interests in equilibrium. Where the people perceive themselves to have a share in government, all are able to feel secure in their honour, property and person.[64] In practice, only a few are likely ever to achieve real influence; but this does not matter, as long as no one feels seriously threatened or resentful.[65] The most successful republic will be one in which each individual is able to enjoy liberty — the freedom to do as he likes in safety — but not to an extent so great that he is able to threaten the liberty of anyone else.[66]

For Machiavelli, therefore, the art of governing a republic is the art of managing the selfish energy of individuals in such a way as to achieve stability and growth and avoid damage and disintegration. He does not value collective or social benefits as such, but only insofar as they contribute to the order and vigour of the State. The laws must be clear and must be made known to all. Citizens who, given half a chance, will always exploit others to suit themselves, must know with a high degree of certainty what they can and cannot do without fear of punishment. When it comes, punishment must be swift, sure and frightening. General economic prosperity should be encouraged, but individual wealth, and the power that goes with it, must be kept in bounds by sumptuary laws. Full recognition must be given to the ambitions and merits of citizens, and advancement in the service of the State should be open to those who desire honour and glory. There should be a State religion for the inculcation and maintenance of civic virtue; religion is an important social glue.[67] This religion should not, however, be Christianity; Christianity is a spineless faith that encourages weakness and submission.[68] There should be a citizen army, both to defend the republic and to extend its possessions by aggressive wars. The army should serve an educational as well as a military purpose: it should instil patriotism, martial virtue and respect for authority. It will also provide a means for individual ambition to find a natural and healthy expression.[69] Social cohesion and vigour are most readily secured in conditions of hardship and crisis.[70] Such conditions make people energetic and resourceful and encourage them to work together, even if only for the sake of self-preservation. Soldiers who must fight or die often find amazing resources of courage and perseverance. Ease and security are inconsistent with public *virtù* not because they make people selfish, but because they turn an already-existing natural selfishness inwards and make it indolent and destructive. Life in a republic must never be allowed to become too easy.

In both *The Prince* and the *Discourses*, then, Machiavelli presents an account of human behaviour that we might fairly describe as a sort of secular Augustinianism. It is secular because entirely divested of the idea that such behaviour is redeemable by grace or capable of being mitigated by the influence of the Church. It is an account that implies a thoroughgoing political realism. The principal force governing human life, and the force that anyone who wishes to survive in politics must keep in the forefront of his mind, is a restless drive for self-assertion. This drive expresses itself as a desire first to preserve and then to advance oneself, where necessary at the expense of one's fellows. Freedom lies in the unrestricted satisfaction of this desire. In essence, the fundamental human drive is what Augustine had called *libido dominandi*, the lust for mastery. In view of it, political activity, for Machiavelli as for Augustine, cannot be regarded as part of the intricate and harmonious working of an ordered social structure. Politics must be conceived as an activity taking place in an open field, characterised by a more or less chaotic play of force. The prince is part of this play of force. He cannot be a man who is simply exercising a particular function within the Divine scheme of things, as he is for St Thomas. In a world governed so completely by the struggle for power, the prince must be one who knows how to attain power and how to hang on to it. His art consists simply in this, and it is exercised to perfection where the play of power is least restrained.

This, then, is all that a study of human nature can tell us about politics. In political life, genuine moral considerations do not arise. The behaviour of the prince will be guided in the domestic sphere by one main operational assumption: that all his companions and subjects are capable of treachery if treachery will serve their turn. Internationally, it will be guided by the principle that every outsider is an enemy. In the *Discourses*, the same assumptions are encountered, and we see human nature analysed in the same way. *The Prince* and the *Discourses* are not different in any radical sense; nor are they contradictory. Both share a view of human nature as individualistic, competitive, and, where necessary, ruthless and unscrupulous. *The Prince* is an essay on how the prince is to control the forces of human nature to his own advantage. The *Discourses* is a treatise on how those forces can be harnessed in such a way as to secure the unity and public safety that Machiavelli, as a product of his own momentous times, valued so highly. But the forces involved in each case are the same.

As a figure in the history of political thought, Machiavelli as it were faces in two directions. On the one hand, he looks back towards the classical past. Contemporary Italy, and contemporary Florence in particular, are his concerns; but most of his examples are taken from the institutions of Athens, Rome and Sparta and the exploits recorded in Greek and, especially, Roman history.[71] Nor is his interest in antiquity a humanist literary conceit only. On the supposition that human nature is something constant and given, he does consistently think that the past has lessons to teach us. He does, in other words, have a genuine philosophy of history. His method arises from the conviction that the behaviour of mankind is subject to general laws capable of being inferred from the events of the past and applied to the present and future. On the other hand, Machiavelli looks forward, towards a kind of political theory from which the traditional moral agendas are excluded. It is a commonplace that Machiavelli is the first political thinker to give serious attention to the idea of *raisons d'état*.[72] This may be so; but it is not the whole story. He esteems adroit political behaviour — the combination of practical qualities that he calls *virtù* — even where no *raison d'état* is at stake. He does so because, at heart, he is impressed by the idea of power itself. Machiavelli's motives, insofar as they are deducible from his writings, are ambiguous; nor is this the 'problem' that it is often seen as being. There is, after all, no reason why Machiavelli's motives should not be as mixed as human motives usually are.[73] He offers 'a wholehearted defence of traditional republican values';[74] but there is a part of his mind to which the values that power is used to serve are of secondary importance. He has a connoisseur's appreciation of efficient means. He admires Cesare Borgia — an individual who, by all ordinary standards, is a cruel and vicious dictator — for his methods, not his purposes. Machiavelli carries us a long step on the way towards those who, especially in the twentieth century, have interested themselves in the analysis of power as a phenomenon divorced from moral considerations.

This is, perhaps, especially obvious in *The Prince*. It is often said, both by those who disapprove of Machiavelli and those who do not, that *The Prince* is a technical manual: a kind of rule book for princes. In one way, this is not a suitable description; in another, it is. On the one hand, the point that *The Prince* makes, reinforcing its argument with a multitude of examples, is that there *are* no rules. The prince has to function in a public world assumed to be governed entirely by the exigencies of power, security and self-advancement. His chance of success depends in some measure on luck, but it depends mostly on his cleverness at improvisation. Rule-bound is exactly what he should not be. He must be able to think on his feet: to read situations, assess his predicament correctly, and do without compunction whatever that predicament requires. On the other hand, there is a sense—a deeply subversive sense—in which *The Prince* is indeed a technical manual. Its purpose is to explain how to practise ruling on the supposition that ruling is a species of art or craft, no different in quality from carpentry or shoemaking. But if this is what ruling is, momentous consequences follow for the definition of political philosophy or political science. It is pointless to explain to the carpenter or shoemaker as such how important it is to be virtuous. It is pointless because it does not make any difference to the practice of his craft whether he is virtuous or not. *The Prince* contains no moral exhortation in addition to practical counsel. It is in this respect that Machiavelli is not quite unique, but certainly very unusual as a political writer. Unlike the great majority of his forebears and contemporaries, he really does seem to believe that politics is a morally neutral activity: an activity capable of being studied and described without regard to moral, spiritual or religious imperatives. The fact that he, more than anyone else, inaugurated this view of how political events and relationships are to be analysed is what makes his thought a suitable point at which to bring this volume to a close.

Notes

Introduction

1. Plato, *Republic* 352D.
2. The definition comes from R. Goodin and H. Klingemann (eds), *A New Handbook of Political Science* (Oxford: Oxford University Press, 1996), p. 7.
3. For these expressions see D. Boucher, *Political Theories of International Relations* (Oxford: Oxford University Press 1998), ch. 2.

Chapter 1

1. For the history of Greece during the period 800–500 BCE, see N.G.L. Hammond, *A History of Greece to 322 BC* (Oxford: Clarendon Press, 1967). See also M.J. Cary and T.J. Haarhof, *Life and Thought in the Greek and Roman World* (London: Methuen, 1968); O. Murray, *Early Greece* (London: Fontana, 1994); R. Osborne, *Greece in the Making: 1200–479 BC* (London: Routledge, 1996); R. Sealey, *A History of the Greek City-States* (Berkeley, CA: University of California Press, 1976). G. Grote, *History of Greece* (10 vols, repr. (from the 1872 edition) Bristol: Thoemmes, 2000), despite its age, is still of great value.
2. But note Waterfield's comment: 'It is...rather naïve to lump all the Presocratics together as if they were somehow identical, although it has been a tendency in the history of philosophy from Aristotle onwards' (R. Waterfield, *The First Philosophers* (Oxford: Oxford University Press, 2000): hereinafter Waterfield).
3. The extant fragments of the presocratic philosophers are in H. Diels and W. Kranz (eds), *Die Fragmente der Vorsokratiker* (3 vols, Zurich: Weidmann, 1951–1952): hereinafter DK. For English translations and commentary see especially Waterfield; also J. Barnes, *Early Greek Philosophy* (Harmondsworth: Penguin, 1987); P.K. Curd and R.D. McKirahan, *A Presocratics Reader* (Indianapolis: Hackett, 1996); M. Gagarin and P. Woodruff, *Early Greek Political Thought from Homer to the Sophists* (Cambridge: Cambridge University Press, 1995); G.S. Kirk and J.E. Raven, *The Presocratic Philosophers* (Cambridge: Cambridge University Press, 1957). And see W.K.C. Guthrie, *A History of Greek Philosophy* (vols 1–3, Cambridge: Cambridge University Press, 1962–1969); G.E.R. Lloyd, *Early Greek Science: Thales to Aristotle* (London: Chatto & Windus, 1970); R.D. McKirahan, *Philosophy Before Socrates* (Indianapolis: Hackett, 1994).
4. For a preliminary account of it, see G.B. Kerferd, *The Sophistic Movement* (Cambridge: Cambridge University Press, 1981), pp. 83–84.
5. DK 11A5; 11A6; 11A20; Waterfield, p. 11.
6. DK 11A12; Waterfield, p. 12.
7. *Metaphysics* 983^{b}6–32; DK 11A12; Waterfield, p. 12.

8. DK 12A9; Waterfield, p. 14. See E. Asmis, 'What is Anaximander's *Apeiron*?' *Journal of the History of Philosophy* 19 (1981); A. Finkelberg, 'Anaximander's Conception of the *Apeiron*,' *Phronesis* 28 (1993); P. Seligman, *The 'Apeiron' of Anaximander: A Study in the Origin and Function of Metaphysical Ideas* (London: Athlone, 1962).
9. J. Engmann, 'Cosmic Justice in Anaximander,' *Phronesis* 36 (1991); G. Vlastos, 'Equality and Justice in Early Greek Cosmologies,' in his *Studies in Ancient Greek Philosophy* vol 1: *The Presocratics* (Princeton, NJ: Princeton University Press, 1995).
10. See C.H. Kahn, *The Art and Thought of Heraclitus* (Cambridge: Cambridge University Press, 1979); G.S. Kirk, *Heraclitus: The Cosmic Fragments* (Cambridge: Cambridge University Press, 1954).
11. Diogenes Laertius 9:6.
12. Cf. DK 22B49a; Waterfield, p. 41; Cf. Cicero, *De finibus* 2:5:15.
13. Plato, *Cratylus* 402A; DK 22A6; cf. 22B12; 22B91; 22B49a; Waterfield, p. 41.
14. DK 22B50; Waterfield, p. 39.
15. DK 22B30; Waterfield, p. 41.
16. DK 22B51; Waterfield, p. 40.
17. DK 22B66; Waterfield, p. 42.
18. Kirk and Raven, *The Presocratic Philosophers*, p. 213.
19. DK 22B80; Waterfield, p. 40.
20. DK 22B53; Waterfield, p. 40.
21. DK 22B114; Waterfield, p. 39.
22. DK 22B33; Waterfield, p. 45.
23. DK 22B54; Waterfield, p. 40. Cf. DK 22B123; Waterfield, p. 40: 'The true nature of a thing tends to hide itself.'
24. DK 22B2; Waterfield, p. 38.
25. DK 22B104; Waterfield, p. 38.
26. DK 22B49; Waterfield, p. 45. Cf. DK 22B29; Waterfield, p. 45: 'The best choose one thing above all: everlasting fame among mortals; but the masses gorge themselves like cattle.'
27. See especially H. Tudor, *Political Myth* (London: Macmillan, 1972), chs 1 and 2. See also G.S. Kirk, *Myth: Its Meaning and Function in Ancient and Other Cultures* (Cambridge: Cambridge University Press, 1970); *The Nature of Greek Myths* (Harmondsworth: Penguin, 1974); S. Price, *Religions of the Ancient Greeks* (Cambridge: Cambridge University Press, 1999); B. Snell, *The Discovery of the Mind in Greek Philosophy and Literature* (New York: Dover, 1982).
28. Cf. C. Brown, T. Nardin and N. Rengger, *International Relations in Political Thought* (Cambridge: Cambridge University Press, 2002), p. 18. See also A.W.H. Adkins, 'Homeric Values and Homeric Society,' in *Journal of Hellenic Studies*, 91 (1971); A.W. Saxonhouse, *Fear of Diversity: The Birth of Political Science in Ancient Greek Thought* (Chicago: University of Chicago Press, 1992), pp. 51, 76; G. Steiner, *Antigones: How the Antigone Legend has Endured in Western*

Notes: Chapter 1

Literature, Art and Thought (Oxford: Oxford University Press, 1986); Woodruff and Gagarin, *Early Greek Political Thought from Homer to the Sophists*.
29. *Iliad* 23:190.
30. Cf. T.W. Adorno and M. Horkheimer, *Dialectic of Enlightenment* (London: Continuum, 1974), p. 8: 'In Homer, Zeus represents the sky and the weather, Apollo controls the sun, and Helios and Eros are already shifting to an allegorical function. The gods are distinguished from material elements as their quintessential concepts. From now on, being divides into the *logos* (which with the progress of philosophy contracts to the monad, to a mere point of reference), and into the mass of all things and creatures without.'
31. *Metaphysics* 983^{b}6–32.
32. See Popper, *The Logic of Scientific Discovery* (London: Routledge, 1959).
33. See Waterfield, p. 49; D. Gallop, *Parmenides of Elea: Fragments* (Toronto: University of Toronto Press, 1984). See also S. Austin, *Parmenides: Being, Bounds and Logic* (New Haven, CT: Yale University Press, 1986); H. Fränkel, *Early Greek Poetry and Philosophy* (Oxford: Blackwell, 1975), p. 349; C.H. Kahn, 'The Thesis of Parmenides,' *Review of Metaphysics* 22 (1968–1969); *The Verb 'Be' in Ancient Greek* (Dordrecht: Kluwer, 1973); 'Being in Parmenides and Plato,' *La parola del passato* 43 (1988); R.J. Ketchum, 'Parmenides on What There Is,' *Canadian Journal of Philosophy* 20 (1990); K. Reinhardt, *Parmenides und die Geschichte der griechischen Philosophie* (Bonn: Cohen, 1916).
34. Kirk and Raven, *Presocratic Philosophers* p. 265. Cf. Guthrie, *Greek Philosophy* vol. 2, p. 4: 'As he develops his strictly logical argument, Parmenides is hampered at every turn...by the *patrii sermonis egestas*. One can feel the struggle to convey philosophical concepts for which the language does not yet exist, and some lines are scarcely amenable to translation at all.'
35. DK 28B4; 28B6.
36. It may be that he wishes us to understand his philosophy as having literally the character of a Divine revelation. Cf. Fränkel, *Early Greek Poetry*, p. 350: 'Whenever he reflected upon his lofty ideas, he felt himself carried away into a realm of light beyond all earthly things. In the introduction to his poem he describes this experience, and since ordinary words are incapable of conveying anything so far beyond the ordinary, he conveys it in images and symbols.' See also Guthrie *Greek Philosophy* vol. 2, p. 7.
37. Waterfield, p. 67; and see P.J. Bicknell, 'Zeno's Arguments on Motion,' *Acta Classica* 6 (1963); N.B. Booth, 'Zeno's Paradoxes,' *Journal of Hellenic Studies* 77 (1957); J.A. Faris, *The Paradoxes of Zeno* (Aldershot: Ashgate, 1996).
38. See J.K. Davies, *Democracy and Classical Greece* (Cambridge, MA: Harvard University Press, 1993); C. Hignett, *History of the Athenian Constitution* (Oxford: Oxford University Press, 1952); A.H.M. Jones, *Athenian Democracy* (Oxford: Blackwell, 1957); C.A. Powell, *Athens and Sparta* (London: Routledge, 1988); R.K. Sinclair, *Democracy and Participation in Athens* (Cambridge: Cambridge University Press, 1988); D.L. Stockton, *The Classical Athenian Democracy* (Oxford: Oxford University Press, 1990).

39. Most of what there is is collected in DK vol. 2. For translations see Waterfield, pp. 205–314; see also K. Freeman, *Ancilla to the Pre-Socratic Philosophers* (Oxford: Blackwell, 1962) and *Companion to the Pre-Socratic Philosophers* (Oxford: Blackwell, 1966); Woodruff and Gagarin, *Early Greek Political Thought*; R.K. Sprague, *The Older Sophists* (Columbia, SC: University of South Carolina Press, 1972). For secondary literature see Guthrie, *Greek Political Thought* vol. 3; S. Forde, 'Classical Realism,' in T. Nardin. and D. Mapel (eds), *Traditions in International Ethics* (Cambridge, Cambridge University Press, 1992); Kerferd, *The Sophistic Movement*; H.D. Rankin, *Sophists, Socratics and Cynics* (London, Croom Helm, 1983); J. de Romilly, *The Great Sophists in Periclean Athens* (Oxford: Clarendon Press, 1992); M. Untersteiner, *The Sophists* (Oxford: Blackwell, 1954).
40. 'It is no exaggeration,' says George Klosko, 'to say that countering the [Sophists' philosophical] tendencies lay at the heart of Plato's philosophic endeavours' (*The Development of Plato's Political Theory* (London: Methuen, 1986), p. 5).
41. *Memorabilia* 1:6:13. The unfavourable sense that we associate with the word Σοφιστής (*Sophistes*) is not intrinsic to it. Originally, a 'sophist' was simply a possessor of σοφία (*sophia*), a term that need denote no more than skill or sound judgment. One's *sophia* might be evidenced in one's accomplishments, and especially one's practical accomplishments, in almost any field: as a shipbuilder, musician, navigator or even wrestler, (see e.g. *Iliad* 15:412; Pindar, *Pythian Odes* 5:115; Aeschylus, *Suppliants* 770 and *Seven against Thebes* 382; Sophocles, *Oedipus Tyrannus* 484; *Philoctetes* 439–440; Euripides fr. 372 and *Iphigenia in Tauris* 1238; Aristophanes, *Frogs* 761). George Grote in the nineteenth century set himself to argue, against the prevailing orthodoxy, that Plato is seriously unfair to the Sophists, and there is undoubtedly much in what he says (*History of Greece*, ch. 67). A number of attempts to rehabilitate the Sophists as credible intellectual figures have been undertaken. See Guthrie, *Greek Philosophy* vol. 3; also Untersteiner, *The Sophists*; Kerferd, *The Sophistic Movement*; Rankin, *Sophists, Socratics and Cynics*.
42. Diogenes Laertius 9:52.
43. Their professionalism is one of the things about the Sophists that Plato most dislikes. He thinks that a teacher's honesty will inevitably be compromised if he allows his livelihood to depend on fees and the popularity that keeps the fees coming. Socrates thought the professional teacher a kind of intellectual prostitute who teaches whatever they want to learn to anyone who will pay (Xenophon, *Memorabilia* 1:2:6; 1:6:5; 1:6:13). Plato says that Protagoras made more money than the famous sculptor Phidias and ten other sculptors put together (*Meno* 91D). He also mentions the large sums made by Gorgias and Prodicus (*Hippias Major* 282D). At *Cratylus* 384B Socrates says that his diction is so bad because he could only afford Prodicus' cheap lecture, not the expensive one. Aristotle has the same joke in mind at *Rhetoric* 1415^{b}12.
44. *Protagoras* 323C–328C.

Notes: Chapter 1

45. Gorgias came to Athens from Leontini in Sicily in 427 BCE on a diplomatic mission. He remained there for some time—evidently long enough to acquire pupils—and 'acquired a great reputation for oratorical skill.' See DK 82A4; Waterfield, pp. 225–226.

46. Callicles is known to us from no source apart from Plato's *Gorgias*. It is possible that Plato invented him, as the spokesman of the particular point of view that he wishes to refute. It has also been suggested that he is the politician Theramnes in disguise. These speculations about the identity of Callicles have no historical foundation, and there seems little point in pursuing them. See Rankin, *Sophists, Socratics and Cynics*, p. 69; also E.R. Dodds, *Plato's Gorgias* (Oxford: Oxford University Press, 1959), p. 13.

47. Sextus Empiricus (*Adversus Mathematicos* 7:65) and Ps.-Aristotle, *On Melissus, Xenophanes and Gorgias* (979^{a}11–980^{b}21) (DK 82B3). The Pseudo-Aristotelian fragment is markedly the less satisfactory of the two. See Waterfield, pp. 232–239, for translations. See also G.B. Kerferd, 'Gorgias on Nature or That Which is Not,' *Phronesis* 1 (1955); 'The Interpretation of Gorgias' Treatise Περὶ τοῦ μὴ ὄντος ἢ περὶ φύσεως,' *Deucalion* 9 (1981).

48. Cf. G. Calogero, 'Gorgias and the Socratic Principle *Nemo sua sponte peccat*,' *Journal of Hellenic Studies* 1957 (I), p. 16, n. 22, who says of *On Not-Being* that 'it is neither a joke nor an exercise, but a highly ironical *reductio ad absurdum* of the Eleatic philosophy.'

49. Cf. Plato, *Sophist* 254A; Aristotle, *Metaphysics* 1026^{b}14; Guthrie, *Greek Philosophy* vol. 3, pp. 192–193.

50. It seems that neither Parmenides nor Gorgias understands the difference between predicative and existential uses of the verb 'to be.' It is from this misunderstanding that the whole ontological puzzle set going by Parmenides, and later to mislead St Anselm so famously, springs. According to Aristotle (*Physics* 185^{b}25), the Sophist Lycophron and others suggested—not altogether seriously, one imagines—that the problem of predication might be avoided by deleting the verb 'to be' from the language. See Guthrie, *Greek Philosophy* vol. 3, p. 216.

51. *Theaetetus* 152A; Sextus Empiricus, *Adversus Mathematicos* 7:60–64; cf. *Cratylus* 386A; Aristotle, *Metaphysics* 1062^{b}13.

52. *Adversus Mathematicos* 7:60–64; and see n. 59 below.

53. *Theaetetus* 151E–152C.

54. See Guthrie, *Greek Philosophy* vol. 3, passim; Kerferd, *The Sophistic Movement*, passim, but especially chs. 6 and 9. See also R. Bett, 'The Sophists and Relativism,' *Phronesis* 34 (1989).

55. The following statement is found in a fragment of Didymus the Blind (b. ca 310), *Commentary on the Psalms*, first published by M. Gronewald, *Zeitschrift für Papyrologie und Epigraphik* 2 (1968), pp. 1–2, and translated in Waterfield, p. 214 (I have slightly amended Waterfield's translation): 'Protagoras says that the being of things that are consists in their being perceived. He says: "If you are here with me, it is obvious that I am sitting, but this is not obvious to someone

who is not here. Whether or not I really am sitting is not clear." They [i.e. the followers of Protagoras] say also that everything that exists consists in being perceived. I see the moon, for example, while someone else does not see it; whether or not the moon really exists is not clear. When I am healthy the apprehension of honey that arises is that it is sweet, but someone else who has a fever apprehends it as bitter; whether it is really sweet or bitter is therefore not clear. In this way they intend to assert the lack of objective apprehension.'

56. Cf. *Theaetetus* 166D–167B. Some commentators speak of this distinction between truth and expediency as if it were a peculiar and slightly disreputable aspect of Sophist thought. In fact, it is a common feature of our relationship with the world. I find it expedient to believe that if I jump out of a high window I shall fall; but I do not *know* that I shall, and it cannot strictly speaking be 'true' that I shall. Students of modern philosophy probably associate this sort of observation with David Hume. Hume's point is that no amount of past knowledge can enable us to predict the future. Protagoras's point seems to be the much more radical one that there cannot be any knowledge at all.

57. Diogenes Laertius 9:51.

58. See, e.g., Kerferd, *The Sophistic Movement*, ch. 9.

59. Diogenes Laertius 3:37. No doubt this was a handbook for students containing examples for use in disputation. The same is probably true of the book called *Kataballontes*. Καταβάλλοντες are, literally, 'wrestling throws'. We may suppose that this was a manual of 'knock-down arguments' or 'arguments to floor you' to be employed in debate. Diogenes Laertius makes the remarkable claim that Plato plagiarised the first part of the *Republic* from Protagoras's *Antilogiai*. This accusation is supported by no other authority, and seems in the highest degree unlikely.

60. Diogenes Laertius 9:51.

61. For some responses to Protagoras' relativism see Plato, *Euthydemus* 286B–287A; *Theaetetus* 171A; Aristotle, *Metaphysics* 1007^{b}18–25; Plutarch, *Adversus Colotem* 1109A. A telling objection, the problem of self-reference, was noted at an early stage. If the statement 'no statement is truer than any other' is true, then it is false; if all knowledge is relative, the knowledge that all knowledge is relative must itself be relative. This argument was known to antiquity as the *peritrope*. See especially *Theaetetus* 171A6–9; DK68A114.

62. *Theaetetus* 167C.

63. Herodotus 3:38; cf. T.H. Irwin, *Classical Thought* (Oxford: Oxford University Press, 1989), p. 60.

64. *The Open Society and Its Enemies* (London: Routledge, 1945).

65. See Protagoras's conversation with Socrates at *Protagoras* 316B–319A. 'What I teach,' Protagoras says towards the end of this passage, 'is the art of making good decisions, both in one's domestic affairs…and in the affairs of the community, so that [the pupil] will be able to conduct political business and manage political matters as well as he can.' Socrates says: 'It seems to me that you speak of political skill and to be promising to make men good citizens of their

Notes: Chapter 1

community.' Protagoras replies: 'Yes, O Socrates, that is exactly what I claim to be able to do.' See also Gorgias's assertion (*Gorgias* 456C–457C) that rhetoric itself is a morally neutral art that may be put to good or bad uses: that it should be used with fairness, and not to undermine others or tyrannise the weak. We note also the almost complete, perhaps embarrassed, silence that Gorgias maintains in the Gorgias while his pupil Callicles defends his own ferocious thesis. See too Gorgias's apparently conservative theory of the virtues as reported by Plato at *Meno* 71D–72A and Aristotle at *Politics* 1260a24–28.

66. See, e.g., *Protagoras* 318E.
67. See G. Kennedy, *The Art of Persuasion in Greece* (Princeton, NJ: Princeton University Press, 1963); R. Wardy, *The Birth of Rhetoric: Gorgias, Plato and their Successors* (London: Routledge, 1996).
68. *Protagoras* 312D.
69. *Gorgias* 456B; cf. 452E–453A.
70. DK 82B11; Waterfield, pp. 228–231. See also D.M. MacDowell, *Gorgias: Encomium of Helen* (London: Bristol Classical Press, 2003); J. Poulakos, 'Gorgias' Encomium to Helen and the Defence of Rhetoric,' *Rhetorica* 1:2 (1983).
71. Cf. *Philebus* 58A–B, where Plato attributes the following sentiment to Gorgias: 'The art of persuasion far outstrips all others and is easily the best, for it makes all things its slaves not by force, but by willing submission.'
72. It has been suggested that we should distinguish two types of Athenian educators: rhetoricians and sophists. There is something to be said for this suggestion; but it is not a distinction that Plato makes in any systematic way. See Irwin, *Classical Thought*, p. 62.
73. *Sophist*, passim; *Republic* 492A–493D.
74. *Republic* 493B–C.
75. Cf. Gorgias, 'It is a law of nature that the stronger is not subordinated to the weaker but the weaker is subdued and dominated by the stronger: the strong lead and the weak follow' (*Encomium of Helen*); see n. 70.
76. Cf. Hobbes, *Leviathan* ch. 6: 'But whatsoever is the object of any man's appetite or desire, that is it which he for his part calleth good; and the object of his hate and aversion, evil; and of his contempt, vile and inconsiderable. For these words of good, evil, and contemptible are ever used with relation to the person that useth them: there being nothing simply and absolutely so; nor any common rule of good and evil to be taken from the nature of the objects themselves.'
77. *Gorgias* 492A–C.
78. Cf. Nietzsche, *The Will to Power*, trans. W. Kaufmann and R.J. Hollingdale (New York: Vintage, 1968), pp. 233–4: 'It is a very remarkable moment: the Sophists verge upon the first *critique of morality*, the very first *insight* into morality: they juxtapose the multiplicity (the geographical relativity) of the moral value judgements; they let it be known that every morality can be dialectically justified...they postulate the first truth that a "morality-in-itself," a "good-in-itself" do not exist, that it is a swindle to talk of "truth" in this field...The

Sophists are no more than realists: they formulate the values and practices common to everyone on the level of values—they possess the courage of all strong spirits to *know* their own immorality.'

79. *Gorgias* 483B–484A.
80. Cf. Hobbes, *Leviathan* ch. 13: 'Nature hath made men so equal in the faculties of body and mind as that, though there be found one man sometimes manifestly stronger in body or of quicker mind than another, yet when all is reckoned together the difference between man and man is not so considerable as that one man can thereupon claim to himself any benefit to which another may not pretend as well as he. For as to the strength of body, the weakest has strength enough to kill the strongest, either by secret machination or by confederacy with others that are in the same danger with himself.'
81. Brown, Nardin and Rengger, *International Relations in Political Thought*, p. 18, quoting T.A. Sinclair, *A History of Greek Political Thought* (London: Routledge, 1967), p. 9.
82. See especially P. Woodruff, *On Justice, Power and Human Nature: The Essence of Thucydides' History of the Peloponnesian War* (Indianapolis: Hackett, 1993).
83. See P. Bobbit, *The Shield of Achilles: Peace and the Course of History* (New York: Knopf, 2002).
84. Thucydides 3:82:1–2; 84:2.
85. C. Schmitt, *The Concept of the Political*, trans. G. Schwab (Piscataway, NJ: Rutgers University Press, 1976).
86. Thucydides 3:82.
87. Hammond, *History of Greece*, p. 420.
88. Thucydides 5:85–111.
89. See e.g. Guthrie, *Greek Philosophy* vol. 3, p. 84; Waterfield, p. 300. Thucydides himself is said to have been a pupil or an imitator of the Sophists Antiphon, Gorgias and Prodicus. See DK 84A9; H. Mayer, *Prodikos von Keos und die Anfänge der Synonymik bei den Griechen* (Paderborn: Schöningh, 1913), p. 61. But see also n. 95, below.
90. *Greek Philosophy* vol. 3, p. 85.
91. Thucydides 5:90.
92. Thucydides 5:98.
93. Thucydides 5:104.
94. Thucydides 5:105.
95. For counter-arguments to the view that Thucydides himself is a straightforward political realist see D. Bedford and T. Workman, 'The Tragic Reading of the Thucydidean Tragedy,' *Review of International Studies*, 27 (2001). See also D.A. Welch, 'Why International Relations Theorists Should Stop Reading Thucydides,' *Review of International Studies* 29 (2003). For the view that the Melians failed to understand the Athenian position see N. Kokz, 'Moderating Power: A Thucydidean Perspective,' *Review of International Studies* 27 (2001).

96. Cf. also Thucydides 3:1–19; 25–50, for the debates in Athens in 427 BCE about how her rebellious ally Mitylene should be treated.
97. Thucydides 5:111. As a postscript, it is fair to note that not all Athenian public figures applauded this deed. Euripides's play *Troades* is a thinly-disguised—and, one may suppose, remarkably courageous—condemnation of the treatment of the Melian women.
98. *Republic* 559D–562A.
99. See Thucydides 2:34.
100. *Euthydemus* 283E–286D; cf. Aristotle, *Metaphysics* 1024^{b}32; *Topica* 104^{b}21.

Chapter 2

1. For the life, works and career of Critias, see Untersteiner, *The Sophists*, p. 313; Guthrie, *Greek Philosophy* vol. 3, p. 298.
2. A. Lesky, *A History of Greek Literature* (New York: Cromwell, 1966), p. 357.
3. Sextus Empiricus, *Adversus mathematicos* 9:54.
4. Xenophon, *Memorabilia* 1:2:31; *Hellenica* 2:3:1; 51.
5. Xenophon, *Memorabilia* 1:2:31.
6. For matters of general history, see the works cited in nn. 1 and 38 of the previous chapter. See also R.K. Balot, *Greed and Injustice in Classical Athens* (Princeton, NJ: Princeton University Press, 2001); K.J. Dover, *Greek Popular Morality in the Time of Plato and Aristotle* (Indianapolis: Hackett, 1974); P. Krentz, *The Thirty at Athens* (Ithaca, NY: Cornell University Press, 1982); J. Ober, *Political Dissent in Democratic Athens. Intellectual Critics of Popular Rule* (Princeton, NJ: Princeton University Press, 1998).
7. This biographical information comes from Plato's *Seventh Letter* (323E–329B), which we here assume to be genuine. For Plato's letters and the questions of authenticity that they raise, see Guthrie, *Greek Philosophy* vol. 4, ch. 7. Plato's letters have been translated by R.G. Bury, *Plato*, vol. 9: *Timaeus, Critias, Cleitophon, Menexenus, Epistles* (Cambridge MA: Harvard University Press, 1929).
8. Despite his attitude to the political opinions associated with Critias, Plato's 'casting' of him in the dialogues *Timaeus, Critias, Charmides* and *Protagoras* suggests that he regarded him with respect or even affection.
9. *Seventh Letter* 325–326.
10. Diogenes Laertius 2:40; Xenophon, *Memorabilia* 1:1:1.
11. Charmides was Plato's uncle. Again, the opening scene of the dialogue called *Charmides* does not suggest that Plato was embarrassed by the connection.
12. Cf. Xenophon, *Memorabilia* 1:2:12; A. Diès, *Autour de Platon* (Paris: Bouchesne, 1927), pp. 166–167; H. Dittmar, *Aischines von Sphettos: Studien zur Literaturgeschichte der Sokratiker* (Berlin: Weidmann, 1912), p. 65.
13. *In Timarchum* 174.
14. It is Socrates who is reckoned to have been 'the first to direct the entire effort of philosophy towards the correction and regulation of morals' (St Augustine, *De civitate Dei* 8:3); but Socrates wrote nothing down, and the 'Socratic problem' is that of how to distinguish the thought of Socrates from that of Plato in

Plato's dialogues. We need not concern ourselves with this problem, but there is no harm in mentioning it. There is general agreement that Plato's earliest dialogues (*Apology, Crito, Euthyphro, Laches, Charmides, Ion, Hippias Minor, Lysis, Euthydemus* and possibly *Protagoras* and *Gorgias*) give us the 'historical' Socrates, whereas the middle dialogues (*Meno, Hippias Major, Cratylus, Phaedo, Symposium, Republic*) and late dialogues (*Parmenides, Phaedrus, Theaetetus, Sophist, Statesman, Timaeus, Philebus, Laws*) increasingly represent Plato's own views as expressed through Socrates. This division seems to be supported by what Aristotle says at *Metaphysics* 987^b, 1078^b and 1086^a. See Klosko, *The Development of Plato's Political Theory*, chs 3 and 4; G. Vlastos, *Socrates: Ironist and Moral Philosopher* (Cambridge: Cambridge University Press, 1991); *The Philosophy of Socrates* (Notre Dame, IN: University of Notre Dame Press, 1971); T. Irwin, *Classical Thought*, ch. 5; *Plato's Ethics* (Oxford: Oxford University Press, 1995). It would be naïve to suppose that Plato's dialogues are straightforward transcriptions rather than, at least to some extent, artistic constructions.

15. *Seventh Letter* 324.
16. *Seventh Letter* 326.
17. Ibid. The same sentiment is expressed in similar words at *Republic* 473C.
18. See G.C. Field, *Plato and his Contemporaries* (New York: Dutton, 1930). See also R.C. Cross and A.D. Woozley, *Plato's 'Republic': a Philosophical Commentary* (London: Macmillan, 1964), Introduction. There is some reason to suppose that the *Republic* is not a single work at all, but a recension of several chronologically-distinct layers of material. Again, this is not something with which we need be concerned; but for some account of the evidence see Guthrie, *Greek Philosophy* vol. 4, pp. 437–438; cf. K.F. Moors, 'The Argument Against a Dramatic Date for Plato's *Republic*,' *Polis* 7 (1987).
19. Unlike Callicles, Thrasymachus is known to us from sources other than, and independent of, Plato. He was by all accounts a distinguished orator and teacher, and the author of several well-regarded works, some or all of which were extant in Cicero's day. One of them, evidently with a nod to Protagoras, is called Ὑπερβάλλοντες (*Hyperballontes*). There seems no reason to suppose that he deserved the bad press given to him by Plato. Everything that we know about Thrasymachus is summarised by Rankin, *Sophists, Socratics and Cynics*, pp. 58–63. For original fragments and references see DK vol. 2, pp. 319–326 and Freeman, *Companion to the Pre-Socratic Philosophers*, pp. 375–381. See also G.J. Boter, 'Thrasymachus and *Pleonexia*,' *Mnemosyne* 39 (1986); L.D. Davis, 'The Arguments of Thrasymachus in the First Book of Plato's *Republic*,' *Modern Schoolman* 47 (1970); S. Harlap, 'Thrasymachus's Justice,' *Political Theory* 7 (1979); T.Y. Henderson, 'In Defence of Thrasymachus,' *American Philosophical Quarterly* 7 (1970); G.F. Hourani, 'Thrasymachus' Definition of Justice in Plato's *Republic*,' *Phronesis* 7 (1962); G.B. Kerferd, 'The Doctrine of Thrasymachus in Plato's *Republic*,' *Durham University Journal* 9 (1947); K. Lycos, *Plato on Justice and Power* (Albany, NY: State University of New York, 1987); B. O'Neil, 'The Struggle for the Soul of Thrasy-

Notes: Chapter 2

machus,' *Ancient Philosophy* 8 (1988); T. Siemsen, 'Thrasymachus' Challenge,' *History of Political Thought* 8 (1987); F. Sparshott, 'An Argument for Thrasymachus,' *Apeiron* 21 (1988); S. White, 'Thrasymachus the Diplomat,' *Classical Quarterly* 90 (1995).

20. J. Annas, *An Introduction to Plato's Republic* (Oxford: Clarendon Press, 1981), p. 9.
21. This at least is what Socrates appears to mean at *Republic* 344D. Professor Bloom's suggestion that the allusion is to the proverbial talkativeness of the attendants at the Athenian public baths seems rather laborious (A. Bloom, *The Republic of Plato* (New York: Basic Books, 1968), p. 445).
22. *Republic* 336B.
23. *Republic* 338C.
24. *Republic* 344C.
25. For the argument in full see *Republic* 338C–344C.
26. See *Republic* 339C–341A.
27. Cf. the position of the radical Sophist Antiphon: 'Doing justice is a matter of not infringing any of the laws of the *polis* to which you belong. One would therefore do justice to his own best advantage if he displayed great veneration for the laws when in the company of witnesses and held the promptings of nature in equally high esteem when alone, with no one to see him' (Oxyrhynchus Papyrus 1364, frag. A, col. 1: DK 87B44 A). For this Antiphon as a teacher of Thucydides see Thucydides 8.68; of Socrates, see Plato, *Menexenus* 236A.
28. *Republic* 344B–C.
29. *Republic* 340D–347D. And cf. Xenophon, *Memorabilia* 1:2:32: 'When the Thirty [Tyrants] were executing many highly-regarded citizens and encouraging so many people to commit crimes, Socrates said: "It seems very strange to me that a herdsman who lets his cattle dwindle and go to ruin should not admit that he is a poor herdsman; but even stranger that a statesman who causes the citizens to dwindle and go to ruin should feel no shame nor think himself a poor statesman".'
30. *Republic* 343A.
31. Cross and Woozley (*Plato's Republic*, p. 51) and Annas, who follows them closely (*Introduction to Plato's Republic*, p. 50), complain especially about what they take to be an equivocation on the verb πλεονεκτεῖν (*pleonektein*: 'to outdo'). Cross and Woozley go so far as to say: 'It is difficult to believe that Plato intended this argument seriously, for it is almost embarrassingly bad' (p. 52). But is the equivocation really so glaring? Even if it is, does this really matter? Here, as so often elsewhere in the interpretation of Socratic argument, such complaints arise from an insistence on taking the language of analogy more literally than it need or should be taken. Illustrative stories and comparisons are not on the whole meant to be read with insistence on minute accuracy and consistency of language. Socrates's argument needs to be received with a degree of sympathy, having regard to the fact that we are supposed to be listening to a conversation and not reading a dissertation. There is

nothing wrong with its gross structure, and its overall point, as elaborated in the rest of the dialogue, is clear enough. Alan Bloom remarks pertinently: 'The Platonic dialogues do not present a doctrine; they prepare the way for philosophizing...One must philosophize to understand them' (*The Republic of Plato*, p. xxi).

32. *Republic* 350D.
33. *Gorgias* 507E–508A.
34. *Philebus* 25E.
35. *Statesman* 283C. R.L. Nettleship expresses the point cogently: 'To Plato and Aristotle alike the natural way of expressing the truth that there is some distinction between right and wrong, or that there is such a thing as moral principle, is to say that there is such a thing as limit or measure, without which it is literally true that human life would be impossible' (*Lectures on the Republic of Plato* (London: Macmillan, 1951), p. 39).
36. *Gorgias* 492E; 507A; *Republic* 477D.
37. *Republic* 576B–592B.
38. *Republic* 353C.
39. *Republic* 353A–354A.
40. *Republic* 368D–E.
41. The kind of city that pigs might live in, as Glaucon describes it at *Republic* 372D. And see D.T. Devereux, 'Socrates' First City in the *Republic*,' *Apeiron* 13 (1979).
42. *Republic* 369B.
43. *Republic* 372E–373A.
44. *Republic* 420B–C.
45. Presumably the translator should say 'Fairville,' or something of the kind.
46. *Republic* 592B.
47. Οι πολλοι are, literally, 'the many': that is, everybody not involved in the executive and administrative tasks of government; but the usual translation 'Producers' best conveys the idea that, according to Socrates, they will be the economically active members of the ideal city. Cross and Woozley suggest (*Plato's Republic*, p. 98) 'Economic Class' as a translation; though, for the reasons given already, we here prefer not to use the word 'class'.
48. For some discussion of the ambiguities here, see Cross and Woozley, *Plato's Republic*, p. 106.
49. *Republic* 428C.
50. *Republic* 429A.
51. *Republic* 430E; 431A–B; 431E; 432A.
52. *Republic* 432D–E.
53. *Republic* 433A.
54. *Republic* 412C.
55. *Republic* 420B–C.
56. See. n. 31.
57. *Republic* 439D–440A.

Notes: Chapter 2

58. *Phaedrus* 253D–254E.
59. *Republic* 367B–C.
60. *Republic* 443A.
61. *Republic* 473C–487A.
62. *Republic* 487C–D; cf. *Gorgias* 484C–485E; Isocrates, *Antidosis* 264.
63. See *Republic* 454B–471C.
64. *Republic* 471C–541B. See Irwin, *Classical Thought*, ch. 6; I.M. Crombie, *An Examination of Plato's Doctrines* vol. 2 (London: Routledge, 1963); N. Gulley, *Plato's Theory of Knowledge* (New York: Barnes and Noble, 1962); D. Ross, *Plato's Theory of Ideas* (Oxford: Oxford University Press, 1951).
65. Aristotle tells us (*Metaphysics* 987^{a}30) that Plato's first teacher was the Heraclitean philosopher Cratylus; (see also the Platonic dialogue of that name). 'Having as a young man become acquainted with Cratylus and the Heraclitean doctrines that all sensible things are always in a state of flux and there is no knowledge of them, he continued to hold these views in later years.' Cf. G.C. Field, 'Aristotle's Account of the Historical Origin of the Theory of Ideas,' *Classical Quarterly* 17 (1923).
66. Diogenes Laertius 6:24.
67. *Republic* 477A.
68. *Republic* 475E.
69. *Republic* 471C–541B.
70. *Republic* 376C–427E.
71. *Republic* 523A.
72. *Republic* 540A–B.
73. *Republic* 514A–517C. See also Cross and Woozley, *Plato's Republic*, chs 9 and 10; N.R. Murphy, *The Interpretation of Plato's Republic* (Oxford: Clarendon Press, 1951), ch. 8.
74. Cf. *Republic* 517D–E (italics ours): 'Do you think it at all remarkable that the man who returns from the contemplation of things Divine and becomes once more involved with the wretched concerns of men should be thought unimpressive and foolish if, while still unaccustomed to darkness and peering in the poor light, *he should be called upon to argue in court or elsewhere about the shadows of justice or the images whereby such shadows are cast with men whose minds have never grasped justice itself?*
75. *Republic* 515E.
76. See. e.g., Guthrie, *Greek Philosophy* vol. 4, pp. 349 and 503; see also A.S. Ferguson, 'Plato's Simile of Light, Part I,' *Classical Quarterly* 15 (1921); 'Plato's Simile of Light, Part II,' *Classical Quarterly* 16 (1922); 'Plato's Simile of Light Again,' *Classical Quarterly* 28 (1934).
77. *Republic* 517B–C.
78. *Republic* 509B.
79. *Republic* 517A.
80. *Republic* 500C.

81. But why would anyone who has achieved the degree of enlightenment that Socrates's philosophers have *want* to return to the cave: why would they want to assume responsibility for government? Socrates says (*Republic* 500D; 519C) that they will govern only under compulsion or necessity. Part of what he means seems to be that they will be compelled to rule by their own sense of duty. He also suggests (*Republic* 520D–521B) that it is a positive advantage to be governed by someone who does not really want the job. See also E. Brown, 'Justice and Compulsion for Plato's Philosopher-Rulers,' *Ancient Philosophy* 20 (2000); R. Kraut, 'Return to the Cave: *Republic* 519-521,' in *Plato: Ethics, Politics, Religion, and the Soul*, vol. 2, ed. G. Fine (Oxford: Oxford University Press, 1999).

82. See, for instance, Professor Popper's comment, that 'with all his uncompromising canvas-cleaning, [Plato] was led along a path on which he compromised his integrity with every step he took. He was forced to combat free thought and the pursuit of truth. He was led to defend lying, political miracles, tabooistic superstition, the suppression of truth and, ultimately, brutal violence' (*The Open Society and Its Enemies* vol. 1, p. 169). This kind of thing has now largely gone out of fashion; but for more examples see the excerpts given in T.L. Thorson (ed.), *Plato: Totalitarian or Democrat?* (Englewood Cliffs, NJ: Prentice-Hall, 1963). See also L. Brown, 'How Totalitarian is Plato's Republic?' in *Essays on Plato's Republic*, ed. E.N. Ostenfeld (Aarhus: Aarhus University Press, 1998); D.L. Cady, 'Individual Fulfillment (Not Social Engineering) in Plato's *Republic*,' *Idealistic Studies* 13 (1983); C.C.W. Taylor, 'Plato's Totalitarianism,' *Polis* 5 (1986).

83. *Republic* 389B.
84. *Republic* 459C–460B.
85. *Republic* 415B–C.

Chapter 3

1. Aristotle was by all accounts a prolific author. Unfortunately, almost all his original works have perished. Ancient library catalogues indicate that what we regard as the 'works' of Aristotle consist mostly of drafts and lecture notes written up and edited after his death, though we do not know who the editors were. (His son Nicomachus and his pupil Eudemus are traditionally thought to have compiled two of the three extant versions of Aristotle's ethical doctrines.) Many of the difficulties that attend the study of Aristotle are due to this fact. For the most part, these are not of a kind that we need spend time on. It should be borne in mind, however, that a chapter-length exposition of Aristotle's thought inevitably glosses over problems and inconsistencies that arise both from difficulties intrinsic to the thought itself and from the nature of the canonical and textual evidence.

    For a summary of some important textual matters see C. Lord, *Aristotle: The Politics* (Chicago: University of Chicago Press, 1984), pp. 1–24; see also A.H. Chroust, *Aristotle: New Light on his Life and on Some of his Lost Works* (London:

Routledge, 1973); I. Düring, *Aristotle in the Ancient Bibliographical Tradition* (Stockholm: Almqvist & Wiksell, 1957); P. Moraux, *Les listes anciennes des ouvrages d'Aristote* (Louvain: Editions Universitaires, 1951).

2. The 'young Aristotle's personal intercourse with the venerable head of the school must have been grievously interrupted during his first ten years in Athens, but it would be useless to adduce this in favour of a thesis that Plato did not have much influence over him at all. Evidence from all sides shows that to be false' (Guthrie, *Greek Philosophy* vol. 6, p. 21).

3. Diogenes Laertius 4:1. For what we know of the philosophy of Speusippus see L. Tarán, *Speusippus of Athens: A Critical Study with a Collection of the Related Texts and Commentary* (Leiden: Brill, 1981); see also J. Dillon, *The Heirs of Plato: A Study of the Old Academy (347-274 BCE)* (Oxford: Clarendon Press, 2003).

4. Aristotle was born at Stagira, a Greek seaport colony on the coast of Thrace. Despite an association with Athens spanning some thirty years, he did not at any point apply to become an Athenian citizen. As a resident alien, he was not eligible, under Athenian law, to inherit the property of the Academy. We may suppose also that the appointment of a foreigner as Plato's successor would have occasioned a certain amount of resentment.

5. On this subject, see especially Guthrie, *Greek Philosophy* vol. 6, pp. 20–48 and the references there given. The classic study of the development of Aristotle's thought is W. Jaeger, *Aristotle: Foundations of the History of His Development*, trans. R. Robinson (Oxford: Clarendon Press, 1948).

6. Diogenes Laertius, who has several discreditable stories about Aristotle, says (5:1:2) that he left the Academy while Plato was still alive, the implication being that he disloyally forsook his teacher. There is a clear thread of tradition unfavourable to Aristotle; as to which see Düring, *Aristotle in the Ancient Bibliographical Tradition*, pp. 256–257.

7. Aristotle's father, Nicomachus, had been court physician to King Amyntas of Macedon. The office was apparently hereditary and had been held by other ancestors of Aristotle. This family connection is the obvious explanation of Aristotle's appointment. Plutarch's story (*Alexander* 7), that Philip sought high and low for a tutor and appointed Aristotle because he thought him the world's greatest philosopher, is pleasant but unlikely to be true.

8. All the extant material relating to Aristotle's biography has been collected by Düring, *Aristotle in the Ancient Biographical Tradition*. For a synopsis see Guthrie, *Greek Philosophy* vol. 6, ch. 2. See also the following articles by A.H. Chroust: 'Was Aristotle Actually the Preceptor of Alexander the Great,' *Classical Folia* 18 (1964); 'Aristotle leaves the Academy,' *Greece and Rome* 14 (1967); 'Aristotle's Sojourn in Assos,' *Historia* 21 (1972); 'Aristotle and the Foreign Policy of Macedonia,' *Review of Politics* 34 (1972).

9. See, e.g. *Nicomachean Ethics* 1164^a30; 1181^a10.

10. *Amicus Plato, sed maior amica veritas*: 'I like Plato, but I like the truth more.' This traditional maxim is adapted from Aristotle's comment at *Nicomachean Ethics* 1096^a16.

11. See, e.g., *Politics* 1261ª10 (on community of wives); 1262ᵇ40 (on common property).
12. *Politics* 1253ª1.
13. Aristotle's two other ethical treatises, the *Eudemian Ethics* and *Magna Moralia*, may for our purposes be disregarded almost entirely. They are partly versions of the same material as we find in the *Nicomachean Ethics*. It has been observed that '[t]he three moral treatises that go under the name of Aristotle present a problem somewhat analogous to that of the three Synoptic Gospels. All three used to be ascribed to the direct authorship of Aristotle with the same simple-heartedness, or the same absence of reflection, with which all three Gospels used to be ascribed to the Holy Ghost' (Introduction to *Ethica Eudemia*, in vol. 9 of *The Works of Aristotle Translated into English*, ed. Sir David Ross (Oxford: Oxford University Press, 1915). All essential information about the literary relationships between the three treatises will be found summarised in this volume.)
14. See especially *Republic* 352E–353E.
15. For Aristotle's doctrine of causes see *Physics* 194ᵇ16 and *Metaphysics* 983ª26. See also Guthrie, *Greek Philosophy* vol. 6, ch. 12.
16. It is, though, difficult to think of an alternative translation that might be in all respects satisfactory. For some pertinent remarks against the translation 'cause' see G. Vlastos, *Plato: A Collection of Critical Essays* (New York: Anchor, 1971) vol. 1, p. 134; see also Guthrie, *Greek Philosophy* vol. 6, p. 223, n. 1 for further references and comment.
17. *Politics* 1253ª9.
18. *Politics* 1252ᵇ30.
19. See, e.g., 'The Problem of Teleology,' in J. Barnes, M. Schofield and M. Sorabji (eds), *Articles on Aristotle* (London: Duckworth, 1977) vol. 1.
20. *Nicomachean Ethics* 1095ª15.
21. See *Apology* 31C–D; 40A–C; *Euthyphro* 3B; *Republic* 496C; *Phaedrus* 242B; etc. Incidentally, what a *daimon* might be is illustrated in Philip Pullman's trilogy of novels *His Dark Materials* (New York: Knopf, 1995–2001).
22. Cf. W.D. Ross, *Aristotle* (London: Methuen, 1964), p. 190.
23. *Nicomachean Ethics* 1097ª30.
24. *Nicomachean Ethics* 1098ª18.
25. *Nicomachean Ethics* 1097ᵇ22.
26. *Politics* 1253ª10.
27. *Nicomachean Ethics* 1098ª10.
28. *Nicomachean Ethics* 1103ª11–1138ᵇ14.
29. For Aristotle's doctrine of the soul, see Ross, *Aristotle*, ch. 5.
30. *Nicomachean Ethics* 1138ᵇ20–1145ª11. We shall here consider only *sophia* and *phronesis*. *Techne* is the intellectual virtue that we call upon when we make things rather than think things or do things. It is 'productive' rather than practical reason.

Notes: Chapter 3

31. For some valuable discussions of the difficulties of Aristotle's ethics see A.O. Rorty, (ed.), *Essays on Aristotle's Ethics* (Berkeley, CA: University of California Press, 1980). Aristotle's account of the good life in the *Nicomachean Ethics* should be read in conjunction with what he says about the good and happy life in the *Politics*, especially Book 7. See also T. Engberg-Pedersen, *Aristotle's Theory of Moral Insight* (Oxford: Oxford University Press, 1983); W.F.R. Hardie, *Aristotle's Ethical Theory* (Oxford: Oxford University Press, 1980); D.S. Hutchinson, *The Virtues of Aristotle* (London: Routledge, 1986); R. Kraut, *Aristotle on the Human Good* (Princeton, NJ: Princeton University Press, 1989).
32. See *Nicomachean Ethics* 1177^{a}12–1179^{a}32.
33. See ch. 1, n. 41.
34. On the rather complex subject of the syllogism in Aristotle, see Guthrie, *Greek Philosophy* vol. 6, ch. 9; also Ross, *Aristotle*, pp. 32–61. Professor Ross points out (p. 32) that '[t]he doctrine of the syllogism may fairly be said to be due entirely to Aristotle.' The first occurrence of the word συλλογισμός occurs in Plato, 'but not in the sense given to it by Aristotle, and no earlier attempt had been made to give a general account of the process of inference.'
35. *Nicomachean Ethics* 1177^{a}15.
36. *Nicomachean Ethics* 1177^{b}30.
37. *Nicomachean Ethics* 1178^{a}8.
38. See, e.g., J.O. Urmson, 'Aristotle's Doctrine of the Mean,' *American Philosophical Quarterly* 10 (1973).
39. *Nicomachean Ethics* 1106^{b}36.
40. R.L. Nettleship again puts it well: 'The whole of the Aristotelian doctrine that virtue is a mean between two extremes is an expression of the same conception of measure [as we find in Plato], that the right, or good, or beautiful, always appears as something which is neither too much nor too little. With the Greeks the presence of such a standard is the symbol of the presence of reason in the world, and in morals, and in the whole of human life. It is not a moral conception, but a perfectly universal conception applied to human life. The characteristically Greek way of describing morality is to say that the moral man is the man who recognizes that there is a principle' (*Lectures on the Republic of Plato*, p. 39).
41. *Philebus* 26D.
42. For a full consideration of Aristotle's conception of justice see especially *Nicomachean Ethics* 1129^{a}1–1138^{b}10; see also W.M. von Leyden, *Aristotle on Equality and Justice* (London: Macmillan, 1985); F.D. Miller, *Nature, Justice, and Rights in Aristotle's Politics* (Oxford: Clarendon Press, 1995).
43. We suspect that the English word 'magnanimity' no longer quite manages to convey what Aristotle means by μεγαλοψυχία (*megalopsychia*).
44. See, for example, Bertrand Russell, *A History of Western Philosophy* (London: Allen & Unwin, 1946), ch. 20. It would be a shame if Aristotle's reputation as a moral philosopher were at all to depend on this trivialised and biased presentation.

45. *Nicomachean Ethics* 1094ᵇ11; 1104ᵃ1.
46. *Nicomachean Ethics* 1094ᵇ15.
47. *Nicomachean Ethics* 1125ᵇ31.
48. See, e.g., *Nicomachean Ethics* 1146ᵇ35–47ᵃ7; *De motu animalium* 701ᵃ7–23; *De anima* 434ᵃ15–21. Aristotle's various examples differ in structure. What he seems to have chiefly in mind is the following process of inference:

> All As in situation B should C;
> I am an A in situation B;
> [He does C].

The conclusion to which the practical syllogism leads is not a statement of truth but an action; though it is presumably possible to have a negative practical syllogism also, the conclusion of which is an abstention, a decision *not* to do something. For instance:

> It is wrong for a soldier under enemy fire to desert;
> I am a soldier under enemy fire;
> [He doesn't desert.]

For some discussion of the practical syllogism and its difficulties see Guthrie, *Greek Philosophy* vol. 6, pp. 349–352; see also the references given in Professor Guthrie's footnotes. Guthrie is rather critical of 'this attempt to squeeze the springs of action into the framework of scientific reasoning. Aristotle seems to have temporarily forgotten his own principle that a *logos* must be adapted to suit its subject, and that no discussion of human action should aim at the precision of formal logic or mathematics' (p. 350). This may or may not be a fair criticism. One is inclined to suggest that the practical syllogism can at least serve as a rule of thumb.

49. Some actions, however, are intrinsically bad and cannot be performed with an eye to a mean between excess and deficiency. The intellectual virtue of *phronesis* is therefore not entirely separable from 'virtue' in the ordinary sense of the term. One cannot be spiteful, envious, or shameless well, or be a good adulterer, thief or murderer. See *Nicomachean Ethics* 1107ᵃ10. See also p. 92.
50. *Nicomachean Ethics* 1144ᵃ6; cf. 1145ᵃ5.
51. Sir David Ross, in the Introduction to his edition of the *Nicomachean Ethics* (Oxford: Oxford University Press, 1980) sums matters up in the following words: 'He who lives [the contemplative life] is, Aristotle says, the happiest man. But he is not the only happy man. The life of moral virtue and practical wisdom, concerned with the feelings springing from our bodily nature, is the life of the composite being which man is, and gives us "human well-being." Aristotle assigns two rôles to the moral life. It is a secondary form of well-being, one forced upon us by the fact that we are not all reason and cannot always be living the contemplative life. And, secondly, it helps to bring the contemplative life into being; the practical wisdom of the statesman provides for the pursuit of philosophy and science, and the moral action of the individual provides for it by keeping the passions in subjection' (p. xxiii). This is a judicious summary of what Aristotle means, except that one is inclined to take is-

52. Needless to say, the literature on Aristotle's political thought is very extensive. The following selection may be consulted. R.C. Bartlett and S.D. Collins (eds), *Action and Contemplation: Studies in the Moral and Political Thought of Aristotle* (Albany, NY: State University of New York Press, 1999); R. Bodéüs, *The Political Dimensions of Aristotle's Ethics* (Albany, NY: State University of New York Press, 1993); D. Keyt, and F.D. Miller (eds), *A Companion to Aristotle's Politics* (Oxford: Clarendon Press, 1991); R. Kraut, *Aristotle: Political Philosophy* (Oxford: Oxford University Press, 2002); C. Lord and D. O'Connor, eds, *Essays on the Foundations of Aristotelian Political Science* (Berkeley, CA: University of California Press, 1991); M. Nichols, *Citizens and Statesmen: A Study of Aristotle's Politics* (Savage, MD: Rowman and Littlefield, 1992); C.D.C. Reeve, *Practices of Reason: Aristotle's Nicomachean Ethics* (Oxford: Clarendon Press, 1992) S.G. Salkever, *Finding the Mean: Theory and Practice in Aristotelian Political Philosophy* (Princeton, NJ: Princeton University Press, 1990); P.A. Simpson, *A Philosophical Commentary on the Politics of Aristotle* (Chapel Hill, NC: University of North Carolina Press, 1998); J.A. Swanson, *The Public and the Private in Aristotle's Political Philosophy* (Ithaca, NY: Cornell University Press, 1991); B. Yack, *The Problems of a Political Animal: Community, Justice, and Conflict in Aristotelian Political Thought* (Berkeley, CA: University of California Press, 1993). See also nn. 31 and 42, above.
53. *Politics* 1252^{a}1.
54. *Politics* 1252^{b}28.
55. *Nicomachean Ethics* 1179^{a}4.
56. *Nicomachean Ethics* 1099^{a}31; 1178^{b}33.
57. *Nicomachean Ethics* 1103^{a}15.
58. See, e.g., M. Burnyeat, 'Aristotle on Learning to Be Good,' in Rorty, *Essays on Aristotle's Ethics*.
59. *Nicomachean Ethics* 1103^{a}31; 1104^{a}27.
60. And cf. Michael Oakeshott, 'Political Education,' in P. Laslett (ed.), *Philosophy, Politics and Society* (Oxford: Blackwell, 1963).
61. *Nicomachean Ethics* 1103^{b}5.
62. *Politics* 1253^{a}30.
63. *Nicomachean Ethics* 1097^{b}7.
64. *Politics* 1278^{b}19.
65. *Politics* 1253^{a}20.
66. *Nicomachean Ethics* 1094^{a}28; 1094^{b}4.
67. *Politics* 1260^{a}30–1269^{a}25. According to Aristotle, Phaleas of Chalcedon, a contemporary of Plato, had suggested that equality of possessions would prevent social disputes and revolutionary movements. Hippodamus of Miletus was an eccentric with some unusual ideas about town planning, law and judgment. Aristotle describes them in some detail and appears to take them seriously.

68. *Politics* 1325ᵇ38.
69. Guthrie, *Greek Philosophy* vol. 6, p. 23.
70. See *Nicomachean Ethics* 1096ᵃ11; cf. *Metaphysics* 986ᵃ22; 1028ᵇ21; 1072ᵇ30; 1091ᵃ29. Aristotle also wrote a work called *On the Ideas*, extant only as fragments: see W.D. Ross, *Aristotelis Fragmenta Selecta* (Oxford: Oxford University Press, 1955), p. 122. See also H. Cherniss, *Aristotle's Criticism of Plato and the Academy* (Baltimore, MD: Johns Hopkins University Press, 1944); G. Fine, *On Ideas: Aristotle's Criticism of Plato's Theory of Forms* (Oxford: Clarendon Press, 1993).
71. *Metaphysics* 911ᵃ21.
72. *Nicomachean Ethics* 1096ᵃ15.
73. *Posterior Analytics* 83ᵃ32.
74. *Metaphysics* 991ᵃ21.
75. *Politics* 1278ᵇ8.
76. *Politics* 1279ᵃ25; 1288ᵇ6–1316ᵇ25.
77. *Politics* 1301ᵃ20–1321ᵇ4.
78. *Politics* 1293ᵇ33; 1295ᵃ35.
79. *Nicomachean Ethics* 1160ᵃ31; *Politics* 1279ᵃ25.
80. Although Aristotle's use of the term *politeia* is somewhat ambiguous: cf. *Politics* 1279ᵃ41; 1293ᵇ33; 1295ᵃ31.
81. *Politics* 1284ᵇ10; cf. 1284ᵇ25.
82. See, e.g., *Politics* 1281ᵃ15; 1281ᵃ40; 1286ᵃ10; 1290ᵃ3–1292ᵃ35.
83. *Politics* 1326ᵃ25–1329ᵃ39.
84. *Eudemian Ethics* 1216ᵇ1; a similar point is made at *Magna Moralia* 1183ᵇ15.
85. See W.M. von Leyden, 'Aristotle and the Concept of Law,' *Philosophy*, 42 (1967); see also J. Ritter, *Naturrecht bei Aristoteles* (Stuttgart: Kohlhammer, 1961); L. Strauss, *Natural Right and History* (Chicago: University of Chicago Press, 1953), ch. 4.
86. *Nicomachean Ethics* 1134ᵃ25.
87. *Nicomachean Ethics* 1134ᵇ20; cf. 1162ᵇ22.
88. *Politics* 1256ᵇ25.
89. *Nicomachean Ethics* 1107ᵃ10.
90. *Rhetoric* 1374ᵃ25–1374ᵇ20.
91. *Politics* 1258ᵇ1.
92. *Politics* 1263ᵃ25–1263ᵇ5.
93. *Nicomachean Ethics* 1134ᵃ35.
94. *Nicomachean Ethics* 1179ᵇ30–1181ᵇ10; *Politics* 1287ᵃ30.
95. *Nicomachean Ethics* 1180ᵃ20.
96. *Politics* 1289ᵃ10.
97. *Politics* 1284ᵃ5.
98. Plato, *Laws* 875C.
99. *Rhetoric* 1374ᵇ1.
100. *Rhetoric* 1374ᵃ25.
101. *Nicomachean Ethics* 1137ᵇ25.
102. *Rhetoric* 1373ᵇ1.

103. *Politics* 1328^{b}25.
104. *Politics* 1253^{b}30–1255^{b}15.
105. *Politics* 1259^{a}39; cf. 1260^{a}13. See also *De generatione animalium* 716^{a}5; 727^{a}2; 727^{b}31; 728^{b}18; 765^{b}8; 766^{a}17; 783^{b}29–784^{a}12.
106. *Politics* 1259^{a}27; cf. *Nicomachean Ethics* 1134^{b}15.
107. *Politics* 1327^{b}20.
108. *Politics* 1334^{b}30.
109. What he seems to mean by 'constitutional' government in this connection is that a husband governs his wife in her interests rather than his own; she, however, has no say. They are equals, but not political equals. At *Nicomachean Ethics* 1160^{b}30, he describes the husband's government of his wife as aristocratic; it is government of the less able by the more able.
110. *Politics* 1255^{b}1; 1259^{a}40; *Nicomachean Ethics* 1160^{b}30.

Chapter 4

1. Cf. D. Boucher, *Political Theories of International Relations*, p. 21: 'Plato and Aristotle could not conceive of a higher association than the *polis*, and both believed in qualitative differences between human beings within and without the community, yet both subscribed to universal moral laws above those formulated by each people for itself.' As Professor Boucher points out (pp. 172–173), the two positions are not incompatible. What is remarkable is that neither Plato nor Aristotle seem to have thought seriously about the relations between them and the implications of those relations for political thought.
2. Cf. T.L. Pangle, 'Justice Among Nations in Platonic and Aristotelian Political Philosophy,' *American Journal of Political Science* 42, 2 (1998).
3. For ancient biographies of Alexander see Plutarch, *Life of Alexander*; Arrian of Nicomedia, *History of Alexander*; Quintus Curtius Rufus, *The History of Alexander*; Diodorus Siculus, *Universal History* vols 16-17: all in Loeb Classical Library editions. For collections of documentary sources see P. Harding (ed.), *From the End of the Peloponnesian War to the Battle of Ipsus* (Cambridge: Cambridge University Press, 1985); M.M. Austin (ed.), *The Hellenistic World from Alexander to the Roman Conquest. A Selection of Ancient Sources in Translation* (Cambridge: Cambridge University Press, 1981); A. J. Heisserer, *Alexander the Great and the Greeks: The Epigraphic Evidence* (Norman, OK: University of Oklahoma Press, 1980). Some recent secondary sources are: A. B. Bosworth, *A Historical Commentary on Arrian's History of Alexander* vol. 1 (Oxford: Oxford University Press, 1980); vol. 2 (Oxford: Oxford University Press, 1995); E. N. Borza, *In the Shadow of Olympus: The Emergence of Macedon* (Princeton, NJ: Princeton University Press, 1990); *Conquest and Empire. The Reign of Alexander the Great* (Cambridge: Cambridge University Press, 1988); *Alexander and the East* (Oxford: Oxford University Press, 1996); R. L. Fox, *Alexander the Great* (Harmondsworth, Middlesex: Penguin, 1973); P. Green, *Alexander of Macedon 356-323 BCE: A Historical Biography* (Berkeley, CA: University of California Press, 1991); N. G. L. Hammond, *Alexander the Great. King, Commander, and Statesman* (London: Chatto and Windus, 1982); C.B.

Welles, *Alexander and the Hellenistic World* (Toronto: University of Toronto Press, 1970); See also W.W. Tarn, *Alexander the Great* (Cambridge: Cambridge University Press, 1948).

4. For comments of this kind see, e.g., D.G. Tannenbaum and D. Schulz, *Inventors of Ideas* (New York: St Martin's Press, 1998), pp. 60; 69. Cf. F.H. Sandbach, *The Stoics* (London: Duckworth, 1975), p. 23; A.A. Long, *Hellenistic Philosophy* (London: Duckworth, 1974), pp. 2–3; E. Bevan, *Stoics and Sceptics* (Oxford: Oxford University Press, 1913), p. 32; L. Edelstein, *The Meaning of Stoicism* (Cambridge, MA: Harvard University Press, 1966), p. 13.
5. See especially Long, *Hellenistic Philosophy*, Introduction.
6. For an excellent general account of Hellenistic philosophy see especially A.A. Long, *Hellenistic Philosophy*. See also A.H. Armstrong (ed.), *The Cambridge History of Later Greek and Early Medieval Philosophy* (Cambridge: Cambridge University Press, 1967); W.W. Tarn, *Hellenistic Civilization* (London: Arnold, 1952). See also E.H. Dodds, *The Greeks and the Irrational* (Berkeley, CA: University of California Press, 1951); W.S. Ferguson, *Hellenistic Athens* (London: Macmillan, 1911); R. Pfeiffer, *History of Classical Scholarship* vol. 1 (Oxford: Oxford University Press, 1968).
7. See D.R. Dudley, *A History of Cynicism* (London: Methuen, 1937); H.D. Rankin, *Sophists, Socratics and Cynics*; F. Sayre, *The Greek Cynics* (Baltimore, MD: University of Baltimore Press, 1948).
8. See Long, *Hellenistic Philosophy*, ch. 4.
9. See F. D. Caizzi, *Antisthenis Fragmenta* (Milan: Varese, 1966), frags 22; 69; 71; 80.
10. See *Metaphysics* 1024^{b}33; 1043^{b}23.
11. Thereby establishing a long tradition of sometimes spectacular acts. To display his indifference to death, the Cynic Peregrinus committed suicide by setting fire to himself himself after the Olympic Games of 167 CE. For Diogenes of Sinope, see Diogenes Laertius 6:24.
12. The pun is a late one, apparently due to Lucian in about 165 CE; but the use of the adjective κύνεος (*cyneos*), 'doglike,' to mean 'shameless' or 'disgraceful' is as old as Hesiod.
13. 'Cynosarges' seems to mean something like 'place of the white dog.' The gymnasium was for the use of people who were not pure Athenians, as Antisthenes was not. Those who used it perhaps had some sense of being despised.
14. For Epicurus's writings and ancient sources for his life and thought see H.K. Usener, *Epicurea* (Leipsig, 1887; repr. Stuttgart: Teubner, 1966); G. Arrighetti, *Epicuro Opere* (Turin: Einaudi, 1960); C. Bailey: *Epicurus: The Extant Remains* (Oxford: Clarendon Press, 1926). For sources in English translation, see E.M. O'Connor, *The Essential Epicurus* (Buffalo, NY: Prometheus, 1993). See also C. Bailey, *The Greek Atomists and Epicurus* (Oxford: Oxford University Press, 1928); N.W. de Witt, *Epicurus and his Philosophy* (Minneapolis: University of Minnesota Press, 1954); H. Jones, *The Epicurean Tradition* (London: Routledge, 1992); J.M. Rist, *Epicurus: An Introduction* (Cambridge: Cambridge University Press, 1972); J.

Warren, *Epicurus and Democritean Ethics: An Archaeology of Ataraxia* (Cambridge: Cambridge University Press, 2002).

15. Epicurus claims to have invented his version of this doctrine for himself, though this seems unlikely to be true. There is more reason to believe that he acquired it from a disciple of Democritus called Nausiphanes of Teos, though Epicurus denies the connection and thinks ill of Nausiphanes, about whom he is consistently rude. See Rist, *Epicurus*, pp. 4–6.

16. Sextus Empiricus, *Outlines of Scepticism*, eds J. Annas et al. (Cambridge: Cambridge University Press, 2000). See also V. Brochard, *Les Sceptiques grecs* (Paris: Vrin, 1959); R. Chisholm, 'Sextus Empiricus and Modern Empiricism,' *Philosophy of Science* 8 (1941); C.L. Stough, *Greek Scepticism* (Berkeley, CA: University of California Press, 1969).

17. *Outlines of Scepticism* 1:12.

18. Carneades and his colleagues Diogenes and Critolaus were expelled from Rome at the insistence of Cato the Censor, who feared that their influence might undermine the patriotism of the city's youth. See Plutarch, *Cato Maior* 22–23: 'As soon as the passion for philosophy first showed itself in Rome, Cato was much vexed. He feared that young people might allow their ambitions to be diverted in this direction, and might come to desire above all a reputation based upon feats of oratory rather than feats of arms...Cato did not [insist on the expulsion of the Athenian philosophers] out of personal dislike of Carneades, as some thought, but because he was opposed to philosophy on principle. His patriotic fervour made him despise the whole of Greek culture and its methods of education.' For an account of Carneades see Lactantius, *Divinae institutiones* 5:15; 17–18. See also Cicero, *De finibus* 5:16.

19. Cf. The Four Noble Truths of Buddhism: life is suffering; the cause of suffering is attachment; release from suffering is possible; the means of release is the noble eightfold path of right understanding, right thought, right speech, right action, right livelihood, right effort, right mindfulness and right concentration. On this subject see, e.g., W. Rahula, *What the Buddha Taught* (New York: Grove Press, 1997); B. Rewatadhamma, *The First Discourse of the Buddha: Turning the Wheel of the Dhamma* (Boston: Wisdom Publications, 1997).

20. See Lactantius, as cited in n. 18, above.

21. For a general account of Stoicism see especially J.M. Rist, *Stoic Philosophy* (Cambridge: Cambridge University Press, 1969); see also A.A. Long, *Hellenistic Philosophy* and *Problems in Stoicism* (London: Athlone, 1971); F.H. Sandbach, *The Stoics*. For a detailed account see M. Pohlenz, *Die Stoa* (2 vols, Göttingen: Vandenhoeck & Ruprecht, 1964). The standard collection of the literary fragments of early Stoicism is H. von Arnim, *Stoicorum veterum fragmenta* (4 vols, Stuttgart: Teubner, 1964): hereinafter SVF. For sources in translation see A.A. Long and D. Sedley (eds), *The Hellenistic Philosophers* (Cambridge: Cambridge University Press, 1967). See also J. Christensen, *An Essay on the Unity of Stoic Philosophy* (Copenhagen: Munksgaard, 1962) and, less useful but still valuable, L. Edelstein, *The Meaning of Stoicism* (Cambridge, MA: Harvard University Press, 1966).

22. Diogenes Laertius 4:62. On Chrysippus in particular see E. Bréhier, *Chrysippe et l'ancien stoïcisme* (Paris: PUF, 1950); J.B. Gould, *The Philosophy of Chrysippus* (Leiden: Brill, 1997).
23. See especially M. van Straaten, *Panétius: sa vie, ses écrits et sa doctrine* (Amsterdam: H.J. Paris, 1946); M. Laffranque, *Poseidonios d'Apamée* (Paris: PUF, 1964); L. Edelstein, 'The Philosophical System of Posidonius,' *American Journal of Philology* 57 (1936).
24. See n. 18, above.
25. See E.V. Arnold, *Roman Stoicism* (Cambridge: Cambridge University Press, 1911): old, but very detailed, with many quotations from original sources.
26. It is one of the minor ironies of history that the enlightened Marcus Aurelius should have been the father of the Emperor Commodus, 'to whom lust-ridden and brutish characteristics ... quickly became second nature' (Dio Cassius 72:1).
27. *De civitate Dei* 2:27.
28. See Long, *Hellenistic Philosophy*, pp. 145–147.
29. See SVF 1:85; 1:88; 1:155; 1:529; 2:300; 2:316; 2:663; 2:1027; 2:1132–1133; Seneca, *De beneficiis* 4:7.
30. *Adversus Hermogenem*, 44.
31. See, e.g., *De Genesi ad litteram* 5:4:7; 6:5:8; *De Trinitate* 3:8:13. St Augustine's expression *rationes seminales*—'seminal principles'—is a literal translation of the Stoic λόγοι σπερματικοί.
32. *Meditations* 6:15.
33. Heraclitus on one occasion (DK, frag. 51) uses (or coins) the word παλίντονος: *palintonos*, which seems to mean something like 'tension of opposites.'
34. See Sandbach, *The Stoics*, pp. 79–82.
35. According to Augustine (*De civitate Dei* 8:2), Anaximander 'thought that things are born not from one substance, as Thales thought from moisture, but each from its own particular principles. These principles...give rise to innumerable worlds and all that arises in them; and these worlds, he thought, are now dissolved, now reborn, according to the age to which each is able to survive.'
36. SVF 1:176.
37. SVF 1:177.
38. The doctrine of eternal recurrence was abandoned by Panaetius in the second century BCE, but it never entirely died out. Posidonius resurrected it, and St Augustine criticises it in Book 12 of *De civitate Dei*.
39. We may guess, for example, that the doctrine of *periodoi* reflects the sort of puzzle that we noticed in connection with Parmenides (see pp. 9–11): if we say that the world is not eternal, how can we explain what happened before it and what will happen after it? For this question as it recurred as a problem in Christian philosophy see R.W. Dyson, 'St Augustine's Remarks on Time,' *Downside Review* 99, 340 (1982).
40. SVF 3:4.
41. On this subject, see especially Rist, *Stoic Philosophy*, ch. 7; see also M.E. Reesor, 'Fate and Possibility in Early Stoic Philosophy,' *Phoenix* 19 (1965).

42. Cicero, *De natura deorum* 2:37.
43. Hippolytus, *Philosophoumena* 21.
44. SVF 1:184; 3:16.
45. Diogenes Laertius 7:87–88.
46. Seneca, *Epistulae* 96:2.
47. Epictetus, *Discourses* 4:1:89–90.
48. *Annales* 15:62–64.
49. See especially Rist, *Stoic Philosophy*, ch. 7.
50. Aulus Gellius 7:2:11.
51. Plutarch, *De communibus notitiis* 1065b.
52. *Academica* 1:10:36; *De finibus* 3:9:31.
53. Diogenes Laertius 8:88, quoting Diogenes of Babylon, Chrysippus's successor as head of the Stoa.
54. *Epistulae* 123:3.
55. The Old Stoa drew the distinction between wisdom and folly very sharply: someone is either wise or a fool, and there are no intermediate grades of enlightenment. From the time of Panaetius onwards this exclusiveness gives place to the idea of moral progress and degrees of wisdom. See Long, *Hellenistic Philosophy*, pp. 213–16.
56. Epictetus, *Discourses* 1:13:4.
57. 1:10:29.
58. See SVF 3:178; Diogenes Laertius 7:85–86; Cicero, *De finibus* 3:16; 4:45.
59. Cf. Seneca, *Epistulae* 121:5.
60. Seneca, *Epistulae* 124:9.
61. Ed. G. Bastianini and A.A. Long, *Corpus dei papiri filosofici greci e latini* vol 1 (Florence: Accademia Toscana di Scienze e Lettere, 1988); also H. von Arnim, in *Berliner Klassikertexte* (1906) vol. 4.
62. See Cicero, *De legibus* 1:5:18–19.
63. Diogenes Laertius 7:87–88.
64. 3:22:33. Cf. his remark at *De officiis* 3:5 that it needs no enacted law to tell us that 'it is more contrary to nature for a man to take something from his neighbour and so to derive benefit from his neighbour's loss than is death, poverty, pain or anything else that can affect either our bodies or our external circumstances.'
65. *De finibus* 3:66; cf. *De officiis* 1:12.
66. SVF 3:314; Cicero, *De finibus* 3:67.
67. *De officiis* 1:57; 3:95.
68. *De Republica*, frag 2.
69. SVF 2:528.
70. *De otio* 4.
71. *Meditations* 4:4.
72. *Meditations* 12:26.
73. *Meditations* 6:43.
74. *De republica* 2:26:48.
75. *De officiis* 3:19.

76. *Meditations* 3:11.
77. Cicero, *De legibus* 1:10:29.
78. *De inventione* 2:53:160; and see *De legibus* 1:5:17–18: 'The most learned men' hold that 'law is the highest reason, implanted in nature, which commands what ought to be done and forbids the opposite. This reason, when firmly fixed and fully developed in the human mind, is law. And so they believe that law is intelligence, the function of which is to command rightdoing and forbid wrongdoing. This quality, they think, takes its name in Greek from the idea of giving to everyone his due, and in our language, I think, from 'choosing' [i.e. choosing fairly]...If this is a correct definition, as it certainly seems to me to be, then the origin of justice is to be found in law, for law is a natural force: it is the mind and reason of the intelligent man, the standard by which justice and injustice are measured.' Cicero here takes it that the Greek word *nomos* is derived from νέμω: *nemo*, 'to distribute.' The suggested Latin derivation of *lex* from *lego*, 'to choose' is almost certainly wrong, however; *lex* more probably comes from *ligo*, 'to bind.'
79. *Epistulae* 91.
80. See A.M. Honore, "The Background to Justinian's Codification," *Tulane Law Review* 48 (1974).
81. J. Harries & I. Woods (eds), *The Theodosian Code* (Ithaca, NY: Cornell University Press, 1993); *The Theodosian Code: Studies in the Imperial Law of Late Antiquity* (London: Duckworth, 1993); J.F. Matthews, *Laying Down the Law: A Study of the Theodosian Code* (New Haven, CT: Yale University Press, 2000).
82. From among the very large secondary literature, the following may be mentioned in particular: W.W. Buckland and P. Stein, *A Textbook of Roman Law from Augustus to Justinian* (Cambridge: Cambridge University Press, 1975); D. Daube, *Roman Law: Linguistic, Social, and Philosophical Aspects* (Edinburgh: Edinburgh University Press, 1969); A.M. Honore, *Emperors and Lawyers* (Oxford: Clarendon Press, 1994); *Law in the Crisis of Empire 379-445 AD* (Oxford: Clarendon Press, 1998); W. Kunkel, *An Introduction to Roman Legal and Constitutional History* (Oxford: Clarendon Press, 1973); B. Nicholas, *An Introduction to Roman Law* (Oxford: Clarendon Press, 1975); O.F. Robinson, *The Sources of Roman Law* (London: Routledge, 1996); F. Schulz, *History of Roman Legal Science* (Oxford: Clarendon Press, 1953); *Classical Roman Law* (Oxford: Clarendon Press, 1951). O. Tellegen-Couperus, *A Short History of Roman Law* (London: Routledge, 1990); A. Watson, *Law Making in the Later Roman Republic* (Oxford: Clarendon Press, 1974).
83. See P. Vinogradoff, *Roman Law in Medieval Europe* (Cambridge: Cambridge University Press, 1969), p. 56.
84. *Medieval Political Theory* (Harmondsworth, Middlesex: Penguin, 1979), p. 47.
85. P. Krueger, W. Kunkel and R. Schoell (eds), 3 vols (Dublin-Zürich: Weidmann 1872-1988).
86. *Digesta* 1:2:2.
87. Ullmann, *Medieval Political Theory*, p. 141.

88. Acts 22:25–29.
89. *Digesta* 1:1:1.
90. *Digesta* 1:1:9.
91. *Institutiones* 1:2:2.
92. See A.M. Honore, *Gaius* (Oxford: Clarendon Press, 1962).
93. *Digesta* 1:1:9.
94. Gaius, *Institutiones*, ed. F. de Zulueta (Oxford: Clarendon Press, 1991), 2:65–66.
95. *Institutiones* 1:2:1.
96. A.M. Honore, *Ulpian* (Oxford: Clarendon Press, 1982).
97. *Digesta* 1:1:1.
98. *Institutiones* 1:2:2; cf. *Digesta* 1:1:5.
99. *Institutiones* 1:11:11.
100. *Digesta* 1:1:10.
101. A.P. d'Entrèves, *Natural Law* (London: Hutchinson, 1972), p. 24.
102. See, for example, R.W. and A.J. Carlyle, *A History of Medieval Political Theory in the West* (Edinburgh and London: Blackwood, 1927–1938) vol 1, p. 9.
103. See Sir Henry Maine, *Ancient Law* (repr. New York: Dutton, 1977), pp. 56–57.
104. See the works cited in n. 23, above.
105. *Aeneid*, 6:853.
106. Virgil, *Aeneid* 1:278–279; 4:229; 6:794–795; Ovid, *Fasti* 1:85–86. For an outline of Rome's conception of herself and its history see H. Tudor, *Political Myth*, ch. 3.
107. 'For Tacitus or for Ammianus Marcellinus, Rome has become the eternal city. Events no longer follow each other to form a coherent and purposeful development...The empire stands fast, as indestructible as the heavens above and the earth below.' Tudor, *Political Myth*, pp. 89–90.
108. See especially Donald Earl, *The Moral and Political Tradition of Rome* (London: Thames and Hudson, 1967); see also C.N. Cochrane, *Christianity and Classical Culture* (Oxford: Oxford University Press, 1943); L.S. Mazzolani, *The Idea of the City in Roman Thought: From Walled City to Spiritual Commonwealth* (London: Hollis & Carter, 1970).
109. Boucher, *Political Theories of International Relations*, p. 183–184.

Chapter 5

1. See, e.g., Acts 15; see also J.D.G. Dunn, *Jews and Christians: The Parting of the Ways, AD 70 to 135* (London: SCM, 1991); E. Ferguson (ed.), *Christianity in Relation to Jews, Greeks, and Romans* (New York: Garland, 1999).
2. See, e.g., R.M. Grant, *Augustus to Constantine: the Thrust of the Christian Movement into the Roman World* (London: Collins, 1972); R. Doran, *Birth of a World View: Early Christianity in Its Jewish and Pagan Context* (Boulder, CO: Westview Press, 1996); J.F. Kelly, *The World of the Early Christians* (Collegeville, MN: Liturgical Press, 1997); R.A. Markus, *The End of Ancient Christianity* (Cambridge: Cambridge University Press, 1990); C. Stead, *Philosophy in Christian Antiquity* (Cambridge: Cambridge University Press, 1994). More generally, see C.N. Cochrane, *Christianity and Classical Culture*; E.R. Dodds, *Pagan and Chris-*

tian in an Age of Anxiety (Cambridge: Cambridge University Press, 1965); A. Momigliano (ed.), *The Conflict Between Paganism and Christianity in the Fourth Century* (Oxford: Clarendon Press, 1963).

3. On this subject see especially D.S. Wallace-Hadrill, *The Greek Patristic View of Nature* (Manchester: Manchester University Press, 1968).
4. The definitive study of Tertullian is T.D. Barnes, *Tertullian: A Historical and Literary Study* (rev. ed. Oxford: Clarendon Press, 1985); cf. C. Mohrmann, 'Saint Jérôme et Saint Augustin sur Tertullien,' *Vigiliae Christianae* 5 (1951); R.D. Sider, 'Approaches to Tertullian: A Study of Recent Scholarship,' *Second Century* 2 (1982). It has been suggested that the jurist Tertullian whose *De castrensi peculio* and *Quaestiones* are cited and excerpted in the *Institutiones* and *Digesta* is the same person as Tertullian the Christian apologist; but on the whole this seems unlikely. See D.I. Rankin, 'Was Tertullian a Jurist?' *Studia Patristica* 31 (1997).
5. *De praescriptione haereticorum* 7; cf. Acts 3:11.
6. J.E.B. Mayor, *Q. Septimi Florentis Tertulliani Apologeticus* (Cambridge: Cambridge University Press, 1918), p. xiv.
7. 'The blood of the martyrs is the seed of the Church,' Tertullian says (*Apologeticus* 50). Beyond what is found in Eusebius of Caesarea (*Historia ecclesiastica* 2:2:4) and St Jerome (*De viris illustribus* 53), little is known of his life; but he himself seems to have died of natural causes.
8. Tertullian himself tells the story of how in 185 a group of Christians approached the governor of Asia and begged him to put them to death (*Ad Scapulam* 5). 'At their trials, martyrs had passed their oral examination: then they waited in prison, assured by their sentence of first-class honours in paradise' (R.L. Fox, *Pagans and Christians* (San Francisco: Viking, 1986), p. 448). See also S. Benko, 'Pagan Criticism of Christianity during the First Two centuries AD,' in *Aufstieg und Niedergang der römischen Welt* 23.2 (1980); *Pagan Rome and the Early Christians* (Bloomington, IN: Indiana University Press, 1984); G.W. Bowersock, *Martyrdom and Rome* (Cambridge: Cambridge University Press, 1995); R.L. Fox, *Pagans and Christians*, p. 419; W.H.C. Frend, *Martyrdom and Persecution in the Early Church: A Study in Conflict from the Maccabees to Donatus* (Oxford: Blackwell, 1965); P. Keresztes, 'The Imperial Roman Government and the Christian Church. I. From Nero to the Severi. II. From Gallienus to the Great Persecution,' *Aufstieg und Niedergang der römischen Welt* 23.2 (1980); R. MacMullen, *Enemies of the Roman Order: Treason, Unrest, and Alienation in the Empire* (Cambridge, MA; Harvard University Press, 1966).
9. For a convenient selection in translation with references, see J. Stevenson and W.H.C. Frend, *A New Eusebius: Documents Illustrating the History of the Church to AD 337* (London: SPCK, 1987).
10. C. Trevett, *Montanism* (Cambridge: Cambridge University Press, 1997); W.H.C. Frend, *The Donatist Church* (Oxford: Clarendon Press, 1952).

Notes: Chapter 5

11. On this subject see especially N. Cohn, *The Pursuit of the Milennium* (London: Secker & Warburg, 1957).
12. A.H. Armstrong, 'The Nature of Man in St. Gregory of Nyssa,' *Eastern Churches Quarterly* 8 (1948).
13. R. Stob, 'Stoicism and Christianity,' *Classical Journal* 30 (1934-1935); see also M.L. Colish, *The Stoic Tradition From Antiquity to the Early Middle Ages* (Leiden: Brill, 1990).
14. See ch. 4, n. 30.
15. John 1:1–4.
16. J.H. Bernard, *A Critical and Exegetical Commentary on the Gospel According to St John* (Edinburgh: T. & T. Clark, 1928), p. cxliii.
17. I.e. the period lying roughly between the third century BC and the end of the first century AD. The term, though common, is of limited usefulness.
18. On this subject see especially A. Harnack, *History of Dogma*, vol. 1 (London: Williams & Norgate, 1905); see also J. Barclay and J. Sweet (eds), *Early Christian Thought in its Jewish Context* (Cambridge: Cambridge University Press, 1996); P. Borgen, *Philo, John, and Paul: New Perspectives on Judaism and Early Christianity* (Atlanta, GA: Scholar's Press, 1987); *Early Christianity and Hellenistic Judaism* (Edinburgh: T. & T. Clark, 1996).
19. *The Gospel of John* (Oxford: Blackwell, 1971), p. 19.
20. The literature on the Christianisation of the *logos* doctrine is extensive; but see especially C.K. Barrett, *The Gospel According to St John* (London: SPCK, 1978); R. G. Bury, *The Logos Doctrine and the Fourth Gospel* (Cambridge: Cambridge University Press, 1940); C.H. Dodd, *The Interpretation of the Fourth Gospel* (Cambridge: Cambridge University Press, 1953); F. E. Walton, *The Development of the Logos Doctrine in Greek and Hebrew Thought* (Bristol: John Wright & Sons, 1911).
21. This is what we take δεισιδαιμονεστέρους to mean, rather than, as the King James Version has it, 'too superstitious' (this English translation evidently owes something to the Vulgate: *viri Athenienses, per omnia quasi superstitiosiores vos video*). δεισιδαίμων can have a pejorative sense; but it seems hardly likely that St Paul would have begun a sermon to a sceptical audience by insulting it.
22. Acts 17:22–28.
23. M. Dibelius, *Studies in the Acts of the Apostles* (London: SCM, 1956), p. 77.
24. Acts 17:18.
25. Ed. D. Kidd (Cambridge: Cambridge University Press, 1997).
26. Stobaeus, *Eclogae*, 1:1:12.
27. *Phaenomena* 1–13.
28. The attribution is accepted by F. F. Bruce, *The Book of Acts* (Grand Rapids, Michigan: Eerdmans, 1988) and J. Munck, *The Acts of the Apostles: Introduction, Translation and Notes* (Garden City, NY: Doubleday, 1967); hesitated over by C. S. C. Williams, *A Commentary on the Acts of the Apostles* (London: A. & C. Black, 1964) and H. Marshall, *The Acts of the Apostles: An Introduction and a Commentary* (Leicester: Inter-Varsity Press, 1980); and denied by E. Hänchen, *The Acts*

of the Apostles: A Commentary (Oxford: Blackwell, 1971) and J.A. Fitzmyer, *The Acts of the Apostles: A New Translation with Introduction and Commentary* (New York: Doubleday, 1998).

29. It seems reasonable to suppose that ὡς καί τινες τῶν καθ᾽ ὑμᾶς ποιητῶν εἰρήκασι at Acts 17:28 means, as we have translated it, 'as some of your own poets have also said,' implying a previous reference to the same poets. Also, it is not obvious why, in this context, St Paul should have wished to appeal to Epimenides. The evident allusion to him at Titus 1:2 is only to the famous 'liar' paradox: such a commonplace that this is hardly to be taken as indicating a Pauline predilection for Epimenides.
30. Matthew 8:11.
31. Galatians 3:28; cf. I Corinthians 12:13; Colossians 3:11.
32. For an interesting if subjective account, see A. Badiou, *Saint Paul: la fondation de l'universalisme* (Paris: Presses universitaires de France, 1997).
33. Romans 2:11–15.
34. *The Epistle to the Romans* (Oxford: Oxford University Press, 1933), p. 65. It is not clear why Karl Barth thinks the 'information' obscure, though the language of the passage certainly is. The Pauline Epistles generally give the impression of someone dictating at high speed in a language with which he is not entirely at home; but the meaning is hardly difficult to see.
35. Barth, *Epistle to the Romans*, p. 66.
36. Romans 3:12.
37. E. Brunner, *The Letter to the Romans* (London: Lutterworth Press, 1959), p. 21.
38. See T. Engberg-Pedersen, *Paul and the Stoics* (Edinburgh: T. & T. Clark, 2000).
39. See C.K. Barrett's comments on Romans 2:11–15 in his *Commentary on the Epistle to the Romans* (London: SPCK, 1991).
40. *Contra Celsum* 5:40.
41. *De corona* 5; 6; *De testimonio animae* 5.
42. *Divinae institutiones* 3:8.
43. *De officiis* 1:84.
44. For numerous references with commentary see R.W. and A.J. Carlyle, *A History of Medieval Political Theory in the West* vol. 1, chs 8–12.
45. *De fuga saeculi* 15.
46. *Etymologiae* 5:4.
47. For authoritative biographies of St Augustine see P. Brown, *Augustine of Hippo* (London: Faber & Faber, 1967); G. Bonner, *St Augustine of Hippo: Life and Controversies* (Oxford: Oxford University Press, 1986). For Augustine's political and social thought see E.M. Atkins and R.J. Dodaro, *Augustine: Political Writings* (Cambridge: Cambridge University Press, 2001); H.A. Deane, *The Political and Social Ideas of St Augustine* (New York: Columbia University Press, 1963); R.W. Dyson, *The Pilgrim City: Social and Political Ideas in the Writings of St Augustine of Hippo* (Woodbridge, Suffolk: Boydell, 2001); J.B. Elshtain, *Augustine and the Limits of Politics* (Notre Dame, IN: Indiana University Press, 1999); P.D. Bathory, *Political Theory as Public Confession: The Social and Political*

Thought of St Augustine of Hippo (New Brunswick, NJ: Transaction, 1981); R.A. Markus, *Saeculum: History and Society in the Theology of St Augustine* (Cambridge: Cambridge University Press, 1970); J.N. Figgis, *The Political Aspects of S. Augustine's 'City of God'* (London: Longmans, 1921). Of interest also are W.E. Connolly, *The Augustinian Imperative: A Reflection on the Politics of Morality* (London: Sage, 1993); G.J. Lavere, 'The Political Realism of Saint Augustine,' *Augustinian Studies* 11 (1980); 'The Influence of Saint Augustine on Early Medieval Political Theory,' *Augustinian Studies* 12 (1981); N.H. Baynes, *The Political Ideas of St. Augustine's 'De civitate Dei'* (London: Historical Association, 1936); E.L. Fortin, 'Augustine's City of God and the Modern Historical Consciousness,' *Review of Politics* 41 (1979); R. Martin, 'The Two Cities in Augustine's Political Philosophy,' *Journal of the History of Ideas* 33 (1972); T.E. Mommsen, 'St Augustine and the Christian Idea of Progress: The Background of the City of God,' *Journal of the History of Ideas* 12 (1951). See also P. Brown, *Religion and Society in the Age of Saint Augustine* (London: Faber & Faber, 1971); F.E. Cranz, 'De civitate Dei, XV, 2, and Augustine's Idea of the Christian Society,' *Speculum* 25 (1950). This is only a selection of a very large literature.

48. Though now very dated and to a great extent hagiographical, E. Gilson's *The Christian Philosophy of St Augustine of Hippo* (London: Gollancz, 1960) continues to be of value. See also J. O'Meara, 'Neo-Platonism in the Conversion of St Augustine,' *Dominican Studies* 3 (1950); *The Young Augustine: The Growth of St Augustine's Mind up to his Conversion* (London: Longmans, 1954); J. M. Rist, *Augustine: Ancient Thought Baptized* (Cambridge: Cambridge University Press, 1994); E. TeSelle, *Augustine the Theologian* (London: Burns & Oates, 1970).
49. *De civitate Dei* 8:5.
50. Genesis 1:31; cf. *Epistulae* 140:2; *De libero arbitrio* 1:8:18; 1:15:32.
51. See e.g. *Soliloquiae* 1:1:3; 1:8:15; *De Trinitate* 12:15:24; 14:15:21; *Enarrationes in psalmos* 57:1; 118:25:4; 119; 145:5; *Sermo* 18:4; 23:1; *De libero arbitrio* 1:6:15; 1:8:18; 2:10:29; 2:19:52; *Contra Faustum* 22:27; *De ordine* 2:8:25; *De civitate Dei* 19:13.
52. *Enarrationes in psalmos* 57:1; *Tractatus in Ioannis evangelium* 49:12; cf. Ambrose, *Epistulae* 73:10; *De fuga saeculi* 15; Ambrosiaster, *Commentaria in epistolam ad Romanos* 3:20; Jerome, *Commentaria in epistolam ad Galatas* 3:2 *Commentaria in Isaiam* 24:6.
53. Psalm 58:1.
54. Tobit 4:15.
55. Genesis 1:26.
56. *Enarrationes in psalmos* 57:1.
57. Cf. Minucius Felix, *Octavius* 16; Lactantius, *Divinae institutiones* 3:21–22; 5:15; 16; Ambrose, *De Ioseph patriarcha* 4; *Exhortatio virginitatis* 1:3; *De officiis ministrorum* 1:28; *Expositio in psalmum David* CXVIII 8; Ambrosiaster, *Commentaria in epistolam ad Colossenses* 4:1; *ad Corinthios II* 9:9.
58. E.g. *De civitate Dei* 19:15–16; *Enarrationes in psalmos* 69:7; 124:7–8; *Tractatus in Ioannis epistulam* 8:14; *De sermone Domini* 1:19:59; 2:4:16; *Sermo* 58:2.

59. E.g. *Enarrationes in psalmos* 39:7; 51:10; 64:9; 83:3; 85:3; 131:18–19; *Sermo* 50:2; 85:4; 113:4; 125:11; *De vera religione* 21:41; 38:69; 47:92; *Epistulae* 93:12:50; 130:2:3; 156:6:26; 157:4:32; *De civitate Dei* 4:3; *Tractatus in Ioannis evangelium* 6:25–26; 40:10.
60. *De republica* 3:23:34; *De officiis* 1:11–13; cf. *De civitate Dei* 22:6.
61. E.g. *Contra Faustum* 22:74; *Quaestiones in Heptateuchum* 4:44–6:10; *Epistulae* 47:5; 138:2:13; 189:4; *De civitate Dei* 1:21; 1:26; 3:10; 4:15; 19:7; 22:6. For a more detailed discussion of Augustine's opinions on slavery, property and war, see Dyson, *The Pilgrim City*, chs 3–4.
62. But Fr Martindale's remark is pertinent here: 'I think that the evidence for an estimate of the "character" of St Augustine is almost equally distributed throughout his works; for in such matters one must look out for unconscious self-revelation...rather than deliberate attempts at self-explanation' (M.C. Darcy et al. (eds), *A Monument to St Augustine* (London: Sheed & Ward, 1930, p. 81)). Quite how profitable attempts to psychoanalyse St Augustine are, however, is debatable. See, for example, T.W. Bryn, *The Psychology of Conversion with Special Reference to Saint Augustine* (London: Allenson, 1935); W.G. Cole, *Sex in Christianity and Psychoanalysis* (London: Allen & Unwin, 1955); K. Power, *Veiled Desire: Augustine's Writings on Women* (London: Darton, Longman & Todd, 1995); J. La Porte and F.E. Weaver, 'Augustine and Woman: Relationships and Teachings,' *Augustinian Studies* 12 (1981).
63. *Confessions* 8:7.
64. *Confessions* 6:15.
65. *Confessions* 2:4–10.
66. *Confessions* 2:6.
67. *Confessions* 1:7.
68. Professor Deane is right to remark that 'if we have really understood [Augustine's] religious teachings, we can virtually deduce from them his views of the nature of man, society and the state' (*The Political and Social Ideas of St Augustine*, p. 14).
69. *De civitate Dei* 13:3; 14:10–15.
70. *De civitate Dei* 14:10.
71. Genesis 2:16–17.
72. See, e.g., *De libero arbitrio* 1:2:4, where Augustine says that the problem of evil 'troubled me greatly as a young man, and so much exhausted me as to drive me into the camp of the heretics,' by whom he means the Manichaeans. See also G.R. Evans, *Augustine on Evil* (Cambridge: Cambridge University Press, 1982); Régis Jolivet, *Le problème du mal d'après saint Augustin* (2nd ed., Paris: Archives de Philosophie, 1936); cf. M.L. Burton, *The Problem of Evil: A Criticism of the Augustinian Point of View* (Chicago: University of Chicago Press, 1909).
73. *Confessions* 7:5.
74. 'Everything that exists is either corporeal or incorporeal. The corporeal is embraced by sensible form, and the incorporeal by intelligible. Everything that exists, then, is not without some form. But where there is some form there is neces-

Notes: Chapter 5

sarily some mode of existence; and a mode of existence is a kind of good. Absolute evil therefore has no mode of existence, for it lacks all good. It therefore does not exist, for it is embraced by no form, and the whole meaning of evil is derived from the privation of form' (*De diversis quaestionibus octoginta tribus* 6).

75. *Enchiridion* 12.
76. See, e.g., *Confessions* 13:9: *pondus meum, amor meus*—'my weight is my love.' Our moral 'resting place' is determined by the weight of the love that pulls us to it. The idea that everything takes up its natural place in the universe by a kind of 'gravity' is one that Augustine inherits unreflectively from Greek physics.
77. *De diversis quaestionibus octoginta tribus*, 6; 21; *Enchiridion* 12; 27; 96; *De civitate Dei* 12:1; 7–8.
78. See, e.g., *De libero arbitrio* 2:1:1.
79. *De peccatorum meritis et remissione* 2:17:27; cf. *De civitate Dei* 14:10–15.
80. *Enchiridion* 23–25.
81. *Epistulae* 190:3:12.
82. *De civitate Dei* 21:12.
83. Romans 9:21.
84. *De civitate Dei* 13:3.
85. *Retractationes* 1:9:4–6; *In Ioannis evangelium* 22:9; *Contra duas epistulas Pelagianorum* 2:5:9; *Ad Simplicianum* 1:2:21.
86. See, e.g., *De libero arbitrio* 2:1:3: 'Justice is applauded as a good because it condemns sin and praises righteous acts; but how could this be done if man did not have free will? An act would be neither sinful nor righteous if it were not done voluntarily'; and *Epistulae* 173:2: 'Who does not know that a man is condemned for no other reason than that his evil will deserves it, and that no man is saved who does not have a good will?' For some discussion of Augustine's understanding of the relation between will, grace and freedom see Gilson, *Christian Philosophy*, ch. 3.
87. Note, for instance, his comment at *In Ioannis evangelium* 29:6: 'Do not, therefore, seek to understand in order than you may believe; rather, believe in order that you may understand: for unless you believe, you will not understand.' See also *De vera religione* 24:45; E. Te Selle, *Augustine the Theologian*, p. 73. No doubt intentionally, the sentiment echoes Tertullian's *credibile est, quia ineptum est* (*De carne Christi* 5:4), usually misquoted as *Credo quia absurdum est*.
88. *Confessions* 3:6.
89. *De civitate Dei* 12:13–14; 20; and see *Contra academicos* 3:19:42 and *De ordine* 2:5:16, on those philosophers who despise the humble form in which God has appeared to mankind; and *De anima et eius origine* 4:2, on those who think that 'man can discuss his own quality or his whole nature as if no part of himself escaped him.'
90. See especially *Confessions* 11:14:12–30:40; *De civitate Dei* 11:4–6; see also R.W. Dyson, 'St Augustine's Remarks on Time'; R. Suter, 'Augustine on Time with some Criticisms from Wittgenstein,' *Revue Internationale de Philosophie* 16 (1962).

91. See especially *De libero arbitrio* 3:7 for a succinct statement of this point.
92. *De civitate Dei* 13:23; 21:12; *Epistulae* 190:3:12.
93. Galatians 5:17.
94. *Ad Simplicianum* 1:2:21; *De civitate Dei* 21:15.
95. *Enchiridion* 105.
96. *Enchiridion* 30; *Ad Simplicianum*. 1:2:7; *De dono perseverantiae* 13:33.
97. *Retractationes* 1:9; *In Ioannis evangelium* 22:9; *Contra duas Epistulae Pelagianorum* 2:5:9.
98. *Ad Simplicianum* 1:2:7.
99. *Enchiridion* 28–30.
100. At one point (*Epistulae* 102:2), Augustine suggests that God offers the gift of grace only to those whom He foreknows will accept it. On the face of it, this is the most plausible of the possibilities. It resembles the theory associated with the sixteenth- and seventeenth-century century Jesuit theologians Luis de Molina, Francisco Suarez and St Robert Bellarmine. See especially Molina's *Concordia*, ed. J. Rabeneck (Oña: Collegium Maximum, 1953). The literature on the subject is, of course, very extensive. There is a lucid and sympathetic account of Augustine's doctrine of grace and predestination, with numerous references, at Te Selle, *Augustine the Theologian*, pp. 319–338.
101. But it seems likely that Pelagius was not, after all, the founder of Pelagianism. There is good reason to believe that it originated with a Syrian teacher called Rufinus. Pelagianism was condemned by the Council of Carthage in 418. Its modified relative semi-Pelagianism was condemned in 529 by the Council of Orange. These condemnations were repeated by the Council of Trent in 1546. See the works mentioned in n. 103.
102. Augustine's anti-Pelagian treatises are: *De peccatorum meritis et remissione*; *De spiritu et littera*; *De natura et gratia*; *De gestis Pelagii*; *De gratia Christi et de peccato originali*; *De perfectione justitiae hominis*; *De nuptiis et concupiscentia*; *Contra Iulianum*; *Contra duas epistolas Pelagianorum*. At his death, Augustine left unfinished a treatise against the semi-Pelagian Julian of Eclanum now known as *Opus imperfectum contra Iulianum*. He also gives an extensive summary of Pelagianism in the last chapter of his *De haeresibus* of 428.
103. See G. de Plinval, *Pélage: ses écrits, sa vie et sa réforme* (Lausanne: Librairie Payot, 1943); Te Selle, *Augustine the Theologian*, ch. 5; B.R. Rees, *Pelagius: Life and Letters* (Woodbridge, Suffolk: Boydell, 1998); P. Brown, 'Pelagius and his Supporters: Aims and Environment,' *Journal of Theological Studies*, n.s. 19 (1968); R.F. Evans, *Pelagius: Inquiries and Reappraisals* (London: A. & C. Black, 1968); J. Ferguson, *Pelagius: A Historical and Theological Study* (Cambridge: Cambridge University Press, 1956); G. Bonner, 'Pelagianism and Augustine,' *Augustinian Studies* 23 (1992). It is important to take seriously Mr Bonner's observation in this article (p. 33) that we should 'see Pelagianism as a religious tendency in its own right and not as mere opposition to prevailing doctrine.'
104. I Corinthians 15:22.

Notes: Chapter 5

105. As Emile Bréhier expresses it, Pelagianism 'presents Christ's work as if it were the work of a model teacher or model doctor, such as a saintly Cynic, and not the work of a victim whose merits justify man' (*The History of Philosophy: The Middle Ages and Renaissance* (Chicago: University of Chicago Press, 1965), p. 4).
106. *Contra Iulianum* 4:3:23; and see 4:3:17: 'If men can...arrive at true faith, true virtue, true justice, true wisdom, without the faith of Christ, then Christ died in vain.'
107. *De genesi ad litteram* 11:15:20. As Peter Brown remarks ('Saint Augustine,' in B. Smalley (ed.), *Trends in Medieval Political Thought* (Oxford: Blackwell, 1965), p. 20, n. 32), this tells against the common belief that *De civitate Dei* was inspired simply by the sack of Rome in 410. No doubt this was its immediate inspiration; but it expresses ideas that were already in its author's mind, and it very quickly outgrew its original purpose. See also J.-C. Guy, *Unité et structure logique de la Cité de Dieu* (Paris: Etudes augustiniennes, 1961), pp. 9–10.
108. Psalm 87:3.
109. *A History of Philosophy* vol. 2 (London: Burns, Oates & Washbourne, 1959), p. 100.
110. See *De civitate Dei* 16:17; 18:2.
111. See *De civitate Dei* 15:1.
112. See *De civitate Dei* 19:24.
113. 'Accordingly, two cities have been formed by two loves: the Earthly by love of self extending even to contempt of God; the Heavenly by love of God extending to contempt of self' (*De civitate Dei* 14:28).
114. *De civitate Dei* 18:54.
115. *Contra Faustum* 13:16; cf. *In Ioannis evangelium* 45:12.
116. See especially *De baptismo* 4:1:1, where Augustine reprises the position of the great Cyprian, that 'No one can have God as his Father who does not have the Church as his Mother' (Cyprian, *De catholicae ecclesiae unitate* 6).
117. *Epistulae* 208:2; cf. *In Ioannis evangelium* 25:10.
118. *Enarrationes in psalmos* 90[2]:1.
119. *De civitate Dei* 18:54.
120. *De civitate Dei* 12:10–13.
121. J.H.S. Burleigh, *The City of God: A Study of St Augustine's Philosophy* (London: Nisbet, 1949), p. 153.
122. The expression is, of course, Oscar Cullman's (*Salvation in History* (London: SCM, 1967)). Professor Markus suggests, for reasons that seem cogent, that the expression 'sacred history' is to be preferred: see R.A. Markus, *Saeculum*, Appendix D.
123. *Sermo* 81:8; *Epistulae* 2:2:2.
124. 'Five ages of the world...have now been completed and the sixth is under way. Of these ages, the first extends from the origin of the human race...down to Noah, who built the ark at the time of the Flood. The second extends from that time down to Abraham...[T]he third age extends from Abraham down to the time of David the king; the fourth from David down

to that captivity under which the people of God passed away into Babylon; and the fifth from that exile down to the coming of our Lord Jesus Christ. With His coming, the sixth age has entered upon its course, so that the spiritual grace that in earlier times was known only to a few patriarchs and prophets may now be revealed to all the nations' (*De catechizandis rudibus* 22:39).

125. *Saeculum*, p. 22.

Chapter 6

1. *De civitate Dei* 19:12.
2. *De civitate Dei* 12:22–23; 14:1; *De bono coniugali* 1.
3. *Epistulae* 130:6:13.
4. *Enarrationes in psalmos.* 57:1; *In Ioannis evangelium* 49:12; *De Trinitate* 14:15:21.
5. Genesis 1:28.
6. *De civitate Dei* 19:15; cf. *In Ioannis epistulam* 8:6.
7. Genesis 4:17.
8. *De civitate Dei* 15:1–8.
9. *De doctrina Christiana* 1:23.
10. *De civitate Dei* 15:4.
11. *Enarrationes in psalmos.* 100:4.
12. e.g. *De civitate Dei* 15:4; 18:2.
13. *De civitate Dei* 5:18.
14. *De civitate Dei* 5:13; 16.
15. See, e.g., *De civitate Dei* 2:2–18; 21; 5:13; 16; 18; 19:21–24.
16. See Cochrane, *Christianity and Classical Culture*, ch. 9.
17. *Retractationes* 2:43:2.
18. For Augustine's detailed treatment of this theme, see *De civitate Dei* 1–10 passim.
19. *De civitate Dei* 2:21.
20. Cf. H.A. Deane, *The Political and Social Ideas of St Augustine*, ch. 4; C. H. McIlwain, *The Growth of Political Thought in the* West (London: Macmillan, 1932), p. 154.
21. Donald Earl is, of course, justified in observing that Augustine's argument involves an equivocation as to the meaning of *iustitia* that is 'wholly illicit from the point of view of strict argumentation' (*The Moral and Political Tradition of Rome*, p. 127). Augustine habitually uses the word *iustitia* to mean either or both of justice in the technical sense, or general 'righteousness.'
22. *De civitate Dei* 5:16.
23. *De civitate Dei* 19:24.
24. *De doctrina Christiano* 1:30.
25. *De civitate Dei* 19:24.
26. *De civitate Dei* 19:23.
27. Ibid.
28. *De civitate Dei* 2:21.

Notes: Chapter 6

29. See pp. 198–208, below. This argument is summarised in a general way in the short treatise called *Quaestio de potestate papae* or *Rex pacificus*, written, probably in France, at the beginning of the fourteenth century: 'Augustine, at *De civitate Dei* 2:21, says this: "A commonwealth cannot be governed without justice." Now there is no true justice in that commonwealth of which Christ is not the ruler. But the commonwealth of the Christian people must be righteous and true. Therefore Christ must be the ruler in it. But the pope is the vicar of Christ...The pope is therefore the ruler of the commonwealth even in temporals' (*Quaestio de potestate papae* (*Rex pacificus*), ed. and trans. R.W. Dyson (Lewiston, Queenston and Lampeter: Mellen, 1999), p. 64). See also the imperialist author Engelbert of Admont, writing in about 1307: 'Augustine... concludes in book nineteen of *The City of God* that outside the Church there never was nor can be a true empire, although there were emperors of a sort, or as such, but not absolutely, who were outside the Christian faith and Church' (*De ortu et fine Romani imperii*, eds and trans. Thomas M. Izbicki and Cary J. Nederman, in *Three Tracts on Empire* (Bristol: Thoemmes, 2000), p. 66).
30. *De civitate Dei* 5:24–26; *Epistulae* 93:5; 155:3:10.
31. See *De Genesi ad litteram* 9:9; *Epistulae* 153:6:16; *De libero arbitrio* 1:15:32–33; *Sermo* 125:5; *De ordine* 2:4:12.
32. *De Genesi ad litteram* 9:9.
33. *De civitate Dei* 19:17.
34. *De civitate Dei* 19:12.
35. *De civitate Dei* 18:54.
36. R.W. and A.J. Carlyle, *A History of Medieval Political Theory in the West* vol. 1, p. 130; and see H.A. Deane, *The Political and Social Ideas of St Augustine*, p. 78.
37. *Epistulae* 153:6:16.
38. *De libero arbitrio* 1:15:32.
39. *De civitate Dei* 1:8.
40. Romans 13:1.
41. *De civitate Dei* 5:21; *De natura boni* 32.
42. *De civitate Dei* 19:6; 20:2; *Epistulae* 95:3.
43. *Epistulae* 153:6:16.
44. *De ordine* 2:4:12.
45. Possidius of Calama, *Sancti Augustini vita*, ed. H.T. Weiskotten (Princeton, NJ: Princeton University Press, 1919), p. 28.
46. *De civitate Dei* 3:14.
47. *De civitate Dei* 3:14, 18–20; 5:12, 17.
48. *De civitate Dei* 3:23–30.
49. *De civitate Dei* 4:6.
50. *De civitate Dei* 17:12–13; *Enarrationes in psalmos* 45:13; 48:2:6; 84:10
51. Psalm 46:9.
52. *Enarrationes in psalmos* 45:13.
53. *De civitate Dei* 19:12.

54. *De Genesi ad litteram* 9:9; *Epistulae* 153:6:16; *De libero arbitrio* 1:15:32–33; *Sermo* 125:5; *De ordine* 2:4:12.
55. *Enarrationes in psalmos* 48:3:6.
56. *De civitate Dei* 15:14; 19:12; *Epistulae* 189:6.
57. *De civitate Dei* 3:10; 5:12, 17.
58. *De civitate Dei* 5:18.
59. *De civitate Dei* 5:12, 18.
60. *De civitate Dei* 2:2–18.
61. *De civitate Dei* 3:14, 18; 5:12, 17.
62. *De civitate Dei* 3:23–30.
63. *De civitate Dei* 3:18–20; 22:6.
64. *De civitate Dei* 1:1–7.
65. The mercy extended by the Visigoths to those who fled to Christian places of worship is commended also by Orosius (*Historia adversus paganos* 7:39) and Jerome (*Epistulae* 27:13). The contrast is not as clear as Augustine thinks. There are similar pagan instances of clemency of which he is perhaps not aware. After the seige of Tyre, Alexander spared those who had fled to the temple of Hercules (Arrian, *Anabasis* 7:24); after the battle of Coronea, Agesilaus showed the same consideration to the Theban hoplites who took shelter in the temple of Itonian Athene (Plutarch, *Agesilaus* 19).
66. Nor was this view exclusive to orthodox Christian teachers. The Manichaeans also embraced what Professor Deane (*The Political and Social Ideas of St Augustine*, p. 161) chooses to call 'a doctrinaire pacifism.'
67. See R.H. Bainton, *Christian Attitudes Toward War and Peace* (New York: Abingdon Press, 1960); C.J. Cadoux, *The Early Christian Attitude to War* (London: Headly Brothers, 1919). It is a long standing view, possibly originating with Edward Gibbon (see *Decline and Fall*, ch. 16) that the Christians' subversive influence upon the army was one of the reasons why the Church was persecuted under the emperor Diocletian.
68. See A.A.R. Bastiaensen et al. (eds), *Atti e Passioni dei Martiri* (Milan: Arnoldo Mondadori, 1987); P. Brock, 'Why did St. Maximilian Refuse to Serve in the Roman Army?' *Journal of Ecclesiastical History* 45 (1994).
69. Sulpicius Severus, *Vita*, ed. K. Halm, *Corpus scriptorum ecclesiasticorum Latinorum* 1 (Vienna, 1866).
70. *Contra Celsum* 8:73.
71. *Epistulae* 189:4; *Contra Faustum* 22:74.
72. *De civitate Dei* 1:21, 26; *Epistulae* 47:5; 138:2:13; *Contra Faustum* 22:75.
73. On 11 April, 1961. See *The Trial of Adolf Eichmann* (9 vols, Jerusalem: Israel State Archives, 1998), vol. 1. Session 1.
74. H. Arendt, *Eichmann in Jerusalem: a Report on the Banality of Evil* (New York: Viking Press, 1992), p. 26.
75. *De libero arbitrio* 1:15:31.
76. *Expositio quarumdam propositionum ex epistula ad Romanos* 72 (italics ours).
77. *Sermo* 125:5.

Notes: Chapter 6 309

78. *Epistulae* 138:2:10.
79. *Enarrationes in psalmos.* 118[31]:1.
80. For an illustration of this practice from the persecution of 249–251 under the emperor Decius, see H. Bettenson, *Documents of the Christian Church* (Oxford: Oxford University Press, 1963), p. 13.
81. *Sermo* 326:2.
82. *Sermo* 62:10:15; cf. *De civitate Dei* 5:17.
83. *Sermo* 62:5:8–10:15; *Enarrationes in psalmos.* 124:7; *Epistulae* 185:2:8.
84. The useful distinction between 'ascending' and 'descending' theories of power originates with Professor Walter Ullmann. See, e.g., his *Principles of Government and Politics in the Middle Ages* (London: Methuen, 1961), pp. 19–26.
85. *De civitate Dei* 19:17.
86. *Sermo* 62:13.
87. I.e. Flavius Claudius Julianus, emperor from 360 to 363. As to why Julian was 'an apostate, a wicked man, an idolater' see R. Panella, 'The Emperor Julian and the God of the Jews,' *Koinonia* 23 (1999); R. Smith, *Julian's Gods: Religion and Philosophy in the Thought and Action of Julian the Apostate* (London: Routledge, 1995).
88. *Enarrationes in psalmos.* 124:7.
89. *De libero arbitrio* 1:6:15:50–51.
90. G. Combès, *La doctrine politique de saint Augustin* (Paris: Librairie Plon, 1927), pp. 152; 416. One suspects that, in making this statement, Fr Combès wishes to evade the conclusion that, in this respect, St Augustine's view is at odds with that of St Thomas (see p. 238), who seems to attach too much weight to a sentence from *De libero arbitrio*. Fr Combès is followed by the authors of a recent textbook: '[B]y defining what a true republic is, Augustine provides a standard of justice by which human law and institutions can be measured. Laws that fail to conform to the higher standards of justice are not real laws' (D.G. Tannenbaum and D. Schultz, *Inventors of Ideas: An Introduction to Western Political Philosophy* (New York: St Martin's Press, 1998) p. 79). See also Deane, *The Political and Social Ideas of St Augustine*, pp. 90–91.
91. At *De libero arbitrio* 1:5:11:33 he does indeed say: 'it seems to me that a law that is unjust is not a law'; but this is only to allow himself to be contradicted immediately by the protagonist Evodius, who makes the 'Augustinian' point that even bad laws are good insofar as they prevent worse things from happening.
92. See also the following passage from the treatise *De vera religione* (31:58), written in about 390: 'In the case of temporal laws, men make judgments about them when they enact them, but after they have been enacted and confirmed it is not lawful for a judge to pass judgment on them, but only in accordance with them. So also the framer of temporal laws, if he is a good and wise man, takes into account that eternal law itself upon which no soul is permitted to pass judgment, so that he may decide what is to be commanded and forbidden for the time being according to immutable rules. Pure souls may, there-

fore, know what the eternal law is, but they may not pass judgment on it.' Here again, the statement is that the framer of temporal laws will take the eternal law into account *'if he is a good and wise man.'* There is not the slightest suggestion that laws enacted by someone who is not a good and wise man should not be obeyed. On the contrary, 'after they have been enacted and confirmed *it is not lawful...to pass judgment on them, but only in accordance with them.'*

93. *Saeculum*, p. 103.
94. Cf. M. Loriaux, 'The Realists and Saint Augustine: Skepticism, Psychology, and Moral Action in International Relations Thought,' *International Studies Quarterly* 36 (1992).
95. More correctly, between temporal and spiritual power, *regnum* and *sacerdotium*. The expressions 'Church' and 'State' are of course not appropriate to the Middle Ages; but they may be used as we do here, as it were in inverted commas, as an innocuous shorthand.
96. See especially W. Ullmann, *The Growth of Papal Government in the Middle Ages* (London: Methuen, 1955).
97. For the *Decretum Gratiani* (also called *Concordantia discordantium canonum*) see *Corpus iuris canonici*, ed. E. Friedberg (Leipzig, 1879), vol. 1. The *Decretum*, with the addition of subsequent official compilations of papal legislation, formed the substance of the *Corpus iuris canonici* of 1580 which, in turn, was to stand as the authoritative legal code of the Church until the promulgation, in 1917, of the much more short-lived *Codex iuris canonici* of Pope Benedict XV. The history of canon law down to the time of the *Decretum* is so complex as almost to defy generalisation. See especially B. Kurtscheid and F. Wilches, *Historia iuris canonici* (Rome: Officium Libri Catholici, 1941–1943); also R.W. and A.J. Carlyle, *Medieval Political Theory in the West*, vol. 2; S. Kuttner, 'The Natural Law and Canon Law,' *Proceedings of the University of Notre Dame Natural Law Institute* 3 (1950); C. Morris, *The Papal Monarchy: The Western Church from 1050 to 1250* (Oxford: Clarendon Press, 1991); K. Pennington, *The Papal Monarchy in the Twelfth and Thirteenth Centuries* (Philadelphia: University of Pennsylvania Press, 1984); *Popes, Canonists and Texts, 1150-1550* (Aldershot: Variorum, 1993); W. Ullmann, *Medieval Papalism: the Political Theories of the Medieval Canonists* (London: Methuen, 1949). A good deal of the secondary literature is now very old and inaccessible (J. W. Bickell, *Geschichte des Kirchenrechts* (Giessen, 1843); F. Maassen, *Geschichte der Quellen und der Literatur des kanonischen Rechts im Abendland* (Graz, 1870); F. C. von Savigny, *Geschichte des römischen Rechts im Mittelalter*, vols 3-7 (Heidelberg, 1843-51); J. F. von Schulte, *Geschichte der Quellen und Literatur des canonischen Rechts*, vols 1–2 (Stuttgart, 1875-77); R. Ritter von Scherer, *Handbuch des Kirchenrechts* (Graz, 1886)). There is an extensive, but highly specialised, journal literature; also numerous collections of documents. A comprehensive modern history of medieval canon law in 11 volumes is planned by W. Hartmann and K. Pennington and will be published by the Catholic University Press of America; but this project is still

Notes: Chapter 6

in its early stages. For the standard method of referring to the *Corpus iuris canonici*, see R.W. Dyson, *Three Royalist Tracts, 1296–1302* (Bristol: Thoemmes, 1999), p. xxxvi.

98. *Decretum*, Dist. 1:5.
99. *Mos* and *consuetudo* may, broadly speaking, be taken as equivalents to what we have called 'convention'; i.e. the human race is governed in two ways: by law that is not man made, and by customary or legal provisions that are.
100. Matthew 7:12.
101. *Decretum*, Dist. 1.
102. *Decretum*, Dist. 1:5:1.
103. Where editions of the glossators exist at all, they are for the most part ancient and inaccessible. 'The political concepts of the medieval canonists—a species of mankind that is virtually known only to librarians—are hidden in dust-covered and worm-eaten tomes which have been relegated to sanctuaries usually inaccessible to the average student of medieval history' (W. Ullmann, *Medieval Papalism*, Preface). See *Die Summa des Paucapalea*, ed. F. von Schulte (Giessen 1890; repr. Aalen: Scientia. 1965); Rufinus, *Summa decretorum*, ed. H. Singer (Paderborn 1902; repr. Aalen: Scientia, 1963); *Die Summa des Stephanus Tornacensis über das Decretum Gratian*, ed. J. F. von Schulte (Giessen 1891; repr. Aalen: Scientia, 1965). For practical purposes, the reader is advised to consult the works of Carlyle and Ullman as cited above, in n. 97.
104. Though such things as slavery and private property are now permitted by reason of sin. Without these institutions to control human conduct, the law of nature could not operate at all in a fallen world; they too, therefore, serve the natural law even though, strictly speaking, they are contrary to it. See Rufinus, *Summa decretorum*, on Dist 1; Stephen of Tournai, *Summa decreti*, on Dist. 1.
105. The converse, however, is not true. In equating the natural law with what is taught in the Scriptures, the canonists encountered an obvious problem: the fact that so much of what is taught in the Old Testament (dietary regulations, for instance) is now not deemed to be binding. How can this be, if the natural law is both immutable and wholly contained in the Bible? The answer is that *ius naturale consistit in tribus: scilicet, mandatis, prohibitionibus [et] demonstrationibus*: 'the natural law consists in three things: namely, commands, prohibitions and recommendations' (Rufinus, *Summa decretorum*, on Dist. 1:1; cf. See also *Decretum*, Dist. 5:1:1; Rufinus, *Summa decretorum*, on Dist. 5). The purely formal and ceremonial regulations of the Old Testament form an additional category, *mystica*, and these no longer hold.
106. *Decretum*, Dist. 8:2.
107. *Decretum*, Dist. 9.
108. Rufinus, *Summa Decretorum*, on Dist. 8.
109. Rufinus, *Summa Decretorum*, on Dist. 9.
110. This term, originally used somewhat more narrowly than we are using it, was coined by F.-X. Arquillière, *L'Augustinisme politique* (Paris: Vrin, 1939). For some account of 'political Augustianism' in its controversial context, see espe-

cially R.W. Dyson, *Normative Theories of Society and Government in Five Medieval Thinkers* (Lewiston, Queenston, Lampeter: Mellen, 2003).

111. For a translation of the whole of this letter, with a few unimportant elisions, see Dyson, *Normative Theories*, pp. 279–289.
112. Dyson, *Normative Theories*, pp. 284–285.
113. *Manegoldi ad Gebhardum liber*, ed. K. Francke (Hanover: Monumenta Germaniae historica, Libelli de lite, 1892).
114. The 'two swords' rhetoric so prevalent in medieval political theory originates with the conversation of Christ with the disciples at Luke 22:38. Its earliest occurrence in a political context is, as far as we know, in a treatise of Cardinal Deusdedit, a partisan of Gregory VII, called *Libellus contra invasores et simoniacos* (ca 1097). The priest, he says in the Prologue to this work, uses the sword of the word; the king wields the material sword; neither should interfere with the other. But the first author to make use of this imagery in the form in which it was thereafter to be cited so often was St Bernard of Clairvaux. It makes its appearance in the little manual of advice called *De consideratione* written by St Bernard between 1145 and 1153 for the guidance of his friend and pupil Bernard Pignatelli—Bernard of Pisa—who had in 1145 become Pope Eugenius III. The *gladius materialis*, the 'material sword,' is also often called the *gladius sanguinis*, the 'sword of blood,' thus appropriating the Biblical impurity of blood in support of the contention that the Church may not pollute her hands with worldly business.
115. For an illustration, see Roger of Hovenden's account of the coronation of Richard I of England in 1189 in *The Annals of Roger de Hovenden, Comprising the History of England and of Other Countries from AD 732 to AD 1201*, trans. H. Riley (2 vols, London: H.G. Bohn, 1853; repr. 1968), p. 117. Note especially that 'They clothed him in the royal robes, first a tunic, then a dalmatic, after which the said Archbishop *delivered to him the sword of rule, with which to crush evildoers against the Church*' (italics ours). On this subject see C.A. Bouman, *Sacring and Crowning: The Development of the Latin Ritual for the Anointing of Kings and the Coronation of an Emperor before the Eleventh Century* (Groningen: J.B. Wolters, 1957). See also W. Ullmann, *The Growth of Papal Government in the Middle Ages*, chs. 3, 5, 8.
116. I Samuel 10, 15 and 16; See also I Kings 1.
117. Matthew 16:18–19.
118. For the Latin text of the *Policraticus*, see C.C.J. Webb, *Ioannes Saresberiensis Episcopi Cartonensis Policratici* (2 vols, Oxford: Oxford University Press, 1909). For translations, see C.J. Nederman, *John of Salisbury: Policraticus* (Cambridge: Cambridge University Press, 1990); J. Dickinson, *The Statesman's Book of John of Salisbury* (New York: Knopf, repr. 1963); and J.B. Pike, *The Frivolities of Courtiers and the Footprints of Philosophers* (Minneapolis: University of Minnesota Press, 1938). See also Dyson, *Normative Theories*, ch. 3.
119. *Policraticus* 4:2: 'And thus, Chrysippus asserted that law has power *over all divine and human affairs*, for which reason it presides over *all good and all evil*

Notes: Chapter 6   313

and is the ruler and guide of things as well as of men. Papinian, a man of the greatest experience in matters of jurisprudence, and Demosthenes, the distinguished orator, would seem to support this and to subject all men to its obedience *because all law is a sort of discovery and gift from God*...It is proper for all who dwell in the community of political affairs to live according to it (Nederman's translation, slightly amended; our italics).

120. See Innocent III's decretal *Novit* of 1204: (*Corpus iuris canonici* X.2:1:13). *Novit* is a quintessential 'political' decretal, and furnished plenty of material for subsequent commentators and political theorists. It was written in defence of the pope's intervention in the quarrel between King John of England and Philip Augustus of France, when Philip invaded John's great fief of Normandy as part of the imbroglio arising from John's marriage to Isabelle, daughter of Count Ademar of Angoulême. Philip Augustus successfully sought the support of the French clergy against the pope. Why, the bishops of France asked, should the pope intrude himself into a purely temporal dispute capable of being resolved in the king's own feudal courts? Innocent III replied: 'Let no one suppose that we wish to diminish or disturb the jurisdiction and power of the king...When we are insufficient to exercise our own jurisdiction, why should we wish to usurp that of another?...For we do not intend to judge concerning the fief, judgment of which belongs to him...but to decide concerning a sin, the judgment of which belongs to us beyond doubt, and we can and should exercise it against anyone...There is no right minded man who does not know that it belongs to our office to rebuke any Christian for any mortal sin and to coerce him with ecclesiastical penalties if he rejects our correction...That we can and should rebuke is evident from the pages of both the Old and New Testaments...That we can and should coerce is evident from what the Lord said to the prophet who was among the priests of Anathoth: "Lo, I have set thee over nations and over kingdoms, to root up and to pull down and to lay waste, and to destroy and to build and to plant" [Jeremiah 1:10]. No one doubts that all mortal sin must be rooted up and destroyed and pulled down. Moreover, when the Lord gave the keys of the kingdom of heaven to the blessed Peter He said: "Whatsoever thou shalt bind on earth shall be bound in heaven, and whatsoever thou shalt release on earth shall be released in heaven."...Although we are empowered to proceed in this fashion against any criminal sin in order to recall the sinner from error to truth and from vice to virtue, this is especially true when the sin is against peace, which is the bond of love...Finally, when a treaty of peace was made between the kings and confirmed on both sides by oaths which, however, were not kept for the agreed period, can we not take cognisance of such a sworn oath, which certainly belongs to the judgment of the Church, in order to re-establish a broken treaty of peace?'

121. See, e.g., Hostiensis on X.4:17:13, *Per venerabilem* (*Summa Domini Henrici Cardinalis Hostiensis* (Lyons, 1537), ff. 215–216); on X. 1:33:6, *Solitae* (*Commentaria in quinque libros Decretalium* (Venice, 1581), f. 171).

122. Giles of Rome, *De ecclesiastica potestate*, ed. R.W. Dyson (*Giles of Rome's 'De ecclesiastica potestate': a Medieval Theory of World Government* (New York: Columbia University Press, 2004)); James of Viterbo, *De regimine christiano*, ed. R.W. Dyson (*James of Viterbo on Christian Government* (Woodbridge, Suffolk: Boydell, 1995)); Augustinus Triumphus, *Summa de potestate ecclesiastica* (Rome, 1584); Alvarus Pelagius, *De planctu ecclesiae* (Venice, 1560). Critical editions of the last two texts are much needed.
123. *De planctu ecclesiae* 1:45. Note the clear echo of the Justinianic principle *quod principi placuit legis habet vigorem*: 'what pleases the prince has the force of law' (*Digesta* 1:3:3; 1:4:1). The implication, which we may assume is intended, is that it is the pope, not the emperor, who has *plenitudo potestatis* to make and interpret law. For the most part, Augustinus Triumphus and Alvarus Pelagius, writing in support of Pope John XXII (1316–1364), repeat what Giles of Rome and James of Viterbo had said on behalf of Boniface VIII.
124. For examples of this literature see B. Tierney, *The Crisis of Church and State, 1050–1300* (Englewood Cliffs, NJ: Prentice-Hall, 1980); Dyson, *Three Royalist Tracts*; John of Paris, *Tractatus de potestate regia et papali*, ed. J. Leclercq, *Jean de Paris et l'ecclesiologie di xiii^c siècle* (Paris: Vrin, 1942), Appendix; also by F. Bleienstein as *Über königliche und päpstliche Gewalt...Textkritische Edition mit deutscher Übersetzung* (Stuttgart: E. Klett, 1969). This work has been translated into English twice (both times with the same title, *On Royal and Papal Power*): by J.A. Watt (Toronto: Pontifical Institute of Medieval Studies, 1971) and A.P. Monahan (New York: Columbia University Press, 1974).
125. *De ecclesiastica potestate* 3:5.
126. See especially Dyson, *The Pilgrim City*, ch. 5.

Chapter 7

1. For his comments see *De regimine principum* 1:8–15; *Scripta super libros sententiarum* 2:44:3:4; *Summa theologiae* IIa IIae 12:2. His position may be summarised as follows. The principal responsibility of kings is to seek the spiritual welfare of their subjects. They should regard this as a consideration superior to any secular one, and they should allow themselves to be guided by the advice of the Church. Also, kings are ultimately subject to the Supreme Pontiff, in whom temporal and spiritual power coincide, in the sense that kings who become apostate can be deposed by the pope. But it is certainly not St Thomas's view that kings are only the executive arm of the Church or that their rule is routinely subject to, or conditional upon, the Church's approval. At most, the pope's authority to judge temporals is exceptional and indirect. St Thomas shows no interest in the more extreme possibilities of the *ratione peccati* principle (see pp. 205–207); and this is clearly in keeping with his general view of the relation between politics and human wellbeing. Given his conviction that kings have so much to contribute to our moral and material welfare, there is no reason why he should make them mere appendages of the spiritual power. Taken as a whole, St Thomas's remarks amount to a moderate

Notes: Chapter 7

papalism: a papalism tempered by his belief that good kings can be trusted to secure for their subjects things that have a value independent of ecclesiastical approval and control. Jean Dunbabin puts it succinctly: 'Thomas was not particularly concerned by the practical problems involved in a clash between king and pope. Indeed, he could not very well be. For his whole political theory demanded that the king be a power for good, and two such powers could not clash—or else the whole castle would come tumbling down' ('Aristotle in the Schools,' in B. Smalley (ed.), *Trends in Medieval Political Thought*, p. 82). See also Dyson, *Normative Theories*, pp. 205–207.

2. Given the 'commanding heights' approach to which we committed ourselves in the Introduction, we here omit, for no better reason than simplicity and convenience, a number of other important contributors to this redefinition. We mention especially Giles of Rome's *De regimine principum* (Rome, 1607; repr. Aalen: Scientia, 1967), a work completely different from his papalist treatise *De ecclesiastica potestate*; and Albertus Magnus's *De Bono* and commentaries on the *Nicomachean Ethics*, eds H. Kühle, C. Feckes, B. Geyer and W. Kübel, (*Opera omnia* (Münster: Aschendorff, 1951). See also S.B. Cunningham, 'Albertus Magnus and the Problem of Moral Virtue,' *Vivarium*, 8 (1969); 'Albertus Magnus on Natural Law,' *Journal of the History of Ideas* 28 (1967); J. Dunbabin, 'The Two Commentaries of Albertus Magnus on the Nicomachean Ethics,' *Recherches de théologie ancienne et médiévale* 30 (1963).

3. St Thomas's earliest biographer, Peter Calo (1300) gives 1227 as his date of birth. See D. Prümmer, *Fontes Vitae S. Thomae Aquinatis, notis historicis et criticis illustrati* (Toulouse: Privat, 1911), pp. 28; 45. Fr Prümmer accepts 1227, but 1225 seems more likely on the whole.

4. The standard edition of the *Summa theologiae* is the *editio Leonina*, prepared by members of the Dominican Order at the command of Pope Leo XIII: *S. Thomae Aquinatis opera omnia iussu Leonis XIII edita cura et studio Fratrum Praedicatorum* (Rome: Commissio Leonina, 1888–1948), vols 4–8. The same text of the *Summa*, with or without *apparatus criticus*, can be consulted in numerous subsequent editions. *Summa contra gentiles* is in vols. 13–15 of the same edition. *De regimine principum* is in R.M. Spiazzi, *S. Thomae Aquinatis opuscula philosophica* (Turin and Rome: Marietti, 1951). R.M. Spiazzi has also edited St Thomas's commentary on Aristotle's *Politics*, as *In octo libros politicorum Aristotelis expositio* (Turin and Rome: Marietti, 1966). *Scripta super libros Sententiarum* is in vols 6-8 of *S. Thomae opera omnia* (25 vols, Parma: Fiaccadori, 1852–1873; repr. New York, 1948-1949). His commentary on Aristotle's *Nicomachean Ethics* (*In decem libros Ethicorum expositio*) is in vol. 20 of this edition. The whole of the *Summa theologiae* is available in the following English translations: *Summa theologica*, translated by Fathers of the English Dominican Province (repr. Westminster, MD: Christian Classics, London, 1981); and *Summa theologiae*, trans. T. Gilby et al. (London: Eyre & Spottiswood, 1964–80). The latter is a bilingual edition printed with the Leonine edition of the Latin text *verso* (without *apparatus criticus*) and the translation *recto*. The Dominican translation is literal and on the

whole accurate; the translation by Fr Gilby and others is so free and colloquial as to be almost a paraphrase. A catalogue of St Thomas's works, compiled by I.T. Eschmann, OP, is printed in E. Gilson, *The Christian Philosophy of St Thomas Aquinas* (London: Gollancz, 1961), pp. 381–430.

5. For a scholarly biography of St Thomas see J.A. Weisheipl, *Friar Thomas d'Aquino: His Life, Thought and Works* (Oxford: Blackwell, 1975). For a general, if tendentious, account of St Thomas's philosophy, see E. Gilson, *The Christian Philosophy of St Thomas Aquinas*; see also F.C. Coplestone, *Aquinas* (Harmondsworth, Middlesex: Penguin, 1970); A. Kenny, *Aquinas* (Oxford: Oxford University Press, 1980); J. Pieper, *A Guide to Thomas Aquinas* (Notre Dame, IN: University of Notre Dame Press, 1987); M. de Wulf, *The System of St Thomas Aquinas* (Cambridge, MA: Harvard University Press, 1922); B. Davies, *The Thought of Thomas Aquinas* (Oxford: Oxford University Press, 1992); T. O'Meara, *The Theology of Thomas Aquinas* (Notre Dame, IN: University of Notre Dame Press, 1997). On St Thomas's moral philosophy see R.M. McInerny, *Ethica Thomistica: The Moral Philosophy of St Thomas Aquinas* (Washington, DC: Catholic University of America Press, 1982); G. Stevens, 'Moral Obligation in St Thomas,' *The Modern Schoolman* 40 (1962–63).

6. There is a valuable account of the recovery of Aristotle by F. van Steenberghen: *Aristotle in the West: The Origins of Latin Aristotelianism* (Louvain: Nauwelaerts, 1970); see also the same author's *Thomas Aquinas and Radical Aristotelianism* (Washington, DC: Catholic University of America Press, 1980); C.J. Nederman, *Medieval Aristotelianism and its Limits: Classical Traditions in Moral and Political Philosophy* (Aldershot: Variorum, 1997); C. Flüeler, *Rezeption und Interpretation der Aristotelischen 'Politica' im späten Mittelalter* (Amsterdam: Grüner, 1992). For St Thomas's understanding of Aristotle's treatment of the virtues, see H. Jaffa, *Thomism and Aristotelianism* (Chicago: University of Chicago Press, 1952); also R. Sokolowski, *The God of Faith and Reason* (Notre Dame, IN: University of Notre Dame Press, 1982); J. Pieper, *The Four Cardinal Virtues: Prudence, Justice, Fortitude, Temperance* (Notre Dame, IN: University of Notre Dame Press, 1966).

7. We must mention also the figure known as Dionysius 'the Areopagite,' usually called Pseudo-Dionysius. 'Dionysius' is a pious fraud of the fifth century who wants us to think that he is the Dionysius converted to Christianity by St Paul at Athens (cf. Acts 17:34). He was also erroneously believed to have been the same person as the martyr Dionysius (Denys) who was the first bishop of Paris. He is the author of a number of works which, because of their emphasis on hierarchy and order, are much quoted by medieval political authors: *De divinis nominibus, De caelesti hierarchia, De ecclesiastica hierarchia* and *Theologia mystica*. Several other works, either specious or now lost, are referred to in the Pseudo-Dionysian writings. It is obvious on internal grounds that these writings are not productions of the first century. Their authenticity was first seriously challenged in the fifteenth century, by the Renaissance scholar Lorenzo Valla. The Pseudo-Dionysian writings, though spurious, are second only to St

Notes: Chapter 7 317

Augustine as a source of Neoplatonist ideas and images in the Christian thought of the west. See C. Luibheid (ed. and trans.), *Pseudo-Dionysius: The Complete Works* (London: SPCK, 1987). Also T. Finan and V. Twomey (eds), *The Relationship between Neoplatonism and Christianity* (Blackrock, Dublin: Four Courts Press, 1992); D.J. O'Leary, *Neoplatonism and Christian Thought* (Albany, NY: State University of New York, 1982).

8. See H. Denifle and E. Chatelain (eds), *Cartularium Universitas Parisiensis* (4 vols, Paris: Delalain, 1889–1897) vol. 1, pp. 59–61; 349; 434.
9. Bonaventure, *In Hexaemeron* 6:2; 6:4.
10. *In Hexaemeron* 6:2–3.
11. Ed. P. Shaw (Cambridge: Cambridge University Press, 1995); see also E. Gilson, *Dante the Philosopher* (London: Sheed & Ward, 1948); U. Limentari, 'Dante's Political Thought,' in his *The Mind of Dante* (Cambridge: Cambridge University Press, 1965); J.R. Woodhouse (ed.), *Dante and Governance* (Oxford: Clarendon Press, 1997).
12. Bonaventure, *In Hexaemeron* 6:4.
13. His distinguished career came to an end when he was assassinated by his secretary. See Dante's comment (*Paradiso* 10:136): *Essa e la luce eterna di Sigieri che, leggendo nel vico degli strami, sillogizzo invidiosi veri;* 'It is the eternal light of Siger, hated because...he reasoned about the truth.' See also the next note.
14. Standard works on Latin Averroism are still P. Mandonnet, *Siger de Brabant et l'Averroisme Latin au XIII^c Siecle* (2nd edition, Louvain: Publications universitaires, 1911) and M. Grabmann, *Forschungen über die lateinischen Aristoteles übersetzungen (Beiträge zur Geschichte der Philosophie und Theologie des Mittelalters* vol. 17 (1918)). See also R.C. Dales, 'The Origin of the Doctrine of the Double Truth,' *Viator* 15 (1984); F. van Steenberghen, *Maître Siger de Brabant* (Louvain: Publications universitaires, 1977). For St Thomas's own views see *On the Unity of the Intellect against the Averroists*, trans. B.H. Zedler (Milwaukee: Marquette University Press, 1968).
15. See D. Piché (ed.), *La condemnation parisienne de 1277. Texte latin, traduction, introduction et commentaire* (Paris: Vrin, 1999); J.A. Aertsen, K. Emery and A. Speer (eds), *Nach der Verurteilung von 1277. Philosophie und Theologie an der Universität von Paris im letzen Viertel des 13. Jahrhunderts: Studien und Texte* (Berlin: W. de Gruyter, 2001); L. Bianchi, *Il vescovo e i filosofi: La condanna parigina del 1277 e l'evoluzione dell'aristotelismo scolastico* (Bergamo: Lubrina. 1990).
16. A number of propositions representing St Thomas's views were included in the condemnation of 1277. Even after his canonisation, his work did not enjoy the recognition it was later to be accorded. The virtually exclusive place occupied by Thomist doctrines in Catholic philosophical education during most of the twentieth century is due to the encyclical *Aeterni patris* (4 August, 1879) of Pope Leo XIII, which recommended St Thomas as an antidote to the threat of liberal thought in the Church. 'Let carefully chosen teachers strive to implant the doctrine of Thomas Aquinas in the minds of students, and set forth clearly his soundness and excellence over others. Let the universities...illustrate and

defend this doctrine, and use it for the refutation of prevailing errors' (*Acta Leonis XIII*, 283-285 (Rome: Vatican, 1879)). *Aeterni patris* made St Thomas an establishment voice; it is easy to forget that, from the point of view of the history of ideas, he is an innovator of enormous significance.

17. It is fair to point out, however, that this prohibition is not as draconian as it may seem. Note the use of the verb *dogmatizare*, as distinct from the more obvious *docere*. Teachers are forbidden to teach *dogmatically*: i.e. to represent the propositions as true. They are not necessarily forbidden to discuss them at all.

18. The whole treatise is available in an edition and English translation by J.M. Blythe, *On the Government of Rulers: De regimine principum. Ptolemy of Lucca with Portions Attributed to Thomas Aquinas* (Philadelphia: University of Pennsylvania Press, 1997). Some account of the manuscript tradition and the difficulties that it presents is given by Fr Eschmann in Gilson, *Christian Philosophy*, p. 412. On questions of authorship, date and authenticity, see especially M. Browne, 'An sit authenticum opusculum S. Thomae *De regimine principum*,' *Angelicum* 3 (1926); A. O'Rahilly, 'Notes on St Thomas IV: *De regimine principum*,' *Irish Ecclesiastical Record* 31 (1929); 'Notes on St Thomas V: Tholomeo of Lucca, Continuator of the *De regimine principum*,' *Irish Ecclesiastical Record* 31 (1929); W. Mohr, 'Bemerkungen zur Verfasserschaft von *De regimine principum*,' in *Virtus politica*, eds J. Müller and H. Kohlenberger (Stuttgart & Bad Cannestatt: Fromann, 1974); J. Echard, 'S. Thomas de Aquino,' in Quétif–Echard, *Scriptores Ordinis Praedicatorum* 1 (Paris, 1719), p. 511. See also A. Black, *Political Thought in Europe, 1250–1550* (Cambridge: Cambridge University Press, 1992), p. 22.

19. The king of Cyprus in question is probably Hugh II of Lusignan, who appears to have had a particular affection for the Dominican order. St Thomas seems to have abandoned the work after Hugh's death in 1267.

20. On the literary structure of the *Summa theologiae* and the standard method of referring to it, see R.W. Dyson, *Aquinas: Political Writings* (Cambridge: Cambridge University Press, 2002), p. xxii.

21. For an edition of St Thomas's specifically political writings see R.W. Dyson, *Aquinas: Political Writings*. See also P.E. Sigmund, *St Thomas Aquinas on Ethics and Politics* (New York: Norton, 1988). The latter volume contains a most valuable selection of secondary material. Less valuable are A.P. D'Entreves, *Aquinas: Selected Political Writings* (Oxford: Blackwell, 1978), which is highly abridged and contains some misleading translations; and W.P. Baumgarth and R.J. Regan, SJ, *Saint Thomas Aquinas On Law, Morality and Politics* (Indianapolis, Hackett, 1988): a comprehensive selection, but with only very sketchy annotation. See also J. Finnis, *Aquinas: Moral, Political and Legal Theory* (Oxford: Oxford University Press, 1998); T. Gilby, *Principality and Polity: Aquinas and the Rise of State Theory in the West* (London: Longmans, Green, 1958); E.L. Fortin, 'St Thomas Aquinas,' in *A History of Political Philosophy*, eds L. Strauss & J. Cropsey (Chicago: University of Chicago Press, 1981); J. Tooke, *The Just War in Aquinas and Grotius* (London, 1965); J. Dunbabin, 'The Reception and Interpre-

Notes: Chapter 7

tation of Aristotle's *Politics*,' in N. Kretzmann, A. Kenny and J. Pinborg (eds), *The Cambridge History of Later Medieval Philosophy* (Cambridge: Cambridge University Press, 1982); J.I. Catto, 'Ideas and Experience in the Political Thought of Aquinas,' *Past and Present* 71 (1976).

22. *Summa theologiae* Ia IIae 2:8.
23. See *Summa theologiae* Ia IIae 3:8; 5:3.
24. *In X Libros Ethicorum* 1 (italics ours).
25. William prefers *animal civile* (see *Aristotelis Politicorum libri VIII cum translatione Guilemi de Moerbeka*, ed. F. Susemihl (Leipzig, 1872)). My own previous failure to notice this point was spotted by Professor Francisco Bertelloni in his review of my *Aquinas: Political Writings* in *The Medieval Review* (2003).
26. See *De regimine principum* 1:1; *Summa theologiae* Ia 96:4, *responsio*; Ia IIae 72:4, *responsio*. On the whole, this translation conveys the meaning of Aristotle's ὁ ἄνθρωπος φύσει πολιτικὸν ζῷον better than the literal translation 'political animal' does.
27. For St Thomas's detailed treatment of justice, see *Summa theologiae* IIa IIae 57 and 58.
28. See especially *De regimine principum* 1:1.
29. See *Summa theologiae* Ia IIae 63:1; 65:2; 92:1.
30. *Summa theologiae* Ia IIae 92 ad 1, quoting *Nicomachean Ethics* 1103^{b}3.
31. *De regimine principum* 1:15.
32. *Summa theologiae* Ia 96:3 ad 3.
33. *Summa theologiae* Ia 92:1 ad 2; 96:4, *responsio*.
34. *Summa theologiae* IIa IIae 104:1, *responsio*.
35. *Summa theologiae* IIa IIae 104:5, *responsio*.
36. *Summa theologiae* IIa IIae 10:10.
37. *Summa theologiae* IIa IIae 104:6.
38. *Summa theologiae* IIa IIae 104:3:2 & ad 2.
39. *Summa theologiae* IIa IIae 10:10, *responsio*.
40. Aristotle, *Historia animalium* 553^{b}6.
41. *De regimine principum* 1:6.
42. Cf. Dunbabin, 'Aristotle in the Schools,' pp. 66–67, where St Thomas's view seems to be seriously misrepresented, particularly in the comment that 'the ideas expressed [at *De regimine principum* 1:6] are not developed anywhere else.'
43. *Politics* 1277^{b}32.
44. Cf. *Politics* 1279^{a}37; 1293^{b}33; 1295^{a}31.
45. *Summa theologiae* Ia IIae 105:1, *responsio*.
46. See, for example, Marsilius of Padua, *Defensor pacis* 1:12:3; cf. Dyson, *Normative Theories*, pp. 246–248.
47. See especially *De regimine principum* 1:4–7; *Summa theologiae* IIa IIae 42.
48. Job 34:30.
49. *De regimine principum* 1:7.
50. *Summa theologiae* Ia IIae 96:4 ad 3.
51. *Summa theologiae* IIa IIae 42:2 ad 3, referring to *Politics* 1279^{b}6 and *Ethics* 1160^{b}8.

52. *Scripta* II 44:2:2 ad 5.
53. His remarks on this subject are worth quoting *in extenso*. 'For it would be a perilous thing, both for a community and its rulers, if anyone could attempt to slay even tyrannical rulers simply on his own private presumption. What is more likely to come of such presumption...is danger to the community through the loss of a king than relief through the removal of a tyrant. It seems, then, that steps are to be taken against the scourge of tyranny not by the private presumption of any persons, but through public authority. First of all, in cases where it belongs by right to a community to provide a ruler for itself, that community can without injustice depose or restrain a king whom it has appointed, if he should abuse royal power tyrannically. Nor should such a community be thought disloyal if it acts to depose a tyrant even if the community has already pledged itself to him in perpetuity; for the tyrant who has failed to govern the community faithfully, as the office of king requires, has deserved to be treated in this way. Thus the Romans who had accepted Tarquin the Proud as their king, then ejected him from the kingship because of his and his sons' tyranny, and substituted a lesser power, that is, the consulate. So also Domitian, who succeeded the mildest of emperors, Vespasian, his father, and Titus, his brother, was slain by the Roman Senate when he exercised tyrannical power, and all the wicked things that he had inflicted upon the Romans were justly and wholesomely revoked and made void by decree of the Senate...If, however, the right to provide a community with a king belongs to some superior, then a remedy against the wickedness of a tyrant must be sought from him. Thus when Archelaus, who began to reign in Judea in place of his father Herod, imitated the wickedness of his father, the Jews made complaint against him to Augustus Caesar, by whom his power was first reduced, the title of king being removed from him and half his kingdom divided between his two brothers; then, when this did not keep his tyrannical behaviour in check, he was banished into exile by Tiberius Caesar to Lyons, a city of Gaul.'
54. *Summa theologiae* IIa IIae 104:6 ad 3; IIa IIae 42:2 ad 3.
55. *Summa theologiae* IIa IIae 40; IIa IIae 64. St Thomas's opinions on just or righteous warfare resemble St Augustine's in all major respects (see p. 149), and there is no need to describe them here.
56. *Summa theologiae* IIa IIae 66; IIa IIae 78.
57. See, for example, his Aristotelian discussion of usury at *Summa theologiae* IIa IIae 78.
58. *Summa theologiae* IIa IIae 66:2, *responsio*.
59. *Summa theologiae* IIa IIae 66:2, *responsio*.
60. *Summa theologiae* IIa IIae 66:7, *responsio* & ad 2.
61. For more detailed treatments see especially R.A. Armstrong, *Primary and Secondary Precepts in Thomistic Natural Law Teaching* (The Hague: Martinus Nijhoff, 1966); D.J. O'Connor, *Aquinas and Natural Law* (London: Macmillan, 1967); J. Finnis, *Natural Law and Natural Rights* (Oxford: Oxford University

Press, 1982); A.P. d'Entrèves, *Natural Law*. More generally, see Y.R. Simon, *The Tradition of Natural Law: A Philosopher's Reflections* (New York: Fordham University Press, 1965).
62. *Summa theologiae* Ia IIae 90:1, *responsio*.
63. *Summa theologiae* Ia IIae 93:1, *responsio*.
64. *Summa theologiae* Ia IIae 90:1 ad 1.
65. *Summa theologiae* Ia IIae 91:1; 93.
66. *Summa theologiae* Ia IIae 93:1, *responsio*.
67. It must be borne in mind, however, that, for St Thomas, the natural order itself is a moral order and not a mere order of facts; necessarily so, for 'God saw everything that He had made, and, behold, it was very good.' This is what enables St Thomas validly to deduce the natural law from the eternal law, and human law from the natural law: validly, that is, in that his reasoning avoids the fallacy or category mistake nowadays called 'deriving ought from is.'
68. *Summa theologiae* Ia IIae 91:1 ad 3.
69. *Summa theologiae* Ia IIae 93:5, *responsio*.
70. *Summa theologiae* Ia IIae 91:2; 94.
71. *Summa theologiae* Ia IIae 94:2, *responsio*.
72. *Summa theologiae* Ia 79:12; Ia IIae 94:1.
73. *Summa theologiae* Ia IIae 94:2, *responsio*.
74. *Summa theologiae* Ia IIae 91:3; 95–97.
75. *Summa theologiae* Ia IIae 91:3, *responsio*.
76. *Summa theologiae* Ia IIae 64: 2 and 3.
77. *Summa theologiae* Ia IIae 91:1, *responsio*.
78. *Summa theologiae* Ia IIae 95:4, *responsio*.
79. *Summa theologiae* Ia IIae 95:2: *obj.* 4 & ad 4.
80. *Summa theologiae* IIa IIae 57:2 ad 2.
81. *Summa theologiae* Ia IIae 95:2, *responsio*.
82. *Summa theologiae* Ia IIae 96:4, *responsio*.
83. *Summa theologiae* Ia IIae 90:4–5.
84. See *Summa theologiae* Ia IIae 90:4; 93:3 ad 2.
85. See n. 16, above. See also J. Maritain, *Man and the State* (Chicago: University of Chicago Press, 1953); *Scholasticism and Politics* (New York: Doubleday 1940); *The Rights of Man and Natural Law* (London: Bles, 1944).
86. See n. 1, above.
87. See Dyson, *Normative Theories*, ch. 6.

Chapter 8

1. J.W. Allen, *A History of Political Thought in the Sixteenth Century* (London: Methuen, 1957), p. 447.
2. Cf. Allen, *Political Thought in the Sixteenth Century*, p. 448: 'He was not very highly educated in a wide sense. His serious training was that of the practical

politician and man of affairs; and a politician he remained to the end of his days, in office or out of office.'

3. See especially his letter to Francesco Vettori in *The Literary Works of Machiavelli*, ed. and trans. J.R. Hale (Oxford: Oxford University Press, 1961), p. 140: 'I am becoming worn out and I cannot carry on like this for long without being harmed by the stigma of poverty, and besides there is my longing that these Medici lords should begin to take me into their service, even if they start by setting me to roll stones, for if I could not then win them over, I should have only myself to blame.'

4. See Niccolò Machiavelli, *Opere*, eds S. Bertelli and F. Gaeta (Milan: Feltrinelli, 1960 *et seqq*.); for English translations see *The Prince*, ed. and trans. A. Grafton and G. Bull (Harmondsworth, Middlesex: Penguin, 1999); *Discourses*, ed. and trans. L. J. Walker and B. Crick (Harmondsworth, Middlesex: Penguin, 1970); *The Art of War*, trans. E. Farneworth (rev. ed. by N. Wood) (New York: Da Capo Press, 1990); *History of Florence*, trans. A. Gilbert (Durham, NC: Duke University Press, 1965). See also *The Literary Works of Machiavelli*, ed. and trans. J.R. Hale; *The Letters of Machiavelli, A Selection*, ed. and trans. A.H. Gilbert (Chicago: University of Chicago Press, 1988). Only *The Art of War* was published in Machiavelli's lifetime (1521). The *Discourses* was published in 1531, and *The Prince* and the *History of Florence* in 1532. The serious disorganisation of the *Discourses* and its very abrupt end at 3:49 suggests, though does not prove, that the work was never finished.

5. From the enormous range of biographical and secondary literature see especially S. Anglo, *Machiavelli: A Dissection* (London: Gollancz, 1969); J. Burckhardt, *The Civilization of the Renaissance in Italy* (Oxford: Phaidon, 1981); H. Butterfield, *The Statecraft of Machiavelli* (London: G. Bell & Sons, 1940); F. Chabod, *Machiavelli and the Renaissance* (London: Bowes & Bowes, 1958); S. De Grazia, *Machiavelli in Hell* (New York: Vintage, 1993); M. Fleisher, *Machiavelli and the Nature of Political Thought* (London: Croom Helm, 1973); F. Gilbert, *Machiavelli and Giucciardini: Politics and History in Sixteenth-century Florence* (Princeton, NJ: Princeton University Press, 1965); J.R. Hale, *Machiavelli and Renaissance Italy* (London: Macmillan, 1961); M. Hulliung, *Citizen Machiavelli* (Princeton, NJ: Princeton University Press, 1983); H.C. Mansfield, *Machiavelli's Virtue* (Chicago: University of Chicago Press, 1998); G.J.A. Pocock, *The Machiavellian Moment: Florentine Political Thought and the Atlantic Republican Tradition* (Princeton, NJ: Princeton University Press, 1975); Q.R.D. Skinner, *The Foundations of Modern Political Thought*, vol. 1: *The Renaissance* (Cambridge: Cambridge University Press, 1978); *Machiavelli* (Oxford: Oxford University Press, 1981); L. Strauss, *Thoughts on Machiavelli* (Chicago: University of Chicago Press, 1995); M. Viroli, *Machiavelli* (Oxford: Oxford University Press, 1998). See also Sir I. Berlin, 'The Originality of Machiavelli,' in *Against the Current: Essays in the History of Ideas*, ed. H. Hardy (London: Hogarth Press, 1979). Still of value is P. Villari, *The Life and Times of Niccolò Machiavelli* (London: Unwin, 1892).

Notes: Chapter 8 323

6. See especially N. Rubinstein, 'Political Theories in the Renaissance,' in A. Chastel et al. (eds), *The Renaissance* (London: Methuen, 1982), p. 153; W. Ullmann, *Medieval Foundations of Renaissance Humanism* (Ithaca, NY: Cornell University Press, 1977), p. 89.
7. See especially Dyson, *Giles of Rome's 'De ecclesiastica potestate': A Medieval Theory of World Government*, Introduction.
8. On these matters see especially Dyson, *Normative Theories*, Postrscript. See also A.J. Black, *Monarchy and Community: Political Ideas in the Later Conciliar Controversy, 1430–1450* (Cambridge: Cambridge University Press, 1970); A. Delaruelle, E.-R. Labande and P. Ourliac, *L'église au temps du grand schisme et de la crise conciliaire (1378–1449)* (Tournai, Belgium: Bloud & Gay, 1962); J.H. Smith, *The Great Schism* (London: Hamish Hamilton, 1970); P.H. Stump, *The Reforms of the Council of Constance (1414-1418)* (Leiden: E.J. Brill, 1994); B. Tierney, *Foundations of the Conciliar Theory: The Contribution of the Medieval Canonists from Gratian to the Great Schism* (Cambridge: Cambridge University Press, 1955); W. Ullmann, *The Origins of the Great Schism* (Hamden, CT: Archon, 1967).
9. *The Prince*, 26.
10. *Discourses* 1:12.
11. *The Prince* 7.
12. S.S. Wolin, *Politics and Vision: Continuity and Innovation in Western Political Thought* (London: George Allen and Unwin, 1961), p. 199.
13. *The Prince* 11.
14. *Discourses* 2:2.
15. Cf. Allen, *Political Thought in the Sixteenth Century*, pp. 458–459.
16. See Rousseau, *The Social Contract and Discourses*, trans. G.D.H. Cole (London: J.M. Dent & Sons, 1966), p. 59.
17. Cf. A.H. Gilbert, *Machiavelli's The Prince and its Forerunners* (Durham, NC: Duke University Press, 1938).
18. *The Prince* 15.
19. Ibid.
20. *Discourses* 1:6.
21. *The Prince* 3; *Discourses* 1, Preface; 3:1.
22. *The Myth of the State* (New Haven: Yale University Press, 1946), p. 153. For some differing views as to Machiavelli's 'political science' see A. Gramsci, *Quaderni del Carcere* (Turin: Einaudi, 1975) vol. 3, p. 1572; Butterfield, *The Statecraft of Machiavelli*, p. 57; Viroli, *Machiavelli*, p. 3.
23. Cf. Viroli, *Machiavelli*, p. 3.
24. Cf. G. Mattingly, 'Machiavelli's Prince: Political Science or Political Satire?' *The American Scholar* 27 (1955).
25. Cf. Allen, *Political Thought in the Sixteenth Century*, p. 448–449: 'It would...be very foolish to suppose that Machiavelli wrote merely to attract attention and obtain a post for himself. His desire to be employed politically must have been largely due to his sense of power and understanding and his conviction that, as adviser to some powerful Prince, he might forward the realization of his

dream of a free Italy. The same reasons and motives that made him desire a post made him write the *Discorsi* and the *Principe*. For even Machiavelli could not escape the idealism that besets us all.'

26. See *Discourses* 1:2; 1:9; 1:16–18; 1:33; *History of Florence* 5.
27. See e.g. *Discourses* 1:9; 1:55.
28. *Discourses*, 1, Preface; 3:43.
29. *The Prince* 17.
30. *Discourses* 1:3.
31. *Discourses* 2, Preface.
32. *Discourses* 3:4.
33. See, e.g., *History of Florence*, 7.
34. Cf. *The Prince* 3–5; 18; 19.
35. *Discourses* 1:37.
36. *The Prince* 3; *Discourses* 1:2.
37. See especially *The Prince* 26.
38. *The Prince* 2; 3.
39. *The Prince* 17–19; and see especially Anglo, *Machiavelli*, chs 2, 7, 8, 9.
40. *The Prince* 12–17.
41. *De regimine principum* 1:11.
42. *The Prince* 17.
43. Cf. *The Prince* 6; *Discourses* 1:11; J.H. Whitfield, 'Savonarola and the Purpose of *The Prince*,' in *Discourses on Machiavelli* (Cambridge: Heffer, 1969).
44. *The Prince* 3.
45. *The Prince* 5; Cf. 4; 12–14.
46. See especially *The Prince* 25; *Discourses* 2:1; 2:29; 3:9. For a detailed analysis of *virtù* see N. Wood, 'Machiavelli's Concept of *Virtù* Reconsidered,' *Political Studies* 15, 2 (1967). For a contrasting view see I. Hannaford, 'Machiavelli's Concept of *Virtù* in *The Prince* and *The Discourses* Reconsidered,' *Political Studies* 20, 2, (1972).
47. *The Prince* 7.
48. *The Prince* 17; *Discourses* 3:21.
49. *The Prince* 25. See also H.F. Pitkin, *Fortune is a Woman: Gender and Politics in the Thought of Niccolò Machiavelli* (Berkeley, CA: University of California Press), pp. 7, 236; J.B. Elshtain, *Public Man, Private Woman: Women in Social and Political Thought* (Princeton, NJ: Princeton University Press, 1981), pp. 96, 99.
50. *The Prince* 18.
51. Ibid.
52. *The Prince* 15.
53. See, e.g., *Discourses* 1:26: 'The life of a private citizen would indeed be preferable to the ruin of so many people. But anyone who is unwilling to adopt the first and humane course must, if he wishes to maintain his power, follow the latter evil course.' See also his remarks about the 'barbarous cruelty and inhumanity' of Agathocles at *The Prince* 8. Even in the 'infamous' chapter 18 of *The Prince*, 'Concerning the Way in Which Princes Should Keep Faith,' he says

that it is 'praiseworthy...for a prince to keep his word and to live honestly rather than by deceit.' The common view that Machiavelli is merely insincere in these statements does not rest upon anything very solid. See also n. 73.
54. See F. Raab, *The English Face of Machiavelli: A Changing Interpretation, 1500–1700* (London: Routledge, 1964).
55. *Discourses* 1:9.
56. *The Prince* 25; *Discourses* 3:9.
57. 'Machiavelli and Vico,' pp. 655–656, in *Philosophy, Poetry, History: An Anthology of Essays by Benedetto Croce*, ed. and trans. C. Sprigge (Oxford: Oxford University Press, 1966).
58. 'We must take it as a general rule that a republic or a monarchy is seldom or never well constituted, or its old institutions thoroughly reformed, except by one individual. It is, indeed, necessary that he whose mind has conceived such a constitution should be alone in bringing it into being' (*Discourses* 1:9). In the case of a State ruled by a decadent nobility, 'the only way to establish any kind of order there is to found a monarchical government. For where the body politic is so thoroughly rotten that the laws have no power to restrain, it becomes necessary to establish some superior power which, with a royal hand, and with full and absolute power, may bridle the excessive ambition and corruption of the great' (*Discourses* 1:55).
59. *Discourses* 1:58; 1:11.
60. *Discourses* 3:6.
61. *Discourses* 1:4.
62. *Discourses* 1:58; he goes on: 'I say that a people is more prudent, more stable and of better judgment than a prince. Not without reason is the voice of the people likened to the voice of God.'
63. *Discourses* 1:4.
64. *Discourses* 1:16.
65. Ibid.
66. *Discourses* 1:2.
67. *Discourses* 1:11–12.
68. *Discourses* 1:12; 2:2.
69. *Discourses* 1:4; 2:2; 3:31; 3:25–37; cf. *The Prince* 12.
70. See, e.g., *Discourses* 2:8; 2:25.
71. For a list of those whom he most admires, see Wood, 'Machiavelli's Concept of Virtù Reconsidered,' p. 161. Only six names on Professor Wood's (incomplete) list—Carmagnola, Cesare Borgia, Francesco Sforza, Gonzalo de Córdoba, Oliverotto Euffreducci and Ottaviano Fregoso—are contemporaries of Machiavelli, and over half of them are Romans.
72. The commonplace was, as far as we know, inaugurated by F. Meinecke, *Machiavellianism: the Doctrine of Raison d'État and its Place in History*, trans. D. Scott (London: Routledge and Kegan Paul, 1957); cf. J.H. Hexter, 'The Loom of Language and the Fabric of Imperatives: The Case of *Il principe* and *Utopia*,' *American Historical Review* 69 (1964); G. Post, 'Ratio publicae utilitatis, ratio status and

"Reason of State",' in *Studies in Medieval Legal Thought* (Princeton, NJ: Princeton University Press, 1964).

73. Cf. Croce: 'Machiavelli seems to be wracked by mental conflict concerning this Politics of which he has discovered the autonomous workings. At one moment it seems to him an odious doom to have to dirty his hands in dealings with the impure. At another moment it seems to him a most sublime calling, to lay and strengthen the foundations of that great institution, the State' ('Machiavelli and Vico,' p. 657).

74. Q.R.D. Skinner, 'Machiavelli's *Discorsi* and the Pre-Humanist Origins of Republican Ideas,' in G. Bok, Q.R.D. Skinner and M. Viroli (eds), *Machiavelli and Republicanism* (Cambridge: Cambridge University Press, 1990), p. 141; cf. M. Viroli, 'Machiavelli and the Republican Idea of Politics,' in Bok et al., p. 144; Mansfield, *Machiavelli's Virtue*, pp. ix, 177, 257.

Select Bibliography

Allen, J.W. *A History of Political Thought in the Sixteenth Century* (London: Methuen, 1957).
Anglo, S. *Machiavelli: A Dissection* (London: Gollancz, 1969).
Annas, J. *An Introduction to Plato's Republic* (Oxford: Clarendon Press, 1981).
Armstrong, A.H. (ed.) *The Cambridge History of Later Greek and Early Medieval Philosophy* (Cambridge: Cambridge University Press, 1967).
Armstrong, R.A. *Primary and Secondary Precepts in Thomistic Natural Law Teaching* (The Hague: Martinus Nijhoff, 1966).
Arnold, E.V. *Roman Stoicism* (Cambridge: Cambridge University Press, 1911).
Arquillière, F.-X. *L'Augustinisme politique* (Paris: Vrin, 1939).
Atkins, E.M. and Dodaro, R.J. *Augustine: Political Writings* (Cambridge: Cambridge University Press, 2001).
Austin, M.M. (ed.) *The Hellenistic World from Alexander to the Roman Conquest. A Selection of Ancient Sources in Translation* (Cambridge: Cambridge University Press, 1981).
Austin, S. *Parmenides: Being, Bounds and Logic* (New Haven, Conn.: Yale University Press, 1986).
Bailey, C. *The Greek Atomists and Epicurus* (Oxford: Oxford University Press, 1928).
Bainton, R.H. *Christian Attitudes Toward War and Peace* (New York: Abingdon Press, 1960).
Balot, R.K. *Greed and Injustice in Classical Athens* (Princeton, NJ: Princeton University Press, 2001).
Barclay, J. and Sweet, J. (eds) *Early Christian Thought in its Jewish Context* (Cambridge: Cambridge University Press, 1996).
Barnes, J. *Early Greek Philosophy* (Harmondsworth: Penguin, 1987).
Barnes, J., Schofield, M., and Sorabji, M. (eds) *Articles on Aristotle* (2 vols, London: Duckworth, 1977).
Bartlett, R.C. and Collins, S.D. (eds) *Action and Contemplation: Studies in the Moral and Political Thought of Aristotle* (Albany, NY: State University of New York Press, 1999).
Bathory, P.D. *Political Theory as Public Confession: The Social and Political Thought of St Augustine of Hippo* (New Brunswick, NJ: Transaction, 1981).
Baynes, N.H. *The Political Ideas of St. Augustine's 'De civitate Dei'* (London: Historical Association, 1936).
Bedford, D. and Workman, T. 'The Tragic Reading of the Thucydidean Tragedy,' *Review of International Studies*, 27 (2001).

Benko, S. *Pagan Rome and the Early Christians* (Bloomington, IN: Indiana University Press, 1984).
Berlin, Sir I. 'The Originality of Machiavelli,' in *Against the Current: Essays in the History of Ideas*, ed. H. Hardy (London: Hogarth Press, 1979).
Bett, R. 'The Sophists and Relativism,' *Phronesis* 34 (1989).
Bettenson, H. (ed.) *Documents of the Christian Church* (Oxford: Oxford University Press, 1963).
Bevan, E. *Stoics and Sceptics* (Oxford: Oxford University Press, 1913).
Black, A.J. *Monarchy and Community: Political Ideas in the Later Conciliar Controversy, 1430–1450* (Cambridge: Cambridge University Press, 1970).
Bodéüs, R. *The Political Dimensions of Aristotle's Ethics* (Albany, NY: State University of New York Press, 1993).
Bok, G., Skinner, Q.R.D. and Viroli, M. (eds) *Machiavelli and Republicanism* (Cambridge: Cambridge University Press, 1990).
Bonner, G. *St Augustine of Hippo: Life and Controversies* (Oxford: Oxford University Press, 1986).
────── 'Pelagianism and Augustine,' *Augustinian Studies* 23 (1992).
Borgen, P. *Philo, John, and Paul: New Perspectives on Judaism and Early Christianity* (Atlanta, GA: Scholar's Press, 1987).
────── *Early Christianity and Hellenistic Judaism* (Edinburgh: T. & T. Clark, 1996).
Borza, E.N. *Conquest and Empire. The Reign of Alexander the Great* (Cambridge: Cambridge University Press, 1988).
Boter, G.J. 'Thrasymachus and *Pleonexia*,' *Mnemosyne* 39 (1986).
Boucher, D. *Political Theories of International Relations* (Oxford: Oxford University Press 1998).
Bouman, C.A. *Sacring and Crowning: The Development of the Latin Ritual for the Anointing of Kings and the Coronation of an Emperor before the Eleventh Century* (Groningen: J.B. Wolters, 1957).
Bowersock, G.W. *Martyrdom and Rome* (Cambridge: Cambridge University Press, 1995).
Bréhier, E. *Chrysippe et l'ancien stoïcisme* (Paris: PUF, 1950).
Brochard, V. *Les Sceptiques grecs* (Paris: Vrin, 1959).
Brown, C., Nardin, T. and Rengger N. *International Relations in Political Thought* (Cambridge: Cambridge University Press, 2002).
Brown, E. 'Justice and Compulsion for Plato's Philosopher-Rulers,' *Ancient Philosophy* 20 (2000).
Brown, L. 'How Totalitarian is Plato's Republic?' in *Essays on Plato's Republic*, ed. E.N. Ostenfeld (Aarhus: Aarhus University Press, 1998).
Brown, P. *Augustine of Hippo* (London: Faber & Faber, 1967).
────── *Religion and Society in the Age of Saint Augustine* (London: Faber & Faber, 1971).
Buckland, W.W. and Stein, P. *A Textbook of Roman Law from Augustus to Justinian* (Cambridge: Cambridge University Press, 1975).

Burckhardt, J. *The Civilization of the Renaissance in Italy* (Oxford: Phaidon, 1981).
Burleigh, J.H.S. *The City of God: A Study of St Augustine's Philosophy* (London: Nisbet, 1949).
Bury, R.G. *The Logos Doctrine and the Fourth Gospel* (Cambridge: Cambridge University Press, 1940).
Butterfield, H. *The Statecraft of Machiavelli* (London: G. Bell & Sons, 1940).
Cadoux, C.J. *The Early Christian Attitude to War* (London: Headly Brothers, 1919).
Cady, D.L. 'Individual Fulfillment (Not Social Engineering) in Plato's *Republic*,' *Idealistic Studies* 13 (1983).
Calogero, G. 'Gorgias and the Socratic Principle *Nemo sua sponte peccat*,' *Journal of Hellenic Studies* 1 (1957).
Carlyle, R.W. and A.J. *A History of Medieval Political Theory in the West* (6 vols, Edinburgh: Blackwood, 1962).
Cary, M.J. and Haarhof, T.J. *Life and Thought in the Greek and Roman World* (London: Methuen, 1968).
Chabod, F. *Machiavelli and the Renaissance* (London: Bowes & Bowes, 1958).
Cherniss, H. *Aristotle's Criticism of Plato and the Academy* (Baltimore, MD: Johns Hopkins Press, 1944).
Christensen, J. *An Essay on the Unity of Stoic Philosophy* (Copenhagen: Munksgaard, 1962).
Cochrane, C.N. *Christianity and Classical Culture* (Oxford: Oxford University Press, 1943).
Colish, M.L. *The Stoic Tradition From Antiquity to the Early Middle Ages* (Leiden: Brill, 1990).
Combès, G. *La doctrine politique de saint Augustin* (Paris: Librairie Plon, 1927).
Connolly, W.E. *The Augustinian Imperative: A Reflection on the Politics of Morality* (London: Sage, 1993).
Coplestone, F.C. *Aquinas* (Harmondsworth, Middlesex: Penguin, 1970).
Cranz, F.E. 'De civitate Dei, XV, 2, and Augustine's Idea of the Christian Society,' *Speculum* 25 (1950).
Crombie, I.M. *An Examination of Plato's Doctrines* (2 vols, London: Routledge, 1963).
Cross, R.C. and Woozley, A.D. *Plato's 'Republic': a Philosophical Commentary* (London: Macmillan, 1964).
Daube, D. *Roman Law: Linguistic, Social, and Philosophical Aspects* (Edinburgh: Edinburgh University Press, 1969).
Davies, B. *The Thought of Thomas Aquinas* (Oxford: Oxford University Press, 1992).
Davies, J.K. *Democracy and Classical Greece* (Cambridge, MA.: Harvard University Press, 1993).
Davis, L.D. 'The Arguments of Thrasymachus in the First Book of Plato's *Republic*,' *Modern Schoolman* 47 (1970).
d'Entrèves, A.P. *Natural Law* (London: Hutchinson, 1972).
De Grazia, S. *Machiavelli in Hell* (New York: Vintage, 1993).

de Plinval, G. *Pélage: ses écrits, sa vie et sa réforme* (Lausanne: Librairie Payot, 1943).
de Romilly, J. *The Great Sophists in Periclean Athens* (Oxford: Clarendon Press, 1992).
de Witt, N.W. *Epicurus and his Philosophy* (Minneapolis: University of Minnesota Press, 1954).
de Wulf, M. *The System of St Thomas Aquinas* (Cambridge, MA: Harvard University Press, 1922).
Deane, H.A. *The Political and Social Ideas of St Augustine* (New York: Columbia University Press, 1963).
Delaruelle, A., Labande, E.-R. and Ourliac, P. *L'église au temps du grand schisme et de la crise conciliaire (1378–1449)* (Tournai, Belgium: Bloud & Gay, 1962).
Dickinson, J. (ed.) *The Statesman's Book of John of Salisbury* (New York: Knopf, repr. 1963).
Dillon, J. *The Heirs of Plato: A Study of the Old Academy (347-274 BCE)* (Oxford: Clarendon Press, 2003).
Dodds, E.H. *The Greeks and the Irrational* (Berkeley, CA: University of California Press, 1951).
Dodds, E.R. *Pagan and Christian in an Age of Anxiety* (Cambridge: Cambridge University Press, 1965).
Doran, R. *Birth of a World View: Early Christianity in its Jewish and Pagan Context* (Boulder, CO: Westview Press, 1996).
Dover, K.J. *Greek Popular Morality in the Time of Plato and Aristotle* (Indianapolis: Hackett, 1974).
Dudley, D.R. *A History of Cynicism* (London: Methuen, 1937).
Dunn, J.D.G. *Jews and Christians: The Parting of the Ways, AD 70 to 135* (London: SCM, 1991).
Dyson, R.W. (ed.) *James of Viterbo on Christian Government* (Woodbridge, Suffolk: Boydell, 1995).
—— *The Pilgrim City: Social and Political Ideas in the Writings of St Augustine of Hippo* (Woodbridge, Suffolk: Boydell, 2001).
—— *Normative Theories of Society and Government in Five Medieval Thinkers* (Lewiston, Queenston, Lampeter: Mellen, 2003).
—— (ed.) *Giles of Rome's 'De ecclesiastica potestate': a Medieval Theory of World Government* (New York: Columbia University Press, 2004).
Earl, D. *The Moral and Political Tradition of Rome* (London: Thames and Hudson, 1967).
Edelstein, L. 'The Philosophical System of Posidonius,' *American Journal of Philology* 57 (1936).
—— *The Meaning of Stoicism* (Cambridge, MA: Harvard University Press, 1966).
Elshtain, J.B. *Public Man, Private Woman: Women in Social and Political Thought* (Princeton, NJ: Princeton University Press, 1981).
—— *Augustine and the Limits of Politics* (Notre Dame, IN: Indiana University Press, 1999).
Engberg-Pedersen, T. *Aristotle's Theory of Moral Insight* (Oxford: Oxford University Press, 1983).

Select Bibliography   331

——— *Paul and the Stoics* (Edinburgh: T. & T. Clark, 2000).
Evans, G.R. *Augustine on Evil* (Cambridge: Cambridge University Press, 1982).
Evans, R.F. *Pelagius: Inquiries and Reappraisals* (London: A. & C. Black, 1968).
Ferguson, A.S. 'Plato's Simile of Light, Part I,' *Classical Quarterly* 15 (1921).
——— 'Plato's Simile of Light, Part II,' *Classical Quarterly* 16 (1922).
——— 'Plato's Simile of Light Again,' *Classical Quarterly* 28 (1934).
Ferguson, E. (ed.) *Christianity in Relation to Jews, Greeks, and Romans* (New York: Garland, 1999).
Ferguson, J. *Pelagius: A Historical and Theological Study* (Cambridge: Cambridge University Press, 1956).
Ferguson, W.S. *Hellenistic Athens* (London: Macmillan, 1911).
Field, G.C. 'Aristotle's Account of the Historical Origin of the Theory of Ideas,' *Classical Quarterly* 17 (1923).
——— *Plato and his Contemporaries* (New York: Dutton, 1930).
Figgis, J.N. *The Political Aspects of S. Augustine's 'City of God'* (London: Longmans, 1921).
Fine, G. *On Ideas: Aristotle's Criticism of Plato's Theory of Forms* (Oxford: Clarendon Press, 1993).
Finnis, J. *Natural Law and Natural Rights* (Oxford: Oxford University Press, 1982).
Fleisher, M. *Machiavelli and the Nature of Political Thought* (London: Croom Helm, 1973).
Flüeler, C. *Rezeption und Interpretation der Aristotelischen 'Politica' im späten Mittelalter* (Amsterdam: Grüner, 1992).
Forde, S. 'Classical Realism,' in T. Nardin and D. Mapel (eds), *Traditions in International Ethics* (Cambridge, Cambridge University Press, 1992).
Fortin, E.L. 'Augustine's City of God and the Modern Historical Consciousness,' *Review of Politics* 41 (1979).
Fox, R.L. *Pagans and Christians* (San Francisco: Viking, 1986).
Fränkel, H. *Early Greek Poetry and Philosophy* (Oxford: Blackwell, 1975).
Frend, W.H.C. *Martyrdom and Persecution in the Early Church: A Study in Conflict from the Maccabees to Donatus* (Oxford: Blackwell, 1965).
Gagarin, M. and Woodruff, P. *Early Greek Political Thought from Homer to the Sophists* (Cambridge: Cambridge University Press, 1995).
Gilbert, A.H. *Machiavelli's The Prince and its Forerunners* (Durham, NC: Duke University Press, 1938).
Gilbert, F. *Machiavelli and Giucciardini: Politics and History in Sixteenth-century Florence* (Princeton, NJ: Princeton University Press, 1965).
Gilson, E. *The Christian Philosophy of St Augustine of Hippo* (London: Gollancz, 1960).
——— *The Christian Philosophy of St Thomas Aquinas* (London: Gollancz, 1961).
Gould, J.B. *The Philosophy of Chrysippus* (Leiden: Brill, 1997).
Grant, R.M. *Augustus to Constantine: the Thrust of the Christian Movement into the Roman World* (London: Collins, 1972).

Green, P. *Alexander of Macedon 356-323 BCE: A Historical Biography* (Berkeley, CA: University of California Press, 1991).

Grote, G. *History of Greece* (10 vols, repr. (from the 1872 edition) Bristol: Thoemmes, 2000).

Gulley, N. *Plato's Theory of Knowledge* (New York: Barnes and Noble, 1962).

Guthrie, W.K.C. *A History of Greek Philosophy* (6 vols, Cambridge: Cambridge University Press, 1962–1969).

Guy, J.-C. *Unité et structure logique de la Cité de Dieu* (Paris: Etudes augustiniennes, 1961).

Hale, J.R. *Machiavelli and Renaissance Italy* (London: Macmillan, 1961).

Hammond, N.G.L. *A History of Greece to 322 BC* (Oxford: Clarendon Press, 1967).

—— *Alexander the Great. King, Commander, and Statesman* (London: Chatto and Windus, 1982).

Hannaford, I. 'Machiavelli's Concept of *Virtù* in *The Prince* and *The Discourses* Reconsidered,' *Political Studies* 20, 2, (1972).

Hardie, W.F.R. *Aristotle's Ethical Theory* (Oxford: Oxford University Press, 1980).

Harding, P. (ed.) *From the End of the Peloponnesian War to the Battle of Ipsus* (Cambridge: Cambridge University Press, 1985).

Harlap, S. 'Thrasymachus's Justice,' *Political Theory* 7 (1979).

Henderson, T.Y. 'In Defence of Thrasymachus,' *American Philosophical Quarterly* 7 (1970).

Hexter, J.H. 'The Loom of Language and the Fabric of Imperatives: The Case of *Il principe* and *Utopia*,' *American Historical Review* 69 (1964).

Hignett, C. *History of the Athenian Constitution* (Oxford: Oxford University Press, 1952).

Honore, A.M. 'The Background to Justinian's Codification,' *Tulane Law Review* 48 (1974).

—— *Emperors and Lawyers* (Oxford: Clarendon Press, 1994).

—— *Law in the Crisis of Empire 379-445 CE* (Oxford: Clarendon Press, 1998).

Hourani, G.F. 'Thrasymachus' Definition of Justice in Plato's *Republic*,' *Phronesis* 7 (1962).

Hulliung, M. *Citizen Machiavelli* (Princeton, NJ: Princeton University Press, 1983).

Hutchinson, D.S. *The Virtues of Aristotle* (London: Routledge, 1986).

Irwin, T. *Classical Thought* (Oxford: Oxford University Press, 1995).

—— *Plato's Ethics* (Oxford: Oxford University Press, 1995).

Jaeger, W. *Aristotle: Foundations of the History of His Development*, trans. R. Robinson (Oxford: Clarendon Press, 1948).

Jaffa, H. *Thomism and Aristotelianism* (Chicago: University of Chicago Press, 1952).

Jolivet, R. *Le problème du mal d'après saint Augustin* (2nd ed., Paris: Archives de Philosophie, 1936).

Jones, A.H.M. *Athenian Democracy* (Oxford: Blackwell, 1957).

Jones, H. *The Epicurean Tradition* (London: Routledge, 1992).

Kahn, C.H. *The Art and Thought of Heraclitus* (Cambridge: Cambridge University Press, 1979).
Kelly, J.F. *The World of the Early Christians* (Collegeville, MN: Liturgical Press, 1997).
Kennedy, G. *The Art of Persuasion in Greece* (Princeton, NJ: Princeton University Press, 1963).
Kenny, A. *Aquinas* (Oxford: Oxford University Press, 1980).
Kerferd, G.B. 'The Doctrine of Thrasymachus in Plato's *Republic,*' *Durham University Journal* 9 (1947).
—— 'Gorgias on Nature or That Which is Not,' *Phronesis* 1 (1955).
—— 'The Interpretation of Gorgias' Treatise Περὶ τοῦ μὴ ὄντος ἢ περὶ φύσεως,' *Deucalion* 9 (1981).
—— *The Sophistic Movement* (Cambridge: Cambridge University Press, 1981).
Keyt, D. and Miller, F.D. (eds) *A Companion to Aristotle's Politics* (Oxford: Clarendon Press, 1991).
Kirk, G.S. and Raven, J.E. *The Presocratic Philosophers* (Cambridge: Cambridge University Press, 1957).
Kirk, G.S. *Myth: Its Meaning and Function in Ancient and Other Cultures* (Cambridge: Cambridge University Press, 1970).
—— *The Nature of Greek Myths* (Harmondsworth: Penguin, 1974).
Klosko, G. *The Development of Plato's Political Theory* (London: Methuen, 1986).
Kokz, N. 'Moderating Power: A Thucydidean Perspective,' *Review of International Studies* 27 (2001).
Kraut, R. *Aristotle on the Human Good* (Princeton, NJ: Princeton University Press, 1989).
—— 'Return to the Cave: *Republic* 519-521,' in *Plato: Ethics, Politics, Religion, and the Soul* vol. 2, ed. G. Fine (Oxford: Oxford University Press, 1999).
—— *Aristotle: Political Philosophy* (Oxford: Oxford University Press, 2002).
Krentz, P. *The Thirty at Athens* (Ithaca, NY: Cornell University Press, 1982).
Künkel, W. *An Introduction to Roman Legal and Constitutional History* (Oxford: Clarendon Press,1973).
Kurtscheid, B. and Wilches, F. *Historia iuris canonici* (Rome: Officium Libri Catholici, 1941–1943).
Kuttner, S. 'The Natural Law and Canon Law,' *Proceedings of the University of Notre Dame Natural Law Institute* 3 (1950).
Laffranque, M. *Poseidonios d'Apamée* (Paris: PUF, 1964).
Lavere, G.J. 'The Political Realism of Saint Augustine,' *Augustinian Studies* 11 (1980).
—— 'The Influence of Saint Augustine on Early Medieval Political Theory,' *Augustinian Studies* 12 (1981).
Lesky, A. *A History of Greek Literature* (New York: Cromwell, 1966).
Lloyd, G.E.R. *Early Greek Science: Thales to Aristotle* (London: Chatto & Windus, 1970).
Long, A.A. and Sedley, D. (eds) *The Hellenistic Philosophers* (Cambridge: Cambridge University Press, 1967).

Long, A.A. *Problems in Stoicism* (London: Athlone, 1971).
—— *Hellenistic Philosophy* (London: Duckworth, 1974).
Lord, C. and O'Connor, D. (eds) *Essays on the Foundations of Aristotelian Political Science* (Berkeley, CA: University of California Press, 1991).
Loriaux, M. 'The Realists and Saint Augustine: Skepticism, Psychology, and Moral Action in International Relations Thought,' *International Studies Quarterly* (1992).
Lycos, K. *Plato on Justice and Power* (Albany, NY: State University of New York, 1987).
MacMullen, R. *Enemies of the Roman Order: Treason, Unrest, and Alienation in the Empire* (Cambridge, MA: Harvard University Press, 1966).
Mansfield, H.C. *Machiavelli's Virtue* (Chicago: University of Chicago Press, 1998).
Maritain, J. *Scholasticism and Politics* (New York: Doubleday 1940).
—— *The Rights of Man and Natural Law* (London: Bles, 1944).
—— *Man and the State* (Chicago: University of Chicago Press, 1953).
Markus, R.A. *Saeculum: History and Society in the Theology of St Augustine* (Cambridge: Cambridge University Press, 1970).
—— *The End of Ancient Christianity* (Cambridge: Cambridge University Press, 1990).
Martin, R. 'The Two Cities in Augustine's Political Philosophy,' *Journal of the History of Ideas* 33 (1972).
Mattingly, G. 'Machiavelli's Prince: Political Science or Political Satire?' *The American Scholar* 27 (1955).
Mazzolani, L.S. *The Idea of the City in Roman Thought: From Walled City to Spiritual Commonwealth* (London: Hollis & Carter, 1970).
McIlwain, C.H. *The Growth of Political Thought in the* West (London: Macmillan, 1932).
McInerny, R.M. *Ethica Thomistica: The Moral Philosophy of St Thomas Aquinas* (Washington, DC: Catholic University of America Press, 1982).
McKirahan, R.D. *Philosophy Before Socrates* (Indianapolis: Hackett, 1994).
Meinecke, F. *Machiavellianism: the Doctrine of Raison d'État and its Place in History*, trans. D. Scott (London: Routledge and Kegan Paul, 1957).
Miller, F.D. *Nature, Justice, and Rights in Aristotle's Politics* (Oxford: Clarendon Press, 1995).
Momigliano, A. (ed.) *The Conflict Between Paganism and Christianity in the Fourth Century* (Oxford: Clarendon Press, 1963).
Mommsen, T.E. 'St Augustine and the Christian Idea of Progress: The Background of the City of God,' *Journal of the History of Ideas* 12 (1951).
Monahan, A.P. (ed.) *John of Paris on Royal and Papal Power* (New York: Columbia University Press, 1974).
Morris, C. *The Papal Monarchy: The Western Church from 1050 to 1250* (Oxford: Clarendon Press, 1991).
Murphy, N.R. *The Interpretation of Plato's Republic* (Oxford: Clarendon Press, 1951).
Murray, O. *Early Greece* (London: Fontana, 1994).
Nederman, C.J. (ed.) *John of Salisbury: Policraticus* (Cambridge: Cambridge University Press, 1990).

―― *Medieval Aristotelianism and its Limits: Classical Traditions in Moral and Political Philosophy* (Aldershot: Variorum, 1997).
Nettleship, R.L. *Lectures on the Republic of Plato* (London: Macmillan, 1951).
Nicholas, B. *An Introduction to Roman Law* (Oxford: Clarendon Press, 1975).
Nichols, M. *Citizens and Statesmen: A Study of Aristotle's Politics* (Savage, MD: Rowman and Littlefield, 1992).
O'Connor, D.J. *Aquinas and Natural Law* (London: Macmillan, 1967).
O'Connor, E.M. *The Essential Epicurus* (Buffalo, NY: Prometheus, 1993).
O'Meara, J. *The Young Augustine: The Growth of St Augustine's Mind up to his Conversion* (London: Longmans, 1954).
O'Meara, T. *The Theology of Thomas Aquinas* (Notre Dame, IN: University of Notre Dame Press, 1997).
O'Neil, B. 'The Struggle for the Soul of Thrasymachus,' *Ancient Philosophy* 8 (1988).
Ober, J. *Political Dissent in Democratic Athens: Intellectual Critics of Popular Rule* (Princeton, NJ: Princeton University Press, 1998).
Osborne, R. *Greece in the Making: 1200–479 BC* (London: Routledge, 1996).
Pangle, T.L. 'Justice Among Nations in Platonic and Aristotelian Political Philosophy,' *American Journal of Political Science* 42, 2 (1998).
Pennington, K. *The Papal Monarchy in the Twelfth and Thirteenth Centuries* (Philadelphia: University of Pennsylvania Press, 1984).
―― *Popes, Canonists and Texts, 1150-1550* (Aldershot: Variorum, 1993).
Pieper, J. *The Four Cardinal Virtues: Prudence, Justice, Fortitude, Temperance* (Notre Dame, IN: University of Notre Dame Press, 1966).
―― *A Guide to Thomas Aquinas* (Notre Dame, IN: University of Notre Dame Press, 1987).
Pike, J.B. (ed.) *The Frivolities of Courtiers and the Footprints of Philosophers* (Minneapolis: University of Minnesota Press, 1938).
Pitkin, H.F. *Fortune is a Woman: Gender and Politics in the Thought of Niccolò Machiavelli* (Berkeley, CA: University of California Press).
Pocock, G.J.A. *The Machiavellian Moment: Florentine Political Thought and the Atlantic Republican Tradition* (Princeton, NJ: Princeton University Press, 1975).
Pohlenz, M. *Die Stoa* (Göttingen: Vandenhoeck & Ruprecht, 1964).
Post, G. '*Ratio publicae utilitatis, ratio status* and "Reason of State",' in *Studies in Medieval Legal Thought* (Princeton, NJ: Princeton University Press, 1964).
Poulakos, J. 'Gorgias' Encomium to Helen and the Defence of Rhetoric,' *Rhetorica* 1:2 (1983).
Powell, C.A. *Athens and Sparta* (London: Routledge, 1988).
Price, S. *Religions of the Ancient Greeks* (Cambridge: Cambridge University Press, 1999).
Raab, F. *The English Face of Machiavelli: A Changing Interpretation, 1500–1700* (London: Routledge, 1964).
Rankin, H.D. *Sophists, Socratics and Cynics* (London, Croom Helm, 1983).

Rees, B.R. *Pelagius: Life and Letters* (Woodbridge, Suffolk: Boydell, 1998).
Reesor, M.E. 'Fate and Possibility in Early Stoic Philosophy,' *Phoenix* 19 (1965).
Reeve, C.D.C. *Practices of Reason: Aristotle's Nicomachean Ethics* (Oxford: Clarendon Press, 1992).
Rist, J.M. *Stoic Philosophy* (Cambridge: Cambridge University Press, 1969).
—— *Epicurus: An Introduction* (Cambridge: Cambridge University Press, 1972).
—— *Augustine: Ancient Thought Baptized* (Cambridge: Cambridge University Press, 1994).
Ritter, J. *Naturrecht bei Aristoteles* (Stuttgart: Kohlhammer, 1961).
Robinson, O.F. *The Sources of Roman Law* (London: Routledge, 1996).
Rorty, A.O. (ed.) *Essays on Aristotle's Ethics* (Berkeley, CA: University of California Press, 1980).
Ross, W.D. *Plato's Theory of Ideas* (Oxford: Oxford University Press, 1951).
—— *Aristotle* (London: Methuen, 1964).
Rubinstein, N. 'Political Theories in the Renaissance,' in A. Chastel et al. (eds) *The Renaissance* (London: Methuen, 1982).
Salkever, S.G. *Finding the Mean: Theory and Practice in Aristotelian Political Philosophy* (Princeton, NJ: Princeton University Press, 1990).
Sandbach, F.H. *The Stoics* (London: Duckworth, 1975).
Saxonhouse, A.W. *Fear of Diversity: The Birth of Political Science in Ancient Greek Thought* (Chicago: University of Chicago Press, 1992).
Sayre, F. *The Greek Cynics* (Baltimore, MD: University of Baltimore Press, 1948).
Schulz, F. *Classical Roman Law* (Oxford: Clarendon Press, 1951).
—— *History of Roman Legal Science* (Oxford: Clarendon Press, 1953).
Sealey, R. *A History of the Greek City-States* (Berkeley, CA: University of California Press, 1976).
Siemsen, T. 'Thrasymachus' Challenge,' *History of Political Thought* 8 (1987).
Simon, Y.R. *The Tradition of Natural Law: A Philosopher's Reflections* (New York: Fordham University Press, 1965).
Simpson, P.A. *A Philosophical Commentary on the Politics of Aristotle* (Chapel Hill, NC: University of North Carolina Press, 1998).
Sinclair, R.K. *Democracy and Participation in Athens* (Cambridge: Cambridge University Press, 1988).
Skinner, Q.R.D. *The Foundations of Modern Political Thought* vol. 1: *The Renaissance* (Cambridge: Cambridge University Press, 1978).
—— *Machiavelli* (Oxford: Oxford University Press, 1981).
Smith, J.H. *The Great Schism* (London: Hamish Hamilton, 1970).
Snell, B. *The Discovery of the Mind in Greek Philosophy and Literature* (New York: Dover, 1982).
Sokolowski, R. *The God of Faith and Reason* (Notre Dame, IN: University of Notre Dame Press, 1982).
Sparshott, F. 'An Argument for Thrasymachus,' *Apeiron* 21 (1988).

Select Bibliography

Sprague, R.K. *The Older Sophists* (Columbia, SC: University of South Carolina Press, 1972).

Stead, C. *Philosophy in Christian Antiquity* (Cambridge: Cambridge University Press, 1994).

Stevens, G. 'Moral Obligation in St Thomas,' *The Modern Schoolman* 40 (1962–63).

Stevenson J. and Frend, W.H.C. *A New Eusebius: Documents Illustrating the History of the Church to AD 337* (London: SPCK, 1987).

Stockton, D.L. *The Classical Athenian Democracy* (Oxford: Oxford University Press, 1990).

Stough, C.L. *Greek Scepticism* (Berkeley, CA: University of California Press, 1969).

Strauss, L. *Natural Right and History* (Chicago: University of Chicago Press, 1953).

——— *Thoughts on Machiavelli* (Chicago: University of Chicago Press, 1995).

Stump, P.H. *The Reforms of the Council of Constance (1414-1418)* (Leiden: E.J. Brill, 1994).

Swanson, J.A. *The Public and the Private in Aristotle's Political Philosophy* (Ithaca, NY: Cornell University Press, 1991).

Tarn, W.W. *Hellenistic Civilization* (London: Arnold, 1952).

Taylor, C.C.W. 'Plato's Totalitarianism,' *Polis* 5 (1986).

Tellegen-Couperus, O. *A Short History of Roman Law* (London: Routledge, 1990).

TeSelle, E. *Augustine the Theologian* (London: Burns & Oates, 1970).

Tierney, B. *Foundations of the Conciliar Theory: The Contribution of the Medieval Canonists from Gratian to the Great Schism* (Cambridge: Cambridge University Press, 1955).

——— *The Crisis of Church and State, 1050–1300* (Englewood Cliffs, NJ: Prentice-Hall, 1980).

Tudor, H. *Political Myth* (London: Macmillan, 1972).

Ullmann, W. *Medieval Papalism: the Political Theories of the Medieval Canonists* (London: Methuen, 1949).

——— *The Growth of Papal Government in the Middle Ages* (London: Methuen, 1955).

——— *Principles of Government and Politics in the Middle Ages* (London: Methuen, 1961).

——— *The Origins of the Great Schism* (Hamden, CT: Archon, 1967).

——— *Medieval Foundations of Renaissance Humanism* (Ithaca, NY: Cornell University Press, 1977).

——— *Medieval Political Theory* (Harmondsworth, Middlesex: Penguin, 1979).

Untersteiner, M. *The Sophists* (Oxford: Blackwell, 1954).

Urmson, J.O. 'Aristotle's Doctrine of the Mean,' *American Philosophical Quarterly* 10 (1973).

van Steenberghen, F. *Aristotle in the West: The Origins of Latin Aristotelianism* (Louvain: Nauwelaerts, 1970).

——— *Thomas Aquinas and Radical Aristotelianism* (Washington, DC: Catholic University of America Press, 1980).

van Straaten, M. *Panétius: sa vie, ses écrits et sa doctrine* (Amsterdam: H.J. Paris, 1946).

Villari, P. *The Life and Times of Niccolò Machiavelli* (London: Unwin, 1892).

Vinogradoff, P. *Roman Law in Medieval Europe* (Cambridge: Cambridge University Press, 1969).

Viroli, M. *Machiavelli* (Oxford: Oxford University Press, 1998).

Vlastos, G. *Plato: A Collection of Critical Essays* (New York: Anchor, 1971).

——— *The Philosophy of Socrates* (Notre Dame, IN: University of Notre Dame Press, 1971).

——— *Socrates: Ironist and Moral Philosopher* (Cambridge: Cambridge University Press, 1991).

——— *Studies in Ancient Greek Philosophy* vol 1: *The Presocratics* (Princeton, NJ: Princeton University Press, 1995).

von Leyden, W. 'Aristotle and the Concept of Law,' *Philosophy*, 42 (1967).

——— *Aristotle on Equality and Justice* (London: Macmillan, 1985).

Wallace-Hadrill, D.S. *The Greek Patristic View of Nature* (Manchester: Manchester University Press, 1968).

Walton, F.E. *The Development of the Logos Doctrine in Greek and Hebrew Thought* (Bristol: John Wright & Sons, 1911).

Wardy, R. *The Birth of Rhetoric: Gorgias, Plato and their Successors* (London: Routledge, 1996).

Warren, J. *Epicurus and Democritean Ethics: An Archaeology of Ataraxia* (Cambridge: Cambridge University Press, 2002).

Waterfield, R. *The First Philosophers* (Oxford: Oxford University Press, 2000).

Watson, A. *Law Making in the Later Roman Republic* (Oxford: Clarendon Press, 1974).

Weisheipl, J.A. *Friar Thomas d'Aquino: His Life, Thought and Works* (Oxford: Blackwell, 1975).

Welch, D.A. 'Why International Relations Theorists Should Stop Reading Thucydides,' *Review of International Studies* 29 (2003).

Welles, C.B. *Alexander and the Hellenistic World* (Toronto: University of Toronto Press, 1970).

White, S. 'Thrasymachus the Diplomat,' *Classical Quarterly* 90 (1995).

Whitfield, J.H. 'Savonarola and the Purpose of the *The Prince*,' in *Discourses on Machiavelli* (Cambridge: Heffer, 1969).

Wolin, S.S. *Politics and Vision: Continuity and Innovation in Western Political Thought* (London: George Allen and Unwin, 1961).

Wood, N. 'Machiavelli's Concept of *Virtù* Reconsidered,' *Political Studies* 15, 2 (1967).

Yack, B. *The Problems of a Political Animal: Community, Justice, and Conflict in Aristotelian Political Thought* (Berkeley, CA: University of California Press, 1993).

Index

Albertus Magnus, 210, 212
Alexander the Great:
    Aristotle and, 67–68, 93, 101–102
    career and influence of, 102–104, 108, 118
Alvarus Pelagius, 205–206
Anaximander of Miletus:
    possible theory of natural law in, 4–5
    science of, 4–5, 9, 111–112
Anaximenes of Miletus, science of, 5, 9
Aquinas, St Thomas:
    and Augustine, 215–244
    on the best constitution, 222–226
    on earthly happiness, 216–221
    on government, 218–221
    importance of, 244
    intellectualism of, 240, 243
    on law:
        Divine law, 239–240
        eternal law, 233
        in general, 232–233
        human law, 234–239
        natural law, 233–234
    life and times of, 209–211
    and the natural law tradition, 241–244
    and Plato, 232
    on political obligation, 226–227, 237–239
    on property, 229–231
    and the 'recovery' of Aristotle, 211–214
    on tyranny, 226–229
Aratus of Chios, 142
Areté, 'virtue,' meanings of, 20, 45, 73, 105, 260

Aristotle:
    constitutional theory of, 86–91
    criticism of Plato, 67–68, 83–86, 90–91
    criticisms of, 95–98
    on equity, 92, 94–95
    eudaimonism of, 70–78
    on intellectual virtue:
        phronesis, 77–78
        sophia, 73–74
    on justice and law, 91–95
    life and times of, 67–68, 101–102
    methodology of, 68–70
    on moral virtue, 73–78
    as a natural law theorist, 98–100
    on the relation between ethics and politics, 78–82
Athens:
    political history of, 12–14
    political realism and, 26–30
    'Thirty Tyrants' and, 33–35
Augustan settlement, 132–133
Augustine of Hippo, St:
    critique of Cicero, 158, 174–178
    on evil, 153–154
    on grace, predestination and free will, 158–166
    legal positivism of, 191–193
    libido dominandi, 170
    on natural law, 146–150
    and Pelagianism, 160–161
    attitude to philosophy of, 156–157
    on political obligation, 188–191
    political realism of, 197
    political theory of, summarised, 193–198
    on property, 148–149

on Rome and Roman history, 171–175
on sin, 150–166
on the State:
　as a consequence of sin, 169–179
　as a disciplinary order, 181–183
　as a remedial order, 179–181
on the two Cities, 161–164
on war:
　just and unjust war, 183–186
　war and moral obligation, 186–188
Augustinus Triumphus, 205
Averroes; Averroism, 211–213
Avicenna, 211

Bonaventure, St, as critic of Aristotle, 212–213
Boniface VIII, Pope, 204, 247
Borgia, Cesare, 246, 249, 260, 269

Canon law, 198–201
Carneades, 107–108, 132
Charlemagne, coronation of, 204
Chrysippus of Soli, 109, 113–115, 120–122
Cicero, Marcus Tullius:
　on fate, 158
　on justice, 123–124, 174–175
　on natural law, 118, 120, 123–124
　and Stoicism, 110
City of God, *see* Augustine of Hippo, St
'Classical' Greek culture, emergence of, 1–3
Cleanthes of Assos, 109, 114, 120, 142
Compatibilism, in Stoic philosophy, 115
Constantine, Roman emperor, 137, 139, 172, 186
Context, importance of, xi
Coronation ceremonies, symbolic significance of, 203–204
Corpus iuris civilis, *see* Roman law
Cosmology, *see* Presocratic science *and* Stoicism

Critias, 33–34
Cynics, 104–105

Dante, *De monarchia* of, 212
Decretum Gratiani, *see* Canon law

Earthly City, *see* Augustine of Hippo, St
Epictetus, 109, 114
Epicureans, 105–107

Fathers of the Church:
　influence on canon law of, 198–200
　doctrine of natural law in, 145–146
　general response to pagan philosophy of, 138–140, 145–146
　attitude to war of, 186

Gaius, Roman jurist, 128
Gelasius I, Pope, 204
Giles of Rome, 205–207
Gorgias of Leontini:
　on rhetoric, 20–21
　political outlook of, 19
　relativism of, 15–18
　treatise *On Not-Being* of, 15
Gregory VII, Pope, 202, 204, 216

Hellenism, *see* Alexander the Great
Heraclitus of Ephesus:
　cosmology of, 5–6
　possible political theory of, 6–7
Homer, 7–8, 27, 37

Innocent III, Pope, 204–205
Isidore of Seville, St, 145–146, 199
Italy, sixteenth-century politics of, 247–250

James of Viterbo, 205
John of Salisbury, 204–205

Logos:
　in Heraclitus, 5–7
　in presocratic science, 3–12

Index

in St John's Gospel, 140–141
in Stoicism, 111–113

Macedonian Empire, *see* Alexander the Great
Machiavelli, Niccolo:
    on Christianity, 250, 267
    on the Church, 248
    on human nature, 253–269
    life and times of, 245–250
    methodology of, 251–252
    on monarchy, 256–260
    on politics and morality, 260–264, 269–270
    on republican government, 264–268
    significance of, 269–270
    unity of political thought of, 252–253, 264–269
    works of, 246–247
Manegold of Lautenbach, 203
Marcus Aurelius, Roman emperor, 109–111, 122–123
Marsilius of Padua, 244, 249
'Melian debate,' 28–30
Moerbeke, William of, 212, 218
Moral relativism, *see* Sophists
Mythos, as form of explanation, 7–8

Natural law tradition, general character of, xii–xiii

Panaetius of Rhodes, 109–110, 121, 126, 131
Papal monarchy, theory of:
    and the natural law tradition, 201–208
    scriptural foundation of, 204
Paris, University of, 212–213
Parmenides of Elea, ontology of, 9–12
Paul, St:
    and natural law, 144–145
    Stoic poets and, 141–143
Peloponnesian War, 26–30
Philip of Macedon, 67, 102

Philo Judaeus, 142, 144
Plato:
    criticisms of, 62–64, 65–66
    on democracy, 31
    dialogues of:
        Gorgias, 22–26
        Laws, 83
        Phaedrus, 51
        Philebus, 44, 75
        Republic, 22–26, 35–66, 83
        Statesman, 44
        Theaetetus, 17
    on the Idea of the Good, 58–61
    on individual justice, 50–52
    on the nature of justice, 40–46
    life and times of, 33–35
    methodology of, 47–48, 62–63
    as a natural law theorist, 64–65
    on the origins of political association, 46–47
    on political justice, 46–50
    and Socrates, 34–35
    attitude to the Sophists of, 1, 12–32
    theory of ideas of, 55–66
'Political Augustinianism,' 198–208
Political realism, general character of, xiii
Pontifex maximus, as papal title, 204
Posidonius of Apamea, 109, 114, 116, 120, 125, 131–132
Presocratic science:
    failure of, 8–9
    nature of, 3–8
    origin and context of, 1–3
Protagoras of Abdera:
    political outlook of, 19–20
    relativism of, 16–19

'Radical' Sophists:
    Callicles, 22–26, 106
    Thrasymachus, 35–40
Ratione peccati principle of papalist ideology, 205–208
Roman law:
    development of, 125–126

divisions of, 126–127
influence on canon law of, 198–201
ius naturale:
    definitions of, 128–130
    ius gentium and, 127–129
    rôle of, in Roman jurisprudence, 130–131
    and Roman imperial ideology, 131–133

Sceptics, 107–108
Seneca, as Stoic exemplar, 114–115
Socrates, *see* Plato
Sophists:
    context of, 12–14
    educational curriculum of, 20–22
    moral relativism of, 18–19
    outlook of, as a possible response to Parmenidean philosophy, 14–18
Stoicism:
    breadth of, as a philosophical movement, 109–110
    on choice, 115–117
    cosmology of, 111–113
    cosmopolitanism of, 121–123
    determinism of, 111–113
    on equality, 117–120
    Heraclitus and, 111, 113, 120
    influence of:
        on Roman imperial ideology, 124–131
        on Roman law, 131–133
    on the law of nature, 120–124, 133–136
    on 'life according to nature,' 109–118
    doctrine of *oikeiosis*, 119–120, 168
    on politics, 121–124

Tempier, Étienne, Bishop of Paris, 213
Tertullian, 111, 138–139, 145, 156, 173, 187, 216
Thales of Miletus, science of, 4, 9.
Theodosius I, Roman emperor, 137
Thucydides, 27–30
'Two Swords' principle, 203–204

Ulpianus, Roman jurist, 129, 234

Vicarius Christi, as papal title, 204
Virtù, in Machiavelli, 260–270

Zeno of Citium, 109, 111, 114, 116, 120–121
Zeno of Elea, 11

MAJOR CONCEPTS IN POLITICS
AND POLITICAL THEORY

This series invites book manuscripts and proposals on major concepts in politics and political theory—justice, equality, virtue, rights, citizenship, power, sovereignty, property, liberty, etc.—in prominent traditions, periods, and thinkers.

Send manuscripts or proposals, with author's vitae to:

>Garrett Ward Sheldon
>*General Editor*
>Clinch Valley College
>of the University of Virginia
>College Avenue
>Wise, VA 24293

To order other books in this series, please contact our Customer Service Department:

>(800) 770-LANG (within the U.S.)
>(212) 647-7706 (outside the U.S.)
>(212) 647-7707 FAX

Or browse online by series at:

>www.peterlang.com